W9-AFM-007

DATE DUE

WILLA

WILLA

The Life of Willa Cather

❈

Phyllis C. Robinson

DOUBLEDAY & COMPANY, INC.

GARDEN CITY, NEW YORK

1983

Lines from "Ode in Memory of the American Volunteers Fallen for France" and from William Archer's Introduction from *Poems* by Alan Seeger are reprinted with the permission of Charles Scribner's Sons: copyright renewed 1944 Elsie Adams Seeger.

Lines from "The Palatine," "The Silver Cup," and "Autumn Melody" from *April Twilights and Other Poems* by Willa Cather are reprinted by permission of Alfred A. Knopf, Inc. and Charles Cather.

Excerpts from *My Ántonia* by Willa Cather. Copyright 1918, 1926, 1946 by Willa Sibert Cather. Copyright 1954 by Edith Lewis. Copyright renewed 1977 by Walter Havighurst. Reprinted by permission of Houghton Mifflin Company.

Excerpts from *Alexander's Bridge* by Willa Cather. Copyright 1912, 1922 by Willa Sibert Cather. Copyright renewed 1950 by Edith Lewis. Reprinted by permission of Houghton Mifflin Company.

Excerpts from *The Song of the Lark* by Willa Cather. Copyright 1915 and renewed 1943 by Willa Sibert Cather. Reprinted by permission of Houghton Mifflin Company.

Excerpts from *O Pioneers!* by Willa Cather. Copyright 1913 and renewed 1941 by Willa Cather. Reprinted by permission of Houghton Mifflin Company.

Excerpts from *Under the Bridge* by Ferris Greenslet. Copyright 1943 by Ferris Greenslet. Copyright renewed 1971 by Magdalena Greenslet Finley. Reprinted by permission of Houghton Mifflin Company.

Quotations from *Willa Cather—a Memoir* by Elizabeth Shepley Sergeant, courtesy of Harper & Row, copyright holder, and J. B. Lippincott Co., publisher.

Library of Congress Cataloging in Publication Data

Robinson, Phyllis C.
    Willa, the life of Willa Cather.

    Bibliography: p. 311
    Includes index.
    1. Cather, Willa, 1873–1947–Biography.
    2. Novelists, American—20th century—Biography.
    I. Title.
    PS3505.A87Z815 1983   813'.52 [B]
    ISBN: 0-385-15254-X
    Library of Congress Catalog Card Number 82–46017

For Ray

Contents

Illustrations

Preface

———— ❀ ————

On April 24, 1947, at four-thirty in the afternoon, Willa Cather, American novelist, died of a cerebral hemorrhage in her apartment on New York's Park Avenue. She was seventy-three.

Park Avenue? New York? How is it possible? What was she doing in the city, in a place of stone and steel? Willa Cather is country air and earth and yellow fields of wheat. Willa Cather is the fresh untroubled face of morning. She is a quiet figure in a rural landscape. She is Nebraska.

But she was in New York when she died. Was she passing through perhaps? Had she recently arrived?

I set out to look for the author of my girlhood. The author who stirred my heart and kindled my imagination with tales of an America and a time I had never known. The author who brought Alexandra Bergson into my life; Ántonia and Lucy Gayheart; Thea Kronborg and the ineffable lost lady, Marian Forrester. Those unforgettable heroines of my youth.

I searched for a woman in a faded portrait, and I found her bursting out of the frame. Passionate, alive, more vivid than any of her characters.

I looked for Willa Cather in the past, in dreaming little towns that barely disturbed the dust. I looked for her in the Middle West and in the desert villages near Santa Fe. And I found her at home, *my* home. I found her in New York.

No, Willa Cather was not passing through. Where she died was where she had lived, for more than forty years.

But was New York really home to her? It is doubtful that she ever called herself a New Yorker, any more than she called herself a Virginian, although she was born there, in Back Creek Valley in the western part of that state.

No, Willa Cather would have called herself a Nebraskan. A Nebraskan who lived most of her life away from home.

WILLA

Introduction

On an unseasonably cool Friday afternoon in late May of 1944 Willa Cather, the novelist, accompanied by her friend and companion of forty years, Edith Lewis, journeyed from her apartment on Park Avenue to Audubon Terrace on upper Broadway where, on the summit of a hill rising steeply from the Hudson River, stood two classic gray stone buildings, the home of the National Institute and the American Academy of Arts and Letters. There in the Cass Gilbert Italian Renaissance auditorium building, at the annual joint meeting of the Institute and the Academy, Willa Cather was to receive the Institute's Gold Medal, the highest award for creative achievement in the arts. The medal was awarded annually but only once in every decade for a particular field. Three other novelists had received the Gold Medal for Fiction before her: William Dean Howells in 1915, Edith Wharton in 1924 and Booth Tarkington in 1933. In the nineteen forties, the prize would belong to Willa Cather alone.

She had already been given the Academy's Howells Medal for *Death Comes for the Archbishop*, and *One of Ours* won her the Pulitzer Prize in 1923. But the Gold Medal was awarded not for a single book, but for an entire body of work, the sustained output of a whole career. It was this honor which came to Willa Cather when she was seventy, three years after her last novel, *Sapphira and the*

Slave Girl, had been published and more than forty years after *April Twilights*, her first collection of poetry, appeared. She would live three more years, but this was to be her last public tribute.

Although she was one of theirs, having been elected to the Institute in 1929 and elevated to the more select Academy in 1938, there were many in the audience that afternoon who had been surprised, when the award was first announced in January, to learn that the author was still alive. She had seemed to belong to another time and place. Now they looked with curiosity at the short, square, self-possessed figure being led to the stage by Arthur Train, the courtly president of the Institute. In a dark tailored suit hanging loosely over her stocky frame, and an ample straw bonnet on which clustered an array of garden flowers and bright cherries, she might have been somebody's maiden aunt come to tea—unless, that is, one chanced to look beneath the hat's broad brim and met the extraordinary gaze of her clear blue-gray eyes. It was a gaze of pure intelligence that quickly dispelled any sentimental image, and it matched the dignity with which she took the seat that had been saved for her.

The program was to begin at three, last two hours and be followed by a reception and exhibition of works by new members. For one afternoon, the progress of the war, the American offensive in Sicily and the imminent Allied invasion of Europe would be allowed to recede while the illustrious figures of the nation's cultural establishment assembled to pay homage to their own, at the traditional "Ceremonial." Paul Robeson was to receive an award that day and so was Theodore Dreiser. Before the program ended eleven new members would be inducted into the 250-member Institute and five would inherit numbered seats in the 50-member Academy. Isabel Bishop, Joe Davidson, W. E. B. DuBois and Upton Sinclair were made members of the Institute and Frederick Law Olmsted, the architect and son of the designer of Central Park, joined the Academy. The annual address, known affectionately as "the Blashfield" after a former speaker, was given by Archibald MacLeish, the Librarian of Congress, and in it he called for a new moral order and a humane conception to combat the sickness of intellectual chaos.

From her seat in the audience Edith Lewis noted old friends among the members filling the auditorium. Many had been guests when she and Willa Cather lived on Bank Street in Greenwich Village and held their Friday afternoons at home. In recent years illness and the war had caused them to curtail their entertaining. Now as she recognized familiar faces, Edith Lewis realized there were some she hadn't seen in years. They brought back happy memories that she would share with Willa later.

Suddenly an unexpected movement on the platform attracted her attention. To her surprise Willa Cather had risen and, with arms outstretched, was walking across the length of the crowded stage to where a very old man was being helped into his chair.

Though he had grown frail and withered and seemed even smaller than she remembered him, Edith Lewis knew at once who it was her friend had risen to embrace. Eighty-seven-year-old Samuel S. McClure, almost forgotten now but once the muckraking editor of the most famous magazine in America, was on the platform to receive the Institute's "Order of Merit" for his services to American letters and journalism. It was fitting that S. S. McClure and Willa Cather should be honored on the same occasion, for a long time ago when she too was a journalist, Willa Cather had been managing editor of *McClure's Magazine*. It was a part of her personal history few present that day were aware of. Edith Lewis, however, knew well the role that the legendary McClure had played in the author's life, and she recognized in the gesture, so publicly demonstrative and so unguarded, how deeply moved Willa was to see her former "chief." For a few brief, emotional moments the two old colleagues clung together in full view of the audience. And later when a news photographer took pictures, the usually austere novelist posed with one arm flung affectionately across McClure's thin shoulders.

Next morning she wrote to him, full of apologies for the years they had been out of touch. She begged to be permitted to see him at his club, or if it suited him better, she would receive him at her apartment. He had only to telephone to let her know when he would come. The sight of him, she said, had released a torrent of happy memories and stirred a flood of gratitude for all that he had done for her. Would he come? There was so much she wanted him to know.

* * *

Willa Cather was teaching English at Allegheny High School and living in Pittsburgh at the home of Judge Samuel A. McClung when her short stories first brought her to the attention of the peppery editor of *McClure's*. After five years of newspaper work and a transient life in Pittsburgh boardinghouses her circumstances had changed markedly in 1901, giving her security and leisure to work at the serious writing she had always hoped to do. She owed her good fortune to the judge's daughter Isabelle at whose invitation she became a member of the McClung household.

They had been introduced two years earlier by a mutual friend, Lizzie Hudson Collier, the popular leading lady of a Pittsburgh stock company. An accomplished and versatile actress, Mrs. Collier had the distinction of being received in fashionable homes not always open to performers. The presence of a devoted husband and the actress' own air of taste and refinement apparently served to reassure the doyennes of Pittsburgh's East End that she was respectable, despite her calling. The meeting that took place in Lizzie Collier's dressing room between the judge's handsome dark-haired daughter and the ambitious journalist from Nebraska marked the beginning of a deep and lasting attachment that was to shape Willa Cather's life for many years to come.

When they met Willa was already well known for her drama reviews and articles in the Pittsburgh *Leader* and Isabelle's fascination with the arts was giving her a reputation as something of a rebel in the staid Calvinist society in which her family moved. One imagines the pleasure of the two young women, exchanging views on the latest books and plays and discovering a variety of shared enthusiasms. Both were ardent lovers of music and the theatre and took a passionate interest in the lives of the artists whose work they admired. Isabelle, with the means to follow her inclinations, had early cast herself in the role of patron of the arts and in her new friend she found not only a companion who delighted in the things that she did, but also an artist whose genius she might help to develop.

In many ways it was an attraction of opposites that drew them to each other. To the sheltered daughter of the McClungs, Willa Cather, living alone in the city, earning her own money, answerable to no one but herself, represented everything that Isabelle's conventional upbringing made impossible. For her part, Isabelle brought personal attributes to which Willa was always susceptible. She was high-spirited and beautiful and she moved through life with a kind of natural grace and authority that made it comfortable to be with her. Her generosity opened up a world of taste and affluence such as Willa had never known before. Over the next two years they were increasingly in each other's company and on occasion, when Willa was traveling and had temporarily given up her boardinghouse, she would stay with Isabelle at the McClungs'—chez the goddess, she called it.

The profound change in Willa's living arrangements did not take place, however, until she had resigned from the *Leader* and accepted a teaching post in the spring of 1901. Isabelle had encouraged her to take the job and she now approached her parents with the idea that Willa should come to live with them.

The judge and Mrs. McClung raised strong objections. They had two daughters and a son and they considered it unseemly to bring a virtual stranger into their home to share their daughter's room. They were unhappy with Isabelle's bohemian interests and looked with misgiving at the free and easy habits of her artistic friends. Judge McClung had presided at the trial of Alexander Berkman, the anarchist lover of Emma Goldman, who had been charged with an attempt on the life of Pittsburgh industrialist Henry C. Frick; the judge had a reputation for severity. His daughter, however, was his match in stubbornness. If Willa could not live with her she would leave home herself. There must have been tense scenes in the McClung home but her parents must have also been persuaded they would lose their daughter if they persisted in refusing her. They agreed finally to a temporary visit and on that basis Willa moved into 1180 Murray Hill Avenue. As it happened, the arrangement worked well and the judge and his wife grew fond of their daughter's unconventional guest. Willa Cather lived with the McClungs for the next five years and she was there in 1906 when S. S. McClure came to get her and take her to New York.

Who was this young woman from the West who cut such a brilliant swath through Pittsburgh's artistic world and was a match even for the McClungs of Murray Hill?

I

❖

Mea Patria

MEMORY OF VIRGINIA

Willa Cather was born in her maternal grandmother's home in the blue-grass country of western Virginia in 1873, a date long obscured by the author herself. In 1909 when she was filling out information for *Who's Who*, S. S. McClure advised her to subtract a few years from her age; she would thank him one day, he said. Her entry that year and subsequent years until 1920 gives her birthday as December 7, 1874. In 1920 she subtracted two more years, and for the rest of her life maintained that she had been born in 1876, the date carved on her tombstone. It was but one of the small deceptions that appealed to her imagination. Her name in the family Bible was Willela, after a sister of her father's who had died, but she rejected both the name and the derivation, preferring to believe that she was called Willa for her grandfathers, William Cather and William Lee Boak, and, even more importantly, for her mother's brother, Willie Sibert Boak, her "namesake," who had died fighting for the Confederacy and for whose memory she had a special fondness.

Names had almost a primitive fascination for Willa Cather. In the early days of her career she used pseudonyms freely and in a postscript to her last novel, *Sapphira and the Slave Girl*, she says that the names she heard in her Virginia childhood stayed with her all her life. She gave her fictional characters names that linger in the mind: the treacherous Wick Cutter; Thea, a name that sounds like music; Jim Burden who carries the weight of memory and disappointment; and that vivid, shining spirit, Lucy Gayheart. They are supremely apt and so imprinted on the memory that long after we have read a Cather story, to recall a name is to bring an entire book to life.

Willa was the first child of Charles Fectigue and Mary Virginia Boak Cather and the eldest of seven, a circumstance that may help to account for her assertive, self-confident personality. The winter she was born the young couple were living with Mrs. Cather's mother, Rachel Boak, in a village near Winchester. The facts of Grandma Boak's life are rendered more faithfully than Willa Cather was accustomed to, in *Sapphira and the Slave Girl* in which she was the model for Sapphira's daughter, Rachel Blake. Widowed at thirty-eight, with five young children, Rachel Boak, like her fictional counterpart, left Washington, where her husband had been an official in the Department of the Interior and, returning home to Back Creek Valley, settled in a house her father purchased for her in the village. There she raised her fatherless family and tended to their needs as well as to the needs of her less fortunate neighbors. Like Rachel Blake, Willa's grandmother was one of those women who just naturally assume responsibility for others.

Her younger daughter, Willa's mother, was a handsome, spirited young woman, accustomed to attention and inclined to be strong-willed and imperious in her manner. Proud and capable, Mary Virginia Boak also had a temper to be reckoned with, as her children would one day learn. The man she married, as is so often the case, was of an entirely different disposition. Gentle and soft-spoken, with easy-going, courteous ways, Charles Cather, even in old age, remained what he had always been, a sweet Southern boy, according to his daughter. Her father's boyishness and undemanding temperament endeared him to Willa, whose own nature was far closer to her mother's.

Charles and Virginia Cather might have felt isolated when they moved out of the village to Willowshade, the home of Willa's Cather grandparents, in the farm country just a little farther east, but they were young and energetic and thought nothing of wrapping up the baby and carrying her with them when they rode horseback into town for a dance. After Grandma Boak came to live with them at

Willowshade the baby was left in her care, and the indulgent father reported to his brother George in Nebraska that "Willie," as they called her, had not cried once while they were gone. She grows very fast, he added, "and is just as good as she is pretty." News of the new Cather baby traveled to Nebraska from other sources, too. A schoolmate of George Cather's wrote that "Charley don't get to church till it is half out on account of having to rock the babe to sleep."

By the time of Willa's childhood the passions of the Civil War were largely spent, but she grew up hearing tales within her own family of both sides of the conflict. Grandfather Cather and his pious, Bible-reading wife Caroline had been staunch Unionists, as were their two sons, Willa's father and his brother George. The rest of the Cather family supported the South, although William Cather's sister, Sydney Gore, a prominent figure in the neighborhood and a heroine to her grand-niece Willa, had been vigorously opposed to slavery and cared for the wounded of both armies all through the war. The Boaks, with relatives in the Deep South and with their own sentimental ties to the old Virginia social order, were loyal to the Confederacy. Willa's mother cherished the rebel sword of her adored brother who fell early in the war, and it held a hallowed place in her home until she died. Yet it was Virginia Cather who acted as peacemaker to the divided family by giving a party early in her marriage to which she invited all the relatives, so that those who had fought on opposing sides for four long years could finally come together. It was a delicate maneuver, requiring goodwill and tact as well as the high-handedness for which she was famous, but the important thing was that it worked.

The divided loyalties of her family in the Civil War gave Willa a feeling for ambiguity that was deeply ingrained. She distrusted causes and put her faith in individuals. She learned very young that experience is many-sided, that human relations are never simple, that motivation is always complicated and springs from many sources. If there was any pattern to experience it lay in conflict and contradiction, rarely in accommodation. In Willa's best work these are energizing principles and she wrote about the conflict between the young and the old, the city and the country, the artist and society, between ideals and realities, between desire and necessity. In her own life self-control was almost an obsession and she struggled to keep

her emotions and her intellect in balance. Her nature was com-
pounded of the sunny romanticism of the South and the chilly hard-
headed practicality of her Cather forebears, and her life was a reflection of the need she felt to make peace between them.

Willa Cather's earliest memories were of the Virginia Boaks and
Cathers and their households. Her first landscape was the land on
Back Creek that her family had farmed from Colonial times for six
generations. It was hilly country better suited to raising sheep than
crops, and Charles Cather would carry Willa on his shoulders when
he went out to visit his flock and herd them into the fold at night.
Willowshade, the family home built by Willa's grandfather, was a
spacious three-story brick farmhouse with five bedrooms, each with
its own fireplace, a two-story wing in back and a white portico with
fluted columns in the front. In Willa's childhood it was the scene of
constant commotion, a whirl of activity, where a friendly little girl
could find scores of interesting people to visit, to learn from, to add
flavor and excitement to her life. Servants and fieldhands, both black
and white, tradespeople, visiting family and friends kept Willowshade humming in every season of the year. Outside the house a child
could roam to her heart's content, visit the old Sibert mill standing a
few yards from the house on the other side of Back Creek, or take
the path across the wooden footbridge leading to the mountains and
stand on the bridge, as Willa did, declaiming poetry.

Willa often passed the time with the local people, like Mrs. Kearns
who wove all of Willowshade's extensive supply of carpets. Sometimes the mountain women would come down from Timber Ridge
and North Mountain to help out with the chores and then Willa
would listen to their stories as they churned butter or did the spin-
ning or made candles for the family's use. Willa's special favorite
among the women from Timber Ridge was Mary Ann Anderson,
the Mrs. Ringer of *Sapphira*. She had a way with children and whenever Willa was sick her mother would send for Mrs. Anderson because she knew it soothed the child to be with her. From her seat beside the window Willa would wait impatiently to catch sight of
Mary Ann Anderson's brisk figure rounding the turn in the road.
Mrs. Anderson would wave and then come up to Willa's room to
make the child comfortable before settling down for a cozy conversation. The lively red-haired lady and the eager youngster had a

common interest in other people's lives. As Willa wrote of Mrs. Ringer, she and Mrs. Anderson were "born interested."

Many years later, when Willa was out of college and visiting her aunt, Mrs. Gore, the two old friends renewed their acquaintance. Either Mrs. Anderson would come down to Mrs. Gore's house to see Willa or Willa would walk up the Hollow Road, the way she used to as a child, to Mrs. Anderson's little house on Timber Ridge where she lived all alone. The mountain woman would fill Willa in on the lives of her Back Creek neighbors, where they were living now, what they were doing, how the older ones had died. Her own memory went back to the years before Willa was born, and much of the flavor of *Sapphira and the Slave Girl* comes from the lore Willa had absorbed from Mrs. Anderson.

More than the past, however, bound the Cather family to their old Virginia neighbor. In their household in Nebraska was a living presence linking them to the days at Willowshade, for when the Cathers were preparing to leave for Nebraska in 1883, Mrs. Anderson had asked Mrs. Cather to take her daughter Marjorie along with them. One of her sons accompanied them as well, but he stayed only two years before taking off for the Far West. Margie, on the other hand, spent the rest of her long life in the Cather home and when she died in 1928, she was buried in the Cather family plot.

Two loving portraits immortalize the simpleminded Margie. She's Mahailey in *One of Ours* and Mandy in "Old Mrs. Harris." Both the short story and the Pulitzer prize-winning novel show Margie as she was in Nebraska in later years. In *Sapphira* we get a glimpse of what might have befallen her had she stayed behind in Virginia. In the book both of Mrs. Ringer's daughters become pregnant and bring their out-of-wedlock offspring home to be raised by their own mother. Mrs. Anderson may well have feared that a simpleminded girl like her Margie could easily be "fooled" the way Mrs. Ringer's daughters were. In the Cather home Margie would be cared for and protected and although it was a wrench to have to part with her, it gave the mother precious peace of mind. As for the Cathers, in Margie they had a friend who lived only to serve them. She would never learn to read or write but she looked after the children, helped with the chores and gave a lifetime of devotion to the family that became her own.

In Margie's last years, on the occasions when Willa, as a famous novelist, came home to Red Cloud for a visit, she loved to care for Margie and cook the simple meals that she enjoyed. The idea pleased her that after so many years of serving others, it was Margie's turn to be waited on. All the Cather children loved Margie but Willa liked to think the two of them shared a special understanding, and that Margie loved her best. The fact that they were both transplants, plucked from the Virginia soil together and set down on the hard Nebraska prairie to find their way, made for a bond and some of Willa's happiest hours were spent with Margie in the kitchen or on the back porch, talking about old times in Virginia.

Willa was in her middle sixties when she at last drew on those childhood memories Margie had helped to keep alive over the years, for *Sapphira and the Slave Girl*. It was to be her last book and her only novel with a Virginia locale, although she had used the setting in several short stories. In 1938 she went on a visit to Winchester to refresh her memory of the physical details of the countryside. She found it much changed, said Edith Lewis who accompanied her, but Willa "refused to look at its appearance; she looked through and through it, as if it were transparent, to what she knew as its reality." She had the characters in mind already, indeed they had been a part of her imagination for as long as she could remember, and it was a matter of selection and arrangement once she decided that she would write her Virginia novel. She could have written two or three Sapphiras out of the material she had, according to Edith Lewis, and she did, in fact, write twice as much in her first draft as finally appeared.

The novel is set in pre-Civil War Virginia and concerns the household of Sapphira Dodderidge, a wealthy slave-owning Southern woman, married to the miller, Henry Colbert. When we first meet them at breakfast they are arguing over the slave girl, Nancy. Jealous of what she perceives to be her husband's interest in the girl, Sapphira wants to sell her but Colbert will not agree. Nancy's mother, Till, is their housekeeper and Aunt Jezebel, her great-grandmother, is still alive. The miller will not allow Nancy to be sold away from her family. Thwarted in her intention to sell Nancy, Sapphira seeks another way to get rid of her. She invites Martin Colbert, Henry's cousin, to visit, knowing that the dissolute young man will force himself upon the helpless girl. Sapphira sets the stage for rape herself by ordering Nancy to sleep in the corridor outside her bedroom door where Martin will be sure to find her. In desperation the frantic Nancy turns to Sapphira's daughter, Mrs. Blake, and she makes arrangements to send Nancy to the North and freedom. One hurdle remains: the trip will cost a hundred dollars. Mrs. Blake appeals to her father who wrestles with the ambiguities of his situation, his loyalty to his wife, his fondness for Nancy and the knowledge that Martin Colbert's behavior has forever tarnished that innocent relationship. Or is it the institution of slavery itself that makes friendship between master and slave impossible? In the end the miller provides the money for Nancy's escape.

The melodramatic tale unfolds in the years before Willa was born but she was a witness to the end of the story and in an epilogue she mixes fact and fiction to describe Nancy Till's homecoming twenty-five years later. It was the greatest experience of her life, said Willa, and it haunted her for sixty years. As she tells it in *Sapphira*, she was sick in bed in her mother's room where the wide front window overlooked the road where she so often watched for Mary Ann Anderson. This day, however, it was not Mrs. Anderson who was awaited but a woman whose romantic story Willa had often heard and who became her fictional Nancy Till. Twenty-five years earlier the woman had been taken across the Potomac by Willa's grandmother, Rachel Boak, on the first lap of her underground railway voyage. Since then she had been living in Canada and she and her mother had not seen each other in all that time.

"The actual scene of the reunion," wrote Willa, "had been arranged for my benefit." Mrs. Cather wanted Willa to be present when the two women met so Aunt Till felt obliged to remain in the bedroom with the little girl rather than greet her daughter as soon as she entered the house. There is something more than a little pathetic, almost cruel, in the woman's gentle acceptance of her position in the household—"'You stay right here, and I'll stay right here,'" she says. "'Nancy'll come up and you'll see her as soon as I do.'" It is doubtful, however, that Willa appreciated either the delicacy of Till's forbearance or the irony of the situation. Like her mother, Willa took for granted certain deferences.

Nevertheless, the reunion is memorable: "Till had already risen; when the stranger followed my mother into the room, she took a few uncertain steps forward. She fell meekly into the arms of a tall, gold-skinned woman, who drew the little old darky to her breast and held her there, bending her face down over the head scantily covered with grey wool. Neither spoke a word. There was something Scriptural in that meeting, like the pictures in our old Bible."

Unfortunately Willa may have waited too long to tell the story. In 1941 when *Sapphira and the Slave Girl* was published Willa was nearing seventy, her health was poor and she was very tired. The book has flashes of perception and intermittent passages of tenderness and affection for the countryside and the country folk, but the narrative drive has slowed, the plot falters before the climax is reached and the individual parts are more impressive than the book as a whole. Powerful forces are set in motion and intricate relationships exposed, between mother and daughter, husband and wife, master and slave, but in the end the author seems to have been too weary to do more than suggest the implications of her grand design.

What gives the book its special flavor is the quiet way in which Willa evokes the ordinary everyday occurrences that made the little society of Back Creek a world unto itself. The rhythm of daily life had not changed very much in the years between the time of which she wrote and the childhood years she remembered so well. The comings and goings at Willowshade when the Cathers lived there were much the same as the life Willa described at the Mill Farm with Sapphira presiding in the parlor and Till holding sway in the kitchen. Grandma Boak had her house in the village and went visiting among the neighbors just as Mrs. Blake did. The old mill still stood alongside the creek when Willa was a child; it belonged to Mrs. Boak's family, the Siberts. Not very much of the book was really fiction, she told a friend. In fact, it was so largely made up of old family stories and neighborhood tales, she hardly knew where her own contribution began.

Undoubtedly, Willa Cather's most notable contribution is Sapphira Dodderidge Colbert herself, the proud and willful woman, accustomed to dominating every situation, who is overtaken by passions she is helpless to control. In her jealousy Sapphira behaves monstrously and it is not difficult to appreciate Edith Lewis' contention that the book is a novel without a heroine. Yet while Sapphira is not admirable, Willa Cather manages to make her human. The character is so complex and the author's understanding of her so sure, it is impossible for the reader to come away from the book without a sense of having been in the presence of a formidable personality for whom one feels repugnance, it is true, but also pity. Edith Lewis may not have wished to see it, but much of the power of the portrait derives from the realization that, of all the characters in the book, Willa Cather identified most closely with Sapphira.

For Willa too was capable of volatile emotions and she admired people who were strong and independent. If along with strength ran ruthlessness and even cruelty, she could recognize some of that in herself and she could understand it. She was not sparing of herself, but neither was she judgmental about others. She had no patience with weakness, however, and she deliberately made Nancy, who is the natural heroine of the tale, a passive character. Rachel Blake, modeled so closely on Willa's beloved grandmother, performs an act of heroism that is central to the plot but she herself is not pivotal. No, it is Sapphira who dominates the book at every turn, untamed and defiant, the last and possibly the strongest of Willa Cather's great heroines.

* * *

Willa's long literary silence about her earliest experiences makes it appear that the Virginia years were a prologue, separate from the drama of her later life. Her statement, when she was a successful author, that a writer's most important years are between eight and fifteen, tends to encourage the idea that Virginia, which she left when she was nine, played a negligible role and that life did not begin for her until Nebraska. Yet significant domestic changes were taking place in the Cather household in Virginia that were bound to have an effect on an impressionable child. Three more children were born at Willowshade, two boys, Roscoe and Douglass, and in 1881, a second daughter, Jessica. The boys, four and seven years younger than their elder sister, became her dearest friends and playmates, but Jessica never shared Willa's tomboy interests and they were never close.

Meanwhile, other members of the Cather family had joined the great westward migration and their letters describing frontier life were read eagerly by the Charles Cathers left behind at Willowshade. In 1877 Willa had said goodbye to her Cather grandparents who left Virginia to settle permanently in Nebraska. A few years earlier they had gone out to visit their eldest son, George, and his wife, Frances Amanda Smith, known as Franc, a former schoolteacher from Massachusetts. Their first home had been a sod hut on the prairie, but now George was a successful farmer and they lived in a comfortable frame house. Accompanying Caroline and William Cather when they moved were their daughters, Alverna and Jennie, with their two small children. Jennie died within months of their arrival in the West and Alverna followed her to the grave six years later. Another daughter had died in Virginia before they left. All three suffered from tuberculosis which the damp Virginia climate had aggravated. After their mothers' death the children, Willa's cousins Kyd Clutter and Retta Ayre and a second child born to Alverna in Nebraska, were raised by their grandparents, just as Jim Burden was in *My Antonia.*

After his parents moved, Charles Cather managed the farm and Willa's mother presided over Willowshade. There they might have remained despite enthusiastic letters from the West except that the climate was a nagging source of worry to them. The Cathers had always been susceptible to TB and now Charles had his own growing family to think about. In 1883, when his barn burned down, he made the decision to join his parents and brother in Nebraska. Grandma Boak would go along with two of her nieces, and Margie Anderson and her brother, as well. Willowshade was sold for six thousand dollars and the furnishings auctioned. Finally, all that remained was to arrange for Vic, Charles Cather's sheepdog and a great favorite of Willa's, to go to a farmer. Edith Lewis tells the story she heard many times from Willa, how just as the family were preparing to board the train, Vic broke loose and came running across the fields, her broken chain dragging behind her. It was one of Willa's saddest memories, wrote Edith Lewis, of a time "that was all of it tragic for a child of her nature."

Tragic does not seem too strong a word to describe the desolation of the nine-year-old Willa. For despite the literary neglect she imposed upon her early memories, as a child she had been passionately attached to Willowshade. She loved the red brick house and "every tree and every rock, every landmark of the countryside, all the familiar faces, all their 'things' . . . all their ways." Interestingly, the few early stories set in Virginia draw their inspiration from the familiar countryside rather than from the people she knew. Willa Cather would be attached to places her entire life and Willowshade was a first love and a lasting one. The pain of separation must have been so intense that she needed to bury the memory of all that she had lost. Loss and change, change and loss, they followed Willa Cather all her life, they helped to form her character and in time became the themes that dominate her fiction.

"THE AWFUL LONELINESS AND LEVEL OF THE DIVIDE"

The journey from the East Coast to the Divide, that stretch of plain and prairie between the Republican and Little Blue rivers that was Willa Cather's destination, is arduous even today. No direct plane service exists from New York to Nebraska. The modern traveler flies first to Chicago and changes planes at O'Hare Airport for the ninety-minute flight to Lincoln. From Lincoln still another aircraft makes the trip to Grand Island. And from Grand Island the journey continues by car down a sparsely traveled two-lane highway. Due south is Red Cloud almost at the Kansas border and within a short distance of the geographical center of the continental United States at Lebanon, Kansas. To the east and west along route 281, under an enveloping sky, mile after mile of cultivated fields of grain stretch endlessly, an artist's palette of yellow corn, bright green patches of newly planted winter wheat and stubborn clumps of crimson milo. Between the road and the horizon only an occasional farmhouse in its circle of cottonwoods gives evidence of a human touch on the otherwise deserted landscape.

In the spring of 1883 the Cather family made the tedious journey to Nebraska by railroad. The earlier covered-wagon and stagecoach days were only memories by then. Old-timers would tell stories of Nebraska when it belonged to the buffalo and Indian hunters and was less a land to be settled than a resting-place en route to somewhere farther west. Once the Mormons had used it as a camping ground on their way to Utah, and in 1849 gold-hunters had crossed it, headed for California. But by the time Willa Cather arrived, Nebraska had been a state for sixteen years. No longer "a highway for dreamers and adventurers," the wagon trails had given way to railroad tracks, and along the route of the Burlington and Missouri Railroad a string of untidy little railroad towns and farm settlements had sprung up. The buffalo and Indians had all but disappeared, and the towns sat like sentinels on the raw prairie.

The railroads that brought the Cathers and other families from the South and East created something entirely new on the great plains of the Middle West. They brought into being an instant polyglot society, the likes of which had never been seen before. Not only were large numbers of foreign workers brought over from Europe to build the railroads, but a vigorous promotional campaign recruited emigrants to settle the untamed land through which the trains would pass. Posters went up in European cities, in Bohemia and Scandinavia, in Germany and Austria, advertising the availability of land, the richness of the soil, the opportunity to start a new life in hospitable surroundings. Agents opened offices to sign people up and facilitate their passage. The railroad companies had acquired extensive tracts of land from the federal government before exact routes had been determined and were anxious to rid themselves of the unused portions before they became a tax burden. In addition, a lively town along the way meant customers for the railroad and a prosperous business moving freight.

State and local governments joined the railroads in competition for foreign settlers. Just as the Burlington vied with the Santa Fe, so Nebraska vied with Iowa and Kansas and even Minnesota. Sometimes a man came alone or with a brother to try out the new land. More often he brought his family. The train would drop them off at a railroad siding where they would spend the first night in the West huddled in a single bare room in a boardinghouse along the railroad tracks. The next day the farmer would set out to find the land that had been promised to him and the sod cave that would be home for him, his wife, his children and his animals in the back-breaking years that lay ahead.

The highly colored brochures and the fast-talking land "boomers" did not prepare the new settlers for the harshness of pioneer life. Some broke and turned back, but most remained and soon others followed. They came from all over Europe. And from the New World, too. The Civil War had caused great dislocation; many homes were lost and farms destroyed. From Virginia came farmers hungering for land. From the crowded cities of the East came restless men and women eager to make a fresh start. Sometimes an entire community from New England or Ohio would move together. Sometimes gold-hunters with empty pockets, returning from California, would remember the campsites on the sunny plains and find their way back again to Nebraska.

They came by rail from both coasts, and at every junction trainloads of settlers, Europeans and Americans, would arrive and depart, their paths crisscrossing, their destinies forever interlocked in the towns and villages of the frontier. One of these junctions was Red Cloud, Nebraska, where eight passenger trains came through daily, traveling between Chicago and Denver. It was here that the weary Cather party arrived one April day, but Red Cloud was not their final destination. They were going on to Catherton, the Virginia settlement sixteen miles to the northwest. It is just possible that on that first day Willa Cather never even saw the little town that her presence was to make famous and that she would write about again and again, calling it Sweetwater or Black Hawk or Moonstone, but always, always, describing Red Cloud.

The last part of the Cathers' journey was made in the bed of a horse-drawn farm wagon, bumping and swaying over the hard red prairie. Nothing in her experience could have prepared the little girl from Back Creek Valley for the country she now beheld. "There seemed nothing to see; no fences, no creeks or trees, no hills or fields . . . There was nothing but land: not a country at all, but the material out of which countries are made."

The words are Jim Burden's in *My Antonia*, but the experience was Willa Cather's and years later she could recall it vividly. She too had felt the erasure of personality, the sense of having made a long journey only to come to the end of everything. In all the loneliness and bleak expanse around her the larks sounded the sole familiar note. They brought back a memory of "something" and just to see them rise into the air and to hear their song clutched at her heart and brought her close to tears.

This then was Nebraska, this vast and lonely sky, this windswept space of earth, this desolate and God-forsaken land. This then was Nebraska that she would one day leave but would never be free of, that was to become the "happiness and the curse" of her life and the source of her deepest inspiration.

* * *

Willa Cather's first home in Nebraska was her grandfather's house on the Divide. Its most characteristic feature which she described faithfully in *My Antonia* was a basement kitchen and dining room with the whitewashed plaster laid directly upon the earth walls just as it used to be in dugouts. Next to the kitchen a long cellar had a stairway and a door leading directly to the outside. In Virginia the kitchen quarters had been separate from the house and it was customary to speak of "out in the kitchen"; in Nebraska it was "down in the kitchen," only one of many bewildering changes for the Willowshade family. When Charles and Virginia Cather arrived with their brood William Cather took the opportunity to go back to Virginia for a visit and his wife Caroline went to stay with their son James and his wife, leaving Charles once again to farm his father's land.

The first months in Catherton were trying. Mrs. Cather was desperately homesick and not well physically, so that it fell to Grandma Boak and Margie to keep the household going and look after the children, with some help from Cousin Bess. Willa too was sick that year. Mildred Bennett who has written extensively about the Cathers in Nebraska thinks Willa may have had a touch of polio.

Willa Cather's Nebraska is so much a part of American literary lore, and she told the story of pioneer life on the Divide in so many guises in her books and stories that it is always difficult, and often impossible, to separate the actual child of nine or ten and her first impressions from her fictional counterparts and from the older author drawing on her early memories. We know that Willa, like her mother, was intensely homesick at first, that she missed the curving land back home, the familiar hills and valleys, and above all the woods, where an imaginative little girl could find a place to hide. Here, when she stepped out of her grandfather's house, she saw only unfenced prairie land, flat and bare as sheet iron, with just a thin line of cottonwood trees in the distance to suggest the course of a vagrant stream. In later years her feelings softened and the hard earth seemed to her to be "young and fresh and kindly." She could even endow the featureless landscape with superior attributes of its own. "The mere absence of rocks gave the soil a kind of amiability and generosity, and the absence of natural boundaries gave the spirit a wider range," she wrote in *The Song of the Lark*.

But that was later, long after she and the country had had it out together, as she put it, and she had made her peace with the wild land. In the beginning, fresh from the gentler world of Back Creek Valley, she was appalled by what seemed the ugliness around her and terrified that she would go under unless she found a way to make the new life tolerable. Another child might have turned inward in despair and lost herself in a fantasy world but to Willa's credit she found an outlet for her sympathies in a consuming interest in her foreign neighbors on the Divide. The people, she said, made up for what she missed in the country, it was as simple as that. She found them, Scandinavians, Bohemians, Spanish and French, in sod houses, on lonely farms and in settlements along the faded wagon trails. "On Sunday," she wrote in later years, "we could drive to a Norwegian church and listen to a sermon in that language, or to a Danish or Swedish church. We could go to a French Catholic settlement or into the Bohemian township and hear one in Czech, or we could go to church with the German Lutherans." Willa's bright, inquisitive nature had always attracted her to people with good stories to tell and she had absorbed everything she could possibly learn from the ex-slaves, the transient tradesman and the mountain women who came and went at Willowshade. Here in Nebraska she found a whole new cast of fascinating characters and a new audience as well, for if Willa was a good listener, she also enjoyed attention and she liked to talk.

A beguiling story is told of the nine-year-old Willa on a shopping trip to Red Cloud to buy shoes soon after the family arrived in Nebraska. Perched on a shelf in Miner Brothers General Store, she discoursed with authority on English history and life in Virginia and quoted Shakespeare to an amazed audience of Mr. Miner's clerks and customers. The town folk of Red Cloud were to become less tolerant of her precocity, but on that early visit they were disposed to be indulgent, and probably praised her and rewarded her with bags of candy just as the Bohemian farmers petted Marie Tovesky and gave her sweets when her uncle brought her into town in *O Pioneers!* In a leopard-skin coat and hat, with her well-bred manners and the soft Southern speech she tried hard to lose later on, Willa, like Marie, must have seemed an exotic little creature. Mr. Miner, with perhaps more than a touch of malice, referred to her as a "young curiosity shop," because she asked so many questions, but on her first visit to his store Willa was herself the curiosity.

Willa chose her own friends and her first playmates in Nebraska were not her cousins or the children of the Virginia colony but the son and daughter of the Fred Lambrechts, German neighbors whose sod house lay along the trail from Catherton to Red Cloud. She didn't like the Virginians who had settled Catherton, they seemed to her narrow and provincial, clinging to their old ways without attempting to learn about the newcomers who had brought with them more interesting and decidedly more colorful customs. Willa was fascinated by the foreign immigrants who lived side by side with the Southerners but were so very different.

She was drawn especially to the older women, the mothers and the grandmothers, who warmed to the little girl's interest and sympathized with her sense of strangeness and the homesickness that came in waves those first lonely weeks on the prairie. They too had been forced to sever ties, to leave cherished homes behind and make a life for themselves in a new land, one that didn't even speak their language. Willa's father told her she must show grit, it was the only way to get along in a new country, and when she met the women on the Divide she knew what he meant. For if their kindness was a comfort to her, they had other qualities that left a deeper mark. They were strong and courageous with a fierce pride that made it possible for them to survive the uprooting of their lives and to endure the rigors of pioneer existence, and the child seemed to have an intuitive understanding of what they had gone through. Despite their hardships, they had kept their spirit and this they shared in abundance with the friendly little girl who liked to visit with them as they went about their work.

In Virginia, Willa had listened to Mrs. Anderson and Grandma Boak talk about the old days and she knew by heart their stories of the Civil War and before. Now she sat in the kitchens of her new neighbors and heard for the first time about an even older world across the sea, where the sun was always shining, the young men were always handsome and the sweet air was filled with melody. It was a world that never was, but Willa didn't know that, and the old women had forgotten the reasons why they had left their old lives behind or they preferred remembering the good times when they were young rather than the drudgery and disappointments. In the harshness of a prairie winter it was good to cling to a romantic picture of a kinder, easier life.

It is an appealing and persistent image, the earnest youngster with her mannerly Virginia ways drawing out the farm women to talk about their lives. One day the stories would find their way into her books, for now it was enough that they were imprinted on her heart. Years later Willa Cather told an interviewer that she had never found any intellectual excitement more intense than she used to feel those mornings she spent with the old women at their baking or butter-making. On the face of it the remark seems sentimental and pretentious until one reflects that Willa was versed in the dramas and melodramas of classical mythology and Shakespeare which her grandmothers had read to her from her earliest childhood. In the child's mind there was little difference between the elaborate plots of Shakespeare and the story she heard when she first came to the Divide about the tragic suicide of the Bohemian farmer Francis Sadilek, who broke his violin across his knees before tying a rifle to his toe and shooting himself. By the time she made the statement to the interviewer Willa had already imposed her own vision upon the raw material. She had become a mythmaker herself who looked back upon her early encounters on the Divide as intellectual no less than emotional experiences.

Yet the days on the Divide that were to remain with Willa Cather for a lifetime, and that she would write about until she died, were over in little more than a year. She had seen the seasons on the prairie change just once, the short, bitter winter followed by the "flower-laden spring," the long, hot summer that gave way to the Western autumn, "that season of perpetual sun, blazing blue skies and frosty nights." By the fall of 1884 it was all over. Charles Cather had decided to give up the farm at Catherton and open an office in Red Cloud where he could use the law training he had received in his youth to make farm loans and write insurance.

Willa's father had a feckless side to his nature that she allows us to see most transparently in a little episode in "Old Mrs. Harris" when Mr. Templeton, an unabashed portrait of Charles Cather, takes off from home "on urgent business" (as he always does in a crisis, observes Mandy) when he learns his wife is going to have another baby. Like Mr. Templeton, Charles Cather avoided unpleasantness and inconvenience when he could. He had never found farm work congenial and he was not a man to stay at a job he didn't like. There were also other reasons, it must be said, for the family to leave Catherton. Mrs. Cather's health continued to be poor and it was generally understood that she might prefer not to live so far from the doctor. The schools in Red Cloud were considered among the best in the state and this too was an incentive for the family. For the first time Willa would not be taught at home by her grandmother but would attend the local school with other children of her own age.

Once again the livestock were sold and the machinery disposed of and the Cather family moved into town in time for the opening of school in the fall of 1884. It was another dislocation for Willa but without the upheaval of the year before when she had traveled half-way across the continent to reach her new home. Catherton was only sixteen miles away and she could expect to return frequently to visit her aunt and uncle. She may even have looked forward to town as a new adventure.

The year in Catherton which was so important for her imaginative life changed Willa Cather in other ways. Her mother's illness and her grandmother's preoccupation with the household and the younger children had given her a freedom that was unusual for the daughter of a Southern family. That she had seized upon it so whole-heartedly was no doubt as much to escape the situation in the crowded house as to become acquainted with the vast new country and her exotic neighbors. It is interesting that as the eldest she was not expected to take on responsibility in the household. That was left to Mrs. Boak and Margie and, to some extent, to Cousin Bess who had come with the Cathers from Virginia. Willa was allowed to roam at will and it gave her a sense of independence she was never afterward to lose. She discovered, earlier than most, a world outside the home and while she was devoted to them she would always de-tach herself a little from the other members of the family. Her range of experience and understanding had widened enormously during those months on the Divide, and by the time she came to Red Cloud she was already the student of human relations she later professed to be.

A TOWN AT THE EDGE OF NOWHERE

Red Cloud when Willa first knew it was a thriving county seat not much older than she was. As a schoolgirl studying local history she was taught that Silas Garber, a former captain in the Union army, took a small party on horseback from Omaha in 1870 and built a stockade on a rise a mile or so above the Republican River. He named the little settlement for a friendly chief of the Sioux and saw it prosper with the coming of the railroad eight years later. By the time the Cathers arrived the town had a population of about twenty-five hundred which grew to five thousand within a few years. In the early 1900s the Burlington railroad decided to move its division point from Red Cloud to Hastings and Red Cloud's influence declined, but in the 1880s and '90s, while Willa was growing up, the citizens of Red Cloud had good reason to think their town was the finest in the state. The *Nebraska State Journal* in 1883 wrote that no town was better off in the line of churches and schools and that "even children in the street show that they are offspring of parents who appreciate advantages." What the *Journal's* writer might have added was that the children reflected their parents' anxious desire to maintain on the raw prairie the dress and the civility of the East.

The white house on Cedar Street to which Charles Cather brought his family was one block west of Webster, Red Cloud's main street, in the part of town where most of the prominent families built their homes. The Cathers didn't own their house, however, but rented it from a German family in town named Newhouse. It was not unusual for people of substance to rent in those days when housing was scarce. Willa said her father thought it made more sense to keep his capital in the business and the Cathers continued to lease the house from Mrs. Newhouse until 1904 when they finally bought a home of their own on Sixth and Seward, a few blocks north. By then Willa had left home and was living in Pittsburgh. The length of time the family rented, and the crowded conditions on Cedar Street, suggest that Charles Cather may have been reluctant to buy a house for another reason, one that his daughter alludes to in her autobiographical story, "Old Mrs. Harris," when Victoria Templeton despairs over her husband's lack of success and the crowded quarters that were all he could provide for her.

Charles Cather's own career as a businessman was only marginally successful and the family's financial situation, though never dire, was over the years often precarious. Charles himself was never certain that he might not have to move on again. He managed property around the state and at one time or another thought of settling in Hastings or possibly in Lincoln. With his temperament and careless

Southern ways, Charles, without a family to hold him to his responsibilities, might well have become one of the drifters Willa wrote about, who somehow charmed their way about the world.

The Cather house behind its picket fence on a tree-shaded corner lot stands today just as it did when Willa lived there. Approached from the street, the narrow front makes it appear smaller than it proves to be. Inside, a warren of small rooms stretches lengthwise. The house is very much as Willa described it in her stories. There's the front parlor where Thea lay when Dr. Archie came to examine her in *The Song of the Lark,* the dining room beyond and two small bedrooms for the parents and the youngest children who shared their room with Cousin Bess. Grandma Boak, like Mrs. Harris, made a bedroom for herself in a corridor off the kitchen. The layout may not have been as haphazard as it seems, since there was another house exactly like it on the other side of town. Nevertheless, for a household that rarely consisted of fewer than nine or ten adults and children at any one time, the quarters must have seemed severely cramped.

The house had a saving grace, however—a commodious attic covering half of it. There, Willa and her brothers, Roscoe and Douglass, shared a dormitory, their beds standing side by side "as in a hospital ward," even as they do today in the restored homestead. The space was actually large enough for each one to have a separate area, but like Lesley Ferguesson and her brothers in "The Best Years," the older Cather children were a triumvirate in the early Red Cloud days and they wanted "to be close enough to share experiences." Upstairs was their private world, a "story in itself, a secret romance." Later Cousin Bess curtained a small area for herself in one corner and a little cubby had already been fashioned for Margie over the kitchen.

When it was time for Willa to give up the dormitory for a room of her own, a move her mother probably encouraged as she saw her daughter starting to mature, a corner of the attic was partitioned off for her as well. Unlike Cousin Bess, however, Willa was provided with a door with lock and key, and the little bedroom under the eaves became her cherished sanctum. She furnished it with an old dresser of her mother's, a night table and a blue washstand, covered the walls with a rose-patterned paper she paid for herself—the younger children referred to it as the Rose Bower—placed her books and other treasures on a narrow bookshelf and declared the room could be entered by invitation only. When she went away to college she locked her door and after she left home for good, the bedroom was passed on to the younger members of the family. Jack, the youngest of the Cathers, took possession in 1900 at the age of eight. Willa was twenty-seven and living in Pittsburgh at the time and she wrote a poem, "Are You Sleeping Little Brother?" in which she expressed her fondness for the snug nest where she had dreamed and planned, and her love for the little boy who slept in her bed and woke as she did to the song of the lark in the morning.

In spite of the sentimental attachment she would always feel for the attic dormitory, recalled so lovingly at the end of her life in "The Best Years," a room of her own had a very special meaning for the young Willa Cather. Thea Kronborg, who often speaks for her creator, considered that moving into her room was "one of the most important things that ever happened to her." For Thea, as for Willa, it marked the beginning of her double life. By day she was one of the children, a part of the group life of the busy household. But at night when she closed the door, in the privacy of her own room, she became a different person. "Pleasant plans and ideas occurred to her," says Thea, "which had never come before."

The theme of the double life intrigued Willa. She caught a glimpse of it in later years in the way performers handled their private affairs and their public careers, and she returned to the theme in an essay about the writer Katherine Mansfield. Her comments about Mansfield's attitude toward family life reveal much about Willa's own sensitivity to the constant rubbing together of personalities. "The mere struggle to have anything of one's own," she wrote, "to be one's self at all, creates an element of strain which keeps everybody almost at the breaking point." Small wonder that Willa felt the need for a place where she could be unreservedly herself, where she could be alone to think things through. It was only in solitude that the other, secret life could come to the surface, "passionate and intense," the real life that "stamps the face and gives character to the voice." Katherine Mansfield, she said, "knew all about the secret accords and antipathies which lie hidden under our everyday behavior," and so did Willa Cather.

It is impossible not to hear Willa's voice in Thea Kronborg's glad cry when her mother gives birth to a boy. "Brothers are better," Thea says. And surely Willa must have seen a look on her own sister Jessie's face like the glance of spite Thea sees on Anna's, which makes Thea realize Anna has always disliked her. Jessica and Willa were often at odds and neither of her sisters claimed the affection Willa lavished on her brothers, although she had loved Elsie dearly as an infant.

"Human relationships are the tragic necessity of human life," wrote Willa Cather, and all that she would ever need to know about the subject she learned in the little house on Cedar Street and among her friends and neighbors in Red Cloud. On the prairie, she had seen men and women in a naked struggle with the elements. In Red Cloud where life was tamer, she was an observer of the more subtle interplay of personalities. After two scant years on the Divide she felt that she had met the challenge of the land and was reconciled to it, but at the end of a lifetime she had yet to come to terms with the town. The ambivalence she felt, the love-hate she was to express over and over in her stories and in letters to her closest friends, was fully reciprocated by the town. It is a hundred years since Willa Cather came to live in Red Cloud and she arouses conflicting passions to this day.

To understand the town's attitude it is necessary to realize that Red Cloud, along with so many other small towns of the West, had been settled by Easterners, many from the South, who brought with them long-established ways of doing things. For those who found the vast spaces of the frontier overwhelming it was as if their personal survival depended on recreating the patterns of social life they had left behind. They were like English colonials holding high teas and cricket matches in the tropics. In such an atmosphere, where safety lay in clinging to traditions, the nonconformist was not appreciated, and when she was a schoolgirl who cut her hair and wore short skirts and performed experiments on animals, the raised eyebrows not infrequently gave way to outright hostility. The Cather family came in for criticism, too, for being too indulgent to their children. At home Mrs. Cather was a stern disciplinarian who used a rawhide whip when she thought it necessary to exercise control, but as far as the town could see, the Cather children did exactly as they pleased, even turning their backyard into a dumping ground for old packing boxes and wooden crates to build a toy town. The sniffs were almost audible, but the Cathers seemed oblivious. They were polite and even friendly, but the Cathers had a way of seeming not to care whether they were liked or not, an attitude that a small town usually finds infuriating. You couldn't get under their skin, and that too irked their neighbors.

Mrs. Cather was a particular target of annoyance. She was accused of giving herself airs, although the town saw nothing for the Charles Cathers to feel superior about. The *George* Cathers were another matter: George was a success. But Charles had trouble making ends meet. Yet here was his wife, dressed to the nines, expecting small attentions, behaving as though she didn't know that they were poor. Family pride might suffice at Willowshade, but it was not enough in Red Cloud. Red Cloud wasn't interested in who you were, they cared for what you did and how well you did at it.

As always, Willa went her own way. She had always been a self-reliant child and her experience on the Divide had given her an added taste of freedom and independence she would not lightly renounce when she moved into the more confining town. She was not so much unconventional as she was indifferent to convention and impatient with standards she considered stuffy and artificial. She didn't feel an obligation to people she didn't like and she had a way of disregarding those who didn't interest her that caused resentment in the town. As she grew older she paid more attention to civility, but she never became tolerant. She liked to tell a story in later life about herself as a child in Virginia, when an old judge came to call and teased her in the patronizing manner of some adults with children. She used the only recourse that was available to her, warning him off with angry words: "I'se a dang'ous nigger, I is." One can imagine the trembling body, see the blazing eyes. The judge may have been amused, Mrs. Cather was mortified, but Red Cloud would have recognized the mutinous little rebel in the Willa Cather they knew.

Considering the temper of the town Willa was fortunate that her immediate neighbors were neither narrow-minded nor provincial. The Charles Wieners who lived next door were a cultured German-Jewish couple who spoke French as well as German and whose home and library were always open to their young neighbor. Willa paid her debt to these old friends in the characters of Mr. and Mrs. Rosen in "Old Mrs. Harris." Mrs. Wiener died when Willa was in college but she continued to dine with Mr. Wiener on Sunday nights whenever she was home. In New York she met his brother, a well-known doctor who numbered Paderewski among his patients. Through Dr. Wiener she was introduced to Alexis Carrel and witnessed some of the early experiments in blood transfusions.

A block away from the Cathers lived the Miner family, four sisters and a brother, the children of the owner of the general store—the one who thought Willa asked too many questions—and his Norwegian-born wife. The Harlings of *My Ántonia* are portraits of the Miner girls and their parents and the book is dedicated to Carrie and Irene Miner "In memory of affections old and true." The Miner daughters and Willa or Willie, as she was known in her family and among her Red Cloud contemporaries, became lifelong friends, and in her later years when she no longer returned to Nebraska, it was Carrie Miner Sherwood, the eldest, who remained in Red Cloud and who died there at the age of 103, who was Willa's closest link to her hometown. Irene, the model for the susceptible Nina Harling who "was rather more complex than the other children," left Red Cloud for Chicago when she married, but she and Willa kept in touch and Willa would stop off and stay with Irene and her husband, "Mr. Weisz," as Willa always referred to him in the formal manner of the day, on the frequent trips she made across the continent. Mary Miner married Dr. Creighton who took care of Willa's parents in their last years and Willa treasured the one season the Creightons spent in New York when she had been able to see them often. Mary Miner had been the first to call on her when she came to Red Cloud, bearing a tiny bottle of perfume in a red plush slipper.

The Miners were her oldest, dearest friends and she clung to them her entire life. They knew her in the sunny years when she was young and life was full of hope, and together they had memories that no one else could share. When Margie Miner died, the first to go, Willa felt that she had lost a part of her own youth. The sisters, in turn, loved their childhood friend devotedly. They read every word she wrote, followed every last detail of her career and, when they were together, catered to her every mood. Carrie held teas for her when she came home and frequently smoothed ruffled feelings, acting as a buffer between Willa and people in Red Cloud she had unthinkingly offended. Dr. Creighton appealed to her on one occasion to be especially kind to a young woman who was pregnant and going through a difficult time, having already lost one baby. He knew Willa didn't mean to be unkind but she could be brusque with people and the girl was sensitive. After his death Willa told Mary that she was complimented that the doctor came to her directly to ask her to mend her manner. Still, he was letting her know in his gentle way that she sometimes behaved badly, and she must have been more than a little chagrined.

As a child Willa was drawn to the Miner house as often by the mother as by the daughters. She said in later years that every one of the fictional mothers she created contained a little bit of Mama Miner, but that Mrs. Harling was so exact a copy as to be a snapshot. Like her special friends on the prairie, Mrs. Miner too had come from Europe and told romantic tales of growing up in Christiania where her father played the oboe in Ole Bull's famous Royal Norwegian Orchestra. Mrs. Miner played the piano and the girls performed as well, giving Willa her first taste of classical music. Mrs. Miner also introduced the Cathers to Professor Shindelmeisser, an old German music teacher who went from town to town giving piano lessons. Willa was his pupil for a while but she preferred to hear him talk rather than learn to play the piano and the lessons ceased. The model for Professor Wunsch in *The Song of the Lark*, Shindelmeisser shared with Wunsch a weakness for the bottle. He was appreciated, nonetheless, by Mrs. Miner and Mrs. Cather whose attitude may be gathered by the comment Thea's mother made about Professor Wunsch, "It's good for us he does drink. He'd never be in a place like this if he didn't have some weakness."

It was in "a place like this," however, that Willa grew up and spent the crucial adolescent years from eleven to seventeen. If the town served as inspiration for the writer she would someday be, and all of the small towns she wrote about are reflections of Red Cloud, we must also turn to Red Cloud to understand the woman she would someday be. To Edith Lewis, who herself had fled Nebraska as a girl, Red Cloud seemed lost in the prairie "as if the hot wind that so much of the time blew over it went on and left it behind, isolated, forgotten by the rest of the world." Seeing it after many years brought back "that forlornness, that terrible restlessness that comes over young people born in small towns in the middle of the continent; the sense of being cut off from all the great currents of life and thought." The young Willa felt those deprivations too, but she was incapable of existing in such an environment without somehow transforming it. If there was little she could do to change the town in fact, she could impose her own vision and desire upon it in fiction. "It was this little town, seemingly so insignificant, so commonplace, so meagre in imaginative material, that became for Willa Cather a rich, an almost exhaustless mine of experience," wrote Edith Lewis. One wonders what her genius would have made of more abundant raw material.

In the same sense that Willa created a Nebraska and a Red Cloud that she could live with, she also created an identity of her own that satisfied her, one that was strong, independent, essentially masculine. According to one story, she cut her hair short because her mother was ill and couldn't comb her long curls, then decided that it suited her and wore it that way until she was halfway through college. She had the bluff and hearty manners of a boy and tried to dress as boyishly as possible and do the things that boys did. She liked to go barefoot and fish and canoe with her brothers on the Republican River, or hunt for buried treasure with them on the little island near the mouth of Indian Creek. Sometimes she would take Roscoe with her when she rode out to see her friends in the foreign settlements at the outskirts of the town. She thought of herself as an outsider who didn't quite fit in with her neighbors, but she was not a loner. Her brothers were her companions, old enough to keep up with her but young enough to follow her lead. When the children built Sandy Point, a toy town in the Cather backyard, Willa was its mayor. She probably ruled it every bit as autocratically as Speckle Burnham in "The Way of the World," before his nemesis, Mary Eliza, brought disaster and ruin on Speckleville. There is a lot of Willa in Speckle's bossiness and efficiency and a lot of Willa, also, in those talents of Mary Eliza's which "peculiarly fitted her to dwell and rule in a boys' town." There are some girls, wrote the older author, "who would make the best boys in the world—if they were not girls." Very likely this was the way Red Cloud's Willie Cather saw herself.

Her ambition was to be a doctor at a time when few women practiced medicine, but she didn't see herself as a feminist or pioneer, opening up fresh avenues to women. The name she adopted was William Cather, M.D., sometimes also adding Jr. It is in this male role that she perceived herself, putting up a shingle on her door and writing William Cather, Jr., in her books. It is interesting that she chose her formidable grandfather to identify with and not her gentle father. Two of Red Cloud's doctors became her friends, Dr. McKeeby who was the model for Dr. Archie in *The Song of the Lark* and Dr. Damerell. She accompanied them both on calls, even helping Dr. Damerell give chloroform to a boy whose leg he amputated. Willa herself caused a great fuss in Red Cloud by performing experiments on animals with a set of medical instruments that somehow found their way into the Cather house.

At the age of fifteen she filled out a form in a friend's album that gives some idea of the direction of her interests, as well as providing a rare instance of her sense of humor. Under the heading "Opinions, Tastes and Fancies of Wm. Cather M.D., October 10, 1888," Willa wrote that "Vivisection" was her favorite amusement, "To be an M.D." her chief ambition and "amputating limbs," her idea of perfect happiness. Her idea of real misery was "doing fancy work." "A cultured gentleman" was her choice as traveling companion and "a good-looking woman" her idea of "the greatest wonder of the world." Yet stirrings of the future storyteller are already discernible. Shakespeare (spelled Sheakspear), Tennyson and Emerson are her favorite book, poet and prose writer respectively; books are the thing for which she has the deepest attachment.

Willa could hardly remember a time in her life when books had not been important to her. As a child she had loved her grandmother to read aloud to her and later when she herself could read she found a small eclectic library to choose from in her own home. The Cathers were an educated, well-read family and they kept adding to the store of books they brought with them from Willowshade. In the Red Cloud parlor were complete sets of Dickens, Scott, Thackeray, Poe, Hawthorne, Ruskin, Emerson and Carlyle, in addition to well-thumbed volumes of Shakespeare and the English poets. Mrs. Cather liked the lighter romantic novels of the day and these too were accessible to Willa who uncritically read everything that came her way. She pored over translations of the Greek and Roman classics and in the Wiener home began to read French with Mrs. Wiener.

While she encountered disapproval from the gossips of the town, Willa also found encouragement from some of the older people like the Wieners and Doctors McKeeby and Damerell who saw through the surface eccentricities to the solid, brilliant girl beneath. She was lucky, too, to find teachers of unusual distinction in the Red Cloud schools. Evangeline King-Case, who taught literature and foreign languages, later became Superintendent of Public Instruction for Webster County. E. K. Brown wrote of her that she "had a remarkable perception of the moral and intellectual flaws in the town's way of life and was an ally in Willa Cather's efforts to find an environment in which her mind could grow more freely." Willa herself said that Miss King, as she was before her marriage, was the first person she cared about outside her family and that she wanted more than anything to please her. It was Willa's first experience in a classroom and she said Miss King made it one of the happiest years she ever spent. When she wrote "The Best Years" she put something of Evangeline King in Miss Knightly. Other teachers were important to her also, A. K. Goudy who taught Latin and his wife who was Willa's high school principal. Mr. Goudy was named State Superintendent of Schools, with his wife as his deputy, and the Goudys moved to Lincoln at about the time Willa left for the University. She saw a lot of them during the time she lived in Lincoln and she corresponded faithfully with Mrs. Goudy for forty years.

* * *

Sadly these letters, like most of Willa Cather's, have not survived. Edith Lewis who read them called it a remarkable correspondence. "Those unguarded early letters, written in a large, immature hand, and filled with the new discoveries she was making about life and people, and about herself—the kind of letters that are only written in the confidence of being infallibly understood—show the crudeness, the extravagance, the occasional bravado of a young, undisciplined talent; and show, too, flashes of rare insight and imagination; a depth of feeling and a capacity for suffering that are found only in exceptional natures." Yet it was Edith Lewis, more than anyone, who bears responsibility for the loss not only of Willa's early correspondence but also the volumes of other letters she wrote during her long life. At Willa's urging, Edith asked the author's friends to return the letters she had sent them and together Edith and Willa burned them, sometimes one at a time, sometimes tied together in bundles. The violinist Yehudi Menuhin said his mother burned Willa's letters herself, in accordance with the author's wishes. After Willa's death Edith frantically bought up everything she could so that she might personally destroy them. With few exceptions, the letters that escaped to find their way into libraries across the country were written when Willa was older and less inclined to reveal herself in the way she did to Mrs. Goudy. The loss is incalculable and we are forced to rely on what she wrote years later for a glimpse of what she must have been in those Red Cloud days, when "the world was full of the summer time/And the year was always June," when she was young and ardent "in the days that were done too soon."

* * *

Just as she had on the prairie, Willa made some of her greatest friends among the older people in Red Cloud who responded to her eagerness to learn and who shared their own interests with her. One of these was William Ducker, an Englishman who had come to town in April 1885, a few months after the Cathers, to clerk in his brother's dry-goods store. Ducker was the kind of man of whom it would probably be said today that he had never found himself. He might have been a teacher had he had more formal education but, as it was, his brothers always found a place for him in their successful business enterprises. Learning was his real love, however, especially the classics, and he imparted his enthusiasm to his young friend. He had the gift of making Latin seem a living language and Willa never lost her love for the Latin tongue and for the literature she and Mr. Ducker read together regularly for many years. He also was interested in science and had fitted up a laboratory in his home where Willa helped him with experiments. She probably learned to dissect animals in Ducker's laboratory. The other children called him "Uncle Billy" but Willa thought it condescending of them and to her he was never anything but "Mr. Ducker."

The truth is that, for all its provincialism, Red Cloud had its share of nonconformists and Willa and the Miner girls spent endless hours talking over the more colorful personalities and speculating about the events in their lives that had brought them finally to the same benighted corner of the world where they were growing up. Most of the wayward types, the remittance men, the dissolute younger sons, the drifters and the drinkers found their way into Willa Cather's stories. They were far more interesting to her than the transplanted Southerners with their teas and clubs and evening socials. Like the Europeans on the prairie, they lent a patch of color to the otherwise dreary sameness of the little town.

The most romantic figure in Willa Cather's childhood and one who lingered for a long time in her imagination before appearing as Marian Forrester in *A Lost Lady*, was the wife of Red Cloud's founder and former governor of the state, Silas Garber. The Garbers lived in a spacious home on the outskirts of Red Cloud where Willa often went to play as a child and later was a frequent guest. The great house was a reminder of the comfort she had left behind at Willowshade, except that even Willowshade paled before the opulence of the Garber house and the grand style of Mrs. Garber's entertaining. Willa fell a little bit in love with everything about it. She was always attracted to strong personalities and to people who lived well. Silas Garber himself was one of her idols. She saw in him, and in the other bankers and businessmen who built the town, the same pioneering qualities she had admired in the farmers who tamed the land. His wife also had color and panache, but in her the sparkle was combined with a kind of fragile and elusive charm that touched the young Willa and to which she gave her heart. Later she would understand that it was a temperament not unmixed with a darker current of mockery and disdain, but by then Lyra Garber was dead and Willa was ready for *A Lost Lady*.

Another heroine of Willa's Red Cloud years, the most famous of them all, was Annie Sadilek, the Miners' "hired girl" who is Willa's Ántonia. The Sadileks, like the Shimerdas of *My Ántonia*, were poor Bohemian farmers living on the Divide in a primitive sod hut, originally nothing more than a cave in the earth, and struggling to work the hard reluctant land. Willa heard the story of Annie's father's suicide as soon as she arrived in Nebraska and she may have known Annie slightly in the early days, but it wasn't until they were both in town and Annie was living with the Miners that she began to capture Willa's imagination. The details of Annie's situation are accurately sketched in *My Ántonia*. She was hard-working and turned her wages over to her family, but Carrie Miner saw to it that she had enough to keep herself in shoes. Mrs. Miner taught her how to cook and sew and she became adept at copying the latest fashions. Like Ántonia, Annie loved to dance and, like Ántonia, she left town with a railroad man she hoped to marry but was deserted by him and forced to return home. Edith Lewis said that nobody else saw anything special in the girl who was agreeable and conscientious but not at all remarkable in any way. It remained for Willa to cast a radiance over Annie Sadilek and invest her simple story with the rare and timeless quality of art. In "Neighbor Rosicky" she did the same thing for John Pavelka, Annie's husband, giving him a nobility of character almost epic in conception. Yet John Pavelka, when he was an old man, did not say that he was Anton Rosicky. "I'm My Ántonia's husband," he would say to strangers when they met him. And one of Annie's sons, then in his seventies, sent a visitor to Red Cloud scurrying for a copy of My Ántonia when he appeared, erect and handsome, and announced, "I'm Leo, the mischievous one."

Even as a girl Willa was aware of the unique personalities of her neighbors. With her imagination and her readiness to look beneath the seemingly smooth surface of everyday life, she found much to absorb and stimulate her in Red Cloud. The little town had its share of domestic dramas and the weekly newspaper, the Red Cloud Chief —"Eternal Vigilance Is the Price of Liberty and One Dollar Is the Price of the Chief"—reported lurid incidents of suicide and murder. Willa read the paper faithfully and knew all about the passions that caused a farmer to behead his wife or a spurned lover to turn a gun upon himself. Her sympathy must have gone out to a young actress from Denver, formerly of Lincoln, who committed suicide at a hotel in Lincoln by taking poison. She had come to the capital to marry a grain merchant from Utica, Nebraska, said the Chief, but his parents raised objections to the match and insisted on postponing the wedding until the spring. On the day she had expected to be married the young woman took poison in her fiancé's presence. The Chief gave her stage name as Kitty Fraser.

Drama of a different sort was to be found in the theatrical companies that came through on tour and played an important part in the lives of Red Cloud's youngsters. The year after the Cathers moved to town an opera house was built on Webster Street, and it was there that the popular plays of the day were performed, The Count of Monte Cristo, The Corsican Brothers, Damon and Pythias and the perennial Uncle Tom's Cabin, as well as the light opera romances of Martha and The Chimes of Normandy.

Willa was fascinated as much by the actors and actresses off the stage as by their performances. The cast generally arrived on the night train, an event widely advertised in advance, and Willa and her friends would walk the half mile to the depot, sometimes pulling younger brothers and sisters along in a sled, to see the company alight. The women would shake out their furs, the men would rub their hands against the cold as they paced the platform while their luggage was being sorted, and then they would drive off, the men in the hotel bus, the women in a "hack." If one of the ladies happened to have a little dog with a blanket on, Willa reminisced many years after, "that simply doubled our pleasure." Everything the players did was a delight, as they settled down in town for a week of plays and parties. The opera house was dark for most of the year, it's true, "but that made its events only the more exciting."

"The excitement began when the advance man came to town and posted the bills on the side of a barn, on the lumber yard fence, in the 'plate glass' windows of drug stores and grocery stores. My playmates and I used to stand for an hour after school studying every word on those posters; the names of the plays and the nights on which each would be given. After we had decided which were the most necessary to us there was always the question of how far we could prevail upon our parents. Would they let us go every other night, or only the opening and closing nights? None of us ever got to go every night unless we had a father who owned stock in the opera house itself."

For children in the little prairie towns the experience was unforgettable. Even the *Uncle Tom's Cabin* companies, admittedly the poorest, had living bloodhounds and "how the barking of these dogs behind the scenes used to make us catch our breath!" "As for old Frank Lindon" playing Monte Cristo "in a frilled shirt and a velvet coat blazing with diamonds," when he stood in Madame Danglars' drawing room and revealed his identity to Madame De Morcery, "his faithless Mercedes," wrote Willa, "when she cowered and made excuses and he took out a jeweled snuff box with a much powdered hand and said softly and bitterly, 'a fidelity of six months!', then we children were not in the opera house in Red Cloud, we were in Mme. Danglars' salon in Paris, in the middle of lives so very different from our own."

The professional players inspired the children to put on their own theatrical performances in which Willa proved herself an uninhibited and accomplished actress, drawing admiring comment in the *Chief*. She loved to dress up in costume and become another person on the stage; it appealed to the creative side of her nature and her need to try on a variety of identities. Her histrionic ability was in evidence as well in the oration she delivered at her high school graduation. She was one of three seniors in the class of June 1890, Red Cloud's second graduating class, and the only girl. The others talked on "Self Advertising" and "New Times Demand New Measures and New Men." Willa chose "Superstition versus Investigation" as her topic and she made her talk a ringing defense of vivisection. Striking the ironic note she would continue in her newspaper columns, she declaimed, "It is generally safe to admire a man who has succeeded . . . but if we bar our novices from advancement, whence shall come our experts?" The girl who dissected cats and dogs and shocked Red Cloud with her experiments was striking back dramatically in what might be considered her farewell performance.

Of the three graduates only Willa was going to the state university at Lincoln in September. There was a difference of opinion in the Cather household as to Willa's immediate future. Her father thought she should teach school first, but Mrs. Cather was adamant that her daughter go on to college. Most Nebraska high school students were required to take two years of preparatory schooling at the University before they were permitted to matriculate, but in Willa's case the first year was not considered necessary and she was accepted as a Second Year Preparatory student, or a "second prep."

Red Cloud had given Willa everything it could and she had taken more from the little town than she yet knew or than she would be willing to acknowledge for many years to come. Her teachers and her close friends sensed, without quite understanding, her uncommon gifts, but the Red Cloud *Chief,* which saw bright futures for her two male classmates, remained silent about the prospects for Willa Cather.

II

—— ❊ ——

Endeavor and Bright Hopefulness

SCHOLARS ON THE PRAIRIE

Willa was not quite seventeen the September day in 1890 when she rode the Burlington to Lincoln to begin her year as a university prep. The trip was less than a hundred and fifty miles and took only six or seven hours, but it was the first step of a greater journey that would carry Willa ever farther from the small Nebraska town where she grew up and from the loving friends and family who saw her off that day. Her college years affected her in profound ways, both emotionally and intellectually, and she made an unforgettable impression on those whose paths crossed hers. Few in the class of 1895 were ever neutral where their famous member was concerned, and Lincoln too retained mixed memories of Willa Cather long after she left the University. She was a girl who made enemies as easily as she made friends, the kind of person who was either liked a lot or thoroughly detested. She was not indifferent to what people thought of her, but she was more concerned with what she could accomplish than with how she was regarded. She was admired by many of her contemporaries, but she was never popular.

* * *

The city Willa came to was almost as young and brash as she was. Considered one of the most attractive state capitals in the West, Lincoln twenty years earlier had been an undeveloped, sparsely populated prairie town slumbering in the middle of the state, but its central location helped it to win out over Omaha as the seat of government, when the Nebraska Territory became a state in 1867. An entirely new city was built on the site and laid out according to the most advanced theories of city planning, to provide generously for public sites and open space. Contained within a rectangular grid set on the open prairie, the young city was notable for broad avenues and handsome public buildings placed to take advantage of long vistas and pleasant views of the surrounding countryside. Three major sites, of four square blocks each, were designed to break the grid and accommodate the University on the north, the capitol on the east and a spacious park in the southwest corner of the city. Five full square blocks were set aside throughout the residential district for public schools, and additional land was reserved for churches and fraternal orders. By the time Willa arrived, business was flourishing along O Street, the capitol and an elaborate post office had been built, and just a few blocks from the University, the depot of the Burlington and Missouri Railroad served as an imposing entrance to the city. The atmosphere in Lincoln was striving, perhaps a bit pretentious, but it was lively enough to be stimulating to a girl from Red Cloud with ambitions of her own.

Like a New England college, the University of Nebraska was set off from the city within an iron fence, the campus consisting of four buildings of institutional red brick, standing solemn and assertive, on University Place. Paths had been laid out and trees planted, but it would be many years before they had grown sufficiently to shade and soften the contours of the young college "that had lifted its head from the prairie only a few years before," as Jim Burden was to describe it in *My Ántonia*. Classes, laboratories and administrative offices were accommodated in the campus buildings, but dormitories had not as yet been built and students were expected to find their own quarters in the town. These informal arrangements—"we lived where we could and as we could"—gave to college life a freedom that was undoubtedly appealing but that could be lonely, too, at times.

Willa lived in two places in Lincoln, first in a boardinghouse at 1019 H Street which had the reputation of serving the best food in town, and later with family friends at 1029 L Street. Her room had a spartan simplicity. When she entertained she sent invitations to a feed "in the crypt of William Cather." She wasn't often in her room, however, preferring in her spare time to explore Lincoln which she discovered was not really very different from Red Cloud, even though considerably larger. She could walk the quiet residential streets that Jim Burden found "almost as oppressively domestic as Black Hawk" just as she so often did at home, and soon find herself in open country. Or she might take the trolley to Lincoln Park and hear a band concert in the spring or walk along the lake shore. Her square figure, striding by or pedaling on her bicycle, soon became as familiar to Lincoln as it had been to Red Cloud.

On campus, in addition to her class work, Willa found a variety of extracurricular activities to occupy her, social clubs and literary societies and several publications devoted to student writing. From the first she attracted attention because of her unusual appearance, and her mannish dress and shingled hair made her a subject of conversation and amusement even to her friends. William Linn Westermann retained for years the memory of the first time he saw Willa. "The door opened and a head appeared, with short hair and straw hat; a deep masculine voice inquired whether this was the class in elementary Greek. A boy nodded yes, and as the newcomer entered and was a girl, the entire class burst out laughing." Most girls would have been afraid of appearing conspicuous, another friend remarked, but Willa had no fear of that. When she finally let her hair grow she did it, she said, to please the mother of a friend. At least that was the way she liked to remember it in future years. Another person who claimed credit, however, was Dr. Julius Tyndale, the debonair drama critic for the Lincoln *Evening News* who squired Willa around town, raising eyebrows and causing talk, and remained her devoted friend until he died. His story was that Willa was extremely boyish when she first came from Red Cloud, but the evening she went to a party at a private home, dressed in boy's clothing, was the last straw and he told her she would have to behave more appropriately.

Willa's associations were never limited to the University community and Dr. Tyndale was only one of many older people in Lincoln who became her friends. His sister, Emma Tyndale Westermann, the mother of six hearty sons, was married to the owner of the Lincoln *Evening News* and frequently entertained young people. Willa modeled the Ehrlichs in *One of Ours* on the Westermann family, and Will Westermann marveled in later years at the accuracy of her description of the Westermann house written so long after she had been a guest there. The Geres were another newspaper family whom Willa knew well in Lincoln. Charles Gere was the owner and editor of the *Nebraska State Journal*, the largest of Lincoln's five major newspapers, and Willa was a close friend of his three daughters, Mariel, Ellen and Frances.

Willa never forgot the first time Mariel brought her home to dinner, when they were both prep students. She was at her most difficult, she remembered, feeling like an awkward country girl, ill at ease and consequently all puffed up with self-importance. Mrs. Gere, however, knew just the way to handle young people who took themselves too seriously. She would laugh when they gave themselves airs, but so kindly that it never gave offense, and that laugh, said Willa, did more good than any amount of scolding. She had a kind of charm and vivacity that were something new in Willa's experience of mothers, but instead of making her feel shy, Mrs. Gere encouraged her and gave her confidence. Only Mrs. Gere, she would say in later years, could have persuaded her to let her hair grow and learn how to spell.

In addition to its solid citizens, Lincoln, like Red Cloud, had also drawn the adventurous and disaffected from Europe and the East, and the University faculty mirrored the town's diversity. The men who taught Willa were quirky, original, dedicated teachers. The Cather scholar Bernice Slote calls the University of Nebraska in the early 1890s "a little Renaissance world—almost a real community of scholars." Classes in the Preparatory School were often taught by members of the University faculty and they insisted on rigorous standards of performance. Willa's first English teacher was Ebenezer Hunt, whose dour words, "Life is a damn grind, Cather," she often quoted over the years. George Woodberry, the Harvard-educated scholar who became a distinguished professor of literature at Columbia University, had left the University by the time Willa entered. A protégé of James R. Lowell and Charles Eliot Norton, he had never adjusted to life in the West, complaining to Norton that it was even worse than he expected. "Well," Norton had replied, "so you may find the rest of your life." Another Harvard graduate, Herbert Bates, joined the faculty in Willa's freshman year and played an important role in her college life. The chairman of the English department was a Yale graduate, Lucius A. Sherman, a brilliant, opinionated scholar and critic but never a friend of Willa's. She rebelled against what she considered his mechanical approach to literature and she mercilessly ridiculed his theories, set forth in his *Elements of Literature and Composition*, in which he analyzed and quantified the language. When she became a critic for the *Journal* and Sherman was writing a book column for the *News*, they frequently took opposing viewpoints, and their differences, amounting to a feud, were matters of common knowledge in the town as well as in the University.

The students in those years were often farmers "straight from the cornfield with only a summer's wages in their pocket" but they were hardworking and serious about their studies and several went on to make names for themselves in later life. A future General of the Armies, John G. Pershing; a future dean of the Harvard Law School, Roscoe Pound; and a future founder and president of New York's New School for Social Research, Alvin Johnson, were all students at the University during Willa's time. It was Willa Cather, however, according to her friend Dorothy Canfield, who was the most brilliant student the college ever had.

Dorothy Canfield was a bright, blue-eyed, winning eighth-grader and Willa was already beginning to be prominent on campus when Dorothy's older brother introduced them. Dorothy was thrilled. "A brilliant freshman in college," she said, "had the prestige of a grown-up to a little girl still in grade school." For her part, Willa was delighted with the younger girl's precocity and charm and the two became friends, despite the six-year difference in their ages. The affectionate admiration, tinged with awe, that Dorothy felt for Willa at their first meeting never changed. She herself would become a best-selling novelist and the only woman for many years on the editorial board of the Book-of-the-Month Club, but all her life, Dorothy Canfield deferred to Willa Cather. At the University, they entered a fiction contest together sponsored by the student magazine, *Sombrero*, and won first prize with their story, "The Fear That

Walks by Noonday." Ever self-effacing, Dorothy always worried afterward lest the tale reflect badly on Willa's later work. It was a *very* early effort, she would say.

The idea for the story was actually Dorothy's. It had come to her one afternoon, she said, while she watched a football game and imagined a player, killed in a scrimmage, whose spirit comes back to help his team. Leaving the field at the end of the game and finding herself in the crowd close to Willa, she mentioned the idea. Willa found the notion picturesque and promptly offered to turn it into a story. She told it as a horror tale from the point of view of the star quarterback of the opposing team, who finds himself playing helplessly against a phantom. When it won the story contest Willa shared the ten-dollar prize money as well as the by-line with Dorothy. That five dollars, said Dorothy, was the first money she had ever received outside her allowance and was therefore a memorable event in her "little-girl life."

Willa's friendship with the daughter of James Canfield, the president of the University, did not go unnoticed on campus, and was still remarked on fifty years later when Willa's classmates were asked what they remembered about her as a student. Several mentioned how often they used to see the two girls together and what an odd pair they always seemed, the sweet-tempered, friendly Dorothy, a universal favorite, and the brusque, stand-offish Willa. Yet the friendship was to survive their differences. Dorothy married John Fisher, raised a family and went to live in Vermont. But although their lives diverged and they saw each other infrequently as time went on, Willa Cather and Dorothy Canfield Fisher, both successful novelists in later years, corresponded regularly and kept in touch literally up until the moment of Willa's death.

* * *

By the time Willa and Dorothy collaborated on their prize story Willa knew that she was going to be a writer. The decision had been made when she was a second prep and Professor Hunt assigned the class a routine exercise on Thomas Carlyle. Willa's two-thousand-word essay was a passionate defense of a misunderstood, tormented genius and a ringing declaration of the artist's eternal creed that would become in time her own personal manifesto: " [Jehovah] says, 'Thou shalt have no other gods before me.' Art, science and letters cry, 'Thou shalt have no other gods at all.'" She wrote brilliantly in what seemed a state of high excitement as if she could not wait to have her say and try out her theories of art and life. Judged on almost any basis, it was an extraordinary effort for a young girl from a prairie town, and a tomboy at that, with only a high school education behind her.

One imagines Professor Hunt's amazement when he was confronted with those confident, exuberant opinions and was first exposed to his student's opulent prose. We know what he did: Without saying a word to her he showed the essay to Charles Gere who published it the next week in his newspaper with an accompanying note introducing the author as a sixteen-year-old from Webster County, and adding the observation that "a careful reading will convince any student of literature that it is a remarkable product, reflecting not a little credit upon the author and the university." Willa knew nothing about it until she saw the essay in the Sunday *Journal*, and the effect she later said was hypnotic. Until then she had taken it for granted she would follow a scientific course and become a doctor, but the sight of her words in print with the initials W.C. changed everything. From that time on medicine was forgotten and she determined to concentrate on writing. In retrospect she confessed the essay was an example of exactly the kind of writing she most disliked—full of high-flown figures of speech—but it had one important saving grace. It may have been florid, but it was honest and it didn't overstate the pleasure she had in reading Carlyle or the delightful sense of bitterness he aroused in her that made her feel grown-up.

She followed the Carlyle essay several months later with a two-part essay on Shakespeare that was another display of versatility and erudition. That too was published in the *Journal* but was unsigned. In her sophomore year she began writing poetry and fiction for the student magazine, the semimonthly *Hesperian*. One of her stories which she titled simply "Peter" so impressed Herbert Bates that he insisted on sending it to the Boston literary weekly, *The Mahogany Tree*, where it was published in May 1892. In later years Willa thought Bates had pushed her too quickly. It encouraged her in bad writing habits, she said, and she warned aspiring young writers against too early publication. But at the time she felt very proud and enjoyed the celebrity her writing was bringing her in Lincoln.

For her early stories in the *Hesperian* Willa turned to subjects close to home. "Peter" is the tale of Francis Sadilek's suicide that made such a strong impression on her when she first came to Nebraska and which she would return to with memorable effect in *My Antonia*. Here it is little more than a sketch, but in it Willa evokes all the harshness of the early days on the Divide and the soul sickness of the old Bohemian who breaks his cherished fiddle across his knees, as much in anger as in despair, and turns his shotgun on himself. But he forgets to break the bow and his thrifty son Anton carries it to town to sell it before the funeral. "Peter" is most striking for the irony with which the young author relates the mournful story. A bitter undercurrent of feeling lies just beneath the surface, mockingly expressed in the neighbors' comment, repeated like a chorus, that Anton was a hard man, but still a better man than his lazy, music-making father ever was.

Willa wrote two other Nebraska stories, "Lou the Prophet" and "The Clemency of the Court," both dealing with the strange benighted types she had known on the prairie who had won her sympathy when she was a child. "The Clemency of the Court" is an especially mean picture of the drudgery of farm life and the terrible punishment meted out to a simpleminded Russian laborer—"he felt the plains were like himself, always lonely and empty"—who kills the man who killed his beloved dog. Two other stories are also about foreigners but these were not drawn from Willa's own experience and are less satisfactory. "A Son of the Celestial" is about a Chinese living in San Francisco and "A Tale of the White Pyramid" goes back to ancient Egypt and is interesting for containing one of Willa's early poems, a chant intoned at the funeral of a great pharaoh. She also wrote a verse as an introduction to the Chinese story, a device she was to use again in her novels.

One of the *Hesperian* stories, "The Elopement of Allen Poole," is set in Willa's native Virginia and throughout the wistful ballad-like tale of young love and early death runs a soft note of nostalgia for the mountains and the creek near Willowshade and the old footbridge she had crossed so many times. She didn't sign the story, as though it did not quite satisfy her, but it is interesting that she strikes a chord in it that comes back often in her work, the theme that it is good to die young when life is fresh and full of hope, before the ordinariness of things takes over and the staleness of age sets in. "It's mighty hard to lose you, Nell, but maybe it's best. Maybe if I'd lived an' married yo' I might a got old an' cross an' used to yo' some day an' might a' swore at yo' an' beat yo' like the mountain folks round here does, an' I'd sooner die now, while I love yo' better'n anything else in Gawd's world." The poor moonshiner says it clumsily but the emotion is real, and the very homeliness is touching.

In the beginning of her sophomore year Willa joined the editorial staff of the *Hesperian* and the next year was named managing editor. She was also elected literary editor of her class yearbook, the *Sombrero*. Another enthusiasm in those years for which she managed to find time was the University's dramatic society. She made a hit in two productions, a spoof of Shakespeare in which she played Lady Macbeth—one friend thought that's when she let her hair grow—and a five-act melodrama in which she gave a long-remembered reading of "Curfew Must Not Ring To-night." In classes that bored her she was something of a cutup and she barely managed to get through math in time for graduation. But when it was a subject that she loved, as she did French, her professors, according to Dorothy Canfield, were astonished and sometimes a bit abashed by her caring more passionately about their subjects than they did. She went well beyond the curriculum to read all the great French literary works that she could get her hands on, and what she could not find in class she read in the library which, in Willa's day, was housed in two musty overcrowded rooms in the University's oldest building, the ornate, red-brick University Hall. A new library was not completed before 1895, the year she graduated.

THE WRITER EMERGES

Willa's editorial responsibilities continued, but her stories for the *Hesperian* tapered off in her junior and senior years when she began writing professionally for the Lincoln press. In the fall of 1893 she enrolled in a special journalism program at the University conducted by the *Journal*'s lively young managing editor, Will Owen Jones. Jones was impressed with her work and invited her to contribute to the *Journal*'s Sunday literary section. Her earliest contributions were vignettes for a column called "One Way of Putting It." The column underwent several name changes and for a long while was headed "As You Like It," but in July of 1895, when Willa was no longer a student at the University, she settled on "The Passing Show" and so it was known for the next five years. Those first brief but pungent character studies with which Willa started her newspaper career read like exercises for her future work and frequently, as in her stories, the observer is a man and the viewpoint male. She must have had a gallery of characters already in mind for stories she would someday write, and the columns gave her an opportunity to try them out.

In one vignette her father was the model for a gentle Southern gentleman who courteously allows himself to be swindled by a lady from the North. Other familiar Cather characters make their appearances as well: a businessman who might have been a writer save for an unsympathetic wife, a crazed evangelist on a small-town street, a German fiddler playing for a dance. Clubwomen and drifters, all the small-town types that Willa knew so well, are there in embryo. Her prejudices are apparent also. In one unpleasant little sketch she describes a baby "with the unmistakable nose of an unmistakable race" grasping for a penny with which his mother tries to comfort him when he cries. "Not an orange or a bonbon," writes Willa, "but a penny. He . . . looks at it carefully on both sides as though seeing if it were genuine."

The greedy infant might be overlooked except that it is the first of many stereotyped portraits of Jews in Willa's fiction. She romanticized other nationalities and cultures, the Bohemians, the Swedes, the French, but where Jews were concerned, she seemed to have a blind spot. For the biblical Hebrews she had respect and admiration, and people she knew, like the Wieners, were certainly not included in her antipathy, but one wonders what they and other Jewish friends who came later made of the obnoxious Jews who populate her stories.

Her prejudice was not uncommon in the Midwest of her day but it was deep-seated. In 1923 she could sit in a New York theatre watching *Loyalties*, John Galsworthy's powerful play about anti-Semitism and, while admiring the performance, still comment to a friend about the fat Jewesses in the audience and suggest that Galsworthy might have changed the ending of his play if he had sat beside them. Ten years later, at the height of her career, Willa Cather surprised a magazine editor by asking him if he was "of the Jewish persuasion." When he said he was, she inquired whether he had experienced anti-Semitism and seemed skeptical when he told her he had not. She questioned him about his background, wanted to know what his mother was like, what she read, what she did for amusement. It interested her that his parents had been born in America and that he had grown up in a small town on the Hudson. Neither he nor his parents matched the Jewish stereotype of her imagination. It was as though, late in life, she was trying to understand a people who had escaped her sympathy for so long, and who fared so badly in her fiction.

* * *

It was not with fiction, however, that Willa established her reputation during her college years, but as a journalist and critic that she was first appreciated. In the spring of 1894 when she was twenty and in her junior year, she became the *Journal*'s drama critic, a post formerly held by her friend George Gerwig. A talented, astonishingly versatile jack-of-all-trades, Gerwig left Lincoln to become Secretary to the Allegheny Board of School Controllers and subsequently Secretary of the Board of Education in Pittsburgh. Willa liked him and probably learned a lot from him about the craft of drama criticism. She was also greatly influenced by her friendship with Dr. Tyndale, her competitor, as Toby Rex, on the *Evening News*. Tyndale knew the theatre world and was almost as stagestruck as Willa. He taught her everything he could and encouraged her to develop the personal style for which she became famous. Her opinions on the theatre appear to have been formulated early, long before she started seeing plays in Lincoln, probably while she was still a child, waiting expectantly for the curtain to go up in the Red Cloud opera house. By the time she began writing for the *Journal* many of her judgments had already been determined and she was well on her way to being the "meat-ax" critic Will Jones later dubbed her.

In Red Cloud when she still hoped to be a doctor, she had chloroformed small animals before dissecting them. In Lincoln, where she had given up the scalpel for the pen, she rarely dealt so mercifully with her victims. Exalted reputations tottered under her attacks and theatrical managers sighed when they knew the *Journal*'s young critic was in the first night audience. She held the least performer to the very highest standards and while she was not ungenerous with praise for her favorites, she probably hurt more feelings than she consoled. She could dismiss Oscar Wilde's *Lady Windermere's Fan* as "not a bad play . . . only driveling," and reprimand the popular but temperamental Mrs. Kendal for "unwomanly tirades." When the dainty Julia Marlowe announced that she would play the boisterous Prince Hal, Willa was aghast: "Is there no kind friend . . . to beseech her not to make of herself one blooming idiot?" Of an aged actress she wrote that "to see a woman of seventy . . . painted and padded and schottishing about the stage is more than most of us can stand with comfort" and as for the prospect of Lillian Lewis in *Cymbeline,* Willa could say only that "when one knows Lillian, her nose and her emotion, one hopes that they dug Shakespeare's grave very deep."

During the season Lincoln was a regular stop for the several hundred theatrical touring companies that came out West from New York and Chicago, and as many as three or four companies might play in a week. The Funke Opera House, with a portrait of Shakespeare looking down over the drop curtain, and a seating capacity of twelve hundred, had opened in 1885, and another, even more elegant theatre, the Lansing, opened the fall of Willa's freshman year and seated eighteen hundred. Unfortunately the new theatre was also notable for possessing a particularly ugly drop curtain. "Atrocious" was Willa's label for the painting which adorned it. Lincoln was a second-run town on the circuit but it nevertheless attracted the great players of the day and Willa saw them all—Modjeska, Julia Marlowe (despite Prince Hal), Clara Morris, the English actress Olga Nethersole and the romantic leading man Richard Mansfield. She saw Joseph Jefferson and Nat Goodwin in a famous production of the *Rivals* and Otis Skinner in *Henry VIII.* Those she didn't see, she wrote about anyway.

For her favorites, like the young actress Maida Craigen, she had sweet words: "She undoubtedly has a great future before her, for she has all those hundred spontaneous, unthought little touches that are so much greater than the great things . . ." But Willa also knew the "great things" when she saw them. On the twenty-second of February 1892, she went to Omaha to see Sarah Bernhardt in Sardou's *Tosca.* Two thousand people filled the theatre to see the performance, which was in French. Six hundred had stood on line for tickets earlier in the day. Outside the night was frosty. Inside Bernhardt was a flame, and the audience rose to its feet again and again to cheer her. Willa was enthralled and for years after she sought images to describe the effect of the actress' personality. "It is like red lava torn up from the bowels of the earth where the primeval fires of creation are still smouldering." And the voice, "one with which a fire worshipper might sing his triumphant chant to the sun, or a snake charmer put his serpents to sleep." Bernhardt didn't play in Lincoln but Willa followed every detail of her career in newspaper accounts. She was impatient with the excesses in the actress' private life, but she had enormous admiration for a quality she was beginning to recognize as more important even than genius. Bernhardt never fails or disappoints her audience, Willa wrote, "because under all those thousand little things that seem so spontaneous there is a system as fixed and definite as the laws of musical composition." Young as she was, the *Journal*'s critic knew that art was nothing without discipline.

Bernhardt's great contemporary, Eleanora Duse, never came to Lincoln either, but her reputation fascinated Willa and she discussed Duse's roles and described her acting style as if she had seen her perform frequently. Undoubtedly there was a good deal of fiction when Willa wrote about the Bernhardts and the Duses, but she wrote with so much authority and was so *au courant* with all the latest news and gossip, as well as with what the New York critics had to say, that her lack of firsthand familiarity was well camouflaged. Art, she wrote, "is Bernhardt's dissipation, a sort of Bacchic orgy. It is Duse's consecration, her religion, her martyrdom." Yet she had seen one of them only once, and the other not at all.

In Duse's personal behavior Willa found a model that had great appeal for her. "In this age of microscopic scrutiny and X rays," she wrote, "to have maintained such absolute privacy is little short of genius in itself." Bernhardt was an artist of a very different temperament, one who "[gave] herself body and soul to the public," but Duse never allowed her audience so much as a glimpse of her private life. "She has kept her personality utterly subdued and unseen and spoken only through her art." Willa leaves little doubt of where her own sympathies lay, but her admiration for Duse's reserve did not blind her to the actress' conscious efforts to cloak her enigmatic personality in mystery. It was the very theatricality with which she insisted on her privacy that made Duse so exciting. Willa's description of her as one who was "utterly alone upon the icy heights where other beings cannot live" might well return to haunt her one day when similar judgments would be passed, not always kindly, on Willa Cather.

The theatre may not have been the shrine for her that it was for Duse, but it was still a special place and it was important enough for Willa to dress formally, unlike most of the students, when she attended opening nights at the Funke or the Lansing. A classmate remembered her costume and the long white kid gloves she always wore for the theatre. "It's queer you should have that one weakness," the friend had said. "Well I must have one," was Willa's answer. She offered another explanation in a column about the proper dress for concerts: "It's worth while to dress for a concert on the same principle that it is worth while to dress for one's wedding. Music calls for the best of everything . . ."

Willa reported on the concert and opera season in Lincoln with the same confidence and verve as when she wrote about the theatre, although, in fact, her musical background was negligible. She covered the scene initially in terms of personalities, meanwhile learning about the music as she went along. In typical fashion she quite demolished Mendelssohn after a concert devoted entirely to his work, calling the composer "pitiably weak and childish," and dismissing his songs as appealing especially to "effeminate minds." Willa frequently deplored effeminacy and what she called "chappieism." She thought it was a characteristic of Eastern colleges and, no doubt, Easterners in general, and that it represented indulgence by the youth of the wealthier classes in dissipations, by which she meant alcohol and tobacco, that sapped their energies. And Willa's cure for such behavior? Unlikely as it seems, she recommended football as one of the few "thoroughly reputable and manly games left in the nineteenth century." It might mean a few broken collarbones but that would not do "Cholly or Fweddy" any harm and she thought anything was worthy that encouraged a young man "to keep his physical manhood perfect." It was the Greek ideal that might still have meaning, even in Nebraska.

Willa often digressed in her reviews to consider ideas she would return to later and develop more fully in her columns where her pronouncements were likely to emerge as full-fledged doctrine. When Lillian Russell wrote an article for the Chicago *Times-Herald*, Willa took the occasion to remind the actress, and any other artist who considered taking up the pen, that "to use that inoffensive article even moderately well requires a study and inspiration and mastery of technique almost as great as that of their own art." A concert by the nineteen-year-old pianist Josef Hofmann brought a discourse on the hazards of the prodigy and was an opportunity to state a principle that came to have profound meaning for her. "The very things out of which an artist is made do not come to a man before he is twenty," she wrote. Helena von Doenhoff, the leading lady of the Tavary Opera Company and one of the singers Willa admired, had said much the same thing to her in an offhand way in her dressing room "as she gave her satin slipper an impatient toss." "Art does not come at sixteen," she had remarked. Von Doenhoff's subsequent marriage and the announcement that she would retire from the stage disappointed Willa. She had hoped the singer would show "a little more endurance," but she was finally forced to acknowledge that "married nightingales seldom sing" and on that reverberating note, she wished her a reluctant farewell. That tension, between an artist's public and private life, became one of the themes that run through Willa's later fiction, and von Doenhoff must have sometimes been in her mind when she was creating Thea Kronborg.

* * *

Writing about books and authors, even more than about plays and players, however, gave Willa the chance to try out her own emerging ideas about the craft she was increasingly making her own. She had a taste for the romantic in fiction, Dumas père's *The Count of Monte Cristo*, Anthony Hope's *The Prisoner of Zenda*, and George du Maurier's *Trilby* which, in her forthright way, she championed against the charges of triviality and immorality which Professor Sherman among others had leveled at it. She loved Robert Louis Stevenson's adventure stories and Kipling's exotic tales. She emphatically did not like the realistic school of writing, particularly when its practitioners dealt in subjects that to her seemed sordid and unhealthy. She was not a prude, passion did not shock her and she had learned very young to be tolerant of human frailty, but she drew a line in fiction between literature and what she considered "social science." William Dean Howells too often crossed the line, she thought, and she found Émile Zola pitiful in his absorption with the ugliness of life. Romance to her was the highest form of fiction and would outlast all the others. The Ibsens and the Zolas, though possibly great in their way, would, in the end, she thought, prove temporary. For Willa, the greatest romancer of them all was Stevenson and she applauded him for keeping his stories free of "heredity, or divorce, or the vexed problems of society." He was her model as a man as well as a writer, and when the news of his untimely death was wired to the *Journal*, she devoted one of her "As You Like It" columns to the gentle traveler from the cold and flinty heart of Scotland who had spent his last years "in the wealth and fragrance of unceasing summer, in the light and starlight of tropic seas and meridian lands," writing books "of fancy, pure and simple."

Willa's tribute to Stevenson says a great deal about her own values and the importance she placed on virtues she had been taught from her earliest childhood and which she had observed daily on the prairie. In a time of conversational novels, Stevenson's were full of action, and in an age Willa thought both cynical and lazy, "he wrote of the glory and the hope of effort and of the completeness which a man's work gives to his life." Those were calls that sounded deep inside her and to which she was already beginning to respond. A few months earlier she had written that "genius means relentless labor and passionate excitement from the hour one is born until the hour one dies." It was true of Stevenson and might one day be said of Willa Cather too.

Willa hoped that Rudyard Kipling might take up the torch from Stevenson, but she was afraid his marriage and transplantation to America, where he seemed to be enjoying domestic life, would prove the young man's undoing. "It would be more encouraging to hear that he had taken to opium or strong drink," was her acid comment. "Don't hang about our cities to study our manners," she scolded, and one can almost see her shaking a plump finger, "they might broaden and deepen a greater man but they will corrupt . . . you." Then she added what must surely be the most impudent words of advice from a college girl to an established author: "So back to the east . . . if the climate is not good for Mrs. Kipling then remember that you were married to your works long before you ever met her. Alas! there were so many men who could have married Mrs. Kipling, and there was only you who could write *Soldiers Three*." And lest she had not made her point, she concluded with a line borrowed from the poet himself, ". . . he travels the fastest who travels alone." Three years later when Willa was living and working in Pittsburgh she had the opportunity to meet Kipling and they talked for forty minutes in her office. It would be amusing to know if any reference was made to the gratuitous marital advice she had tendered him at twenty-one. Perhaps he and Mrs. Kipling had laughed about it, though it is more likely they had never seen it, not being in the habit of reading the *Nebraska State Journal* in Vermont.

Whether she was castigating authors or admiring actresses Willa was ready with opinions on every conceivable subject, and she entered vigorously into the fray when controversy was in the air. On the subject of whether critics should write reviews on the night of a performance or at the end of the week, a matter of debate in London and New York, she did not hesitate to come down on the side of first instincts as being the truest. When that guardian of public morality, the "Gerry" Society, stopped thirteen-year-old Essie Graham from appearing in the cast of *Under the City Lamps*, Willa thought they would do better to remove all actresses over fifty, rather than under fifteen. The requirements of writing, however, were different from those of the stage and she condemned youthful novel writers who tried to project a personality before they had any personality to project. "The talent for writing," she believed, was "largely the talent for living."

For Oscar Wilde, then serving a prison term for sodomy, she had no sympathy and considered that he had deserved his sentence. To her mind, however, he had committed an even more serious crime as an artist by being "insincere." She loathed his artificiality, his flippant epigrams and mannered witticisms. They represented everything she most disliked in art and literature, and she denounced the aesthetic movement as the basest school of art that had ever "voiced itself in English." Willa admired what she called "the healthy commonplace." She took her stand early on the side of sense, action and control as opposed to sensibility, introspection and emotional profligacy. These attitudes remained with her all of her life, only intensifying as she grew older and as the natural optimism and exuberance of youth had faded.

She saved her highest praise for Shakespeare, for whom she had a passionate regard, and considered that his works and the Magna Carta were the treasures of the English mind as well as of the English tongue. But she disliked the idea that the academics had taken

Shakespeare over, and she liked to say that if he were suddenly to appear in Lincoln it would not be as a member of the faculty of the University but rather as the manager of the Lansing or maybe even as a stagehand. She loved the man of action with a smell of greasepaint about him, even more than the litterateur, though she was prepared to state in an early exercise in hyperbole, that "for him [Shakespeare] alone it was worth while that a planet should be called out of Chaos and a race formed out of nothingness. He justified all history before him, but sanctified all history after him."

About her own sex Willa was inclined to be uncharitable, and her opinions regarding women writers could hardly have endeared her to the feminists of her day. "Sometimes I wonder why God ever trusts talent in the hands of women, they usually make such an infernal mess of it," she wrote. She thought women—always "they" never "we"—were sentimental and "horribly" subjective and that they let their adjectives run away with them. Only the "great Georges," George Eliot and George Sand, were spared her scorn, along with Charlotte Brontë and Jane Austen. Women poets fared slightly better, though she questioned whether they had any place in poetry at all. When a woman did write poetry worth reading, she said, it had to be "emotional in the extreme, self-centered, self-absorbed, centrifugal." The trouble with women, Willa thought, was that they wrote exclusively about their feelings. Only when a woman wrote "a story of adventure, a stout sea tale, a manly battle yarn, anything without wine, women and love" would she begin to look for something great from women. If she seems to be saying, "Why can't a woman be more like a man?", that may be precisely what she meant.

Nevertheless, she included in that same captious article on women poets an almost offhand observation that shows she was not being frivolous but was always shaping her beliefs and working toward her own artistic creed. Literary women, she wrote, had yet to learn what their sisters on the stage had discovered, that "to feel greatly is genius and to make others feel is art." It was Willa at her very best, simple, serious and sound. She had staked out her interests early and she continued to develop and enlarge those principles she had enunciated so triumphantly in that first essay on Carlyle. "An author's only safe course is to cling close to the skirts of his art, forsaking all others, and keep unto her as long as they two shall live." She was twenty-one when she wrote those words at the start of her junior year in college.

A RUPTURED FRIENDSHIP

Willa plainly took the role of critic seriously. She considered herself part of a great literary tradition and the allusions with which she teased and stimulated the readers of her columns were drawn from sources which came as naturally to her as the air she breathed. She knew the Greek and Roman classics intimately. From her grandmothers she had received a thorough grounding in the Bible, and her own reading had given her a wide acquaintance with French, English and American contemporary literature. As a critic she was not always consistent, sometimes peevish and often affected, but she was young and spirited and had energy to spare. She had a capacity for ideas, she was hungry for experience and she had a sumptuous way with language. She could think and she could write and she had the added good fortune to be the protégée of two men, Charles Gere and Will Jones, who recognized her brilliance and were willing to give her her head. Willa always said she owed her first editors a debt for allowing her to riot in excessive writing until she grew to hate it. A twinkle in Mr. Gere's eye might give her pause and cause her a moment's distrust of her high-stepping rhetoric, but he was too wise to correct her. He knew, she said, that you can't hurry nature and so he let her alone to work out her own salvation. It was probably hard on the *Journal*'s readers, she said many years later, but it was good for her.

As a schoolmate of his daughters, Willa saw Charles Gere in his home as well as in the office and she came to love him dearly and to value him equally as a friend and as an employer. She liked nothing so much as to sit alone with him in his library, a fire crackling on the hearth, and confide her ambitions and her youthful troubles. He always listened sympathetically, stroking his dark beard with a hand that seemed to Willa to have a singular elegance. She used to think that if she could ever write anything that was like Mr. Gere's hands in character, it would be the greatest happiness that could befall her. Dark, sinewy and curiously alive, they fascinated her and one day she would give her Archbishop Latour those singularly elegant hands of Mr. Gere.

A constant visitor in the house, she also had a chance to observe him as a father and when he died some time after she left Lincoln, she told Mariel that she could not bear to think of the Gere family without him. In most of the families she knew, the father, no matter how beloved, was nevertheless a good deal of an outsider—it must have been the way she saw her own father—but Mr. Gere had always been a part of everything that touched the lives of his wife and daughters and their friends as well. Mr. Gere's kindness, his easy wit and his serene smile remained with Willa and gave her pleasure to remember all her life.

Among her contemporaries at the University it was another member of the Gere family, the eldest daughter Mariel, who became Willa's friend and confidante and the person to whom she looked for stability and support, especially during her emotional crises. No evidence exists that Willa ever had a serious boyfriend in college. Her classmates said she scared the boys away because she was so mannish herself. But she fell in and out of love with any number of actresses who played in Lincoln. She was beguiled by their raffish beauty and air of frenzied helplessness, and the young women in turn were flattered by her attention. They also knew she could be depended on not only for adulation, but for loans of cash when they fell short and wanted some trinket or other bit of extravagance that caught their fancy. They can't live without paste diamonds and champagne, she would tell her friends. She often found herself in financial difficulties because a loan had not been repaid but she could not bring herself to press some pretty thing for money.

The most serious romantic attachment of Willa's college life, however, was not to an actress but to a schoolmate, the daughter of a prominent Lincoln family, Louise Pound. Louise with her small intense face and burnished red hair was a striking figure on the Nebraska campus, a brilliant student who was also an accomplished pianist and a formidable athlete. A year older than Willa, she too had been taught at home, not by her grandmother but by her mother, a former teacher in New York, who considered the Lincoln public schools unsatisfactory for her children. Louise's father, Stephen Bosworth Pound, was a greatly respected judge, an intellectual, who also played an active role in the civic affairs of the state. Their imposing home at 1632 L Street boasted a well-furnished library, and the Pound children had been encouraged by their parents to develop independent, inquiring minds. Louise and Olivia Pound were referred to by classmates simply as "the sisters" and no one questioned who the sisters were.

A fellow student, who knew both Willa and Louise, described Louise Pound in later years when she was teaching at the University and had become a world authority on folk literature, as having had a hold upon the imagination that was hypnotic. "There was something enigmatical about her personality, almost cryptic," he wrote. She had "a type of innerly contained and controlled expression quite out of the ordinary gamut." This was the personality that exercised its spell on Willa from her freshman year. Before she went home to Red Cloud for the summer in June of 1892, she presented Louise with an illustrated copy of the *Rubáiyát* which of all the books she knew was the one that she loved best. She wrote several notes which she tore up but finally sent a sad but restrained letter of farewell, signing herself "William," which was what the Pound family called her.

For the next two years Louise was an obsession. Willa's infatuation was common knowledge in her family and among her friends and she openly expressed herself to Mariel. From her reports to Mariel it appears that Louise, although elusive, was not entirely indifferent. In the summer of 1893 she consented to visit Red Cloud and the day before her arrival Willa made preparations by bribing seven-year-old James—with two nickels and a bottle of pop—to go out in the country where their father was working on some property he owned, because Louise was not used to children. She had neglected, however, to specify how long he was to remain away, and the very next night he appeared back home, having begged a ride of a farmer coming into town. Louise was forced to put up with the little boy and his affectionate caresses, but he struck the same ice, said Willa, that she had encountered for so long. For Willa the visit was all too short and only made her miss Louise the more when she went back to Lincoln.

And then it ended, painfully, totally, irrevocably, and Willa had brought it on herself. Louise's older brother, Roscoe Pound, a student at the University several years earlier, had returned after a year at Harvard Law School and admission to the Nebraska bar, as a graduate instructor while studying for a doctorate in botany. At the time, Willa was writing profiles in the *Hesperian* called "Pastels in Prose" and she devoted one of them to a vitriolic attack on a "university graduate" who was unnamed but was unmistakably Roscoe Pound. The Pounds were outraged. Willa had often been a guest in their home and Mrs. Pound considered her behavior an unforgivable breach of etiquette. Willa was forbidden to enter the Pound house ever again and Louise and Olivia refused to have anything further to do with her. In later years Louise and Willa picked up the threads and resumed a friendship of sorts. They corresponded from time to time and Willa always addressed Louise warmly. Louise was less charitable and in the future when she referred to Willa there could often be detected a note of mockery. Whatever the feelings of the Pounds toward Willa, however, Louise and her parents were kindness itself to Elsie Cather during the many years Willa's sister lived in Lincoln.

What possessed Willa to lash out at Roscoe Pound so savagely and wreck her friendship with Louise? She could hardly have believed the Pounds would overlook her intemperate language: "In his early youth, he was a notorious bully . . . Now he bullies mentally just as he used to physically . . . He had ability enough but he just seemed to quit growing when he graduated . . . He is a University graduate and that's all he ever will be in this world or that to come." There is no doubt the words were meant to wound. But why? Dorothy Canfield said she knew about the Pound affair but it was too painful to speak about. It is true that Willa never liked the elder Pounds; she found them cold and self-important. But why did she hate Roscoe? Willa never offered an explanation and neither have any of her biographers.

Yet something must have provoked her. What had Roscoe Pound done to cause her outburst? He must have hurt her in a way she could not forgive and one can only speculate about the things that might have passed between them. Had he found himself attracted to her and been rebuffed? Had he lashed out and bullied her for preferring his sister to himself? Perhaps he made fun of her attachment to Louise? Perhaps he did more than laugh at her. With his greater sophistication and knowledge of the world did he say ugly things about her to Louise? Perhaps he called the friendship unnatural and his sister's friend perverse. He may even have used the term "lesbian" to describe her. We do not know. We do know, however, that losing Louise caused Willa the most intense suffering she had ever known. In despair, she vowed to herself to be more cautious and less impetuous in her affections in the future.

She could not do without friends, however. They had always been important to her and she had thought a great deal about the mutuality of need and obligation involved in friendship. In her freshman year essay on Shakespeare she fastened on the friendship between Hamlet and Horatio as one of the most interesting aspects of the play. She called it a love that "came unbidden [and] grew unforced, until it was stronger than the men themselves . . ." And she went on to say that, "It is not often that two souls are delicately joined enough to experience a friendship like that of Hamlet and Horatio. It is hardly covered by the word friendship; it is an almost awful thing."

Two years later, reviewing a play called *Friends*, she was more circumspect: "The great virtue of friendship is to keep itself to itself; if it imparts itself gratuitously to the unhappy object of affection it ceases to be friendship and becomes a bore." The idea of one man's loving another man better than himself, which the play dramatized and which Hamlet and Horatio had epitomized, Willa conceded was "a beautiful idea, perhaps" but it did not exist outside a girl's boarding school.

In a story written after she left Lincoln and had moved to Pittsburgh she gave the most explicit statement of her own experience. As so often, her alter ego is a young man, in this case Harold Buchanan, a recent college graduate living in a Chicago boardinghouse who encounters a fellow boarder but hesitates to push the acquaintance "lest he should exhaust it too soon. His tendency had always lain that way. In his intemperate youth he had plunged hotheaded and rapacious into friendship after friendship, giving more than any one cared to receive and exacting more than any one had leisure to give . . ." The ideal persists, however, for Buchanan as for Willa. "There are so few minds that are fitted to race side by side, to wrestle and rejoice together, even unto the paean. And after all that is the base of affinities, that mental brotherhood. The glamor of every other passion and enthusiasm fades like the brilliance of an afterglow, leaving shadow and chill and a nameless ennui."

The openness with which Willa talked about her feelings for Louise suggests that most people did not regard their friendship as perverse or as anything but a not uncommon college "crush." Even the intensity of her emotional involvement with Louise was not unacceptable between close women friends. Willa herself said it was unfair that female friendships should be thought unnatural. What makes the attachment significant is that Willa went on to form other intimate relationships in her life that were always and exclusively with women, and it may be that the painful episode with Louise served the purpose of making Willa, if not the people around her, aware of her sexual nature. For all that she could tell Mariel how she suffered when the thing she had lived for was torn away, Willa nevertheless understood the limits the tight-knit society of Lincoln and the University imposed. And perhaps even more, she feared the revulsion she might encounter if she pressed her affections beyond the bounds. The idea of women loving women in any but a romantic sense would have shocked and horrified the people she knew and cared about. With her psychological acuity she may have understood herself and may even have begun to come to terms with her own needs, but if Roscoe Pound thought he had seen through her and charged her with loving his sister like a man, it would have been enough to make Willa fear and hate him, and being Willa, she would have punished him with her pen.

AFTERMATH

The explosion with the Pounds occurred in the spring of 1894 and by the time she returned home for vacation in June, Willa had begun to recover her spirits somewhat, although she still believed the scars would never heal. It took courage to face her family and friends and get on with her life that for so long had focused on Louise. The younger children helped her greatly. When she arrived in Red Cloud she found them all decked out to welcome her. Four-year-old Elsie was just as cute as ever, she told Mariel, and the baby was entrancing with his big gray eyes and long black lashes. Jack, who had been born in Willa's sophomore year, was Mrs. Cather's last child and made the family complete.

Willa enjoyed being with the family and she loved the freedom of summertime in the country. To her friends at school she tended to romanticize her situation: life in the provinces, she called it. If Mariel and her sisters came to visit around July 10, wrote Willa, the folks would be harvesting and the fields would be pretty. Mariel must understand that they lived in rather primitive style and she had only the solitude of semi-barbarism to offer, but she hoped the Gere girls would decide they could endure it. She reported the younger children's bright remarks, sounding more like a doting aunt or grandmother than a sister, but at the same time she promised her friends the youngsters would not be allowed to bother them. If Mariel would only come, she wrote the summer before the break with Louise, she gave her solemn word not to talk about Louise more than once a day. To Ellen (or Ned as she was called) Willa gave assurances that the Cather boys would not bore her with their learning and to Frances, who had a sweet tooth, she dangled visions of whipped cream every day.

Nevertheless, summers were a mixed blessing. The hard reality was that Willa returned to an overcrowded, anxious household and to a town that had less patience with her than her loving family. In Red Cloud she was not the celebrity she had become in Lincoln, but only the Cathers' difficult, nonconformist daughter. She might have let her hair grow finally, but she still went around like a tomboy, and Red Cloud's attitude was that if Willie Cather was as special as her family seemed to think she was, she had yet to prove it to the town. The Miners, of course, remained loyal and country people like the Lambrechts looked forward to her homecoming each June. Her small circle of friends and champions diminished sadly, however, with the loss of three of the most important people in her life, Grandma Boak, Mrs. Wiener and Mr. Ducker. Grandma Boak and Mrs. Wiener had been ill but Mr. Ducker's death came suddenly and unexpectedly. Willa had just left him one evening when his daughter ran after her to say that he was dead. They had been walking home together from his store and almost his last words were, "It is as though the lights were going out, Willie." They parted at his front door, he entered the house and suffered a fatal heart attack.

She and Mr. Ducker had resumed their reading of the classics whenever she was home from school, and after his death she continued the practice with her brother. One summer she made Roscoe read thirty lines of Caesar a day and the next vacation saw them both translating Vergil, at lightning speed, she boasted to Mariel. Her brother Roscoe had gone to teach high school in a neighboring town without attending college, but like Willa he came home in the summer. Douglass always managed to find odd jobs and one year he spent his vacation cultivating ninety acres of corn all by himself, pretty steep work for a little boy, his sister thought.

* * *

Although comments in her letters allude to the serious drought in the state, and her infant brother Jack was dangerously ill, frightening them all, the summer of 1893 seems to have been one of the most contented periods in Willa's life. She hadn't started working for the *Journal* yet so that her time was her own, and she was more carefree that summer than was ever likely to be the case again. A stint in her father's office in June, where she was in charge while he was off on one of his cattle farming ventures, gave her a sense of self-importance and she wrote to friends on office stationery with the letterhead, C. F. Cather, Real Estate and Loan Broker. It was the summer, too, of Louise's memorable visit and after she left Willa cheered herself, as she informed Mariel dramatically, by journeying westward with Roscoe to spend a few days at their uncle's house in the country near Bladen. When Mariel came to visit they would treat her to some of Bladen's famous ice cream.

Several events during that hot dry summer so impressed themselves on Willa that she went back to them years afterward in her fiction. Even nursing Jack through his illness served as inspiration for a later tale about a small boy, also called Jack, who had all of her brother's engaging qualities, but who, unlike Jack Cather, succumbed to the epidemic and died. The other incidents were more cheerful and Willa exercised her storytelling skills and entertained her friends with full accounts of her adventures. Once she and Roscoe were invited to attend a country "literary" presided over by Aunt Franc, who did her share of distributing manna in the wilderness, according to her niece. Her aunt and uncle, she told Mariel, had come out to Nebraska at about the time of creation, and lived in a small colony of Virginians who had clannishly stayed together. Her aunt was a graduate of Smith and Mount Holyoke, and her "literaries" tended to be of a higher caliber than most. On this particular day the discussion was about Emerson and Willa decided that the hayseeds understood transcendentalism about as well as most university students.

The highlight of the afternoon, however, was a recital by a young lady who, to Willa's merriment, unfortunately could not sing. The girl's mother stood beaming in the doorway much as Mrs. Livery Johnson beamed at Lily Fisher in *The Song of the Lark*, while the daughter ran through twelve songs, not counting encores, in a voice that grated like a file. Later, the mother bought up fifty copies of the local newspaper, which had printed the full program, to send to her friends back East.

One of their favorite amusements when she and Roscoe visited their uncle was to climb to the top of his fifty-foot windmill at night and survey the scene for miles around. Roscoe called it being right off the edge of the world and Willa loved it especially in the moonlight when whatever was ugly was obliterated and what was beautiful was raised almost to the divine. Once she and Roscoe were caught on their little four-foot platform in a great storm, just as Jim and Ántonia would be in *My Ántonia*. They saw the storm coming and watched the cattle huddle together in one end of the corral and the corn leaves stir restlessly and hold up their long blades as if to receive the rain. When the wind struck, Roscoe took command and ordered his sister to take off her skirts or they would never get down. She did as he told her to, removing all her skirts save one light one, but she told Mariel that it was Roscoe's strong grip that really saved her. If he had not held on to her she would surely have fallen in. As it was, she emerged with only blistered hands.

Before the summer ended she and Roscoe made a pull up the river once again to brave the island as they used to. Willa seemed to sense that there would never be another summer like it and she tried to crowd as many memories as possible in those few brief, carefree months. By the next summer, the last vacation before her senior year at college, she had been a working journalist for several months and had less time for play. For two weeks in early July of 1894 the Lincoln *Evening News* sent her to nearby Crete to cover a meeting of the Chautauqua Society and she reported daily on the program of recitals, lectures and physical fitness exercises that transformed the little town into a great open-air classroom. In August on a blistering day, "the hottest day I ever knew," she was to call it, she and Roscoe, with Mariel and Grace Broady, made a party to visit Brownsville which was celebrating its fortieth birthday as the oldest city in the state.

Willa's story in the *Journal* commemorating the event was hardly likely to make her friends in Brownsville. In fact, she told Grace, from now on she had better get everything about a town on her first visit, because it was certain she could never visit the same town twice. Brownsville, Nebraska, was a river town that had flourished on the steamboat trade in its early days, but when the river channel changed its course the shipping business disappeared and Brownsville with it. Now, Willa said, it was the tiredest town she had ever seen, with a picturesque sort of decay "that made it look as if it had gone to sleep in the hills like Rip Van Winkle . . ."

Willa never tried to make it up to Brownsville. Instead, she made matters even worse with a short story she wrote in 1897 called "Resurrection" that was set in the poor dispirited town that once had been so lively. "No real estate ever sells in Brownsville," she wrote, "except cemetery lots."

After the Brownsville adventure she made no further trips but spent the last weeks of vacation at home in Red Cloud. Mr. Wiener was boarding at Mrs. Garber's and Willa often joined them for Sunday dinner at Mrs. Garber's invitation. Mr. Wiener had acquired a new trotting horse and he took her out driving almost every afternoon. Evenings she spent playing cards with Roscoe and enjoying the younger members of the family, although she complained that purchasing kisses at a chocolate drop apiece from James was rather an expensive business. She stayed at home as long as she could, not returning to Lincoln until mid-September, just in time to begin her final year at the university.

* * *

Between September 1894 and June 1895, her last semesters, Willa had close to a hundred pieces in the *Journal*. A full-time reviewer might not have produced much more than she did and her school work suffered accordingly. Nevertheless she managed to fulfill the mathematics requirement that had nagged her throughout her college career, and she received her diploma in June with the class of '95. Willa always worked hard at subjects she liked but she never felt obliged to spend time and effort where her interest was not engaged, and her final record as a student was rather lopsided. She was brilliant in English and in languages, and went well beyond the curriculum in those classes, but even in her literature courses, required reading was anathema to her. She thought it ruined a book for a student to be made to read it, and when she was a famous novelist, she often said she didn't want her books assigned to students as part of the grind. She would much prefer, she said, to be read on the sly. And she refused to allow her work to be reprinted in cheap paper editions for classroom use.

* * *

In addition to her newspaper work and her academic courses Willa did some practice teaching in her senior year as an aid to Herbert Bates. Alvin Johnson, who was a prep then, recalled that his themes were passed on "by a rather mannish young woman with a head that seemed vast under her jungle of hair. 'You write not badly,' she told him, 'but you don't *see*. Learn French, a little French, and read Flaubert or even Maupassant. They *see* . . .'" It was always best, she felt, to read on one's own.

De Maupassant, who was one of Willa's favorite authors, figures peripherally in a famous encounter with another author, the young Stephen Crane, that took place in the winter of 1895, although in describing it several years later, Willa placed it a year earlier, in the spring of her junior year. She was "Maupassant mad" at the time, she wrote, and tried frantically to get Crane to comment on "Le Bonheur" but all she could get from him was a sarcastic grin and the remark, " 'Oh, you're moping, are you?' " She never referred to the meeting with Crane either then or afterward except in an article at the time of his death in 1900 and she was careful then to use a pseudonym, Henry Nicklemann. Her silence, however, does not necessarily suggest that the meeting was apocryphal, but rather that Crane was probably preoccupied during the time he was in Lincoln with his series of articles on the drought, and that he had little time for conversation with a schoolgirl journalist. When he died and it was appropriate to write a lengthy obituary, Willa embroidered the details of their brief acquaintance and took the occasion, as she so often did, to express her own artistic principles. The quote attributed to Crane in her article, " 'The detail of a thing has to filter through my blood, and then it comes out like a native product but it takes forever,' " is pure Cather.

Willa herself had the last word on Crane's behavior many years later when she wrote in a preface to his collected works that "there is every evidence that he was a reticent and unhelpful man, with no warmhearted love of giving out opinions." Undoubtedly she did at least *see* Crane in Lincoln and probably at the *Journal*'s offices. In her account she said that he had come to see the managing editor and that when she heard his name, she found a spot where she could sit and stare at him unobserved. He was the first man of letters she had ever met in the flesh, a statement that rings true, and she meant to observe him and, if possible, get him to talk seriously with her about his work. He was in Lincoln as a journalist and, like herself, wrote "stuff that would sell" and earn him a living, but he also wrote poetry and stories and Willa felt they shared what Crane called "a double literary life." *The Red Badge of Courage* had been published serially in the *Journal* in 1894 and, according to the article, Willa did some copy editing on his story. It was the sort of thing she might have been called on to do. Crane's grammar was appalling, she wrote, but even through the careless sentence structure, she had been able to discern "the wonder of that remarkable performance."

It was typical of Willa to make herself a year younger than she really was and to call herself a junior rather than a senior. And it was also typical of her to make her subjects conform to her romantic picture of them. It was exactly what she would do with her fictional characters. Whatever the truth of the encounter, the idea of a meeting somewhere in a Western town between Willa Cather and Stephen Crane, the one still in the cocoon, the other with his wings already clipped at twenty-four, has enormous imaginative appeal. For the novelist and critic Wright Morris "the meeting of youthful minds on a sultry plains night" was one of "the star-crossed moments in American letters."

Willa could only have met Crane in February when he is known to have been in Lincoln. The very next month an opportunity arose that must have eclipsed in importance everything else in her senior year, even the meeting with Crane. In March she had a chance to visit Chicago during the week the Metropolitan Opera was performing there. Her friends encouraged her to go; Mary Jones, the acting librarian at the University of Nebraska would accompany her, and Dr. Tyndale helped defray the cost. It was Willa's first taste of grand opera and she was enraptured. Now she had a touchstone and could write with more authority than ever, knowing she had at last seen the greatest company of the day. Chicago was a wonder also, and Willa stored impressions of the unique urban mixture of brashness and civility that made the city infinitely fascinating and that she would use so effectively one day in *The Song of the Lark*, *The Professor's House* and *Lucy Gayheart*.

Willa brought back from Chicago an awareness of a new dimension of sophistication that made her understand how much there was to learn and how far she had yet to go. The experience had a polishing effect like the first coat of varnish on an unfinished surface. It would take further applications for the polish to sink in but the refining process had begun. At twenty-one, her school days were behind her.

III

❧

Nebraska Coda

THE DOUBLE LITERARY LIFE

After graduation Willa went home to try the double literary life in earnest. Her plan was to go on with her newspaper work and, as often as she could, to retreat to the little bedroom under the eaves and devote herself entirely to her writing. She had the feeling the family was waiting for her to do something extraordinary, but her own aspirations were the real spur. The first few months at home were a restless time for Willa and when she was offered a chance to work in Lincoln she grasped it eagerly. In July she rechristened her column "The Passing Show" and in August transferred it from the *Journal* to the *Courier*. A note in the *Courier* at the same time announced that she would also join the staff, adding that her services were a valuable acquisition to any paper. The next several months found her living in Lincoln, working for the *Courier* as an associate editor and columnist, and for the *Journal* as its drama critic. The *Courier* association proved short-lived, however.

She had been hired by her friend Sarah Harris, who, with a young but experienced newspaperman from the East, W. Morton Smith, had bought the *Courier* from its former owner in early August. Under the reorganized company Smith was made editor and Sarah

Harris and Willa were listed on the masthead as associate editors. Willa had known Sarah Harris since her first days at the University and they had always liked each other. At thirty-five, Sarah Harris was one of those spirited women the West could produce, attractive, independent, warmhearted. Her family were railroad builders and she had means as well as intelligence. She married later on but in the years that Willa knew her best, Sarah Harris was a single woman wielding a considerable amount of influence in the small metropolis of Lincoln. Willa and she worked together on the *Courier* for only a short while, when something appears to have gone wrong. By the end of December "The Passing Show" went back to the *Journal* and, to all intents, so did Willa. She asked Mariel in early January to get back a copy of Daudet's *Sapho* which she had loaned to Sarah Harris because she said she would feel uncomfortable asking for it herself under the circumstances. Whatever the "circumstances," it put an end to Willa's job on the *Courier* but not, in the long run, to her friendship with Sarah Harris. They argued frequently, sometimes in print. Sarah was an ardent feminist and a political activist; Willa was interested in personalities, not politics. Nevertheless, at the core of their relationship was a strong feeling of affectionate regard and mutual admiration and when Sarah Harris died in 1918, Willa knew that she had lost not just a colleague but a friend.

Coming back to Red Cloud in midwinter, after a busy few months at the newspaper office, was a letdown. Consider me dead, Willa wrote in one letter, and she datelined another, in Siberia. A short visit to Beatrice in December helped enliven things a bit and a New Year's dance which Douglass took her to provided amusement of sorts. Douglass had prevailed on her to go, she told Mariel, so he could avoid the sixteen girls who expected him to ask them, and he had ordered a lot of flowers sent to her from Lincoln. The hall was big and the floor was heaped with shavings and chunks of wax that one had to clamber over with an alpenstock. The seats were long rough planks resting on chairs and the refreshments consisted of ice water, coffee and ham sandwiches passed in a potato basket. The real entertainment, however, was the dance itself. The men caught the girls by the arm as high as their sleeves allowed and then hung on tight. When they fell, as they did every now and then on the slippery floor, it was up to the girls to help the men up. Yet this boisterous occasion was attended by the *bon ton* of Red Cloud, Willa said.

The Miner girls were there with their brother and Willa's cousin Retta Ayre.

Douglass did his sister proud by being the most civilized-looking object in the crowd, in her opinion, and she agreed to go to another dance with him later in the season. On that occasion the dance was held twenty miles away at Blue Hill, and Willa stayed the night with a professor and his wife who had a young teacher, a Miss Gayhardt, boarding with them. Well educated and extremely pretty, according to Willa who was much taken with her, the girl was teaching for the first time and was as starved for companionship and "civilized" conversation as Willa herself. The dance ended at three in the morning and the two girls sat up and talked until dawn. It was a chance meeting that made a lasting impression and affected Willa poignantly. She used a variation of the girl's name when she wrote *Lucy Gayheart*, but she waited almost a lifetime to tell the story of a young teacher, very like the ardent Miss Gayhardt, in "The Best Years." In both the novel and the short story the enchanting heroines die young in tragic accidents, a not-infrequent occurrence in Willa Cather's fiction, but it was memory, and not death, that preserved the girl in Blue Hill from the erosion of time.

Again it was home to solitude and unfinished manuscripts, but an important event took place in January 1896 that made all the loneliness and hard work seem worthwhile. Her story "On the Divide" appeared in the *Overland Monthly*, a small but prestigious publication with a national circulation. Like the best of her early work in the *Hesperian*, this too was a Nebraska tale and the setting was one which she knew intimately. In the story of the lonely, tormented Norwegian farmer, Canute Canuteson, "the wreck of ten winters on the Divide" and his drunken courtship of his neighbor's daughter, Willa evoked all the primitive mystery and terror of the heartless land where men brought "only the dregs of the lives they had squandered in other lands and among other people," and where insanity and suicide were everyday occurrences. Willa makes Canute an almost epic figure in his desire and his rage, and the fact that the provocative Lena ultimately submits and that Canute shows a shamefaced delicacy in the end does nothing to diminish the man's passion or the ferocity of his pursuit. Some of Willa's neighbors undoubtedly found the character repellent, but her handling of the strong theme was so controlled and her vision so assured, it was as though she defied her readers not to see the larger truth in everything she wrote, however shocking.

She spent the early months of 1896 in Red Cloud with an occasional visit to Lincoln, once to attend a meeting of the Nebraska State Press Association where she delivered an address on "How to Make a Newspaper Interesting." Characteristically she spoke for a personal approach to journalism, declaring a neutral newspaper to be an abomination. When she was in Lincoln she reviewed plays for the *Journal*, but she wrote "The Passing Show" in Red Cloud and relied for material on books and personalities rather than performances. By March she was complaining once again of bitter exile in the provinces. Roscoe came once a week, Douglass was sent home from school daily for misbehavior and all she did was get the mail, read the newspaper, eat and sleep. Occasionally she tried to cook and when it was not too cold she rode her bicycle. Any diversion was welcome and when her cousin Retta Ayre, the "heiress," married Hugh Miner, Willa gave them a stylish wedding breakfast, ordering strawberries, fresh tomatoes and watercress from Chicago. Another time her parents went to Hastings and Willa found herself the harried mother of a large and turbulent brood. Jack swallowed two pennies, Jim cut his upper lip and Willa said she felt like the matron of a hospital. Nevertheless, Douglass was good company, quite a model brother, Willa thought, and when Roscoe came they called on friends, had card parties and generally entertained themselves sportily in a small way. If they weren't going anywhere, Willa read to the children. She was happily taking a rest from *Alice*, she reported to Mariel, and putting James through the *Arabian Nights*.

In mid-March her routine was interrupted by an unexpected flurry of excitement. Herbert Bates abruptly announced his resignation from the University, leaving a vacancy in the English department for which Willa immediately applied. She wanted the job desperately and asked Mr. Gere to intercede for her with the chancellor. She had taken all of Bates's classes she told him, and could count on the professor's recommendation. She knew that her age and sex were against her, but the University was pressed for funds and she thought they might like to hire her since she would go in as an instructor for five hundred dollars less than the man they were considering, who would be an adjunct professor.

Her logic and her friends' support were of no avail, however, against the intransigence of her old antagonist, Professor Sherman, who flatly refused to consider her appointment. It was petty revenge for a man in Sherman's position to deny her the post, but as chairman of the English department he had the final word and his opposition prevailed. Willa was stung but, in spite of her disappointment, it is unlikely that she regretted her past behavior.

Of all the might-have-beens in Willa Cather's life, no single incident probably made more of a difference to her future than her not being hired by the University. Had she joined the faculty at that stage of her life and career she might well have remained there all her life, like her friend Louise Pound. She would have been a writer, too, of course, and a brilliant one as her early stories attest, but her best work was always done out of memory and reflection and at a distance from her subject. Her novels of Nebraska, translated into a dozen different languages, impressed an image of the prairie on readers all over the world, but she wrote them in other places. She needed to get away from Nebraska to write about it, and one wonders what her stories would have been like, had she never left home. She never made another attempt to become an academic, and she had no further professional association with the University, although the University would be proud to claim her as a graduate.

* * *

Losing the University appointment made it harder than ever for Willa to settle down again to the daily routine. It was one thing to be a temporary visitor at home during school vacations, knowing that she would be returning soon to Lincoln, but the prospect of remaining indefinitely in Red Cloud dismayed her. She had grown away from her family and their way of looking at things during the years she was at school, and she was feeling increasingly isolated from the town. Writing disconsolately to Mariel, she complained that she was played out and she wondered how she would ever accomplish anything worthwhile. Herbert Bates was sending happy letters from a place, she said, where people cared about Paderewski and Swinburne. (The place was Cincinnati.) She could believe that he had come into his kingdom, but how was she to write when she had seen so little of the world?

Nevertheless, for all her depression and frustration, Willa was working constantly, exhibiting the energy and dedication that would in time come to dominate her life. The *Journal* was lavish in the amount of space they gave her. Once a week, page nine, and later page thirteen, literally belonged to "The Passing Show." A single day might find her recommending a new novel by Anatole France; deploring the namby-pamby literary fare served up to children—"The whole category of child literature is largely farce anyway"—and discussing the acting styles of Richard Mansfield and Minnie Maddern Fiske. "The Passing Show" for January 1896 contains reviews and observations on everything from Yvette Guilbert and Lillie Langtry to two poets on either side of the Atlantic, England's new poet laureate, Alfred Austin, and the American Walt Whitman.

Austin fulfilled every requirement of his post as poet laureate, Willa wrote, by being totally unknown and by not being a poet at all "by any stretch of courtesy or imagination." But Whitman was a different phenomenon. Willa likened him to a "joyous elephant" who had no code but to be natural. He never bothered to select the poetic but took everything in the universe "from fly-specks to fixed stars." His lack of discrimination bothered her but she knew a poet when she saw one and she found his primitive elemental energy irresistible. She would not have borrowed the title of her first Nebraska novel from Whitman as she did in *O Pioneers!* had she not been deeply affected by his poetry.

A month after the Whitman column, writing an appreciation of the Midwestern author Eugene Field and his posthumously published *Love Affairs of a Bibliomaniac*, Willa perceived another model that had great appeal for her. Field had been a man of letters who lived in a big city, who loved the classics and read them daily, yet had also been a journalist. She thought it unfortunate that the contrasting elements in his life appeared to be such a rare anomaly.

When she wasn't writing Willa was usually reading, in those long cold winter months of 1896. Words and ideas preoccupied her and the thoughts that found their way into her columns cast long shadows that revealed themselves again and again in her later work. It was never enough for her simply to express an opinion. Every statement had to reflect a philosophy, fit into a comprehensive theory that emerged slowly and deliberately and would stand the test of time. Her own taste was eclectic and could embrace both Bliss Carman and Verlaine, George Eliot and Mrs. Humphrey Ward, but Willa always knew the difference. "Comparisons may be odious in art," she wrote, "but they are the only means of keeping your taste pure and inviolate. People who never make them have no stability or judgment." By the time she left school she had already passed beyond Bohemianism, although she could admit its lure. She cared too much for order, however, to be quite comfortable with attitudes that seemed to her to verge on anarchy. She had dipped into the gaudy and the frivolous but they had no lasting substance. She needed solid nourishment and it was only to be found in work. "The business of an artist's life is not Bohemianism, for or against," she wrote, "but ceaseless and unremitting labor."

Still, she was a worshipper of beauty and could say with Ruskin that "to know is little and to feel is all" and "the highest end of an individual life is to create, or, at least to see and feel beauty." To Tolstoi setting forth on his ascetic venture, clothed in moral purpose, she could point out that "art itself is the highest moral purpose in the world." All of Ruskin's lectures on political economy, she said, were designed "to induce men to live more simply that they may live more beautifully." Here at the beginning of her life's work was the great message of the *Archbishop*. She was expressing Ruskin's creed, but she was making it her own.

"TOMMY, THE UNSENTIMENTAL"

Spring came slowly to the prairie and then summer and in June Willa had her deliverance. Her work on the *Courier* and *Journal* had brought her to the attention of a publisher in Pittsburgh who offered her the editorship of a new magazine, the *Home Monthly*. The firm of Axtell, Orr and Company, which heretofore had been known only for its farm journals, saw an attractive possibility in the women's magazine field which the *Ladies' Home Journal* had recently entered with spectacular success. Charles Axtell knew the Geres and Will Jones in Lincoln and was acquainted with George Gerwig in Pittsburgh and they all had enthusiastically recommended Willa for the post. It was a bold step to go from living at home and working part time for a Nebraska newspaper to editing a major magazine and moving East to an unfamiliar city. But Willa was confident and courageous and, besides, she was mad to get out into the world.

The East was where books were bought and sold, and Pittsburgh was only 350 miles from New York, so Pittsburgh it would be. On June 17 the *Journal* announced her departure and by the end of the month she was gone, having stopped briefly in Chicago on her way to Pittsburgh.

Willa was only twenty-two when she left home and she never again lived in Nebraska, although she went back often to visit as long as her parents were alive. Fortunately she left a picture of the girl she must have been that last year in Red Cloud, in the glowing story of "Tommy the Unsentimental" which she wrote while she was still at home and used in the very first issue of the *Home Monthly*. There is no better introduction to the young Willa Cather.

Tommy's real name is Theodosia and, like her creator, she is blunt, energetic and competent, the kind of no-nonsense girl who gets along best with older men who appreciate her qualities and are not concerned with her deficiencies. The "Old Boys" in this case are seven friends of Tommy's father and they serve as a cackling Greek chorus, warning, prophesying and mourning the outcome of the drama that unfolds in the small Nebraska town of Southdown. Tommy has a head for business and runs her father's bank when he is out of town. She also does the work of his cashier, Jay Ellington Harper, good-looking, but incompetent and something of a wastrel. Tommy is smitten, however, and the Old Boys look on helplessly, finally maneuvering to get Jay started in his own bank in a town twenty-five miles away. It isn't far enough, unfortunately, and Tommy finds excuses to bicycle the distance to straighten out the young man's business for him.

The Old Boys don't like it any better when she goes East to school, where "she took rather her own way with the curriculum," and brings back with her a girl she had grown fond of, a "Miss Jessica," "a dainty, white, languid bit of thing, who used violet perfumes and carried a sunshade." (There is more than a touch of Willa's sister Jessica in the portrait.) The inevitable befalls, of course. As one of the Old Boys puts it, "The heart of the cad is gone out to the little muff . . .", and he prepares to leave for Kansas City rather than stay and see "the abominable suffering of it." Knowing she is losing Jay to Jessica, Tommy makes one last bid. At ten-thirty one morning she gets word that Jay is in trouble, there's a run on his bank and he must have help by noon. Like the Western heroine she is, Tommy grabs her bike and makes up her mind to "wheel it." Jessica pleads to go along and, smiling to herself, Tommy agrees, though not without a warning that "it's twenty-five miles uppish grade and hilly, and only an hour and a quarter to do it." But Jessica will do anything for Jay and so off the girls go on their rescue mission, Jessica riding behind and Tommy in front pedaling furiously. The ride is memorably described: "The whirr of the seventeen-year locust was the only thing that spoke of animation, and that ground on as if only animated and enlivened by the sickening, destroying heat. The sun was like hot brass, and the wind that blew up from the south was hotter still. But Tommy knew the wind was their only chance."

Jessica, nearly fainting with thirst, begs to stop for water, but Tommy only shakes her head. " 'Takes too much time,' " she mutters and bends over the handlebars, "never lifting her eyes from the road in front of her." It flashed upon Miss Jessica, wrote Willa, "that Tommy was not only very unkind, but that she sat very badly on her wheel and looked aggressively masculine and professional when she bent her shoulders like that." (Willa knew exactly how she was viewed in Red Cloud!) Halfway there, Jessica slips off the bike and Tommy heroically finishes the ride alone, arriving in the nick of time. The field is hers and the temptation all but irresistible to claim the prize. But Tommy, above everything, is a realist and she sends Jay off to marry Jessica, knowing those two belonged together and that she was different from them both.

On the surface the plot is uncomplicated. A clever girl falls for an unworthy man, introduces him to her best friend and loses him to her. Undoubtedly this is the way Willa intended her story to be read. Only a very subtle shift of emphasis is required, however, to perceive the characters in a somewhat different triangle, one in which a clever girl is attracted to a clinging maiden, introduces her to a man of her acquaintance and loses her to him. It is not possible that Willa was unaware of the ambiguities; it is more probable that she intended them and even took a wicked satisfaction in them. The Old Boys state the case right out: "It's a bad sign when a rebellious girl like Tommy took to being sweet and gentle to one of her own sex, the worst sign in the world." Exactly what they meant by this observation is never quite established but it remains as explicit a statement of Willa's own susceptibility as anything she ever wrote and serves as the purest example of her self-awareness of the duality of her nature.

By the time the August *Home Monthly* came out with "Tommy the Unsentimental," Willa was a long way from Nebraska and already starting to miss it painfully, just as Tommy did when she went East to school. " 'It's all very fine down East there,' " Tommy says when she returns to Southdown, " 'but one gets mighty homesick for this sky, the old intense blue of it, you know. Down there the skies are all pale and smoky. And this wind, this hateful, dear old everlasting wind that comes down like the sweep of cavalry and is never tamed or broken . . . I used to get hungry for this wind! I couldn't sleep in that lifeless stillness down there.' " Perhaps Willa felt that this paean to the Nebraska sky would make up to her family and friends in Red Cloud for the ambiguity of "Tommy" and the confession that lay hidden in her defiantly revealing self-portrait.

IV

❀

Apprenticeship in Pittsburgh

A CITY OF HILLS AND RIVERS

Pittsburgh in the last years of the nineteenth century, when Willa first saw it, was busier, dirtier, noisier and more alive than any place she had ever known. Three hundred thousand people lived in the smoky city between the Allegheny and Monongahela rivers, while Allegheny to the west, long since incorporated into Pittsburgh, was then a separate city almost as large and booming. The great mills along the river that spewed flares and smoke and roared right up into the hills seemed to charge the town with "the very incandescence of human energy." Year round the sky glowed red with the garish lights of huge furnaces so that it sometimes seemed the city was actually breathing fire. The air itself, Willa was to write, snapped with "a feverish, passionate endeavor."

Pittsburgh's rich resources and mighty industries had spawned great fortunes, and the wealth of the empire builders—Carnegie, Frick, Schenley, Heinz—was visible everywhere, in their opulent homes and handsome office buildings and in the stately parks and monuments that bore their names. Only the year before Willa's arrival the Carnegie Institute had opened with its Music Hall and art gallery in addition to the already famed Carnegie Library. Willa had never seen so much marble, she said, not even in the University of Nebraska Library, nor so many books, all the books in the world, she imagined. The newly formed Pittsburgh Symphony led by Frederic Archer played in the sumptuous Carnegie Music Hall and Willa wrote to Neddy Gere that she had gone there one Saturday night to hear the versatile conductor give a brilliant recital in which for the first time she had the thrilling experience of hearing Schumann's *Träumerei* played on an organ. All the leading theatrical companies played in Pittsburgh and stars of the Metropolitan Opera on tour performed regularly. The Casino Theatre was near the office and when one of Willa's actress friends from Lincoln, Pauline Hall or Maida Craigen, happened to be playing there, Willa would stop in on matinee days as often as she could, to watch them once again.

Moreover, the city was visually exciting, with stunning natural features that the iron furnaces and smokestacks could not obliterate. The wide rivers and the hills, unfamiliar sights to the girl from the flat, dry prairie, would compensate for anything, she wrote. Later she would see the city's meanness and the way it could numb the senses with its crude pursuit of commerce and what she called "its hard-handed practicality." In "Paul's Case," the city is a cause of Paul's malaise and its stifling presence the goad that sends him on his desperate journey. "Paul's Case" was the only story Willa wrote while she still lived there to use Pittsburgh as a background, and she did not write it until she had been in the city for almost ten years. In 1907, shortly after she had moved away, she set a portion of "The Namesake" in Pittsburgh. But she waited twenty years before going back to it again in "Uncle Valentine" and "Double Birthday," where once more the city is portrayed as oppressive and inimical to art and creativity. Yet Willa's personal associations with Pittsburgh were happy ones and she never lost her affection for the smoky city on the Monongahela and for the friends she made there.

* * *

The Axtells felt responsible for Willa when she first arrived in Pittsburgh to take up her post as editor of the *Home Monthly*. Until she could find a place of her own they invited her to stay with them. Living with her employer and his wife, she soon learned, was a little like doing penance. They were kind and well-meaning people but fun was not in their nature. In fact, their coldness reminded Willa very much of Judge and Mrs. Pound. Even with each other the Axtells were stiff and formal and their brand of Presbyterianism, though it was not the "infant damnation sort" which she would have found intolerable, was still chilly enough to depress her. When their daughter Lydia who was going to Vassar the next year had a party she invited the members of her *Sunday school class*, Willa reported in mock horror to her friends. Otherwise Lydia's social engagements were confined to her five thousand, seven hundred cousins, one of whom asked Willa how she had found time at the University of Nebraska to take so many courses along with her newspaper columns and her *church work*. In the Axtell family, Willa said, a girl had her church work just as other girls have powder boxes. A niece who was a member of the household confided to Willa she'd rather not live at all than live as they did, never going anywhere and rarely associating with anyone except relatives. Willa was sympathetic, but since her own stay was to be temporary she could afford to be accommodating, even to singing hymns with the family. For comfort, there was Philly, the youngest of the Axtells, who at least had the virtue of being small, said Willa. Between going to church and telling tall tales about Indians to Philly, who expected them of her because she came from the West, Willa told her friends she was afraid she was losing all sense of the truth.

Fortunately for Willa she did not have to depend on the Axtells to introduce her into Pittsburgh society. For that she had her old friend George Gerwig and his wife who, no doubt, were familiar with the gloomy atmosphere at the Axtells and very soon after her arrival, with great kindness, took her under their wing. Social life for the wives and daughters of the city's prosperous burghers centered on a multitude of women's clubs which, according to Willa, literally ruled Pittsburgh, and it was to one of the most prestigious of these clubs that Mrs. Gerwig brought Willa for high tea on a warm summer afternoon. It was the custom at club meetings for members to discourse on a selected topic of the day and on this occasion they had chosen Thomas Carlyle as their subject. When the new editor of the *Home Monthly* was politely invited to speak, she astonished her audience by delivering a lengthy and impassioned dissertation. She had remembered almost word for word her essay on Carlyle written for

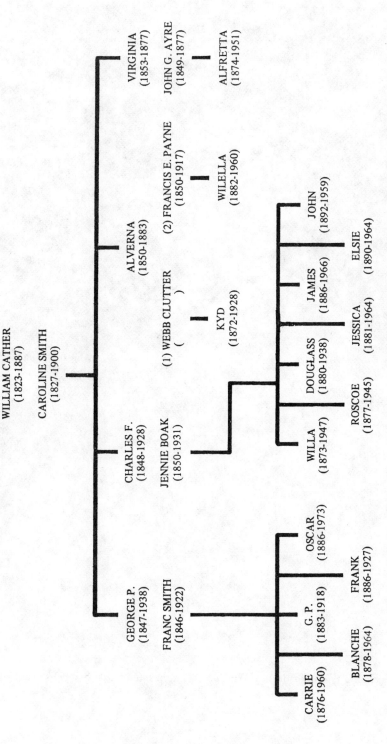

1. Adapted from Mildred R. Bennett, *The World of Willa Cather*, this chart appeared in *Nebraska History*, Volume 54, Number 4, Winter 1973, Nebraska State Historical Society.

WILLIAM CATHER
(1823-1887)

CAROLINE SMITH
(1827-1900)

GEORGE P.
(1847-1938)

FRANC SMITH
(1846-1922)

CHARLES F.
(1848-1928)

JENNIE BOAK
(1850-1931)

ALVERNA
(1850-1883)

(2) FRANCIS E. PAYNE
(1850-1917)

WILELLA
(1882-1960)

VIRGINIA
(1853-1877)

JOHN G. AYRE
(1849-1877)

ALFRETTA
(1874-1951)

(1) WEBB CLUTTER
(   )

KYD
(1872-1928)

CARRIE
(1876-1960)

BLANCHE
(1878-1964)

G. P.
(1883-1918)

FRANK
(1886-1927)

OSCAR
(1886-1973)

WILLA
(1873-1947)

ROSCOE
(1877-1945)

DOUGLASS
(1880-1938)

JESSICA
(1881-1964)

JAMES
(1886-1966)

ELSIE
(1890-1964)

JOHN
(1892-1959)

2. Willa as a child at Willowshade, near Winchester, Virginia. (Nebraska State Historical Society)

3. Mary Virginia Cather. Willa's mother was a proud woman but, like Mrs. Kronborg in *The Song of the Lark*, she also had "an unusual capacity for getting the flavor of people and of places." (Nebraska State Historical Society)

4. Charles F. Cather. Her father, Willa said, remained a sweet Southern boy until the end of his life. (Nebraska State Historical Society)

5. The house on Cedar Street, Red Cloud, Nebraska, was never quite big enough but the Cathers lived there for twenty years, from 1884 to 1904, and it is the setting for many of Willa Cather's stories. (Willa Cather Pioneer Memorial Collection, Nebraska State Historical Society)

6. The attic was "a story in itself." Willa and her brothers shared a dormitory, their three beds side by side as "in a hospital ward."

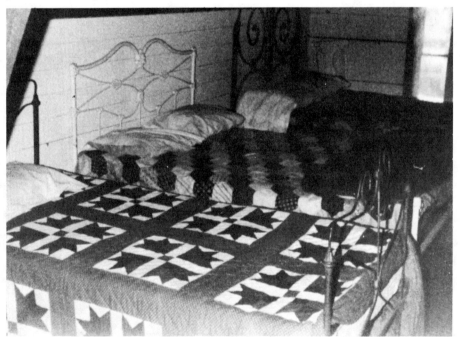

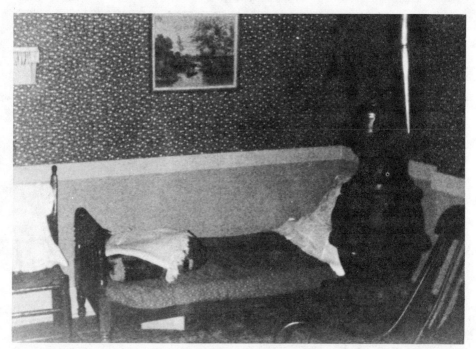

7. Like old Mrs. Harris, Grandma Boak had her corner in a corridor off the kitchen. Her bed was a narrow spindle-frame lounge "with a thin mattress and a red calico spread." Nearby was her black rocker and the chair that usually held her darning basket. They are seen here in the restored homestead.

8. Willa and her brothers Roscoe (left) and Douglass were a triumvirate. When she dedicated her first book to them she remembered how they "lay and planned at moonrise,/On an island in a western river,/Of the conquest of the world together." (Nebraska State Historical Society)

9. Jessica Cather. At least, said Willa, her mother would have one daughter who was a lady. (Nebraska State Historical Society)

10. Jack, the youngest of the Cathers, was born while Willa was at the University of Nebraska. When she was feeling blue she found comfort in her little brother's big gray eyes. He was just made to love people dearly, she said, and she was afraid that he would suffer for it. (Willa Cather Pioneer Memorial Collection, Nebraska State Historical Society)

RED CLOUD, *Bulkley,* NEBRASKA.

11. Willa's classmates at the University of Nebraska never forgot their first impression of "Billy" Cather, age sixteen, as a Second Prep. By the time she graduated she had let her hair grow and dressed more fashionably. (Nebraska State Historical Society)

12. G. P. Cather, seen here in uniform, was killed in France. Her cousin's short life and his death in battle haunted Willa and inspired her to create the character of Claude Wheeler in *One of Ours*. (Willa Cather Pioneer Memorial Collection, Nebraska State Historical Society)

13. Frances (Mrs. George P.) Cather. A graduate of Mount Holyoke, Aunt Franc, according to her niece, did her share of distributing manna in the wilderness. She was the model for Claude's mother, Mrs. Wheeler, in *One of Ours* and Aunt Georgiana in "A Wagner Matinee," although neither portrait does her justice. (Nebraska State Historical Society)

Professor Hunt's class six years before and, once the idea seized her, she allowed herself to soar with it.

It was a tour de force that made her famous in Pittsburgh. The women fell over each other to shake her hand, she told Mariel, and, with the unkindness of youth and the arrogance she could sometimes display, she dismissed them as awfully stupid for believing she had actually made up the talk as she went along. It seems more likely that the ladies were not quite so taken in as Willa thought, but were applauding what must indeed have been a superb performance. When a few months later Dorothy Canfield brought her mother for a visit, it gave Willa particular satisfaction to introduce Mrs. Canfield to the clubwomen of Pittsburgh. By then Dorothy's father was president of Ohio State University and the Canfields were living in Columbus, but Willa knew that Mrs. Canfield's friends in Lincoln would hear about the Pittsburgh visit and she gloried in the thought that they would learn of her improved social standing. No matter how she was thought of in Lincoln, she was "in it" in Pittsburgh. She had fifteen calls to return, she boasted to Mariel, and it was a matter of pride to have been called on so soon.

She was meeting young men, too. On a magical moonlit evening George Gerwig took her on an excursion with the Press Club up the river in a steam launch. A catered supper was served on board to the accompaniment of banjos strumming "Lover's Serenade" and "Last Night," and a delightful Princeton boy was in attendance. The hills of the city, she wrote, glowed with a thousand lights of a thousand colors, so close they looked like great honeycombs of fire.

Within a few weeks she was able to leave the Axtells and move into a boardinghouse at 304 Craig Street. It suited her, being well located on Pittsburgh's proper East End and close enough to the office for her to ride her bicycle back and forth, racing the electric streetcar all the way. If she was sometimes lonely in her little room with only the "prim old maid" who ran the boardinghouse for company, she managed in the office to be fully occupied. The Axtells went West on a month's vacation leaving her to get out the entire magazine by herself. It was all great rot, she wrote, home and fireside stuff about babies and how to make mince pie, but her position was responsible and the experience was invaluable. Besides, it allowed her to prove to herself and to her doubting friends that she could work hard and stick to a job that was less than congenial. The *Home*

Monthly might not be all that she could wish for from a literary standpoint but that was the publisher's business, not hers, and she would try to do the best she could with the material at hand.

YOUNG EDITOR

The August 1896 issue was almost wholly Willa's. It contained "Tommy the Unsentimental" which she signed with her own name, a tongue-in-cheek fairy tale called "The Princess Baladino" which carried the by-line Charles Douglass and a poem, "My Little Boy," attributed to one John Esten. In fact, all of them, as well as an unsigned editorial, were written by the editor herself. Her good taste is already evident; she used her own by-line for the best of the lot. As for the cheerful "Princess Baladino," it was exactly the kind of story she made up for the younger children in the family—she may even have told it to them before writing it—and the "author's" name combined her father's and one of her brother's.

For September she planned an in-depth article on the wives of the two Presidential candidates, Mrs. William McKinley and Mrs. William Jennings Bryan. Her landlady had known Mrs. McKinley well in her youth and Willa had "worked her" for all she was worth. Willa was prepared to go to Canton, Ohio, herself to get photographs of Mrs. McKinley, but she couldn't easily get to Lincoln for material on Mrs. Bryan. For that she turned confidently to her old friend Mrs. Gere. Could Mrs. Gere send her all the facts she knew about Mrs. Bryan—her literary tastes, her home, her club standing? It was the personal touch she wanted.

Mrs. Gere obliged, and the finished article is an astute character study of the two women, contrasting the fragile invalid charms of Ida Saxton McKinley, all social grace and elegance, with the energetic "new woman" from Nebraska who was Mrs. Bryan. Willa's sure professionalism and crisp ironical style save "The Women the World Is Watching" from the usual bland treatment reserved for the wives of famous men. Willa was not political, but she did allow herself the observation that Washington would be a dull place with Mrs. Bryan at its head because she had neither the taste nor the aptitude for society.

When she asked Mrs. Gere to help her Willa promised that she would keep the Gere name out of it; she would keep her own name out of it too, she said. When the story on the political wives appeared in September, the author's name was discreetly listed as Mary K. Hawley, one of a string of inventive pseudonyms that Willa used for as long as she worked on the *Home Monthly*. Sometimes they were women's names, Clara Wood Shipman, Gilberta S. Whittle, Emily Vantell; sometimes they were men's, John Charles Asten, Charles Douglass, John Esten. Undoubtedly it appealed to her imagination to assume a variety of identities. It was a little like putting on a costume and becoming someone else, but her motivation in this case was less romantic than practical. She had pages of a magazine to fill and, at least in the beginning, a shortage of material. In time, as stories began coming in from other sources, her own contributions tapered off, though never entirely.

Many years later Willa told an interviewer that "when you are buying other writers' stuff, it simply isn't the graceful thing to do, to do any writing yourself." But in the early years the opportunity to see her words in print was irresistible. Besides, she felt she was giving her readers full value. She had shown one of her longer stories, "The Count of Crow's Nest," to a reader for *Cosmopolitan* and he had offered to buy it on the spot and pay her a hundred dollars for it. She couldn't let him have it, however tempting the offer, since her work was committed to the *Home Monthly*, but it was encouraging to know that she could sell her stories elsewhere if she chose to.

She had never worked half so hard, she wrote to Mariel, but the job was absorbing and she was enjoying it. She didn't even mind the proofreading which she had feared she would find tedious. She was meeting interesting people all the time, including a number of New York drama critics, and she had talked forty-six minutes with Rudyard Kipling which alone was worth coming to Pittsburgh for. Her head was teeming with new ideas for articles and stories and she was doing better work than ever before. She may not have appreciated Mr. Axtell in his role as *pater familias*, but in the office he was the ideal boss, allowing her to do pretty much as she pleased with the magazine, as long as she followed certain broad policies. She even had a real live stenographer of her own, she told her friends, and dictated all her business letters. Best of all, her time was flexible and she could take a day off to write whenever she wanted it.

One of Willa's closest friends in Pittsburgh, the writer and librarian George Seibel, saw her for the first time in the office, and it is to this ebullient man, lover of music, literature, good food and good conversation that we owe an appealing portrait of the young editor. He had dropped by with an idea for a story about the composer Richard Wagner and found the *Home Monthly*'s editor sitting in a room whose walls were decorated, inappropriately, he thought, with pictures of prize pigs and silos from Axtell, Orr and Company's other magazine, *The National Stockman and Farmer*. Seibel was as unprepared for the editor as for the office. She looked about eighteen, he thought, "plump and dimpled with dreamy eyes and an eager mind." She didn't seem to object to the pigs at all, found them and the silos amusing. She liked his Wagner anecdotes and was charmed by the exuberant Seibel himself. She bought the article and commissioned others and before long he had become a regular contributor to the *Home Monthly*.

What began as a professional relationship quickly ripened into friendship. Willa was invited to the Seibel home where the warmth and hospitality of Seibel and his wife reminded her of her European neighbors in Nebraska. They discovered many tastes in common, including an enthusiasm for French literature, and soon a routine was established, with Willa coming once or twice a week to read French with the Seibels. Mrs. Seibel served a simple supper of noodle soup, potato salad with cucumbers, and "crisp and crackling" cookies, and after supper they started on their reading. "I had a faculty for instantaneous rough-and-ready translation," Seibel remembered. "Each of us held a copy of the French text. I read aloud—in English. If anyone dissented, or knew better, I was interrupted. Sometimes there was a 'what-the-hell-does-that-mean pause,' especially when the author was Flaubert and the text *La Tentation de Saint Antoine*." The readings at the Seibels continued for as long as Willa lived in Pittsburgh and before they ended, the little group had ranged widely over a vast territory—Gautier, Hugo, Huysmans, Verlaine and Baudelaire, as well as their "adored Flaubert."

On occasion George Seibel would read to them in German, in particular the poetry of Heine who was a favorite of his and Willa's. Sometimes Willa brought along manuscripts and "under the green student lamp which would occasionally gurgle" she read her own poetry in a voice whose "velvet cadence" Seibel never forgot. Willa was also in the habit of bringing along new books which she received as a reviewer, and when they weren't reading aloud, they would talk about books and authors and about their own ambitions. They both despised Marie Corelli and Hall Caine and were in high-minded agreement that even to think of making a million dollars writing such trash was "philistine, bourgeois, blasphemous." They disagreed about Henry James, however. "I hated his style or lack of it," said Seibel. "Willa thought it was the last word—and I hoped it was."

Most of all they both loved owning books, and they vied with each other in serious collecting. One of Willa's first acquisitions in Pittsburgh of which she was very proud was a red buckram set of Stevenson in Scribner's Thistle edition that remained in her personal library until her death. She bought a copy of Eugene Field's posthumous *Love Affairs of a Bibliomaniac* for the Seibels, and one Christmas she presented them with Edward FitzGerald's *Omar Khayyám* in a green corrugated cardboard edition for which she paid the "prodigal price of 25¢."

Christmas at the Seibels was a traditional celebration and Willa spent every Christmas Eve with them for as long as she lived in Pittsburgh. She always helped to trim the tree and George Seibel recalled her "peculiar taste for eating the needles of the fir or pine." She told him she wished she could eat all the needles "and curl up under the tree like a contented boa constrictor." One year she brought Dorothy Canfield along for what Dorothy later said was "the most concentrated essence of Christmas I've ever had." The Seibel house was swathed in greens, the talk was cosmopolitan and Dorothy felt very grown-up, staying up late and being allowed an extra cup of coffee. Willa was relaxed and happy and seemed thoroughly at home, munching on Mrs. Seibel's Christmas treats and playing with the Seibels' baby daughter who called her "Wee you." George Seibel read a Christmas poem by Heine in his rich German and Willa took down the book from the shelves and copied it. Before Dorothy left Pittsburgh Willa had made a rhymed translation of the poem. It was the first translation she had ever seen made, said Dorothy, and it was very thrilling to her.

The visit held several memorable "firsts" for Dorothy. She had never gone alone to stay with a friend before and she confided to

Willa that it was the first time she had been treated as a young lady. Willa's friends rose nobly to the occasion with theatre parties, excursions and drives in the park and it amused Willa to see the haughty, offhand manner with which her little guest received the attentions of the young men who clamored to escort her. George Seibel must have spoken for them all when he described the young Dorothy Canfield as "vivid, vivacious, full of sparkle and wit." For Willa, Dorothy was a cherished link with home, the only one of her Nebraska friends to come to Pittsburgh often. She had always been a bright spirit in Willa's life and now it was a comfort and a joy to have her close. When the visit ended Willa told Mariel that it was hard to come home from the office in the evening and find no one cuddled on the divan waiting for her.

Some time during that first winter in Pittsburgh, in addition to her work for the *Home Monthly*, Willa revived "The Passing Show" in the *Nebraska State Journal* and began doing drama reviews for the Pittsburgh *Leader*, the largest newspaper in Pennsylvania, signing herself in the *Leader* simply Willa, or more often, Sibert, a family name she later adopted as her own middle name. Her output was astonishing: she published nine short stories in the *Home Monthly*, many foreshadowing later themes and moods and, like "Tommy" and "The Count of Crow's Nest," suggesting her preoccupation with scenes of her girlhood on the one hand and, on the other, the problems of artists struggling in a hostile environment. She was also writing articles, as well as fiction, on everything from European royalty to the origin of Thanksgiving, and she established a book page in which she commented on current books and authors and on the classics of world literature. Using the by-line "Helen Delay," she answered queries from readers and volunteered to give information on new and cheap editions and where to procure them. She would even be pleased, she wrote, to give personal advice on "what to read."

Her own literary taste was eclectic as ever. She loved that "dear old book" *The Count of Monte Cristo* and that other "dear old romance of the last generation" *John Halifax, Gentleman*, and recommended Anthony Hope's *The Prisoner of Zenda*. Stevenson and Kipling were still great favorites, though she had feared that marriage might be the latter's undoing. A fresh enthusiasm was a little volume of poems called *A Shropshire Lad* by A. E. Housman. She had no idea who the author might be, save that he was an English-man and had written "some of the most musical lyrics that have been done in England for many a long day."

She was devoted to the novels of George Eliot, especially *The Mill on the Floss*, and she wrote one of her finest columns on the story of the Tullivers and the tender love between a brother and a sister that had always touched her heart. Such a love she thought of as "the strongest and most satisfactory relation of human life." Certainly her relationship with her own brothers seemed to her to be just that, and since she never had a husband they were the men she knew most intimately. Like Tom and Maggie, Willa and her brothers had also "laughed and sorrowed and learned the world together from the first." They too had entered into each other's lives and minds more completely than any of them ever would again. *The Mill on the Floss*, with its contented scenes of childhood, spoke to Willa's own attachment to her home and family. It was true that when she was at home she railed against the boredom and sought ways to escape, yet she knew deep in her consciousness that "when you have travelled the wide earth over . . . what spot is it that your heart cries out for with unassuaged longing but the spot, no matter where, no matter how desolate, where you have been good and happy and a child!"

The readers of the *Home Monthly* were entering into the sensibility of an artist when Willa Cather was at her best, as she sometimes was during those hectic months when her typewriter was never busier and stories, articles, reviews, editorials and interviews came pouring forth. She was writing for three separate audiences: the housewives who read the *Home Monthly* for its high-minded tone and useful household information; the more sophisticated readers of the *Leader*, who appreciated her wide-ranging knowledge of music and the theatre; and the people back home in Nebraska who wanted a taste of what life was like in a big city back East.

It was in her Nebraska columns that she began to take an increasingly bitter tone toward the city from which she wrote. What she could not say about Pittsburgh in the *Leader*, she wrote with venom in the *Nebraska State Journal:* "All of Pittsburgh is divided into two parts—Presbyterian and Bohemia—and the former is the larger and more influential kingdom of the two." And "Anyone who has not lived here cannot realize how incongruous, how little short of miserable it is for an artist to come out of Pittsburgh."

By the summer of 1897 she had been in Pittsburgh a full year. She was tired and lonesome and it was time to go home. In June she wrote to Mariel Gere that she would stop off in Lincoln on her way to Red Cloud because she knew that once she was home, she would not want to leave an hour earlier than she had to. She spent a few days in Columbus with the Canfields first—that became a regular stop on her way to and from Pittsburgh—saw her Lincoln friends, and was in Red Cloud by July. During the summer word came of a change of management at the *Home Monthly* and she resigned, although she continued to write "Old Books and New" under the name Helen Delay.

At home Willa led a quiet country life. Red Cloud restored her in a way she could always depend on, and she enjoyed becoming a part of the family again and entertaining the younger members of the household. Elsie was seven and Jack five that summer and she never tired of their company. She was also writing again in her little bedroom under the eaves. When she was working well it seemed to her that Red Cloud was the best place for her to be, that she could do better work there than anywhere else. She might have stayed at home then, helping her father in his office, going on with the stories that flowed so easily, and Pittsburgh might have been no more than an interlude, but other influences were at work and journalism had not finished with her yet.

Just as the job on the *Home Monthly* had seemed to fall into her lap the year before, so now she received another providential offer. In early September, the *Leader* wired her to come back to Pittsburgh as its full-time drama critic at a handsome seventy-five dollars a month. She wrote immediately to her old friend on the *Journal*, Will Jones, to tell him about the offer and to explain why she had decided to accept it. She just couldn't let the chance go by, she said. She knew it meant postponing her own work, but there was next summer and the summer after that and lots of other summers to come. (In fact, although she did manage to get home for summer vacations, it would be several years before Willa Sibert Cather's stories appeared regularly again.) Besides, she wrote, Pittsburgh had attractions she was not ready to give up. No only were Emma Calvé and Sarah Bernhardt and all the great performers there, but that flinty-hearted city had been good to her. They didn't take to strangers easily as a rule, but they had gone out of their way to make her welcome. She had admirers in Pittsburgh, a new experience for Willa Cather.

Would Mr. Jones please send transportation for her (he gave her newspaper passes on the railroad to save fare) so she could spend a few days in Lincoln? And could he get her to Chicago as soon as possible?

HOW WE LIKE TO BE LIKED

Willa's return to Pittsburgh in the fall of 1897 was in the nature of a personal triumph. She was met at the station by five young men and, refreshed from her summer at home, was soon doing the social act, as she put it, even more vigorously than she had the year before. When an international committee of artists came to Pittsburgh to judge an exhibition of paintings at the Carnegie gallery, Willa was invited to a dinner in honor of the judges. "These gentlemen," she called them, although they happened to include, besides William Merritt Chase, John La Farge, Winslow Homer and Frank Duveneck, the fashionable painter, *Miss* Cecilia Beaux. Her costume did not meet with Willa's approval, however. "She paints such pretty clothes, I wonder why she wears such awful ones," Willa wrote in the *Courier*. Will H. Low was also a member of the committee and Willa said she "basely bribed" the hostess to ask Will Low to take her in to dinner, not because he was Will Low, but because he was Robert Louis Stevenson's dearest friend. A week later the President arrived to present the five-thousand-dollar Carnegie award to the winning picture and Willa was again a guest, this time at a luncheon for Mrs. McKinley. "Never before was I present at anything so truly gorgeous," she told her readers. The floral arrangements had come from New York and New York's Sherry's provided the catering. "It was one of those rare things that are not overdone and yet leave nothing to be wished for."

Life had never been so pleasant, she thought, though she was working harder than she had anticipated. She had come back to Pittsburgh prepared for the relatively easy schedule of a reviewer, but within a few days of her arrival the day telegraph editor left for

New York and it fell to her to do his work as well as her own until the *Leader* could find a man to replace him. She found the new responsibilities stimulating and decided to propose herself for the job, though she knew her age, sex and inexperience were all against her. Nevertheless, the publishers said she might try it for a few weeks, just as an experiment.

Willa plunged into the work, sifting through the avalanche of material that descended on her desk every day, selecting the most important items, rewriting news stories, and trying not to let herself be rattled while a dozen copy boys stood waiting at her elbow. The job, she told her friends, required discretion, a general knowledge of foreign affairs and history and a knack for writing headlines. The last taxed her ingenuity; once she had to think up different headlines for twelve suicides, she told Louise Pound. She must have done them satisfactorily, however, because after she had been at the *Leader* only a month, the paper's directors met and gave her the day editor's job. Her male colleagues held a supper in her honor and the other papers ran stories about her.

She was not yet twenty-four and already she had achieved a degree of prominence in the city. If she was surprised that the *Leader* gave her the job when Pittsburgh had so many unemployed reporters, no doubt the explanation occurred to her that the publishers were businessmen and that they paid her less than they would have had to pay a man in the post. Nevertheless, she was content because they paid her extra for free-lance reviews. Her hours were from 8 A.M. to 2 P.M. and after that she was completely free, except for Saturday, when she was required to work until midnight. The schedule gave her time for diversion and also allowed her to go on with her columns, "Old Books and New" for the *Home Monthly* and "The Passing Show" which she transferred, for the last time, from the *Journal* to the *Courier*. On occasion she could even take an afternoon off to work on her short stories.

As for her social life, she wrote to her friends that she was getting a good deal of attention. She found it necessary to make clear to Mariel that it was not Hugh Conway who called her back to Pittsburgh. She had other suitors who were equally persistent. A young doctor wanted to marry her and though she acknowledged it would be an excellent match, and Dorothy Canfield had met him and approved, Willa knew she really didn't care for him. Another friend, the English teacher Preston Farrar, was also beginning to make demands upon her. She appreciated his friendship, it was warm and comforting, but she wanted no emotional entanglements. For the present all she asked was to be free, to work and to do with her money whatever she liked. Her protestations ring true; too much was happening to Willa at that stage of her life for her to wish to settle down. She appreciated having young men to escort her about the town but she was not interested in getting married, at least not yet. She was enjoying her popularity, it was a novel experience for her. " 'Gad, how we like to be liked,' " she wrote, quoting Charles Lamb to an old friend.

In her more serious essays she wrote about the artist's dedication to his work as being all-encompassing and all-rewarding and in a letter to Mariel she stated her own creed: Art was her religion and it demanded absolute devotion. Even then she knew that Pittsburgh was not to be the end of her journey, nor was journalism to be her life's work. They were merely stops along the way and she would give almost the best she had to them because they would help her to her goal. But she knew, as she told George Seibel, that "no man can give himself heart and soul to one thing while in the back of his mind he cherishes a desire, a secret hope for something different." The best that Willa had, she was storing up for the time when she could devote herself entirely to her art.

Meanwhile, there was the city to explore, picnics and boat rides, theatre, opera and a circle of faithful friends. Almost the first person Willa had met in Pittsburgh was May Willard, the head of the children's room in the Carnegie Library. One of two sisters, she took an interest in the young journalist from the little Nebraska town with the amusing name, and Willa always considered May Willard the most vital and vivid part of her early years in Pittsburgh. Another one who became a lifelong friend was Ethel Jones Litchfield who had been a concert pianist before her marriage and still played with the Pittsburgh Symphony on occasion and accompanied artists when they came through the city. Willa regularly attended musicales in the Litchfield home and many of the details about the concert world, which she would make such effective use of in *The Song of the Lark,* she learned during evenings spent with Ethel's musician friends. When her husband died, Ethel Litchfield moved to New

York and she and Willa renewed the friendship begun so many years before.

The Edwin Hatfield Andersons—he was the chief librarian of the Carnegie Library—were also kind to her and Willa saw them often. George Gerwig and his wife continued to be attentive and she still went to the Seibels for the weekly French readings. She was also a frequent guest at Mrs. John Slack's more formal musical parties in Sewickly, the comfortable suburban community across the river. The Slacks lived next door to Vineacre, the rambling old home of the composer Ethelbert Nevin whose family owned Willa's paper, the *Leader*, and Willa used the setting of the two houses in "Uncle Valentine." It was probably at Mrs. Slack's that she met Nevin himself and first felt the enchantment of that "boy-man with the girlish laugh." Later Nevin and his wife entertained her at Vineacre and on one memorable afternoon Nevin took her shopping and bought her a bunch of violets as big as the moon. She used the episode in "Uncle Valentine" when Valentine Ramsay, who is closely modeled on Nevin, goes Christmas shopping with his old friend Charlotte Waterford.

In the way she often did, Willa Cather took clearly recognizable characters and actual events and rearranged them for her fictional purposes. The real Nevin steps right off the pages of the story, but Valentine is not meant to be Ethelbert Nevin, nor is the tragic circumstance of Valentine Ramsay's loveless marriage to a coarse and venal woman, drawn from Nevin's own life. Willa was very fond of Mrs. Nevin and considered her the ideal partner for her artist husband, but it suited her story to depict a very different woman and a very different marriage. When "Uncle Valentine" appeared in the *Woman's Home Companion* in 1925 Nevin was long since dead. For Anne Paul Nevin, who was to outlive her husband by forty years, there was comfort, if such was needed, in the portrayal of Charlotte Waterford who was said to resemble her, and whose sensitivity and kindliness are counterpoints to the rapacity of Mrs. Ramsay. It is unlikely that Mrs. Nevin took offense, but Willa Cather was not always spared the hostility of those who saw treachery in her fictional portraits. She was to leave in her wake, as the years went by, a score of irate friends and relatives who resented deeply what they read as insults to people and places that were dear to them. But that was in the future. For the present, Willa was intent on being agreeable and making people like her.

It was while she was in Pittsburgh that Willa's work habits took on a pattern that she followed, one way or the other, for the rest of her life. She had great powers of concentration and she proved on the *Home Monthly* that she could throw herself into an assignment and work hard when she had to, but she also required frequent breaks in the routine in order to find the stimulation and refreshment that were essential to her. Although she formed strong attachments to people and places, she also needed to escape from time to time. When she became a successful author she never stayed longer than two or three months in any one place during the course of the year, and even her days were broken up and varied. At the height of her career, it was her custom to write for three or four hours only in the morning, finishing in time for lunch and freeing her to enjoy a leisurely and varied afternoon. During the busiest time at the *Home Monthly* she had managed to take a bicycle trip to the Shenandoah Valley, and when she accepted the job on the *Leader*, it was with the understanding, at least on her part, that she would spend her summers at home. In the early months of 1898 she found two opportunities to get the change of scene that was so important to her.

Her by-line was sufficiently known and respected by this time for the New York *Sun* to invite the Pittsburgh *Leader*'s drama critic to fill in for its own reviewer, Franklin Flyes, who was ill. Willa had a glorious week of theatre-going in New York, capped by Nellie Melba's final performance at the Metropolitan Opera. Her description of that occasion in the *Courier* is typical of her style, intimate, informed, a mixture of serious criticism and sprightly gossip that exactly captured the flavor of an event and made her Nebraska audience feel they had shared it with her.

"To sit in the Metropolitan on a gala night is an experience. I was there at Melba's last appearance in concert there this season and I will never forget it," she began. "[The singer] was magnificently got up in pink and silver and she was thinner than when I heard her in Pittsburgh several months ago. She subsists on grapes and crackers to keep her proportions down, poor thing, but the result is satisfactory. She was down for two solos, but the audience got five out of her. The impetuous, insistent, peremptory applause was new to me.

Nothing like it is ever heard in the provinces; it goes to your head; you feel as though you were at a fire or the triumph of a conqueror." The house broke loose after the final encore and Willa said it was the first time she had ever seen flowers "thrown promiscuously upon the stage. The men in boxes rose as when a royal personage enters, and the women pulled the violets from their corsages and threw them at her."

Willa saw at least five plays that week in New York, including *The Country Girl* with Ada Rehan and *Mary Stuart* with Helena Modjeska. She lunched with the Polish actress and found her to be a thorough gentlewoman and, even higher praise, a sound scholar. Many years later Modjeska makes an appearance in a scene in *My Mortal Enemy* in which she comes to Myra Henshawe's New Year's Eve party. "She looked a woman of another race," says the narrator, "no less queenly than when I had seen her . . . as Marie Stuart." Another day during that same visit to New York, Willa was lunching at Gilsey House "with a party of player folks" when Ada Rehan and Augustin Daly, the critic and dramatist who was then her manager, came in and took a table near her. Daly kept his overcoat buttoned to his chin and proceeded to dribble soup down the front of it until Ada Rehan "absently handed him a napkin." She was not in much better shape than he was, Willa noted. "Her hair was iron gray, straight and carelessly arranged, there were black circles under her eyes and she looked deadly tired." These two people, Willa felt, lived all their life in the theatre. Their days "were just stretches of time between stations, merely preparations for the nights, and it seemed a waste of time to begin to think about clothes until half past seven." They appeared to care nothing for how they looked or what others thought of them; they had been touched by the "divine madness" of art, and for Willa, as she presumed for the great actress and her companion, that was enough to justify all else and to excuse the most eccentric behavior.

By mid-February Willa was back in Pittsburgh in time to handle the *Leader*'s coverage of the sinking of the *Maine*, but in May she was able to get away again for two weeks, this time to Washington, D.C., where she visited her cousin Howard Gore and his fascinating Norwegian wife. Her summer vacation was delayed by the Spanish-American War and the bottling up of Pascual Cervera's fleet in the harbor of Santiago de Cuba, news events that required her presence in the office, but she was in Red Cloud by August and spent the month exploring the Black Hills and Wyoming with Roscoe. On her way back to Pittsburgh in September she stopped as usual in Columbus to see the Canfields, a visit which had to be extended when she came down with the grippe. It was not until October that she returned to the office and resumed her columns for the *Leader* and the *Courier*. Sometime during the year, possibly in March when Lizzie Hudson Collier was performing in a play called *Jane*, Willa met Isabelle McClung in the actress' dressing room and when she returned from a vacation in Red Cloud in October 1899, it was Isabelle who met her at the train and brought her to Murray Hill to stay until she could get settled.

ENTER ISABELLE

Writing to Dorothy Canfield who was in Europe, Willa said that Isabelle was so good to her it was making her childish, she'd be playing with dolls next. She told Dorothy they went everywhere together, on picnics, on long hikes in the hills, to the Damrosch concerts in the Music Hall and, all in all, were having a completely frivolous time. As if in apology for so much frivolity, she added that she was studying Greek and that Ethelbert Nevin had sent her a copy of Shakespeare's *Sonnets*. (She had learned to spell Shakespeare!) One afternoon at the Willards', the guests had included someone from California, someone from Europe, the Pittsburgh contingent, of course, and Willa Cather from *Red Cloud!* She was still amazed and a little shy to find herself among them. Nevertheless, a wistful note creeps in. Too many things were happening, too fast. She had been taken up by Isabelle and it excited her, but she also held back a little. Change was never easy for Willa and always made her long for old friends and familiar scenes that seemed to offer safety and protection. Now she begged Dorothy to write and do it quickly; she needed almost desperately to bridge the distance between them.

She was given little chance, however, to be more than momentarily blue. The cultural scene was livelier than ever and life for Willa was a steady round of entertainment and a constant struggle to meet deadlines. Olga Nethersole, Lillian Nordica, Joseph Jefferson, the Kendals, Ellen Terry and Henry Irving all played Pittsburgh that season. Maude Adams came with her production of James M. Barrie's *Little Minister*, but the actress herself was never to Willa's taste. Her comments, as usual, were personal. "To me," she wrote, "she is merely a clever ingenue, very unattractive to look at. Her perpetual 'girlishness' bores me to extinction, and the nasal twang in her voice is unpardonable." Julia Marlowe's charms fare better: "How has she preserved that beautiful immaturity of figure which lends an almost sacred attribute to the parts of virtuous maidenhead she plays?" she asks. But it is Richard Mansfield's Cyrano that brings out the critic's most rapturous prose. "Each night you seem to wear the livery of a new master and to make your body the receptacle of a different soul. Each night your limbs seem moulded, your cheek seared, your eyes burned by the despotic usage of the particular passion you assume, as a house, long occupied, seems at last to conform to and even share the caprices of its tenant."

She was also interviewing visiting celebrities and was every bit as stagestruck as she had been in Nebraska. When Minnie Maddern Fiske came to town Willa spent an hour in the actress' dressing room, "an hour to be singled from among the rest, an hour touched with highlights and standing out boldly in the long calendar of hours so gray and so like each other." To her *Courier* readers she confided that "the whole secret of talking to artists . . . is to enter completely into their mood, not to ask them to come to yours; for the moment to make their gods your gods, and to make their life the most important thing on earth to you."

The preceding spring she had interviewed Lillian Nordica when the Metropolitan Opera Company added Pittsburgh to its spring tour for the first time and when, according to Willa, "this dirty, gloomy city arrayed itself in dress coats and imported toilettes and just got up and did itself proud." The engagement of four operas opened with Jean de Reszke in a brilliant performance as Lohengrin, a triumphant Madame Schumann-Heink singing Ortrud and Nordica in the part of Elsa. Willa had only praise for Nordica's artistry but found her "less attractive physically this season than I have ever seen her, for she happens to be unpardonably stout." However, she was "a mere sylph" beside Schumann-Heink with "her peasant face and her absurd dumpy little figure."

It was for comments such as these that readers back home in Nebraska loved to read her columns. And also for such asides as, "Madame Nordica told me in the afternoon when she was running over the score at her hotel . . ." or "I was talking with Mme. Nordica about Elsa's particular variety of stupidity after the performance, when she was getting . . . into a Paris street dress."

Another singer, however, an English contralto named Clara Butt, may well have wished she had never sung in Pittsburgh. "Conceive if you will," wrote Willa remorselessly, "a woman six feet two by actual measurement . . . long, long arms, narrow shoulders, a trifle stooped, almost epicene . . . a face common and middle class, and a nose which belongs to the genus of Cheapside, and you have Clara Butt." Furthermore, the young woman had "absolutely no musical intelligence; no musical memory, no musical taste" and to hear her sing gave the *Courier's* critic "a creepy feeling," she couldn't say just why.

When she reviewed books—and she read hundreds every year— Willa was no kinder to authors than to actresses, even some like Stephen Crane whose work she had often admired. "It is a grave matter for a man in good health and with a bank account to have written a book so coarse and dull and charmless as *Active Service*," she scolded. But there was a newspaper novel by Frank Norris that she liked very much, a new translation of the *Rubáiyát* she enjoyed but thought unlikely to rival FitzGerald's, a new play by George Bernard Shaw and translations of Maupassant and Gautier she recommended.

With so much going on, Willa was too busy to leave Pittsburgh. She had moved to a boardinghouse on Harvard Street where she put up a screen to separate the bed from the work table and tried to get home for an afternoon as often as possible to work on her stories. Her sympathetic landlady, Marie Eyth, would provide her with a cup of strong, black coffee while she worked and Willa would repay her by discreetly placing a coin in a little dish on the mantel. Mrs. Eyth had a piano in the parlor and sometimes Willa brought home a new piece by Nevin and asked the landlady to play it for her. It was not an unpleasant life, but Willa was beginning to tire of it.

"SLEEP, MINSTREL, SLEEP"

January brought a new century as well as a new year. The mood in Pittsburgh, as in the country, was optimistic and aggressive and more than a little smug. A spirit of anticipation was in the air, a sense that everything was possible, that change and movement were the order of the day. The restlessness around her matched Willa's own mood and she found herself vaguely hoping for, if not actually pursuing, something new in her own life.

The daily reviews, frequently rewritten for her column in the *Courier*, had grown tedious. Even the theatre itself was losing its luster. She began increasingly to resent the demands of her job on the *Leader* which took so much of her energy and left her so little time for her own work. She was too conscientious to do a sloppy job but she was aware of her impatience. In the almost uncanny way that things worked out for her when she was ready, relief was on the way from an unexpected source.

A young man with a small fortune had decided that what Pittsburgh lacked and had to have was a literary journal, something on the order of the London *Spectator*. With a $20,000 legacy and supreme self-confidence, he established *The Library*, hired an editor from New York and put Willa Cather and George Seibel on the staff. Charles "Chuck" Clark's venture lasted only six months, but Willa made the most of it. She resigned from the *Leader* in April and discontinued "The Passing Show" in May. Just as when she worked on the *Home Monthly*, she now flooded the new magazine with articles, poetry and stories, resorting once again to pseudonyms to hide the extent of her own contributions and possibly to dissociate herself from some of her more trivial efforts.

Her favorite pen name on *The Library* was Henry Nicklemann. George Seibel said she had borrowed it from a folklore figure in a book by Gerhart Hauptmann which they had read "as an interlude" in their French reading. She used the pseudonym freely for poems and articles and on the first of her short stories, "The Dance at Chevalier's," which appeared in the issue of April 29. She had four more stories in *The Library* before it ceased publication but she employed a pen name only for "The Dance at Chevalier's." She may have had misgivings about the story but it is more likely that she decided to disguise herself in this instance because she did not want to detract from another story that appeared the same month, not in *The Library*, but for the first time in a major magazine with a national circulation. The April issue of *Cosmopolitan* carried "Eric Hermannson's Soul" by Willa Sibert Cather.

No one reading the two stories that month could fail to see that they had been written by the same person. The characters and setting bear unmistakable similarities, but the *Cosmopolitan* story is a far more accomplished piece of work that transforms an overwrought tale of passion and revenge into a genuinely emotional encounter between two ill-matched but interesting people—the possibly overbred but vulnerable young woman from the East, and the inarticulate, clumsy fellow, a Caliban, out of the West.

"The Dance at Chevalier's" is pure melodrama; "Eric Hermannson's Soul" begins to have the resonance of myth. In it Willa began to work out major themes that would repeat themselves again and again in her work—the hardships of the foreign-born on the frontier, the conflict between East and West, between temperament and reason, and the eternal seduction of the land. The story is sometimes crude and the dialogue is artificial but in its ambitious scope, its feeling for the country and its brief incisive portraits, "Eric Hermannson's Soul" is almost a microcosm of Willa Cather's later fiction and none of her stories in *The Library* comes close to it.

In the summer of 1900 Willa was too busy working on *The Library*'s last issues to get home to Red Cloud for her usual visit. Her mother was ill and it appeared for a time that the family would be moving to Lincoln. Willa herself expected to spend the winter there, and she let Will Jones know that she would not be too proud to accept work for the *Journal* if he could arrange it. She had lost the art of loafing, she told him, and since she could only work on her stories and verse three or four days of the week, that left her with time for journalism. She was in high spirits when she wrote to him in September. The year was the happiest of her life, she said. She had a lot of new things coming out, both prose and verse, in *Harper's Weekly*, *Lippincott's*, *Youth's Companion* and *New England Magazine*. She was becoming known outside of Pittsburgh and Lincoln, and she was finding the world a good place to live in.

As it happened, she was not to be in Lincoln that winter, but in Washington, D.C. She made the decision to go sometime in the early fall and when she arrived in the capital she came with assignments from the *Nebraska State Journal* and the *Index of Pittsburgh Life*, the publication which had absorbed the short-lived *Library*. Her columns for both were similar to "The Passing Show," interspersing criticism and interviews with comments on the Washington cultural and social scene. She did not deal with the city's political life, which did not interest her. To supplement her income she took a job as a translator in a government office, an experience she recalled many years later in *The Professor's House* when Tom Outland voices his depression at seeing "all the hundreds of clerks come pouring out of that big building [the War Department] at sunset. Their lives seemed to me so petty, so slavish . . ."

In November, Willa had an article on Ethelbert Nevin in the *Ladies' Home Journal*. Called "The Man Who Wrote 'Narcissus,'" and essentially an expanded version of a *Courier* column, it told about Nevin's early years, his marriage to "a Pittsburgh girl" and their happy life together at Vineacre. She described the informal Sunday afternoon gatherings which she was privileged to attend, when Nevin sang and played for his friends and relatives, and she reported an exclusive account of the actual composition of his most popular song although, she confided, the composer himself considered "Narcissus" to be one of the most trivial of his compositions. Another of his songs, "La Lune Blanche," he dedicated to Willa Cather.

And then in February came the shocking news of Nevin's death in New Haven at the age of thirty-nine. His widow brought the body back to Pittsburgh and Willa came up from Washington for the burial "on one of the hillsides where he played when he was a boy and gathered May flowers through many a spring . . ." His death touched Willa deeply, as indeed the man himself had touched her in life. He was probably the first real artist she had ever known more than casually, and if she tended to romanticize him, it was because his qualities of temperament and disposition were those that always made a unique appeal to her sympathies. Like Stevenson, Nevin was a grown man whose "personality had preserved all the waywardness, freshness, enthusiasm and painful susceptibility of youth." For Willa that was the ultimate triumph, to escape the erosion of time, to stay young forever. Just a month after Nevin's death Willa had a short story in the *Saturday Evening Post*, a morbid little tale called "Jack-a-Boy" that in a curious way makes explicit her belief that death may be the only way to avoid change, and that a perfect little boy must necessarily never grow up.

Willa's affinity for Nevin may have been a recognition of a restlessness in him with which her own nature profoundly identified. "Frequent change in his environment," she wrote, "was almost necessary to him, and all his life he was torn by the conflict between his love for the old and intimate surroundings of his childhood and the feverish restlessness that periodically took possession of him." That passage from her obituary for Nevin in the *Nebraska State Journal* could as truly have been written about Willa Cather herself.

Significantly, grief has no part in the obituary, only an acceptance, almost a sense of fulfillment, that "Whom the gods love dies young." Nevertheless, although resigned to Nevin's death, Willa had been devoted to him and his family and she was keenly aware of having suffered a personal loss. From Washington just four days after his death she wrote William Alexander at the *Ladies' Home Journal* to ask if he could, without inconvenience, return the photographs the magazine had purchased for the Nevin piece but had not used. They would probably be of no use to them, she wrote, but of great value to her and she promised never to use them as illustrations for any other publisher but to keep them as her own personal property.

That was one of the last letters she was to write from the capital. "I remember Washington chiefly by these beautiful, hazy, sad sunsets, white columns and green shrubbery, and the monument shaft still pink while the stars were coming out," Tom Outland was to say.

In March Willa gave up her job, packed her things at 237 R Street and returned to Pittsburgh where she had been hired to teach the spring term at Central High. She had many close ties to the school community in Pittsburgh and undoubtedly she had let her friends know she would be receptive to an offer should an opening occur. It was not so much that she wanted to be a teacher, but that she thought it would be easier to combine teaching with writing than it had been to combine writing with journalism. She was looking forward to a teacher's hours and an entirely new routine. In the end it was to prove a more reverberating change than any she could possibly have imagined.

V

❧

At the McClungs'

"THE HELPING FRIEND"

It was when she came back to Pittsburgh from Washington that Willa went to live with Isabelle at the McClungs'. And it was there that a young writer, Elizabeth Moorhead, came to call on her one Sunday afternoon. She had written spontaneously because she liked one of Willa's stories and Willa had invited her to tea. Years later Elizabeth Moorhead could remember every detail of the visit: "At the appointed hour I set out to climb the poplar-shaded Murray Hill Avenue. It was quite a pull to the top of the hill where the Judge's house stood high on a sort of ridge. Steps led up to the front porch, a bank thickly planted with honeysuckle sloped down to the cross street on the other side."

She described Isabelle, who came to the door, as the most beautiful girl she had ever seen. "She gave me a friendly welcome, then quickly disappeared after ushering me into the little parlour, typical room of a hostess, cool, impersonal. Blinds were drawn against the afternoon sunlight." Willa had been standing in the shadows and when she stepped forward Elizabeth Moorhead was surprised to find that she was young. "Short, rather stocky in build, she had a marked directness of aspect . . . 'Pretty' would indeed be a trivial word to

describe a face that showed so much strength of character as hers
. . . She looked me straight in the face as she greeted me, and I felt
her absolute frankness and honesty." Willa made tea and the two
young women sat around the tea table and became acquainted.

Before long Elizabeth Moorhead had joined the close circle of
friends that formed around Isabelle and Willa. "I discovered at
once," she wrote, "that Isabelle was distinctly an individual in her
own right, quite apart from the reflected glow of Willa Cather." Her
first impression of the girl at the door never changed: Isabelle was
"beautiful to look upon, large of mind and heart, entirely frank and
simple, with natural dignity of manner" and although not herself an
artist, said Moorhead, she had "an infallible instinct for all the arts.
She never mistook the second-best for the best" and for Willa she
became "what every writer needs most, the helping friend." Young
as she was—she was only twenty-four when Willa went to live with
her—there was a grandeur about Isabelle that others also felt. Dorothy
Canfield described her as beautiful "in a sumptuous sort of way,"
and George Seibel called her presence "stately."

Teaching, which Willa counted on to free her for her own work,
proved more demanding than she expected. Not only were the hours
long, but she had students to see and student themes to read. Isabelle
had fitted a small room on the third floor for her as a study but it
was only on weekends that she could work there undisturbed. Isabelle would undoubtedly have been pleased had Willa chosen to
devote herself full time to writing but Willa was not a rich woman
like her friend, and she felt keenly the need to earn her own living
while staying at the McClungs'. Someday, perhaps, she would be able
to support herself by writing alone but that time had not yet come.
At this stage of her life teaching seemed to provide a solution and,
besides, it suited her. One of her early biographers, E. K. Brown,
quotes a student about Willa Cather as a teacher: "Her voice was
deeper than is usual. She spoke without excitement; her manner was
quiet, reposeful, suggesting reserves of energy and richness of personality. Her teaching seemed natural and human but without conta-
gious sparks." Willa herself felt that she gained confidence and became a better teacher as the years went on.

Meanwhile she wrote when she could in her spare time and kept
her hand in journalism by contributing articles to still another publication, the Pittsburgh *Gazette,* in addition to working on poems and

stories. She felt less pressure in her new life but she was just as busy as she had ever been. There was "the calculated round of social engagements" that Isabelle provided and that Willa enjoyed, even as she enjoyed the comfort and serenity of the McClung home. On Sunday afternoons Isabelle held teas for neighbors and special friends on Murray Hill Avenue. "These informal affairs became very popular," wrote Moorhead. "One was sure of good tea and good talk. Sometimes the little 'parlour'—a larger room across the hall was kept for the Judge's use—would be crowded but Isabelle was a born hostess, equal to any emergency; she would open doors, bring in more chairs, redistribute her guests." Willa was meant to be the chief attraction at these gatherings but, it being Sunday, she was frequently at work in the little attic room and would not put in an appearance in the parlor. However the other guests felt about it, Isabelle was entirely sympathetic, feeling always that it was her responsibility to protect her friend from interruptions and intrusions.

During her first months at the McClungs', Willa had a poem in *Lippincott's* and a short story in *New England Magazine*. The steady stream of work had slackened but it picked up again in the summer when she went home to Nebraska. Instead of staying quietly in Red Cloud, she was prevailed upon to spend three weeks in Lincoln as guest editor of the *Courier*, writing columns, reviews, articles and editorials on topics as diverse as municipal corruption in Denver, a new theory to explain the drought, and the private life of Carrie Nation. It was to be Willa's last editorial stint until she went to *McClure's* and it was the last time ever that she would work in a newspaper office.

In the fall when she returned to Pittsburgh she wrote a few Henry Nicklemann pieces for the *Gazette*, but for the most part she tried to do her own work while living at the McClungs' and continuing to teach. By spring she was feeling restless and out of sorts. Life on Murray Hill was pleasant but it was also confining, and Willa sometimes needed to get away even from the people and places she loved best. However, it was not to be Nebraska that would provide the change of scene when school ended in the summer of 1902. This year, an entirely new experience awaited Willa. On June 14, she and Isabelle sailed from Philadelphia on the Noordland American line for a three-month stay in Europe. It was her first trip abroad.

Though she would be traveling through places she had never seen before, for Willa it was a kind of homecoming.

Steeped as she was in the literature of the Old World, it was natural for her to want to visit scenes familiar from her reading, to see with her own eyes the landscapes that were an inspiration to the writers she most admired and even to make pilgrimages to the homes of favorite authors. But the affinity went beyond literary sympathy. Europe was the first home of her dearest friends and neighbors on the Divide and from childhood she had been stirred by their tales of the old country. For Willa it was the working out of a strange yet fitting destiny, that she should reverse the journey of these pioneers and make her way back across the sea to the land from which they had traveled so many years before.

LETTERS FROM ABROAD

The *Nebraska State Journal* gave Willa an assignment that made it possible for her to earn money on her European trip and she sent back regular travel letters from abroad. The day that she and Isabelle landed in Liverpool was to have been the coronation day of Edward VII but the king's illness had forced a postponement. The city had dressed for the occasion, however, and Willa reported that they drove to their hotel "under canopies, arches and flags." Indeed, she wrote, "Liverpool presented such an array of color, flowers and banners as very nearly disguised the grimness of the city itself." That first impression of the contrast between the pomp and ceremony and the underlying ugliness of much that she saw in England was never to desert Willa. England never won her heart or drew from her more than a cool appreciation. She liked the quaint old town of Chester, especially the Cathedral, and when she and Isabelle paid a visit to Shropshire she felt that "the remoteness, the unchangedness and time-defying stillness" of much of that country helped to explain Housman as well as "its own singularly individual beauty." But while it was possible to appreciate the countryside and view the landscape with approval, Willa took a decidedly jaundiced attitude toward the people. The English might have been players on the stage and she a critic passing judgment from her seat on the aisle.

The dress of the English working class she declared to be shocking, "no matter how Catholic one may be in such matters." The posture of the women was so unfortunate as to amount to a "national disfigurement." Hats were "something beyond belief." The English working girl with "her passion for cheap jewelry" could learn from the American idea "of neatness, of being genuine as far as you go, of having little and having it good." Some of her cruelest derision was reserved for the London street people, both male and female, and she painted a Hogarthian portrait of London life that must have vastly entertained her readers in Nebraska. Of the London shopgirl she wrote, "Sometimes she is sober, oftener she is not . . . We have nothing at all at home to correspond to her." And, anticipating Shaw's Eliza Doolittle, she described the flower seller's voice as "harder than her gin-sodden face, it cuts you like a whiplash as she shouts, 'Rowses! Rowses! Penny bunch.'" With one eloquent judgment she summed up her opinion: "Of all the shoddy foreigners one encounters, there are none so depressing as the London shoddy."

Nevertheless, despite the unflattering things she had to say about the English in general, Willa wrote to Mariel that she and Isabelle personally had met the nicest kind of people ever since they started out. Dorothy Canfield was with them in London for three weeks and a friend of Louise Pound showed them around. When the time came to leave, Willa actually hated to say goodbye.

In one of Willa's "Letters" she reported on a visit to the Kensington studio of the painter Sir Edward Burne-Jones who had died four years earlier. The story makes colorful reading but there is reason to believe Willa may have fictionalized her account. James, the valet, "wide and red of countenance, with diminutive mutton chops and a keen grey eye . . . ," who, Willa says, acted as her guide, appears to have been a figment of her imagination. Mildred Bennett, who tracked down the reference, was informed that Burne-Jones never had a valet nor anyone in his household named James and that the studio had been cleared out by 1902!

The poet A. E. Housman whom Willa also visited was decidedly not imaginary. Yet Willa did not write either then or at any time in her life about the occasion when she and Isabelle, with Dorothy Canfield, called on him. She talked about it many times and the story of the visit became rather famous over the years, a garbled version appearing in Ford Madox Ford's *Return to Yesterday*, but Willa refused to write about it. Thirty years after the event she was still sensitive on the subject when Cyril Clemens, Mark Twain's nephew, applied to her for the facts in 1936 in connection with a biography of Housman. Willa sent off an angry letter, blaming her reluctance to discuss the incident on Housman's intense dislike of personal publicity. But she also cited the purely personal nature of the meeting and chided Clemens for pressing her for information about when or where she happened to meet someone when she had no wish to give the information.

A year later she wrote again to Clemens, this time less truculently. Madox Ford was the Prince of Prevaricators; there was not a word of truth in the story he had circulated. She had been greatly annoyed by the matter, she told Clemens, and besieged by demands to tell what she knew about Housman. It seemed a heavy price to pay for a very brief acquaintance. One's memories were one's own, after all. However, she had just about decided, since so many false stories had been given out on the subject, that she would probably one day write a statement setting forth the very brief and simple facts.

Another ten years went by before she returned to the matter. On April 17, 1947, in a letter to Dorothy Canfield Fisher Willa recalled the long-ago afternoon. She wished at last to make her plain statement of an uninvited call on a scholar and a gentleman—a stiff and angular gentleman at that. She hoped Dorothy would help to refresh her memory.

Dorothy Fisher returned a long and loving letter to "Dear dear Willa." She appeared to have total recall of the afternoon. Isabelle and Willa, she remembered, had secured Housman's address in "some rather drab London suburb." As they started out Willa said it was odd that nobody knew a thing about the poet personally, he might turn out to be a blacksmith for all they knew. The landlady was surprisingly cordial and went upstairs to announce to Housman that some American ladies had come to see him. He in turn came running downstairs to greet them, his cordiality explained by his mistaking them for Canadian cousins he had never seen who were expected at any minute. Nevertheless he was courteous and invited them to go upstairs to his study, which Dorothy described domestically as "a plain, rather thread-bare room with boarding-houseish cheap furniture—not ramshackle but not a bit good and badly needing wax and rubbing." As for the "thin, ascetic-looking scholar with straggly mustache," both the man and the setting "were just what scholars had always been, from medieval times down to Nebraska University." Dorothy recalled that at first she took little part in the conversation. Isabelle and Willa had just come from Ludlow and tried unsuccessfully to get Housman to join in their talk about the castle, the countryside and the people. The visit was becoming awkward when Housman turned to Dorothy and asked politely if she had been to Ludlow. No, she told him, no such luck, she'd been in the British Museum "slugging away at manuscripts." When he heard that her subject was Romance languages and that she had done some work in his own field of pre-classic Latin, his interest was thoroughly aroused and he held forth at length.

Dorothy remembered feeling most uncomfortable, sure that Isabelle and Willa must be bored to death. But Housman kept talking to her and she could think of no way to get off the subject without being impolite. In retrospect Willa acknowledged that Dorothy had saved the day by her Latin scholarship, but at the time she was frustrated and impatient. She had come as to a shrine and she wanted to hear the great man talk about his poetry. The poet was shy, however, and clung to the safely impersonal topic Dorothy's research provided. From Willa's point of view the afternoon was a complete failure and on the bus going back to their rooms Dorothy saw that she was crying.

Her heart was simply broken, Dorothy said, because she thought she had spoiled the whole occasion for Willa. But Willa had reassured her young friend that her tears had nothing to do with anything Dorothy had done during the visit.

Forty-five years later Dorothy Canfield Fisher wrote that she thought it at the time, and still thought it, characteristically greathearted of Willa not to have minded. And she signed herself, "With all my love, dear old comrade, Your devoted Dorothy." Her letter arrived on the day that Willa Cather died and was returned to her by Willa's secretary, Sarah Bloom.

ACROSS THE CHANNEL

By the end of July, Willa and Isabelle felt they had seen enough of England and were ready to push on. Willa had a taste for the exotic that the English could never satisfy. It was the foreign flavor she was after and she was longing to see France. She had always loved French literature and those evenings at the Seibels had heightened her appreciation of the French language and culture. Now that it was within her reach, she was impatient to begin the truly European portion of the trip. They made the channel crossing from Newhaven to Dieppe at night on a boat crowded "with French people from all over the world." Dorothy went with them as far as Paris, where she left to join her parents on a trip through the Scottish highlands.

Like many a traveler before her, Willa quickly made the discovery that "so small a body of water as the English Channel never separated two worlds so different." Every railway poster in Dieppe, she wrote, was a thing of grace and beauty and the cries of the street boys were like music. The little seaside town charmed her with its sanded yards splashed with beds of bright red geraniums. After the fogginess of London she was dazzled by the glare of the sun on the white stone and yellow sand of the beach. Everything had its own perfection. A little boy was flying a red and green kite on the hotel's terrace and Willa declared it to be "quite the most magnificent kite I have ever seen." When the kite went up and up her heart, she said, went just as high.

From Dieppe they rode away "through miles of brook-fed valleys and yellow wheat fields sown thick with poppies . . ." and made their way to Rouen. The Cathedral was to Willa the most beautiful thing about Rouen, but of more personal interest to her was the Flaubert monument in its place of honor in the very wall of the museum, Rouen's "holy of holies." In France, she wrote, "it seems that a town will forgive the man who curses it if only he is great enough." The comment carries a measure of prescience, for the day would come when Willa Cather would wish for a little of Rouen's generosity from her own town, but Red Cloud would prove less forgiving. There is no monument to Willa Cather in Red Cloud.

In Paris, Willa and Isabelle stayed at a pension at 11 rue de Cluny and made expeditions from there. A favorite walk was to the cemeteries of Montmartre and Père Lachaise where they spent endless hours at the tombs of the great men buried there—the Goncourt brothers, Dumas fils, Heine, Alfred de Musset, Chopin. Balzac's monument Willa thought conspicuously ugly but the man himself seemed "more a living fact than a dead man of letters. He lives in every street and quarter; one sees his people everywhere." Although there was a monument in every square in Paris and a dozen in every park, Willa thought the French had an even better way of commemorating their historic figures by naming streets after them. With *rue Racine* and *rue Molière* the great names of the past were always on the tongues of the living.

Much as Willa enjoyed Paris and its attractions, as she wrote to Mariel Gere, she liked the countryside even more. One Sunday she and Isabelle had gone by train to Fontainebleau and walked from there to Barbizon, the little village so admired by Millet and Rousseau. They took rooms at the Hôtel des Artistes, less interesting, she apologized to her Nebraska readers, than Les Charmettes, but more reputable for women traveling alone. The little forest town was desperately poor but the villagers had made it beautiful, with grapevines along garden walls and masses of flowers in the small, well-tended gardens. Beyond the town stretched long flat fields of wheat broken, here and there, by tall Lombard poplars, reminding Willa of the country around Bladen and Campbell back home, a resemblance sharpened by the sight of an American-made reaper, "very like the one on which I have acted as super-cargo many times." Years later Willa could still recall the pang of homesickness the familiar landscape had aroused in her. It was a sensation that caught her by surprise when she least expected to give a thought to home, and she never forgot it. That single stab of recognition made her feel an intimate connection with the French soil and the farmers who worked it, but even more significantly it was an intimation, as yet not fully acknowledged, of her emotional attachment to the land around her prairie home and the irresistible hold it had upon her imagination.

Willa's European articles, like everything she wrote during her newspaper years, whether "The Passing Show" or the columns she sent home from Washington and Pittsburgh, are vividly subjective and colored by the superior intellect with which she was equipped and by a richly endowed imagination. At twenty-eight, even as at twenty, she had decided views about the world and confidence in her power to express them. Her temperament was ardent but it was also disciplined, and her understanding was both subtle and alert. Historical and literary allusions came naturally to her. Henry James, she informed her readers, had liked a certain hotel in Avignon and wrote affectionately about it in one of his essays. Barbizon was where Robert Louis Stevenson met and fell in love with his American wife. The

Italian garden at Avignon was as beautiful as when Pope Clement VI planted it in the fourteenth century. Observing the Roman ruins at Arles, she thought the Roman colonists who stayed to settle Gaul had shown "a sort of Chicago-like vehemence in adorning their city and making it ostentatiously rich."

Not yet a novelist, she was already a supreme storyteller for whom the daily lives of simple men and women were the stuff of legends, and she filled her columns with lively anecdotes and telling portraits of the people she and Isabelle encountered. There was the little boy on the channel steamer, hoisted on his father's shoulders, crying "with small convulsions of excitement, 'Is it France? Is it France?'" as the coastline rose out of the fog. Or the French family at Barbizon, the bourgeois papa with his white waistcoat, the mama "stout and puffing as she plodded, her skirts held up under her elbows" and the half dozen sons and daughters all singing a drinking song "for joy of life and companionship." It was a scene that Breughel might have painted, but that Willa brought to life with words.

She told about the half-naked baby, like an infant Bacchus, who slept sucking on the straps of her suitcase in the third-class carriage from Lyon to Avignon. And the young house painter singing airs from *Rigoletto* as he worked, while the olive oil buyer "rumbles" *Il Trovatore* on his way to the post office, sounding like a big bumble-bee.

The fabled Monte Cristo which she had always longed to see was exactly as she had imagined it. Every sailor on the dockyards of La Seyne was an Edmond Dantes. The island and the Château d'If were as important and as moving to contemplate as Westminster or Notre Dame. And she had also to consider its attraction, she said, "for a certain small brother of mine and bear all his thrills upon me."

In a letter to Mariel Gere just before she and Isabelle set out on a walking trip through Provence, Willa made a personal statement to her old friend that it was people who counted more than places. In time she would come to believe that such an intimate connection existed between them that it was often impossible to separate her affection for a person from her feelings for a place. Temperament, behavior, customs all derived from the land. In later years her interest would fasten upon the papal town of Avignon, but on that first visit, when everything was fresh, a variety of images came crowding in on a consciousness that was eager to respond, and Willa felt her senses bombarded by a continual novelty of impressions: the green pines, blue sea and porcelain sky of Le Lavandou which, more than any place she had seen in England or France, gave her a "sense of immeasurable possession and immeasurable content"; the scent of dried lavender in the air in the little village of Cavalaire, itself a place "not a little like certain lonely way stations in Wyoming and Colorado"; the perfect grouping of a family eating their figs and sea grass salad and drinking their sour wine under an olive tree; and with September, the smell that was everywhere of drying fruit, of ripe things and making wine. "One cannot divine nor forecast the conditions that will make happinesss; one only stumbles upon them by chance in a lucky hour at the world's end somewhere, and holds fast to the days as to fortune or fame."

The ancient town of Arles in the heart of Alphonse Daudet's country brought the four-month journey to a close and it was there that Willa glimpsed a culture and a way of life that were to be her ideal. Removed from the world of modern commerce, Arles was the center of a large pastoral district, "a great country of shepherd kings, and farmer barons, of fat priests, of old customs and simple living." The villagers, wrote Willa, kept their ancient festivals and were content to farm as their fathers had for generations before them. They asked nothing more than to drink their wine and eat the snails and fried tomatoes that had always been their fare. Their ambitions were simple, but to Willa they expressed "nearly the whole will and need of the people of Provence," and she was profoundly sympathetic to their values. Above all, the desire to avoid change and innovation struck a deep responsive chord in Willa that would echo in her work and in her own life in the years to come.

By the time the travelers reached Arles the weather had changed sharply. Along the banks of the Rhône the mistral blew fiercely and in Arles itself the sycamore leaves were beginning to turn and the chill of autumn was in the evening air, "the strange homesick chill that always makes one want to be at home." Willa concluded her travel letters with a strange disturbing image of "these fine, subtle, sensitive, beauty-making Latin races" withering before a cold wind from the north. That too was one of Willa Cather's constant themes

—the blighting of the creative spirit by an indifferent society, the grinding down of the artist in an insensitive materialistic culture. Willa's own spirit had been lifted by the country she and Isabelle had traveled through and she returned to Pittsburgh and another school year refreshed and deeply stimulated. But although she wrote several poems that drew upon her travels, characteristically it was not for many years that her European experience was directly reflected in her fiction.

A SPLENDID YEAR

Willa's "letter from Provence" appeared in the *Nebraska State Journal* in mid-October and was the last journalistic writing she was to do for her old friends in Lincoln. Settled once again in Pittsburgh, she was more than ever determined to concentrate on serious writing, and in whatever spare time she could manage to take from her teaching chores and the social engagements that were expected of her, she would retreat to the little attic room to work on her stories undisturbed. The year and a half she had been living at the McClungs' had been productive and she was selling regularly to major magazines. *New England Magazine* bought three stories, the ironic "El Dorado —A Kansas Recessional," "The Professor's Commencement" and "The Treasure of Far Island," the first telling of a tale of childhood fellowship that would reappear in different guises in *Alexander's Bridge, O Pioneers!* and *My Ántonia. Scribner's* published "A Death in the Desert" and *Critic, Harper's Weekly* and *Youth's Companion* all carried poems by Willa Sibert Cather.

Willa had always written verse, sometimes for a column, or as a prologue to a story and often to fill a page when she worked on the *Home Monthly* and *The Library.* Most of it she considered trivial, but in the last year she had worked hard on her poetry and when the Boston publisher Richard Badger expressed an interest in her work, she was not unwilling to put together a selection. In January 1903 she told Will Jones proudly that Badger would bring out a volume of her verse in the spring, as part of a series by young poets. Willa was accustomed to discussing her business affairs with Will Jones.

She told him that the publisher's terms were liberal and confided that if the book had a decent sale she could expect to make a tidy sum. Badger intended sending out circulars and she asked Jones to lend her a Lincoln directory or telephone book so that she could make up a mailing list of people who were acquainted with her and might buy her book. When the circular appeared announcing *April Twilights* it showed a picture of the author looking very young and wistful, and it described her first volume of poems as "a little book worth while." Eleven of the thirty-seven poems had been previously published, the others had not been seen before. The book, said the publisher, was handsomely printed and bound and would sell for a dollar.

The *April Twilights* poems of 1903 exhibit, far more than Willa Cather's fiction up to this time, the full extent of her impressive learning and the breadth of her frame of reference. Art, music, literature, history, all were sources of inspiration. Her themes are traditional, love and loss and longing, nature and the way it feeds the human soul. But she was richly read and rigorously trained and she knew a variety of poetic forms and meters. She drew on other poets, and echoes come through of Housman, Keats, Daudet and Stevenson, but her material was distinctively her own. She wrote about her family, her home, her friends, the Europe she had visited and the ancient worlds of Greece and Rome she knew so well. Her imagery is sometimes deceptively simple but it is carefully wrought and is almost never banal. An elegiac mood and sense of underlying sadness hint at muffled passions, stirred but unsatisfied.

The loveliest verses have a blithe, singing grace—several were subsequently set to music—and a delicate rhyme scheme that make an unforced appeal to the imagination: the seemingly artless refrain from "In Rose Time," *Oh this is the joy of the rose; / That it blows, / And goes;* or the sighing chant of the elegy to Nevin, *Sleep, minstrel, sleep; the winter wind's awake, / And yellow April's buried deep and cold.* The short sweet phrases of "The Hawthorn Tree" are pure melody: *Across the shimmering meadows— / Ah, when he came to me! / In the night time, / In the starlight, / Beneath the hawthorn tree.*

The most popular poem in the collection, however, and the one most frequently reprinted and anthologized, is the less lyrically romantic but more personal "Grandmither, Think Not I Forget."

Recalling Grandma Boak and the years she lived with the family when Willa was small, the poem is written by an older troubled woman looking beyond the grave for the love she had known as a child and longing for her grandmother's comfort at a moment of desperate unhappiness in her adult life. *Grandmither, gie me your still, white hands, that lie upon your breast, / For mine do beat the dark all night, and never find me rest . . .* The source of the poet's pain is left obscure but the bleak despair is heartfelt and clearly came out of Willa's own experience of loss and suffering. In an intuitive understanding of the poem's emotional content, another poet, Sara Teasdale, included it as one of a hundred love lyrics by women in an anthology she called *The Answering Voice.*

Willa dedicated her first book to those dear companions of her childhood, her brothers Roscoe and Douglass, in a verse evoking fond memories *Of the three who lay and planned at moonrise, / On an island in a western river, / Of the conquest of the world together.* Twenty years later, when Alfred Knopf brought out a revised edition of *April Twilights and Other Poems*, she removed the dedicatory verse and thirteen other poems and dedicated the new volume to her father "for a Valentine." Her attitude toward her early work had changed in the years since her proud announcement to Will Jones and she had been earnestly trying to suppress all evidence of what seemed to her mistaken examples of a youthful talent by buying up as many copies as she could lay her hands on of the original edition and burning them. Some of the early poems had touched on powerful emotional experiences, but she no longer used poetry as an outlet for her deepest feelings and among the verses she would not permit to be reprinted are those she judged too sentimental and revealing. A few were sonnets and suggest she may not have been entirely at ease in the sonnet form.

She retained "Grandmither, Think Not I Forget" but she eliminated two other poems that described actual people and events: "The Namesake," about the death in battle of her uncle, Willie Sibert Boak, and "The Night Express," about a local boy who died away from home, whose friends waited at the railway station for his body to be brought back. In both cases she reworked the material and subsequently told the stories in fiction.

For the revised edition Willa added twelve poems, five not previously published and seven that had first appeared during the prolific period between 1907 and 1915 when she was writing her first three novels. Ballads and longer narrative verse, the new poems are closely related to her Nebraska stories in mood and theme, even when the setting is Gaul or Roman Britain. The last lines of the Palatine (in the "Dark Ages") might have been spoken by Alexandra Bergson: *Saxon boys by their fields that bide / Need not know if the world is wide. / Climb no mountain but Shire-end Hill, / Cross no water but goes to mill; / Ox in the stable and cow in the byre. / Smell of the wood smoke and sleep by the fire; / Sun-up in seed-time —a likely lad / Hurts not his head that the world is sad. / Back to your play, little brother.* The dark ages, the poet suggests, are not so far behind us and, in certain small Nebraska towns, may still exist. In poems like "The Swedish Mother," "Macon Prairie" and "Poor Marty" (the only poem added in a 1933 edition) the authentic voice of the prairie novelist is heard.

Less romantic and less delicate in feeling, the new poems show a vigor and authority the earlier volume lacks. Willa was fifty in 1923, no longer the eager, hopeful young woman singing that *Joy is come to the little / Everywhere.* She was not sure anymore that hope would indeed come back with the spring. For years she had struggled to subdue an impetuous disposition and restrain an ardent and explosive temperament and the mature poems seem less spontaneous, more tightly disciplined than the 1903 verse. The mood is harsher and the air of rueful melancholy has undergone a transformation to reveal a darker strain of personal bitterness. "The Streets in Packington [Chicago]" is a bleak foray into social realism, and in "The Silver Cup" Willa gives vent to her distaste for aspects of city life in a swift and savage portrait of New York as *a city full of exiles, / Short marriages and early deaths and heart-breaks.*

Nevertheless, there are rhythms in the later book that bring back echoes of the younger poet and phrases of pure poetry that still have power to catch the heart. The mood may be autumnal—*Long forgot is budding-time and blowing*—but in "Prairie Dawn" the note is emphatically triumphant and the vibrant words ring out with an unforgettable sweetness.

The modest sales of Willa's first book unfortunately disappointed her optimistic expectations, but *April Twilights* was important nonetheless. It introduced her to a new and wider audience and for the first time brought her critical attention. The Pittsburgh and Nebraska press, as might be expected, were flattering—George Seibel was the reviewer for the Pittsburgh *Gazette*—and other good reviews appeared as well, although, as Bernice Slote observed, for the most part they were "passive." Still, at a time when books of poetry went largely unregarded, for a first effort to be mentioned at all and even praised was a rarity and gave Willa's small circle of intimates in Pittsburgh, and Isabelle in particular, reason to believe that their friend's genius was at last on its way to being recognized.

* * *

At the same time, in New York, the name Willa Cather was causing something of a stir in the offices of *McClure's Magazine*. *McClure's* had an especially fine reputation for fiction but Willa had never sold a story to them. She had submitted several but they had been promptly returned with form letters of rejection. Then in May, just a month after the publication of *April Twilights*, she received a telegram from S. S. McClure himself, characteristically demanding that she come to see him in New York at once. Behind the scenes her old friend Will Owen Jones had been at work again on her behalf. He had seen a cousin of S. S. McClure's in Lincoln and had talked to him about his protégée, whose first collection of poems had just been published. H. H. McClure in turn spoke to the publisher. The timing could not have been more auspicious. S. S. McClure inquired of his staff and learned that Willa had indeed submitted manuscripts, that there were some in the office at that very moment. He read them and wired her to come.

Willa's memorable first visit to the McClure offices on West Twenty-third Street took place on a clear spring morning in May. The publisher was waiting for her, an energetic, restless little man with snapping blue eyes and a manner of barely suppressed excitement that Willa would soon learn was habitual. S. S. McClure had prowled all over Europe and America in search of writers for his magazine and publishing syndicate. He had worn down Stevenson and Kipling until they agreed to write for him, and he had published Arnold Bennett, Arthur Conan Doyle, George Meredith and Thomas Hardy. Mark Twain, Walt Whitman, Julia Ward Howe, all had appeared in the pages of *McClure's Magazine*. Now as he rose to greet still another promising new author, he found himself being measured in turn by a sturdy, alert young woman with the look of a scrubbed-cheek country girl. When she came into his office she seemed to bring the springtime in with her. McClure was a quick judge of people and something in her modest manner and air of wary confidence drew him to her from the start.

He sat her down and began to pepper her with questions. She answered in her rapid, breathless way and before long he knew everything there was to know about Miss Cather from Pittsburgh and Nebraska. Their conversation went on for two hours with the usually reticent Willa telling the publisher more about herself than she would have dreamed possible before that morning. At first McClure just listened, then he began to make plans for her. There wasn't a circumstance of her life he did not go into, she told Will Jones. McClure said that he would bring out her stories in a book but that first he would use them in his magazine. He would take whatever she wrote and if he could not use something himself, he would undertake to find another publisher.

Willa felt that she had been transformed. When she walked into his office at ten, she said, it would not have mattered if she'd been run down by a streetcar. But when she left at one, she had become someone worth saving. McClure had made her feel valuable. He had so strengthened and encouraged her that she felt she wanted to do well for him as much as for herself. Willa was not the first to come under the spell of the man's personal magnetism. If he'd been a preacher, she told Will Jones, he'd have had people going to the stake for him.

A revealing little episode occurred in the course of Willa's first interview that might have proved embarrassing. Actually it gave her considerable satisfaction. McClure sent for the two readers who had so summarily rejected her stories. It was sweet revenge for Willa and she held her chin high as the publisher demanded an explanation from the staff.

She had several more conversations with McClure and one evening he took her home to Westchester to meet his wife. They both urged her to stay with them for a few days but she declined the invitation. The Canfields were in New York and she had promised to visit them. She spent a day in the country with the McClures, however, and met Mrs. Robert Louis Stevenson, who was also a guest. Mrs. Stevenson had read her stories and talked about them helpfully. In the end, McClure took them without a change, Willa said.

Reluctantly McClure saw his newest acquisition leave New York, but he was not about to let her slip away from him entirely. He brought her back at least twice during the next few years and one summer she spent two weeks in the office. Plans were in the wind for her but they would have to wait. Meanwhile Willa returned to Red Cloud for the summer with a light heart. She was not yet thirty and it seemed that she'd been launched at last.

Still, the splendid year that saw the publication of her first book and brought S. S. McClure into her life was not yet finished with her. Another momentous event lay in store for Willa, this one of a more personal nature. When it came it took place casually and its significance would not be perceived until long afterward but it was a fitting climax to a year that changed her life.

She was in Lincoln in late summer of 1903, visiting Sarah Harris, when she made the acquaintance of a young friend of her hostess'. Edith Lewis was a Lincoln girl who had gone East to college but had come home after graduation to see her family and renew old ties, one of them with the *Courier*'s editor, who had published a few of her college themes. Growing up in Lincoln and an aspiring writer herself, she had followed Willa's drama criticism and columns ever since they began appearing in the Lincoln press. Then in January, while she was still at school, she had seen the familiar by-line in *Scribner's* on "A Death in the Desert" and she had read the story with "fervent admiration." Sarah Harris knew of her enthusiasm and when Willa came through Lincoln on her way back to Pittsburgh, Edith was invited to meet her.

A maid brought her into the parlor where Willa, wearing a gray and white striped cotton dress and sitting upright in a straight-backed chair, was engaged in an animated discussion with Sarah Harris. Neither of them acknowledged the new arrival who sat silently, "a fascinated spectator," while the duel of words went on. When Edith rose to go after a brief visit, however, Willa accompanied her to the door, perhaps to make amends for her unintended rudeness, and stood and talked with her for fifteen or twenty minutes. Edith had plans to go to New York and take whatever job she could find, which Willa found marvelously enterprising. They saw each other a few more times, and before Willa left Lincoln she invited Edith to stop in Pittsburgh on her way to New York and spend a night at the McClung house.

Of that first encounter which began so disconcertingly, Edith Lewis reminisced half a century later: "It was one of those unimportant incidents that later, when seen from a long perspective, become to one very important. If I had not met Willa Cather at this time, the chances are that I would never have met her, and our long friendship and association, which lasted until her death, would never have happened."

PITTSBURGH IS "MCCLURED"

A change took place in Willa's circumstances when she came back to Pittsburgh in the fall of 1903. Her good friend Preston Farrar had given up his teaching post at Allegheny High School and recommended Willa for the job. It meant a salary increase and pleasanter surroundings than the grimy red-brick Pittsburgh High and Willa gladly accepted the offer when it was made to her. She was given two assistants, a Miss Wilson of Hastings and a Wellesley girl, who eased the burden of reading and correcting student themes and gave her added hours to do her own work and assemble material for McClure. She published only one story during 1904 but its reverberations were profound. The unexpectedly explosive tale appeared in the January issue of *Everybody's Magazine* and was called "A Wagner Matinee."

The story is simple. A young man receives a letter from his uncle in Nebraska announcing the imminent arrival of his aunt, who must come to Boston on business. The aunt before she married and went West had been a music teacher at the Boston Conservatory and the nephew, wishing to give her some pleasure during her visit, gets tickets for a Wagner concert at the Symphony. The story's power lies in the contrast between the primitive life the woman has endured for over thirty years and her ultimately undiminished sensibility.

The effect of the music on Aunt Georgiana, however, was as nothing compared to the effect of Aunt Georgiana on Nebraska. A hue and cry erupted and even Will Jones scolded Willa for an unfairly harsh description of life in the West. In addition, enough details were drawn from Willa's own experience to cause resentment in her family.

Willa defended herself to Will Jones and denied that she had set out to insult the state. A story, she insisted, was a personal impression and not a real estate advertisement and she slyly suggested that what her family objected to was that she had told the truth. She assumed that everyone admitted the old days were desolate and she had only wanted to pay tribute to the uncomplaining women who survived them. Of the woman in the story she said nothing to Will Jones, but the George Cathers found enough resemblances to Aunt Franc's life for them to take offense. The character seems actually to be a composite of those silent, careworn farm women, grown old and misshapen from years of thankless labor in the fields, whom Willa had known well in her youth. But it must be said, in fairness, that if she had not intended to depict Aunt Franc, a certain ambiguity in the portrait could conceivably have led to other interpretations. Willa once described her aunt to a friend as one of the ugliest, smartest and most eccentric of human kind. In the story the narrator recalls his aunt as a pathetic and grotesque figure and there is nothing of Aunt Franc's spunk and independence. Willa may have made her private peace with the aunt she truly loved, but the wound lasted.

For Willa's debut in *McClure's* it was decided to use one of her most characteristic stories, in which she gave play to the twin themes that animated her work while she was in Pittsburgh, the struggle of the artist to create and the withering effect of a narrow small-town environment. "The Sculptor's Funeral" reworked the episode she had first used in her poem "The Night Express," but this time the body that is awaited at the depot is that of a celebrated sculptor, Harvey Merrick, who long ago had fled the little Kansas town but asked to have his body brought back home in the end. The story is peopled with the small-town types Willa drew so well, the bankers, real estate agents, coal and lumber dealers, ministers and lawyers. She could bring a character to life with a few deft strokes and reproduce the local speech with uncanny accuracy.

Not a little of the author herself comes through in the portrayal of the young Harvey Merrick, "cast ashore upon a desert of newness and ugliness and sordidness." Willa liked "The Sculptor's Funeral" well enough to include it along with "A Wagner Matinee" and the story that Edith Lewis had so admired, "A Death in the Desert," in the collection of stories McClure brought out in the spring of 1905. She called the book *The Troll Garden* and dedicated it to Isabelle. The publishers, McClure, Phillips, bound it handsomely in embossed red buckram with the name Willa Sibert Cather in bold gold lettering.

Three of the stories written especially for the book were never afterward reprinted in Willa's lifetime, but a fourth, "Paul's Case," became her most frequently anthologized work and has long been considered among the finest short stories in the English language. (A version of "Paul's Case" became the first of Willa Cather's stories to be adapted for television when its copyright ran out.) As if to underscore her own intuition in regard to the story, Willa gave it the subtitle "A Study in Temperament," and to the modern reader the pathological attributes of Paul's malaise are more persuasive than the romantic aspects. Willa told George Seibel that she drew on two boys who had been in her classes for the character of Paul, but to others she confessed how much of her own hunger and frustration were embodied in the unhappy boy's flight from the drab reality of his daily life and in his instinctive reaching out for beauty.

In later years Willa Cather would have been the first to chide the moody, reckless Paul for seeing in the glitter and gold of the Rialto the answer to his heart's desire. But she was in Pittsburgh when she wrote "Paul's Case" and she understood too well Paul's anger and impatience and New York's lure. One day she would explain the impulse behind "Paul's Case" and others of her early stories as the raging bad temper of a young person kept away from the things she wanted. The stories were warped, she said, even the Western ones, by the author's note of personal discomfort. For Paul the discomfort proved fatal. But of herself, Willa wrote that she had learned to come to terms with her youthful dissatisfactions. If a young woman sits down in the cornfield and howls because she can't hear music, she said, it does not mean she has fallen out with the cornfields. Give her all the music she wants and take her about the world a little and she will come out all right with the corn.

Poor Paul destroyed himself rather than spend his life swimming in the "tepid waters of Cordelia Street," which was the only future he could envision. Willa too had moments of despair, times when she could not see beyond Pittsburgh. Her case was very different from Paul's, however. Paul may have had the sensitivity of an artist but, unlike his creator, he was without discipline, without direction and, saddest and most hopeless of all, he was without talent. Willa knew that she was gifted and she was confident that in the end her talent would prevail. Meanwhile, she had chosen a field that was rigorous and demanding and she was willing to work hard at her apprenticeship. Although she was not yet ready to leave Murray Hill Avenue she was certain that one day she would. Sometimes she thought she might go back to Red Cloud for a year or so, but at other times she must have sensed that her destiny lay elsewhere.

The Troll Garden won for its author a spate of reviews around the country, most of them finding promise in the stories rather than fulfillment, which would seem to accord with Willa's own later judgment. She was criticized in the New York *Times* for being too ambitious. Nevertheless, the *Times* critic saw deep feeling and real ability in several of the stories. The reviewer for *The Bookman* was offended by what he called "a collection of freak stories that are either lurid, hysterical or unwholesome . . ." This morbid judgment was not shared by the *Reader*, however, which found the stories "vivid, strong, true and original" and detected in them a richness of quality that was like a contralto voice. In two stories where the influence of Henry James is most pronounced—"Flavia and Her Artists" and "The Garden Lodge"—the authentic Cather voice is scarcely heard at all. Nor is it heard in another contrived Jamesian tale, "The Marriage of Phaedra."

Of the stories in *The Troll Garden* only "A Wagner Matinee" and "The Sculptor's Funeral" are Western. Although the setting of "A Death in the Desert" is Cheyenne, the characters meet there by chance, and the real action of the story takes place offstage, primarily in Europe, where the central figure, the composer Adriance Hildegarde, has lived and worked most of his life. The sentimental story, with its Browning title and its heroine dying Camille-like in a wretched little town at world's end, is redeemed by flashes of genuine emotion and by the portrait of the artist Hildegarde, for whom

Nevin was the inspiration. The story belongs properly to the tales of artists and their lives, its several motifs suggesting that Willa was experimenting with a number of ideas and images and was, perhaps, as the *Times* thought, trying to do too much at one time. But Edith Lewis liked "A Death in the Desert" very much and it was republished along with "A Wagner Matinee," "The Sculptor's Funeral" and "Paul's Case" in Willa's second collection of short stories.

Following the publication of *A Troll Garden* Willa took a two-month holiday in the West. This time Isabelle went with her and they spent a week visiting Douglass in Cheyenne, where he was a station agent with the railroad, and another week camping and fishing in the Black Hills with Roscoe. The Cathers had moved the year before into their own house at Sixth and Seward and while she was in Red Cloud Willa was helping her father fix it up. Jessica too had left home by then; she had married a young banker in town and she and her husband were expecting a baby. Her small niece or nephew to be, said Willa. The younger children in the Cather house were growing up, but they kept many of their childish ways and were still pets to their big sister. In a contented letter to Mariel she described the lazy summer days and said the West was the only place she really wanted to live. She had seen a lot of Mrs. Garber who, though charming as ever, seemed greatly aged and saddened by the governor's death. There were still many people in Red Cloud of whom she was very fond, she said, but Lincoln was not the same for her. Mr. Gere had died the previous autumn and Willa missed him every moment of the time she was there. It particularly pained her that Isabelle and he had never met; he was one of the people she had always wanted Isabelle to know.

From Nebraska at the end of the summer she went directly to New York to see S. S. McClure and stayed with Edith Lewis on Washington Square. Willa had been working on a Pittsburgh novel that she may have wanted the publisher to read, and no doubt they talked about her future. But nothing was decided and, as she had every year for almost a decade, she returned to Pittsburgh in the fall. Now it was no longer to a solitary life in boardinghouses, but to the warmth and solid comfort of the house on Murray Hill Avenue, to the room she shared with Isabelle, to the little attic study where she worked, and to her teaching.

The shine had not worn off, but the years had smoothed some of the rough edges and polished Willa's country ways. Though she still favored tailored shirtwaists and mannish ties, she also wore soft dresses that Isabelle helped choose for her, and her brown hair, usually pulled back and parted in the middle, was sometimes piled becomingly on top of her head, like a Gibson girl's. The secure and gentle world that Isabelle had fashioned had enabled her to write, and in two years she had brought out *April Twilights* and *The Troll Garden*. Years before, when she first came to Pittsburgh, she had told Mariel Gere that it was like beginning a new life in broad daylight, away from the old mistakes. That was before she met Isabelle but the words were prophetic. Yet in the spring, when McClure made one of his flying visits to Pittsburgh especially to offer her a job, she gave it all up—the sheltered life at the McClungs, the teaching job at Allegheny High, the daily intimacy with Isabelle. Why?

Willa herself gave a clue when she wrote, while she was still at the University, that "our necessities are so much stronger than our desires." An inner sense of timing perhaps, and a drive for independence that was almost an instinct for self-preservation, impelled her to accept Mr. McClure's offer to join the staff of his magazine. To be in the thick of things at *McClure's*, to come to New York, not as a novice struggling for recognition but as a journalist, sought after by the publisher, was a heady proposition. She had been attracted from the first by McClure's charismatic personality and she believed implicitly that her own future might safely be entrusted to him. He appreciated that she must work to earn a living now. He also understood that one day she would give up journalism to devote herself entirely to her writing and he supported that goal and was helping her to reach it. He had already started her on the road when he published *The Troll Garden*. What he was offering her now was the inevitable next step.

Other considerations, more personal and infinitely more complicated, must also have been at work causing Willa to grasp at the opportunity McClure held out to her. All her instincts as well as her good sense told her that she could not go on living with the McClungs indefinitely; that had never been her intention. Her life there was undoubtedly serene but it was also confining. The rhythm of the household had long since been established. Although the judge and his wife were kind and hospitable, they were conventional people who expected Isabelle and Willa to conform to the family routine. Even more significantly, Willa must have had sufficient self-awareness by this time to know she would not be satisfied unless she and Isabelle were on their own. She must often have thought how splendid it would be if they could set up house together. It wasn't possible in Pittsburgh; the McClungs would never allow it. In New York, however, there might be a chance. Once she was settled perhaps Isabelle would find the courage to make the break and join her. In any event, Willa knew she could no longer go on as they were.

When McClure, who until then had been "a mere name, a sort of far-off benignant deity," arrived in Pittsburgh in the flesh, the McClungs invited him to dinner. The hushed, sedate dining room had never seen anything like it. The publisher took over the conversation and dominated the evening. He never stopped talking, his words fairly bouncing off the paneled walls, striking sparks from the heavy silver and shivering the crystal goblets. No man was more fascinating than McClure when he put his mind to it and he was determined to make a good impression on Willa's friends. He talked world affairs with the judge and entertained the ladies with the latest literary gossip.

By the time he left the house Isabelle and her dazzled parents, in the words of Oliver Wendell Holmes, had been "'McClured.'" And before he left Pittsburgh Willa had promised to consider a move to New York. He must have known he had won her. She had spent ten years in Pittsburgh, and it was time to bring her apprenticeship in the provinces to an end.

VI

❋

A Red-hot Magazine of Protest

THE VILLAGE AND THE SQUARE

New York in 1906 was moving at a rapid pace into the booming, brazen twentieth century, but traces of an older, slower, more intimate city survived in the narrow, twisting streets and small red brick houses of Greenwich Village and in the tree-shaded, Georgian tranquillity of Washington Square. Once the Square had been a potter's field and at another time the scene of public hangings with a gallows swinging from a huge elm tree. The tree had outlived its grisly purpose but had since been removed, and Stanford White's great Romanesque arch now dominated the Square. Standing astride the north end, the marble arch served as an imposing gateway to Fifth Avenue and the spreading city beyond. The houses on the north side were dignified and substantial as befitted New York's first families—the Rhinelanders, DeForests, Delanos and Hoyts—who had built them and still lived in them. This was the world of Henry James, who found in Washington Square "a kind of established repose."

The south side of the Square was a different matter. There the "very solid and honorable dwellings" of the north gave way to some of the oldest buildings in the Village, shabby, wooden structures which in time were replaced by modest red brick dwellings inhabited principally by artists, writers and musicians. In the Square, a roadway wound between small green parks containing trees and benches and play areas for children. Horse carriages were already giving way to the automobile, but in the summer of 1906 when Willa took her first apartment in the studio quarter on the south side at Number 60, it was still possible to see carriages and cars alike driving through the Square.

Willa's arrival antedated the heyday of the Village by several years. Margaret Anderson did not appear before 1910 to start the *Little Review* and it was not until 1912 that the flamboyant Mabel Ganson returned from Europe with her second husband, Edwin Dodge, and established her salon at 23 Fifth Avenue on the corner of Ninth Street. Willa was never a contributor to the audacious *Little Review* nor was she one of the regular guests at Mabel Dodge's, although she had many friends among the entourage that gathered there on Wednesday nights. She liked Mabel and, later, Tony Luhan, the full-blooded Indian who became Mabel's fourth husband, but for herself Willa preferred not to be a part of any set. She had chosen to live in Greenwich Village because she knew it from her visits to Edith Lewis and because its friendly domestic atmosphere appealed to her. The informal neighborhood of little shops and restaurants, with its mixture of the tidy and the slightly tawdry, had retained an individuality and an air of *bonhomie* that she enjoyed. It reminded her of Europe. The presence of creative people made it stimulating, but it was the sense of civility and privacy that Willa found not only attractive but also absolutely essential to her temperament.

With Edith living nearby in the same house, Willa settled contentedly into the life of the small apartment building, which was next door to Number 61, the so-called "House of Genius," where Stephen Crane, O. Henry and her great contemporary, Theodore Dreiser, had all lived. If she remembered her words to Mariel ten years earlier, that she would go to New York one day but it would not be as a Bohemian, she must have been amused to find herself in an environment that was the classic setting for *la vie Bohème*. The neighbors who greeted her on the stairs or in the narrow hallways, who shared the bath at the end of the corridor and waited patiently on line in bathrobes and slippered feet, were mostly young and poor. Painters, poets, singers, they practiced their craft and lived hardworking, precarious lives. Willa enjoyed the stir they created, their optimism and exuberance. She approved their ready sympathy for one another and, above all, she admired their dedication and discipline. One day she would write a story about struggling artists in New York and faithfully describe the red brick building on the Square. But at thirty-two, she was not really one of them. Art for art's sake had not brought her to New York. She had not come to the big city to starve like Mimi in a garret. She had come as a journalist with a job she had not sought but that had sought her, and with expectations already on their way to fulfillment. It must be said, however, that it was as unlikely a job for Willa Cather as could be imagined.

THE OFFICE

McClure's had built a reputation as a powerful, muckraking publication, the scourge of mighty corporations, the flayer of corrupt politicians, a voice raging against the ills of an industrial society. A strange setting, indeed, for a young woman who, if she was not a Bohemian, was emphatically not a reformer either. The critic who disliked Zola and Tolstoi in their reforming moods had no use for reformers when she met them in the flesh. They offended her by always seeming to press for the destruction of something. She thought they spent so much time in the company of horrible ideas that it made them mad, like Electra. In Pittsburgh, Isabelle's philanthropy had been directed exclusively to artists, not to the objects of "causes." Isabelle and Willa both drew back from people who "rode a hobby" as they called it. Yet here was Willa working for *McClure's*, still the most successful reforming magazine in America despite a recent series of difficulties that had almost brought the magazine to an end and S. S. McClure's own career along with it.

At the heart of the trouble was the man himself and his intemperate behavior, both personal and financial. McClure was an editorial genius, but his private affairs were messy and mismanaged. The brilliant editor who could conceive an exposé of Standard Oil and get Ida Tarbell to write it, who could give Lincoln Steffens carte blanche to bring in a story of municipal corruption, who could uncover demons in the body politic, was incapable of exercising self-control. He had an agile mind, crammed with bold and imaginative ideas, but he was hopeless with money and appallingly inept when it came to his romantic attachments. His restless nature demanded that he be constantly on the move, and he had grown accustomed to spending months at a time out of the office, usually in Europe, sometimes traveling in the United States. An able staff, headed by John Phillips with Ida Tarbell, Lincoln Steffens and Ray Stannard Baker, managed the magazine without him.

In the beginning the arrangement seemed to work well. It was something of a respite for the staff to have the manic presence removed, and for McClure it was an opportunity to look around for new talent—he had first met Ida Tarbell when she was working in Paris—and to develop new markets. He had not only the magazine to occupy him but also a publishing house and a highly successful syndicate. Most of the illustrious authors who wrote for the magazine had previously been signed for the syndicate. For ten years McClure had been able to keep his own needs and those of the magazine in some sort of balance, but it became increasingly evident that even the most heroic measures on the part of the staff and his own frequent acts of contrition were insufficient to prevent an explosion.

Willa left her own impression of McClure in the person of O'Malley, who appears in the 1918 short story "Ardessa" as the editor of a "red-hot magazine of protest" called *The Outcry*. Like McClure, O'Malley had bought the magazine to make a stir and he had built up an organization of which "he was somewhat afraid and with which he was vastly bored. There were five famous men on his staff and he had made every one of them." In perhaps the most incisive description of her own boss, Willa wrote: "Constraint was the last thing O'Malley liked. The most engaging and unusual thing about the man was that he couldn't be fooled by the success of his own methods, and no amount of 'recognition' could make a stuffed shirt of him . . . O'Malley went in for everything, and got tired of everything; that was why he made a good editor."

But by 1904 McClure's staff was tired of him. They hadn't minded the absences from the office, the working trips abroad, but when word came back of his more notorious escapades, of the young women who accompanied him on his grand sweeps through Europe, of the vast sums of money he was spending, the office was disgusted. Ida Tarbell, in a private letter to John Phillips, called McClure a "canny, scheming, unstable soul—now at the height of aspiration and ambition and now in the mire." His wife had taken to coming to the office and was given a room and a desk where she could keep an eye on things, but her seeming indifference infuriated Ida Tarbell. "Mrs. McClure," wrote Tarbell, "is stone blind and deaf and dumb. She makes me wild."

Only a woman who had never been married could seriously have believed that Hattie McClure was unaware of her husband's philandering. No one knew him better than she did, his formidable weaknesses as well as his formidable gifts, but in her own way Hattie was as canny as he, and even more tenacious. For seven years, while Sam McClure worked his way through Knox College in Galesburg, Illinois, Hattie had held out against her parents' opposition to the penniless young Irishman who courted her. So strongly did her father disapprove of Sam McClure that he sent his daughter away to school and forbade the young couple to correspond. He made it very clear that the front door of the Hurd home would always be closed to Hattie's suitor. Still they persisted, until one day Hattie informed her parents that she intended to marry Sam with or without their blessing. At his wife's urging Professor Hurd grudgingly permitted the wedding to take place at home, but he took the occasion to reiterate his opinion of the groom in a letter to the bride. Calling him "conceited, impertinent and meddlesome," he nonetheless reassured his daughter that he would not cease to love her.

McClure's subsequent success somewhat mollified his in-laws, but the professor's sentiments never really changed. For Hattie the marriage had been achieved with too much heartache to turn against her husband now when his staff was closing ranks to battle him. Besides, Hattie Hurd McClure was a proud woman who could keep her feelings to herself and not allow herself to be disconcerted by office gossip. She thought by working in the office she would be able to look out for McClure's interests, but the atmosphere was deteriorating daily. Meetings were held in corridors and behind closed doors to compare notes about the publisher's latest offense. Writers and editors who had addressed themselves to the sins of society in the pages of McClure's magazine, were now charging the publisher himself with the most heinous defects of character.

His face, according to one of the memos circulating about the office, was "streaked with cruelty." Ida Tarbell's language became so hysterical it is difficult to escape the conclusion that her reproaches to her boss may not have hidden more than a touch of wounded personal vanity. "He's a Mormon," she wrote in one of her letters, "an uncivilized, unmoral, untutored natural man with enough canniness to keep himself out of jails and asylums."

Matters had finally gone too far to be salvaged. Phillips presented an ultimatum, demanding that McClure surrender control of the magazine. When he refused—he simply couldn't let it go, he said—Phillips, Tarbell, Steffens and Baker resigned in a body. McClure might keep his magazine; he would not keep his staff.

This was the situation in the office when Willa came to work in the summer of 1906. The great upheaval had already taken place. Of the old group only a few loyal confederates remained—Viola Roseboro, Witter Bynner and Burton Hendricks on the editorial side, and Albert Brady, who stayed on as business manager. Bynner, who had come to McClure's right out of Harvard in 1902, was serving a brief stint as managing editor, when the "ex-schoolteacher from Pittsburgh," as he called her, joined the staff. From the beginning a coolness existed between Bynner and Willa Cather that may have had its origin in an episode that took place the year before, when Willa spent a week in the office at McClure's invitation. Bynner had been asked by the publisher to cut what he remembered forty years later as "hundreds of words" from "The Sculptor's Funeral," the Cather story that was to appear in the January 1905 issue. Bynner recommended that the cuts be spread throughout the piece to prevent having to eliminate entire paragraphs, and McClure agreed. The author had not been told about the cuts, however.

"I can still hear her explosion in his office and see her enraged expression toward me," he wrote, "when Mr. McClure pretended that the cutting had been entirely my own idea." Willa was to learn that injured innocence was a not uncharacteristic pose of her new boss.

And, as a rule, she accepted criticism when it came from quarters she respected. In fact, she once said that all good writers consented to cuts because they knew there were "plenty more words where those came from." Nevertheless, it was not an auspicious start and the relationship never fully recovered. The fact is, Bynner was always ungenerous where Willa was concerned and she continued to regard him as something of a literary dilettante.

For Viola Roseboro, on the other hand, Willa had the respect of a younger person for an experienced professional in her field. A striking, dark-eyed woman, some sixteen years older than Willa, Viola Roseboro had come to New York from Tennessee, where she had worked on a local newspaper, to take a job on the *Daily Graphic* before joining McClure's syndicate as a manuscript reader. When McClure started his magazine in 1893 she began to read manuscripts for both enterprises, becoming in time the powerful literary editor who saw every short story and every poem submitted to the magazine.

In New York she lived the life of a "female bachelor," smoking when cigarettes still scandalized, admired by both men and women, and sending shock waves back to the community of Rock Creek, Ohio, where she had grown up and where her parents continued to live. Like Willa she was intolerant of small-town manners and held herself aloof from the neighbors, resenting their polite inquiries about her mother's health, for instance, as curiosity, and their interest in her own career, as an invasion of her privacy. Like Willa she had used a variety of pseudonyms in her newspaper days, many of them male. Hired to write a gossip column which was the only spot on a newspaper considered appropriate for a woman, she managed to get in her opinions on the broader cultural life of the city.

During the tempest at *McClure's*, Viola Roseboro had stayed unmoved to a remarkable degree. Loyalty to S. S. McClure alone would probably have kept her from joining the rebellion and from leaving with the other editors, but her own peculiar working arrangements also helped to insulate her from the worst of the gossip and the passions that shook the office. Very simply, she spent almost no time at all *in* the office. Manuscripts were delivered in a suitcase to her home and she read them there or in the park, working on a park bench, penning her notes to authors and her comments for McClure.

A messenger would call for the finished work and deliver new manuscripts. In the summer, manuscripts were mailed to the vacation homes she maintained over the years in Massachusetts. When authors or members of the staff had business with her she received them in her apartment—she lived on Bank Street for a long time—or she might invite them to join her in the park.

To new arrivals on the staff Viola Roseboro was almost a legend, and many who stayed only briefly on the magazine never got to see her at all. Those who did, remembered a regal figure, her long skirts trailing the floor or held up with one hand, her musical voice calling out a greeting as she swept past the desks on her way to McClure's office. She was known as a brilliant conversationalist, an admirer remarking once that "to listen to Miss Roseboro talk is to have a memorable experience." McClure agreed. "I know," he is said to have acknowledged, "but often I can't keep quiet long enough to listen."

In her role as reader for the magazine Viola Roseboro was probably the first to see Willa Cather's early stories and no doubt she was the person who had rejected some of those that were subsequently published elsewhere. She said later that she had recognized Willa Cather's genius from the start but that it had taken time for the author's talents to develop, and that she had wasted herself in some of her first attempts. Nevertheless, as McClure's chief story editor, almost his alter ego, Roseboro must have had a hand in selecting the stories that were collected in *The Troll Garden*. The subject of artists in the city would have had a special appeal for her. She had been on the stage herself once and she was drawn, as Willa was, to the theatre and theatre people. It would have been a bond between them when they became acquainted. Viola Roseboro may even have encouraged McClure to bring Willa to New York; at least her friends always thought this was the case.

A natural rivalry between the young editor and "Miss Roseboro," as Willa always called the older woman, was inevitable, but it was kept in check by Viola Roseboro's infrequent appearances in the office, as well as by Willa's confidence in the publisher's support. McClure, meanwhile, had the services of two of the most brilliant women of the day. He had always seen the advantage of hiring women, especially those without family responsibility who would be willing to devote themselves entirely to their jobs, and at a time when few women held positions of importance in business, the McClure office was unique.

In his attitude toward employing women, McClure was not unlike another publisher, in England fifty years before, who had offered a young woman a job on his magazine, in large part because he felt he could count on her giving all her time and energy to her work. John Chapman's professional association with Mary Ann Evans began when he published her translation of David Friedrich Strauss's *Life of Jesus,* and he again sought her out when he bought *The Westminster Review.* For five years Mary Ann Evans worked as a writer, critic and editor for Chapman's magazine before she published her first fiction, as George Eliot. As for Chapman, he was as erratic in financial matters as McClure, and his domestic life was even more chaotic.

During the years Mary Ann Evans was assistant editor of *The Westminster Review* she lived in Chapman's house along with his wife and his mistress. Hopelessly in love with the publisher, she extricated herself from the unsavory situation by a deliberate and heroic act of will, finally leaving both the household and the magazine, though maintaining her friendship with Chapman and continuing as a contributor to the *Westminster.*

Fortunately for Willa she was never emotionally involved with McClure and was therefore spared George Eliot's anguish. As an admirer of the "great George," however, she could not have failed to appreciate that she was following in a splendid tradition while she worked on *McClure's,* and it must have pleased her to remember that the English novelist had also apprenticed as a journalist.

Within a few months of Willa's arrival McClure had assembled a whole new staff, many of whom were writers rather than editors. Will Irwin came over from the New York *Sun,* where his stories on the San Francisco earthquake had impressed McClure, to relieve Witter Bynner as managing editor. Bynner went back to reading manuscripts for Viola Roseboro and was also made poetry editor. Characteristically, McClure assigned another writer, George Kennan, not Irwin who was a native of San Francisco, to do a muckraking series on the politics of the Bay City. McClure held the firm conviction that a good writer could write on any topic as long as he was given sufficient time to learn about the subject. He was the first editor to put his writers on a retainer so that they were paid—and paid well—while they were traveling and doing research for a story. A political historian might know the facts about corruption in municipal government, but he would probably write a dull story. A fiction writer, on the other hand, knew how to stir readers with his prose, and it was essential that readers of McClure's be shaken up.

George Kibbee Turner, a short-story writer and novelist, was added to the staff and put to work on "certain immediate problems of American civilization and government," according to an advertisement of the magazine's plans for 1907. Ellery Sedgwick and McClure's son-in-law, Cameron Mackenzie, completed the editorial lineup and the advertisement made it clear that, despite the loss of the old guard, *McClure's* would continue to run the same kind of provocative material the public had come to expect.

Thanks to Viola Roseboro and McClure's own missionary efforts abroad, the magazine had established a reputation for publishing fiction of unusually high quality. Robert Louis Stevenson's *The Ebb Tide* and *St. Ives* had appeared in *McClure's*. So had Anthony Hope's *Rupert of Hentzau* and Rudyard Kipling's *Captains Courageous*. The prospectus for 1907 promised short stories by Joseph Conrad, O. Henry and Viola Roseboro herself. It also announced the publication of "The Namesake" by Willa Cather. "Our list of stories by this writer," read the copy, "has made a mark in proportion to its strength rather than its length." Actually only two Cather stories had appeared in *McClure's* before Willa went to work there, "The Sculptor's Funeral" and "Paul's Case." None of the other stories in *The Troll Garden* had been reprinted in the magazine, though the book itself was published by McClure, Phillips and Company.

As soon as Willa was on the staff, however, her stories began appearing regularly, causing not a little resentment among her colleagues, who claimed she ignored the fiction editor and put her own stories in the magazine without showing them to anyone except McClure, and not always to him. Certainly Viola Roseboro thought she made a mistake publishing the banal "Eleanor's House" and "The Willing Muse" and such overwrought romantic melodramas as "The

Profile," all of which appeared during 1907. Her poetry was another matter. "Autumn Melody" and "The Star Dial," were both published in *McClure's* during 1907 and Viola Roseboro was enthusiastic about them. In later years she said she had loved Willa's poetry before she had ever written anything worthwhile in prose, that it had taken her a long time to come to herself except in verse.

In the case of "The Profile" Viola Roseboro's attitude may have had as much to do with a peculiar aspect of the story's content as with her literary judgment of its merits. The plot turns entirely on a woman's disfiguring scar that covers half her face, "like the shameful conception of some despairing medieval imagination . . . as if some grotesque mask, worn for disport, were just slipping sidewise from her face." The fact that the woman was otherwise very beautiful and that an artist, a worshipper of beauty, falls in love with her and marries her, gives the tale an ironic twist. Apparently the story caused an uproar in the office. As Witter Bynner tells it—and he is not unbiased —friends came to Willa asking her to withdraw the story from the magazine because they feared that publication might ruin the life, possibly even cause the suicide, of a mutual friend of hers and theirs whose face was similarly disfigured. According to Bynner, the woman's plight had suggested the story to Willa.

A "tense session" was held in McClure's office. It is possible that some members of the staff may also have been disturbed by the unmistakable erotic overtones in the painter's fascination with the scar. Willa was an acute observer who was well aware of psychological subtleties in human behavior long before Freud's concepts had found their way into the average piece of fiction. The staff's concern was unavailing, however. Willa remained obstinate and, at least in Bynner's version, insisted, " 'My art is more important than my friend.' "

It is certainly the kind of thing she might have said in anger if she were forced to defend herself against the united opposition of her colleagues. It is also possible, however, that she expressed herself with a little less self-righteousness and that Bynner remembered only what he chose to. Where Viola Roseboro stood in the matter is not recorded. She may have felt that Willa's "art" was not much in evidence in "The Profile" and that the story was of too little significance to risk the consequences. At any rate, with or without Viola

Roseboro's approval, the story was published in June 1907. In the end, Bynner says, the friend survived. He says nothing about the friendship.

AN ASSIGNMENT IN BOSTON

Undoubtedly *McClure's* commitment to fine fiction was one of the magazine's chief attractions for Willa. Her first assignment, however, had nothing to do with fiction, except insofar as the story she would be working on turned out to be as fascinating, as bizarre, as filled with human interest as any novel. When Phillips, Ida Tarbell and the others left *McClure's* and started their own magazine, *The American*, they made sure to take with them most of their uncompleted projects. Among those they preferred to leave behind was a strange, dog-eared manuscript that had been around the office for over three years and which they were probably relieved to see the last of. A comprehensive life of Mary Baker Eddy and the Christian Science Church she founded, it was considered by McClure to be one of the most important stories he had ever accepted for publication. Written by a free-lance writer, Georgine Milmine, and worked on by several members of the staff, the vast, disorganized manuscript was badly in need of editing, checking and rewriting. This was the formidable task McClure turned over to his new associate.

In regard to Willa Cather, McClure's judgment was astute. She was, he knew, a complicated woman whose feelings ran deep and whose emotions he might guess at from her youthful poems and stories. He'd glimpsed the intensity that was reined in at the McClungs' dinner table and he admired the loyalty to family and friends that she had exhibited during their early conversations. Now he liked what he saw of her in the office. She was cool and level-headed and she took what was assigned to her and worked hard. Despite Witter Bynner's unfortunate first impression, Willa was not temperamental in the office. Opinionated, stubborn perhaps, but not temperamental. Viola Roseboro and others must have made her familiar with the events that led to the "revolution" at *McClure's* and she may have concluded that the publisher had temperament enough for all of them. As for herself, it was not in her nature to indulge in behavior she would have considered unprofessional.

Even before Willa began the serious task of reworking Milmine's material, the magazine was preparing its readers for revelations to come. The story, promised an editorial announcement, would take Mrs. Eddy from her birth "in a New Hampshire farmhouse" through her "strange, hysterical childhood and equally strange youth"; follow her through her marriage and "her wanderings"; and would explore the "peculiar phenomena of mind and emotions which mark her character." "Wilful [sic], ungoverned and dominant in her youth," the ad went on, in her old age she became "all dominating" and "holds over her Church a control more absolute than any other leader in the western world."

Milmine's manuscript was full of potentially libelous material, provocative but undocumented. Verification would require tracking down people who had known Mrs. Eddy in the little towns around Boston, interviewing them and getting signed statements attesting to the truth of their assertions. It was a laborious undertaking and since the job might conceivably take several months it was decided that Willa should move to Boston temporarily. She had left Washington Square by this time for a room at the Hotel Griffou on Ninth Street and she was not averse to exchanging one transient life for another. She was ill on the bitterly cold January day in 1907 when she left New York, but the magazine's deadline would not allow a delay and she checked in at the Parker House in the middle of the month as planned. The first installment of the Mary Baker Eddy story had already run in the January issue and was found to contain errors; it seemed especially important that the subsequent articles be accurate. Within a few days of her arrival in Boston Willa was writing to Mrs. McClure that she had come upon several persons who had not been seen before who proved helpful. She would proceed slowly until she felt stronger, but she was encouraged.

Willa was to write often to Hattie McClure over the next years. Indeed, she seemed to go out of her way to keep in touch with her boss's wife. Knowing the office gossip, she may have wanted to reassure Hattie that she need have no apprehension on her account. Significantly, she signed her letters, "With loyalty to you and yours." If Willa sometimes felt the need to assert her independence of Viola Roseboro, it did not trouble her to defer to Mrs. McClure. She treated Hattie as her husband's surrogate in office matters and was quite willing to keep her informed of the progress of her assignments. In later years her letters to S. S. McClure invariably included warm concern for his wife.

Willa remained in Boston through most of 1907 although she managed short trips to New York whenever the work, or Mr. McClure, required her presence there. The project was even more demanding than she had anticipated. Not only was she checking facts and conducting interviews, but before she finished she had taken Georgine Milmine's hundreds of pages and thousands of words of text and completely rewritten them, shaping the material into a brilliant series of articles that ran in fifteen installments over a period of a year and a half. It was decided to retain Milmine's name as author, but *The Life of Mary Baker Eddy* which appeared in *McClure's* has long since been acknowledged to be the work of Willa Cather. Willa's style is unmistakable—the brisk narrative, the clarity, the compression: "All the members of her household live as if they were exactly as old and as much enfeebled as Mrs. Eddy," reads the article describing the lady's retirement to Pleasant View in Concord, New Hampshire. "They rose early, retired early; never went out of the house except upon her commissions; never dined out, received visits or went to Boston for a holiday."

Of a piece of childish verse that Mrs. Eddy had allowed to be published in a volume of autobiographical sketches, this judgment rings with familiar Cather scorn: "Many another girl certainly has written verses just as bad, but the fact that at the age of seventy, Mrs. Eddy had actually published this doggerel, indicates that her taste had not greatly changed." The gentler environs of Boston had not changed Willa either; Pittsburgh would have recognized the critic's caustic tone. Nevertheless, by not having her name connected with the series, Willa was spared the outrage that descended on the magazine from the Christian Science Church. As, month after month, the tantalizing story unfolded, newsstand copies of *McClure's* were bought up rapidly by the Church while library copies vanished from the shelves or were found to have the Mary Baker Eddy articles neatly excised. An unmutilated copy of *McClure's* during those months became a collector's item. One wonders how Georgine Milmine fared while Willa remained safely cloaked in anonymity, at least until the furor subsided.

THE LADIES OF CHARLES STREET

Although she was working hard, Willa found time to enjoy the city. Her temperament responded to Boston's understated manner and its uneasiness with excess of any kind. She felt very much at home in the city's cultivated atmosphere, so reminiscent of London, yet with an air of intellectual endeavor and Puritan pride that made it like no other place on earth. She also found its scale congenial, the little squares and gardens along Beacon Hill, the quaint cobbled streets and the decorous avenues bordered with sedate town houses built to outlast generations of Boston brahmins. From the Parker House and later from a small apartment she took on Chestnut Street, she could walk down to the Charles River or wander through the Commons and the Public Gardens and watch the swan boats on the pond.

She soon had her favorite bookshops and restaurants and a circle of friends who helped to make her stay a pleasant one. In New York she had seen a lot of the Goldmark sisters, Josephine and Pauline, and when she made the move to Boston they introduced her to their sister Alice, who lived on Otis Place with her husband Louis Brandeis, then a successful Boston attorney with a reputation for championing economic and social reform. Later Woodrow Wilson would appoint him to the United States Supreme Court. Willa was instantly attracted to the brilliant lawyer and his perceptive wife. They shared her love of art and music and they took a sympathetic interest in her work.

Mrs. Brandeis was to play an especially important role in Willa's life. It was she who took Willa one afternoon to call on a legendary Boston lady, the widow of James T. Fields of the publishing firm of Ticknor and Fields. The firm's name was familiar to Willa from volumes of Longfellow and Hawthorne in her father's library and she was surprised that a widow of one of the partners could still be living. Mrs. Brandeis explained that when Fields married the nineteen-year-old Annie Anderson he was a widower and already in middle life. At seventy-four, when Willa met her, the still beautiful Annie Fields had been a widow almost as long as she had been a wife.

For sixty years the Fields house on Charles Street had been a gathering place of the "aristocracy of letters and art." There was "scarcely an American of distinction in art or public life who was not a guest in that house," Willa wrote many years later, "scarcely a visiting foreigner of renown who did not pay his tribute there." On the afternoon of Willa's first visit she found her hostess in the drawing room having tea with another lady who turned out to be the writer Sarah Orne Jewett. Annie Fields was "reclining on a green sofa, directly under the youthful portrait of Charles Dickens (now in the Boston Art Museum)." Sarah Jewett sat opposite, with the low tea table between them.

One remembers Elizabeth Moorhead's first impressions of the house on Murray Hill and of Willa at the tea table. Now it was Willa Cather's turn to be awed and enchanted. "I do not at all remember what we talked about. Mrs. Brandeis asked that I be shown some of the treasures of the house, but I had no eyes for the treasures, I was too intent upon the ladies." For their part the ladies found Willa distinctly original and almost equally exotic. Her robust personality was something new in that rarefied atmosphere. Soon Mrs. Fields was treating her like a Midwestern grandchild, delightfully amiable, but perhaps in need of just a little toning-down. If Willa was overwhelmed by the idea of knowing someone who had invited Emerson and Lowell to her table and who remembered and quoted what they said there, Annie Fields found Willa's experiences as a journalist just as fascinating. She and Sarah Jewett hung on every word when Willa told stories about Mary Baker Eddy and the odd Christian Science Church on Huntington Avenue that belonged to a Boston so near and yet so strange to them.

From Mrs. Brandeis, Willa no doubt learned something of the history of the two friends. They had met when James Fields was still alive and it was he who introduced the young writer to his wife. Annie Fields's courtly biographer, Mark de Wolfe Howe, treads lightly on the relationship between the two women and the role played by James Fields in bringing them together. Anticipating that he would probably die many years before her, says Howe, Fields saw in Sarah Orne Jewett "the ideal friend to fill the gap in Annie's life. He must have realized that the intensely personal element in her nature would require an outlet through an intensely personal devotion." From the time of James Fields's death in 1881, Sarah Jewett was the center of Annie Fields's life. Helen Howe, Mark Howe's daughter, was more explicit than her father in her own book, *The Gentle Americans:* "Such an alliance I was brought up to hear called 'a Boston marriage.' Such a 'marriage' existed between Mrs. Fields and Sarah Orne Jewett."

When Mrs. Brandeis brought Willa to tea in 1908 Sarah Orne Jewett and Annie Fields had been together for over twenty years and their lives had fallen into a pattern. The spring and fall Sarah spent at her own home in South Berwick—when they were apart the friends wrote to each other every day—but Christmas found her ensconced in Charles Street for the winter. In the summer, when they weren't traveling in Europe, she and Annie were together in the Fields's house on Thunderbolt Hill in Manchester-by-the-Sea. Winter and summer their routine was invariable. They wrote in the mornings and early afternoons, but came together in the library for tea and read aloud before the open fire. Saturday afternoon was Annie Fields's "at home" in Boston, and there Sarah Jewett acted as co-hostess, entertaining her own friends as well as Annie's.

The idyll ended with Sarah Jewett's death in 1909, only sixteen months after Willa's meeting with her. Ironically, Annie Fields was to outlive the younger woman by six long years, during which she occupied herself and kept her friend's memory alive by editing a volume of Jewett's letters. Mark Howe lent his friendly editorial assistance and gently advised eliminating most of the baby talk and the endearments with which the friends were accustomed to address each other.

Acceptance by Annie Fields introduced Willa to a world she might not otherwise have known. "Sometimes entering a new door can make a great change in one's life," she was to say. It was in the Charles Street parlor that she had a chance at last to meet George Woodberry, the brilliant poet, critic and teacher who had made such a vivid impression on his students at the University of Nebraska when he taught there in the 1870s and '80s. At the time that Willa met him he had recently resigned from Columbia University and was embarking on an itinerant career, teaching at various colleges across the country. He and Willa had books and poetry in common as well as the University in Lincoln, and he told a friend he found her pleasant to talk to and have around.

An amusing story is told of a visit Willa and Woodberry made together to Sevenels, Amy Lowell's Victorian mansion in Brookline. They went expressly to see the poet's collection of Keats memorabilia—manuscripts, letters and books. After a considerable delay while the lady of the house remained in bed dictating to her secretary, the guests were at last admitted to the inner sanctum where the Keats treasures were displayed. Woodberry stepped forward eagerly, his right hand outstretched, to have a closer look, at which Miss Lowell put her fists down firmly on the item before he could examine it, and informed him in her haughtiest manner that he might not *touch* anything. If he wished to see a book, *she* would turn the pages. Willa was furious that Amy Lowell should treat the distinguished professor as though he were a child with dirty hands. She had never cared for Lowell's poetry. For years after the incident, the mere mention of her name was enough to make Willa splutter with remembered rage.

Other guests of Annie Fields who became good friends of Willa's were the painter Laura Hills with whom she corresponded as long as she lived, and the novelist Margaret Deland. Deland, whose *Awakening of Helen Richie*, a tearful novel of sin, suffering and redemption in the little New England town of Old Chester, had caused a critical stir the year before, was a Bostonian by adoption, having married Lorin Deland and settled in Boston. The fact that she was born and raised in Pittsburgh was a bond between her and Willa. Willa was extremely fond of the Delands and once when she was ill she went to stay with Margaret and her husband until she felt well enough to go back to her own place.

Still another member of the Fields entourage was to be important in Willa's life. Ferris Greenslet was not a native Bostonian either, having been born along the shores of Lake George in upper New York State. Educated at Wesleyan and Columbia, where he came under the influence of George Woodberry, Greenslet had long since taken on the coloring of the Boston publishing firm of Houghton-Mifflin which he joined after a stint on *The Nation* and a short-lived career as a free-lance journalist. It was in his free-lance period that he had reviewed *April Twilights* and been haunted by the lines beginning, "How sure a thing is Beauty . . ." To his surprise, the poet when he met her was not a pale, shy, Emily Dickinson figure, but "a fresh-faced, broad-browed, plain-speaking young woman," who stood her ground "with a singular solidity." He was to see Willa often at Mrs. Fields's and in time would become her editor.

In spite of his assumption of the manner of a Boston publisher, Ferris Greenslet, nevertheless, brought a little of the outsider's perspective, and some of his reflections on the Fields ménage are amusing. Thunderbolt Hill, he said, provided the "acme of refined comfort," so refined, in fact, "that in the guest chambers all articles of domestic china possessing lids were provided with knitted sound-dampeners." If for any reason the lids were removed, they could be replaced in "nothing less than a luscious silence." The ladies themselves he found charming, if perhaps a trifle frivolous, always ready "to giggle girlishly at any slightly malicious anecdote of the Boston great." Their joint philosophy of the happy life "consisted quite simply in taking short views." Ferris Greenslet was undoubtedly a perceptive gentleman with not a little touch of malice of his own.

Annie Fields might well have been a Cather heroine with her romantic, flower-like beauty, the "quick flashes of humor" in her clear eyes, her "large, generous, mobile mouth, with its rich freshness of color." "A *woman's* mouth," Willa called it, "not an old woman's!" But although she felt the spell of Annie Fields's personality, it was Sarah Orne Jewett who had the more profound influence on Willa Cather. For with Sarah she could talk about her writing and what it meant to her, and despite her fragile health, Sarah Jewett was tough-minded when it came to her profession. Sam McClure himself had discussed his ideas for a literary syndicate with her and he had found her advice sensible and business-like as well as kind. She knew the marketplace, having sold dozens of books and stories, and she had a high regard for the independence a woman achieved by earning her own money. Besides, she too was something of an outsider who, though she moved easily in the world of Boston letters, was not a Bostonian by birth. Her home was the village of South Berwick, Maine, and she still lived there part of the year in the house where she was born.

As a child Sarah Jewett, like Willa, was drawn to older people and she too had grown up listening to their tales of an earlier time. Sarah Jewett's stories, however, came not from pioneers but from old sea captains who talked of their adventures, of storms they had survived and exotic places they had sailed to. The sea became for Jewett what the prairie was to Willa, a limitless source of mystery and fascination and the ultimate inspiration.

Like Willa also, Sarah Jewett enjoyed the conversation of her neighbors, the local men and women who came to do their shopping in Berwick's general store. Many were patients of her doctor father and from him she learned all about their lives in the little towns of North Berwick, Wells, York and Eliot. When as a young girl she began to suffer from painful rheumatism, her father prescribed fresh air and took her with him on his country rounds. "The quiet village life, the dull routine of farming or mill life early became interesting to me," she is quoted as saying. "I was taught to find everything that an imaginative child could ask, in the simple scenes close at hand."

There was a time she had even thought of becoming a doctor herself, just as Willa had, but her health was frail and after graduation from the Berwick Academy she chose to settle down at home with her sister Mary. But unlike Mary, who enjoyed a sedentary life, Sarah's temperament was restless and she was soon making trips away from Berwick, sometimes to visit school friends as far as Cincinnati, but more often in the vicinity of Boston or Newport. John Green-leaf Whittier was a childhood friend and through him and other family connections she met congenial people with the inclination and the leisure to enjoy the things that she did, art exhibitions, lectures, concerts and the theatre. A tall, graceful woman, with elegance rather than beauty, Sarah Jewett was "a lady, in the old high sense," Willa wrote, echoing Ferris Greenslet. "There was an ease, a graciousness, a light touch in conversation, a delicate unobtrusive wit." She had a singular gift for friendship and the capacity to form close attachments, almost always to women, both single and married, most of whom were older than she, some by many years. One of these older friends bequeathed her membership in the Boston Atheneum to Sarah along with a gift of twenty thousand dollars.

Except for a few like the author and critic Harriet Waters Preston, Sarah was unique among her Boston friends in pursuing an active professional life. She had started writing when she was still in school and she was eighteen when she published her first story in a Boston weekly. Her goal was to write for the *Atlantic Monthly* and it was through William Dean Howells who edited the magazine and bought her story, "Mr. Bruce," that she met the owner and publisher, James Fields, and was subsequently introduced to his wife.

Her first book, *Deephaven*, was published in 1881 and was followed by *Country Byways, Mate of Daylight* and *A Country Doctor*. She wrote her best-known work, *The Country of the Pointed Firs*, in 1897. Willa called the *Pointed Firs* sketches, "living things caught in the open, with light and freedom and air-spaces about them. They melt into the land and the life of the land until they are not stories at all, but life itself."

Most of Sarah Jewett's books are collections of short stories, some little more than vignettes, but her 1884 *Country Doctor* is a full-scale novel with a spunky heroine through whom she gave voice to some of the most advanced feminist thinking of the day. Nan Prince is an orphan, the ward of Dr. Leslie, the country doctor of the title, who raises her according to Rousseau-like principles to "work with nature," as he puts it, "not against it." He considers it unlikely that she will marry. "Nan's feeling toward her boy-playmates is exactly the same as toward the girls she knows," he says. "You have only to look at the rest of the children together to see the difference; and if I make sure by and by, the law of her nature is that she must live alone and work alone, I shall help her to keep it instead of break it, by providing something else than the business of housekeeping and what is called a woman's natural work, for her activity and capacity to spend itself upon." When a neighbor protests that a married life is happiest, the doctor does not disagree but replies that "a rule is sometimes very cruel for its exceptions; and there is a life now and then which is persuaded to put itself in irons by force of custom and circumstances, and from the lack of bringing reason to bear upon the solving of the most important questions of its existence."

Nan shares the doctor's views and both reason and her own nature impel her to follow in his footsteps and become a doctor herself. When she meets a young man who asks her to marry him she is forced to serious self-examination but in the end she rejects his proposal. She would like to have had him for a brother, she decides. To the well-meaning women who insist that she will change her mind as soon as " 'Mr. Right' comes along," she puts up a spirited defense: "Most girls have an instinct toward marrying, but mine is all against it . . . I should only wreck my life and other people's. I have never since I can remember thought of myself and my life in any way but unmarried—going on alone to the work I am fit to do."

Undoubtedly Nan's life and her choice of a profession are what

Sarah Jewett would have wanted for herself had she been stronger, but although she gave up the idea of going on with her father's work, the sentiments expressed by Dr. Leslie and Nan Prince were those of Sarah Jewett. "The preservation of the race is no longer the only important question; the welfare of the individual will be considered more and more," Dr. Leslie asserts. "I won't attempt to say that the study of medicine is a proper vocation for women," says Nan, "only . . . that it is the proper study for me. It certainly cannot be the proper vocation of all women to bring up children, so many of them are dead failures at it; and I don't see why all girls should be thought failures who do not marry."

Willa had appreciated Sarah Jewett's astringent opinions when she was still in Pittsburgh and sharing books with George Seibel. She had given him a copy of *The Country of the Pointed Firs* and she had also liked the "austere and unsentimental" *Country Doctor*, Seibel said. Meeting her, Willa found they shared many attitudes and were alike in their approach to work and its importance in a woman's life, although in Sarah Jewett's case it was friendship rather than her writing that took first place. Willa never overestimated Sarah Jewett's range—"She was content to be slight if she could be true"—but she admired the sensibility that Jewett brought to bear upon her characters and the delicacy of her perceptions. Now that finely tuned and probing sensibility was turned upon Willa and the work she was doing for *McClure's*.

As soon as the last Mary Baker Eddy article had appeared in the spring of 1908 Willa went on a long holiday with Isabelle in Europe. This time they took the Mediterranean route and visited Italy as well as France. In August when she returned, Willa went to stay with Annie Fields and Sarah Jewett at Thunderbolt Hill and in the fall she went alone to visit Sarah Jewett at South Berwick. There they went walking in the woods and talked about their work.

Sarah had not written for several years since suffering an accident in which she had been thrown from a carriage, and Willa had been trying to persuade her to do something for *McClure's*. "No story yet . . . but do not despair," Jewett wrote in August. "I begin to dare to think I could get something done for you, and it should be for you . . ." "I envy you your work, even with all its difficulties," she added. But she worried about Willa. She agreed with Viola Roseboro that Willa had wasted her talent in most of her stories in the last years, and she blamed the responsibilities she had assumed at *McClure's*. "It is impossible for you to work so hard and yet have your gifts mature as they should," she told Willa. When the visit ended she was too tired to drive with Willa to the station but she followed their talks with several remarkable letters filled with concern and advice for her young friend.

"If you don't keep and guard and mature your force and above all, have time and quiet to perfect your work, you will be writing things not better than you did five years ago," she warned. Her affections did not impede her critical objectivity. "I want you to be surer of your backgrounds," she wrote. "You have your Nebraska life, a child's Virginia and now an intimate knowledge of 'Bohemia,' of newspaper and magazine-office life. These are uncommon equipment but you don't see them quite enough from the outside." She acknowledged the "vivid, exciting companionship in the office" but reminded Willa, "They must not be your audience. You must find a quiet place near the best companions (not those who admire and wonder but those who know good things with delight!) . . . You must find your own quiet center of life and write from that to the world that holds offices, and all society, all Bohemia; the city, the country—in short you must write to the human heart . . ."

Sarah Orne Jewett must have known that she was writing—with almost her last ounce of energy—to a heart that was ready to respond. "I am sure that Willa Cather never forgot this letter," Edith Lewis wrote long afterward. "She could not act on it at the moment . . . but I think it became a permanent inhabitant of her thoughts." In a few months Sarah Jewett would be dead. "To work in silence and with all one's heart is the writer's lot," she had told Willa. "He is the only artist who must be solitary and yet needs the widest outlook upon the world." And "you must know the world before you can know the village."

A PERSONAL DECISION

Returning to New York in the fall of 1908 Willa made an important personal decision. After her transient existence of the past two years in New York and Boston she took an apartment on Washington Place just off the Square with Edith Lewis. At the time it seemed to her no more than a convenient living arrangement that suited her for the present, but the implications of the move were significant. It was a tacit acknowledgment that Isabelle would not be coming to New York to share her life and it was another manifestation of that intuitive understanding of her own nature that had guided her before. "Our necessities are so much stronger than our desires," she had written, and once again she was responding to needs she may not have fully appreciated but that were essential to her.

For despite what later became an increasing withdrawal from the outside world and a narrowing of her personal relationships, Willa was not a solitary person. She was happiest in a domestic setting and she wanted a place to live that would give her a feeling of home and family, that was neither transient nor lonely. Her physical surroundings were important to her and so was the companionship of an attentive and loving friend. Annie Fields and Sarah Jewett provided a model for the sort of household Willa may have wished she could share with Isabelle. If so, she was deluding herself.

It is true that the atmosphere of Charles Street was cheerful and harmonious. But it was also sentimental and more than a little precious. Willa would never have been able to exist for very long in such rarefied air. There was a lusty, earthy side to Willa and her passionate nature would have required a physical relationship that went beyond the playful tenderness her Boston friends expressed so freely for each other. Willa undoubtedly needed sexual fulfillment as well as intellectual and social stimulation. With Isabelle there were complications that made a life together impossible, at least in the foreseeable future.

Isabelle was dependent for money on her father, who was indulgent, but only up to a point. He allowed her to make visits and she could spend freely on gifts and travel, but the judge drew the line at his daughter's leaving home to set up her own establishment with her friend. Willa was always welcome as a guest in the McClung house for as long as she wished to stay, but it was to be understood that Isabelle's home was with her parents. Whatever conflict ensued between father and daughter, Isabelle by her own nature was incapable of making a break. She had no means of earning a living; she had not been brought up to expect to work. She was used to pampering, to being cared for and waited on. She had expensive tastes and it would have been unthinkable for her to give up the little luxuries she took for granted. For Willa, even if Isabelle had defied her parents, it would have meant a responsibility she could not possibly assume at a time when she was working so hard to achieve her own independence. In Pittsburgh, Isabelle had been able to provide her with peace and privacy and a place to work. Willa had no way of giving Isabelle the life to which she was accustomed in New York. One day she might be able to, but in the meantime she turned to Edith Lewis.

Edith, too, came from a well-to-do home. Her father was a prominent banker in Lincoln but he had raised his scholarly daughter to be independent and had encouraged her to plan for a career. Her mother and sister, on the other hand, were conventional clubwomen of the sort Willa knew so well and they were hostile, when they were not merely indifferent, to Edith's ambitions. Though her father was on her side and she was devoted to him, a degree of tension was invariably present in the household. Once Edith went away to school she rarely returned home and, in effect, severed ties with her family. In New York Willa became all the family she wanted.

The two women from Nebraska had many things in common. At Willa's urging Edith had been hired as a copy editor for *McClure's* and she was sent to Boston frequently while Willa was working on the Mary Baker Eddy pieces, to read proof and consult with her on stories. They had always been compatible and those Boston visits and their mutual involvement with the magazine drew them even closer. Younger than Willa by several years, Edith was a plain, unpretentious woman with a keen mind and a lively sense of fun. Like Willa she loved to travel, enjoyed music and had simple tastes. Her disposition was equable and pleasant, an ideal counterpart to Willa's darker, more mercurial moods. Willa was not yet ready, however, to make a permanent commitment. Indeed, it would be many years before she was prepared to acknowledge the place Edith had already begun to assume in her life.

For although they suited each other so well and she was fond of Edith, Willa did not feel the intense emotional attachment she felt for Isabelle. Besides, the future was uncertain. Willa had no idea where she would be living or what she would be doing in two or three years. Her work might take her anywhere. She was at a stage in her life when everything was possible to her both professionally and personally, and she was unwilling to tie herself down. Stability was important but she also wanted to be free.

The timing of the move to Washington Place proved fortuitous. No sooner had Willa returned to New York in the fall than Sam McClure rewarded her for her handling of the Christian Science stories by making her his managing editor. He considered that she had a genius for administration and he was only too pleased to leave the daily running of the magazine to her. That she was loyal to him he had no doubt. The work was draining, as Sarah Jewett knew, and Willa more than ever needed a quiet place to come home to after a day in the office. As managing editor, in addition to developing articles, buying material and performing executive chores, Willa had also frequently to act as a buffer between the editor-in-chief and writers who felt themselves underpaid or who complained that the magazine's decisions were not made promptly enough. Her business letters were patient, cordial and encouraging, but it was often a trial to explain some of McClure's bizarre behavior. Manuscripts had a way of disappearing or languishing for months in McClure's desk and Willa had often to suggest to writers and their agents that they be sure to send stories to her personally. She would see to it that McClure read them as soon as possible and if she could not get a quick decision from him or could not get permission to make a decision herself she guaranteed to return them to the writers promptly. Sometimes she almost wheedled disaffected authors to stop by and see her so that they could patch up misunderstandings. She was guided in handling young writers, she once told Will Jones, by remembering the patience he had shown to her. She admitted that theirs was a mysterious office, but it was getting less mysterious all the time, she promised.

Mysterious or not, the office had lost none of its liveliness, however, and though McClure may have been temporarily deflated by the treachery, as he saw it, of his brilliant staff, he had not been defeated. "His electric energy keyed the whole office to a high tension which never relaxed so long as he was in the place; and he seemed to be everywhere at once," Edith Lewis wrote. It was like "working in a high wind, sometimes of cyclonic magnitude" and the storm center was, of course, McClure himself. Yet both Edith and Willa spoke also of his gentleness, his courtesy that extended to everyone from staff writer to office boy, and his particular kindness to the young. Years later Willa told her former "chief" that she thought the secret of his success with young people was that he often thought them a little more able than they really were, which encouraged the best of them to work all the harder to come up to his expectations. She was probably thinking of herself as she had been in those days. She was always eager to please him, she remembered, and he was eager to be pleased. It was one of the happiest associations of her life and even during the years when they saw little of each other, Willa counted McClure among her closest friends.

In 1913, after the magazine had at last been taken out of his hands and Willa, too, had gone on to other ventures, McClure asked her to help him write his autobiography. Actually Willa wrote and McClure talked. Pacing the floor in Willa's apartment, he told her about his boyhood and early struggles. The story of his life was published in *McClure's* in installments over a period of eight months, and Frederick A. Stokes Company brought it out in book form in 1914. The only reference to Willa in the entire book is a succinct note at the beginning that, "I am indebted to the cooperation of Miss Willa Sibert Cather for the very existence of this book." It was McClure's way of acknowledging that *My Autobiography* by S. S. McClure was in fact the work of Willa Cather.

After Willa's death Edith Lewis paid a visit to McClure in the hospital where he lay critically ill at the age of ninety-two. His daughter had given Edith permission to see the dying man. When she spoke of a posthumous collection of Willa's stories that had just appeared, his face lit up. "'She was wonderful, a wonderful girl,'" he kept repeating. And when she told him that a biography of Willa was being planned, he roused himself to say, "'I will help you with it.'" A short while later an intern came in and asked him how he felt. He took a minute to answer, Edith Lewis wrote, and then he said, "'I think—I am still Mr. McClure.'" He died the following week.

"SOMETHING OF A MASQUERADE"

There is no doubt that Willa found working with McClure exhilarating. Nevertheless, the job required every bit of energy that she possessed and left her with no time for her writing. On occasion she would follow Viola Roseboro's example and steal an afternoon to stay at home, but they were other people's stories she worked on in the peace and quiet of the apartment, not her own. Most of Willa's stories that appeared during 1907 were written earlier, probably while she was still in Pittsburgh. During 1908 she published only one, "On the Gull's Road," that appeared in *McClure's* in December. She was dissatisfied with it but it brought warm praise from Sarah Jewett, who was beguiled perhaps by the strongly Jamesian flavor of the tale.

The story is a conventional shipboard romance, the "gull's road" is the sea, and the events are recalled twenty years later. The American narrator, returning home after two years in Italy to take up his first consular appointment—the tale is subtitled, "The Ambassador's Story"—falls in love with the wife of the ship's chief engineer, a florid, mean-spirited woman-chaser, some years older than his wife. She responds to the young American but refuses to run away with him; she has a child and, besides, she is very ill and hasn't long to live. She leaves her husband's ship, however, when it docks in New York and returns alone to Norway where she dies in her father's home a few months later. The lover is left with his memories, a sketch he drew of her and a swatch of her red-gold hair which she gave to him at parting.

The effect of a beautiful woman on the people around her, especially on an impressionable young man, was a theme Willa returned to often. Sarah Jewett remarked on the "wonderful tenderness" with which she had drawn the figure of Alexandra Ebbling, the wife. She felt, however, that Willa had been less successful with the lover because it was always "something of a masquerade" when a woman wrote in a man's character. And then she added, without a trace of self-consciousness, "you could have done it as yourself. A woman could care enough to wish to take her away from such a life."

These words, so simply stated yet so full of meaning, must have struck a chord when Willa read them, but it was advice she could not take. Sarah Jewett, shaped by the notions of the nineteenth century, was comfortable with the idea of love between women. She had her own experience of an intimate relationship that was free of overt sexual expression. But Willa, in the emerging Freudian age, was both more sophisticated about the nature of her feelings and more guarded in expressing them. She wrote romantically about women, again and again, but always in the person of a man. Though she would movingly describe intimacy between men, between Tom Outland and Roddy Blake, or between Father Vaillant and Archbishop Latour, the loving relationships with women that were so important in her personal life are nowhere reflected in her fiction, unless they involve family members or characters separated by age or station in life. In her books friendship is a sentiment of childhood or it exists between men or between a man and a woman, but she never wrote about an attachment between two women.

Sarah Jewett's gentle caution to Willa raises provocative questions. Would *My Antonia*, for one, or *A Lost Lady* have been better books if they had been told from the point of view of women instead of men? Perhaps, but then they would not have been the books we know. Jim Burden's role in *My Antonia* sometimes seems contrived, but Willa pointed out that she had known Annie mostly from hearing men talk about her. She had observed her heroines as men responded to them and it was their effect on men she evoked so hauntingly in both books. She was not denying that she too had been stirred by Annie's warmth or disturbed by the elusive beauty of Lyra Garber, but she chose Jim Burden and Niel Herbert to speak for her. Besides, Willa felt that the time she had spent with McClure had given her practice in getting inside the skin of a man, and she told a friend she considered that in the autobiography she had even written "better and truer McClure than McClure himself."

Significantly, it is in the most palpably erotic of Willa Cather's stories, "Coming, Aphrodite!" that the author's own voice seems most androgynous. The setting is the studio building on the south side of Washington Square where Willa lived when she first came to New York, and the young painter, Don Hedger, who spies on Eden Bowers through a knothole in the closet wall adjoining their apartments and watches her as she performs her daily exercises, could as easily be a woman as a man. At first he regards her naked body with the cool impersonal eye of an artist, but when the two finally meet the attraction between them is fiercely sexual and their affair, while it lasts, is passionate and clearly mutually satisfying.

Nevertheless, the male and female roles seem interchangeable and the ambiguity is underscored in the story within a story, the legend that Hedger recounts to Eden of "The Forty Lovers of the Queen." The normal civility between the sexes is stripped away to be replaced by elemental lust in which the queen, her lovers and the emasculated captive all share. Small wonder that Eden understands that Hedger was not trying to please her with the brutal story but "to antagonize and frighten her."

Willa wrote "Coming, Aphrodite!" in 1920. By then she had abandoned the Jamesian influence of "On the Gull's Road" which, Sarah Jewett to the contrary, seemed to stifle her natural exuberance. The romance of the young consul and Mrs. Ebbling is tepid and unreal beside the physical excitement that flows between Eden Bowers and Don Hedger. Willa herself knew the difference between sentiment and passion and when she is at her most uninhibited in describing sexual passion between a man and a woman, she also reveals the dual perspective from which she wrote. She had absorbed both the male and female roles, and her voice seems primitive and androgynous. But that was later. When she wrote "On the Gull's Road," she was still experimenting, trying out styles and themes, still trying to find her pitch.

In January 1909 she sent Sarah Jewett a little story that was to appear in *Harper's* in April. For it she went back to Nebraska, to the river and the island where she had played with her brothers and which had been so important a part of her imaginative life as a child. She had used the setting seven years earlier, in "The Treasure of Far Island" in which she told the story of Douglas Burnham, grown up and a successful playwright but still the Speckle Burnham of "The Way of the World," who comes home to Sandtown after an absence of twelve years. With the almost forgotten companion of his youth, the tomboy Margie Van Dyke, now a lovely and desirable woman, he revisits the river to find the treasure they had buried long ago when they had pretended to be pirates and the little world was theirs to rule. No doubt Willa winced in later years at the false and sentimental ending. She never included "The Treasure of Far Island" in collections of her stories, but her childhood adventures on the river were important to her and when she reworked the material for "The Enchanted Bluff," memory and imagination combined to produce a flawless tale.

"The Enchanted Bluff" is set in childhood. The boys who were first introduced in "The Way of the World" and who keep appearing in Willa's fiction—Jimmy Templeton, Shorty Thompson, the Hassler brothers—are spending a last evening on the river before going back to school. Stretched out on one of the sandbars, they drift into conversation about the stars, the Mound Builders and the Aztecs, about Spanish gold brought by Coronado and whether gold might yet be hidden in the river. One of the boys has heard about "a big red rock" rising nine hundred feet out of the sand somewhere in New Mexico. They call it the Enchanted Bluff, he says, and no white man has ever climbed to the top. One by one, the boys vow they will be the first to reach it.

The banter of the boys, the starlit night, the lazy river evoke a sense of time suspended. All that has happened to the little band of friends, all that lies waiting for them and all that they will lose, is contained in a few brief pages. Willa was to write years later, in a preface to Sarah Orne Jewett's stories, that every great story must leave in the reader's mind "an intangible residuum of pleasure; a cadence, a quality of voice that is exclusively the writer's own, individual, unique." Willa was on her way to finding her unique voice in "The Enchanted Bluff" but she was tentative about it. She was still susceptible to other influences and it would be several years more before she was ready to claim Nebraska as her territory. When she again returned to the river and the sandbar it would be triumphantly in *My Ántonia*.

VII

❀

People and Places

NEW SCENES AND A NEW FRIEND

"The Enchanted Bluff" was Willa's last story for the next two years. In May 1909 she made the first of several trips abroad on assignment for *McClure's*. Sam McClure was of the strong opinion that an editor needed to get away from the office to keep from growing stale and he encouraged Willa to travel. Her mission was to find fresh material, meet with established authors, discover new ones and bring back manuscripts for the magazine. It was just what she had hoped to do when she accepted McClure's offer to work with him. "I wasn't out to spy on life. I was out to live it," she said in later years about those trips to Europe for *McClure's*. Her stay in London on that first visit was a round of literary and theatrical events and on subsequent visits she went everywhere and met everybody of importance in the arts and publishing—Edmund Gosse, Sidney Colvin, G. K. Chesterton, H. G. Wells and John Galsworthy. When the Abbey Players gave their first London performance Willa was with Yeats and Lady Gregory in their box. Through the critic William Archer, who became a good friend, she was introduced to London's backstage world which always fascinated her. And on one of her visits Archer took her along with him to George Meredith's funeral where she found herself in an illustrious company of mourners. McClure was delighted with the way his protégée had been accepted and he applauded her "splendid and successful stay in London."

Willa's attitude had mellowed since her first trip to England with Isabelle. Perhaps she had absorbed some of Mrs. Fields's lifetime Anglophilia, or perhaps it was that she herself had changed and was no longer the raw young woman from the prairie who felt herself an outsider, ill at ease and awkward in the presence of the "hallowed shades." As managing editor of *McClure's* she brought her own considerable credentials and moved comfortably and confidently in a world which before had been closed to her and which she had seen only at a distance.

The European trips were marvelously stimulating and important to Willa, but so too were the visits home to Red Cloud, the camping trips with Roscoe and Douglass and the frequent visits to Isabelle in Pittsburgh. Willa had resumed the schedule she had begun so many years before, periods of intense work, followed by vacations and a change of scene. She went up to Boston as often as she could to be with Mrs. Fields. While she was in England she had received word of Sarah Jewett's death and she knew how lonely Annie Fields must be. Mary Jewett too was living on alone and Willa stayed with her in Maine on several occasions in the house in South Berwick which seemed to Willa to be permeated by a presence as no other place she knew. To sit at Sarah Jewett's desk and look out upon her garden gave her a sense of perfect rest and contentment.

She had her routine in New York as well. On her very first trip to the city she had discovered Central Park and now, when she felt she absolutely had to have a respite from the noise and pace of New York life, she would take a bus up Fifth Avenue from the Square and walk around the reservoir or write letters, sitting on a bench beside the pond where children sailed their model boats.

To a new friend who met her in the winter of 1910 and who was soon to be admitted to her small circle of intimates, a trip to Central Park with Willa on the open top of a Fifth Avenue bus was a memorable experience. "Willa Cather's Fifth Avenue . . . halfway between the Age of Innocence and the Age of the Skyscraper," Elizabeth Sergeant called it. When Willa cared about something, she wanted her friends to feel about it as she did, and Elizabeth Sergeant never forgot their first journey up the avenue together and Willa's enthusiasm for the landmarks along the way. Passing Admiral Farragut on his pedestal in Madison Square, she spoke excitedly about the American sculptor Augustus Saint-Gaudens, who had so magnificently evoked the French tradition in the squares of New York. She was proud that she had been able to secure his letters for publication in *McClure's*. At Thirty-fourth Street the Waldorf Hotel reminded her of evenings following the opera when she had watched the "copper kings from Denver pouring their admiration and their jewels on the opulent knees of the stars." It was the thing to do, she confided, to go to the Waldorf and eat oysters at midnight. She herself went to the opera twice a week during the Metropolitan's season. It was a luxury to attend the opera with no thought but for her personal enjoyment after her years of reviewing in Pittsburgh.

Sometimes, when she had walked around the reservoir, she made the return trip in style by hansom cab as far as Delmonico's or another of her favorite restaurants. Many years later Elizabeth Sergeant recalled one such afternoon at Delmonico's and the poise with which Willa ordered a sumptuous tea—brioche, petits fours, a napoleon, two babas au rhum—and commanded the waiter to bring tea that was "hot, Hot, HOT!" The headwaiter had smiled as he helped Willa to remove her coat and revealed her costume—luxurious, ornate and conspicuously embroidered in red. As Elizabeth Sergeant was to learn, Willa had a taste for bright colors and elaborate fabrics, in spite of her "blithe made-in-Nebraska look" and the lisle stockings, low-heeled Oxfords and easy sports coat that were her customary attire. She still enjoyed dressing up when she had the chance and her friends knew she appreciated nothing so much as a gift of finery. In this she was not unlike her mother, although Mrs. Cather disapproved of some of her daughter's more garish color combinations.

Elizabeth Sergeant, however, was eight years younger than Willa and more than a little in awe of her. She had experienced the kindness of which Willa was capable when she cared about a person. But she had also seen the icy way she could withdraw when she was displeased, as she was with the waiter at Delmonico's who failed to conceal his surprise at her outfit. Her behavior was full of contradictions that fascinated Elsie Sergeant and, at least in the beginning of their friendship, Elsie was indulgent of them. She too was something of a rebel.

A New Englander of firm principles and eclectic sympathies, she was the first woman in her family to go to college. When the time came, she chose Bryn Mawr outside Philadelphia over one of the Boston schools closer to home. There she came under the influence of strong-minded educators like Bryn Mawr's president, M. Carey Thomas, who believed young women from privileged homes had an obligation to alleviate the conditions of those less fortunate than themselves, and to help right the evils of society. In Elsie Sergeant, Miss Thomas had one of her staunchest disciples. During the six years or so since her graduation Elsie had climbed stairs and toured slums to investigate working conditions of women in Europe and New York. She was working on an article about the sweated tenement workers in New York when her friend, the social worker Pauline Goldmark, suggested she go to see Willa at *McClure's*. Expecting to find another Ida Tarbell, whom she had once met briefly at the home of William James, she was unprepared for the buoyant, youthful figure who came to greet her. "No trace of the reforming feminist . . ." was her first thought. "Her eyes were sailor-blue, her cheeks were rosy, her hair was . . . parted in the middle like a child's." All belied the muckraking editor she had anticipated.

For her part, Willa found the interview equally surprising. She had her own notions about reformers and nothing about this shy, eager-faced Bostonian matched the image in her mind. She looked over the tenement pieces with a practiced editorial eye and found them good enough to buy and feature prominently in the magazine, but she wondered why their author had chosen to join the " 'reforming pamphleteers . . . Aren't short stories more in your line?' " Willa wanted to know; " 'You look like a Jamesian.' " Elizabeth Sergeant was flattered but also somewhat disconcerted. She *did* have literary interests but she was sincere as well in her commitment to the causes of the day. She soon realized, however, that if she and Willa were going to be friends, she would have to mute her social and political concerns. Willa wanted to talk about books and authors, not about the exploitation of Italian immigrants.

Characteristically, once Willa made up her mind that Elizabeth Sergeant was someone she could talk to about the things that really mattered to her, her interest in the young journalist quickly became personal. It was the old, impulsive Willa embarking on a new relationship, and she revealed herself to Elsie Sergeant as she did to very few people. It was a full year before she began writing to Dear Elsie and not to Dear Miss Sergeant, but her affection comes through nonetheless. She wanted Mrs. Fields and Isabelle to meet her new friend. Isabelle, who cared so much for lovely things, would appreciate her in spite of Elsie's New England propensity for reform, Willa promised.

Willa would never have considered taking a casual acquaintance to call on Annie Fields, but she felt that Elsie was a kindred spirit who would understand how important the house on Charles Street was to her. She brought her there at teatime just as Alice Brandeis had once brought her, and Elsie Sergeant observed another side of her Nebraska friend in Willa's tender homage to their hostess and the way her forceful personality seemed to retreat in the presence of that faded figure in the black lace cap.

At their first meeting in Willa's office Elsie Sergeant had been uncertain whether her new editor was a writer also, but in the course of conversation Willa confided something of her own ambitions. Journalism was only a temporary means to an end; the day would come when she would leave the magazine to write. She could not afford to give up her job as yet but it was what she was working toward. She had already had a book of stories published, she confessed, but now those early efforts seemed to her pretentious and deformed by the mood of anger and frustration in which they had been written. When Elsie later wrote to say she had come upon a copy of *The Troll Garden* in the Boston Public Library, Willa's reply was to suggest she take a look at the "Enchanted Bluff" if she wanted to read a candid little Western tale that satisfied its author.

For ten years Elizabeth Sergeant was one of Willa's closest friends and one of the two or three people with whom she discussed her work. They weren't often in the same place during those years and their friendship was carried on in letters to a great extent. Elsie was frequently in Boston and spent long periods in France, but she visited Willa when she was in New York and at one time took her own apartment in the city. Willa valued Elsie's cool New England judgment on literary matters and she felt a strong personal attraction to the young Bostonian. When Elsie returned from a stay in Europe in 1913 it was Willa who met her at the boat and brought her back to her apartment. Edith was away and Elsie stayed with her. Whether Willa ever considered the possibility of Elsie's replacing Edith in her life is impossible to know. Significantly, Edith Lewis never mentions Elizabeth Sergeant in her book, although she talks of other friends, and Willa's letters to Elsie are remarkable for their few references to Edith.

As time went on, the friendship between Willa and Elizabeth Sergeant that had begun so spontaneously, with so much curiosity and anticipation on both sides, gradually cooled and the friends grew apart, although they never completely lost touch with one another. A potential for friction had always been present in their relationship. Elsie represented Boston and the rarefied Eastern literary world that Willa scoffed at but to which she aspired also, and in Willa's admiration there may have been a trace of envy and resentment. Next to Elsie she would sometimes feel the outsider, still pushing her way into polite society. She would like to be " 'a lucky Bostonian . . . living in a house' " instead of always living like a transient, with her suitcases under the bed.

Their real differences, however, were matters of temperament and ideology and these divided them more deeply and completely than the superficial difference in their backgrounds ever could have. Elsie Sergeant was *engagée* in a way that Willa never would be and that she came increasingly to deplore. As Elsie grew more confident and independent—she became a reporter for the *New Republic*, a war correspondent and an ardent New Dealer—it wasn't possible to keep their opposing viewpoints from interfering with their friendship. Willa's bitterness and Elsie's stubbornness made poor company and it was better to see less of each other than to quarrel.

Yet when they met, as they did up until Willa's death, their old affection remained a bond between them. The best part of their friendship, the place where it " 'clicked,' " as Elizabeth Sergeant wrote, had always been their shared love of literature and their devotion to the creative process. Elsie may have despaired at Willa's political opinions but she never doubted her friend's genius as a writer.

PLEASE LIKE BARTLEY

In 1911, while still at *McClure's*—you need simple tastes to give up a good job, she told Elsie Sergeant—Willa took a step that would ultimately lead to freedom from the office grind. She began working on a novel which she finished in the fall. *McClure's* serialized it in three parts in the early months of 1912 under the title *Alexander's Masquerade*, and Houghton Mifflin brought it out in book form in the spring as *Alexander's Bridge*, the name by which it has since been known. At the same time she submitted the novel to Ferris Greenslet at Houghton Mifflin and while it was being read in those austere premises Willa indulged in a little masquerade of her own. She sent a copy of the book to *McClure's* using the name Miss Fanny Cadwallader, and to protect her anonymity even further, she had the typescript mailed from St. Louis. Perhaps she wanted to prove that she could sell a story to the magazine on the story's own merits and not because of her position or maybe it was just the old Willa, hiding behind a pseudonym. At any rate, her quixotic deception did not go undetected for long and her own by-line appears in both the magazine and the book.

Bartley Alexander, the Western engineer who comes East to build bridges and establishes himself on Boston's Brimmer Street, was Willa Cather's first hero. From that time on, for the rest of her life, she was never without a novel, or a hero or a heroine to occupy her. If Willa's men and women made lasting impressions on her readers, they filled their creator's life. Willa cared about her family and friends, as one of them remarked, but her deepest feelings were reserved for her characters.

Please like Bartley if you can, she begged her friend, the poet and playwright Zoë Akins. Annie Fields, she said, had found him appealing in spite of his bad manners, especially in comparison to the Emersons, whom she disliked. Others, too, found Bartley interesting. The critic Maxwell Geismar considered him one of Willa's most attractive men and he thought it curious that she disparaged her first novel in later years. It was well received when it appeared and won praise for its psychological acuity as well as for its graceful prose, but looking back on it, Willa saw it only as "shallow" and "superficial." The trouble was that the story had not come to her spontaneously as she believed a story should, but was the result of meeting some interesting people in London and deciding that a book had to be made out of "interesting material." At the time, she said, the new had seemed more exciting to her than the familiar.

Moving between Boston where Bartley lives with his wife and

London where he begins an affair with the fascinating Irish actress he had known in Paris in his youth, the novel's sophisticated setting caused some critics to conclude that Willa was laying claim to territory already marked out by James and Wharton. In fact, Bartley Alexander is too original, too distinctively a Cather creation, to fit into anybody else's mold. He is an engineer, but he has the qualities that Willa associated with the pioneers, the vigor and the vehemence, the force that "takes us forward" and "builds bridges into the future, over which the feet of every one of us will go." Bartley's old professor, seeing him after a lapse of many years, is struck anew by his former pupil's "powerfully equipped nature," but he also detects something close to desperation in Bartley's recognition that he is approaching middle age without having lived out all his potentialities. The twin themes of middle-aged disillusion and the divided self which Willa introduced in *Alexander's Bridge* were expressed often in her letters and in her later work.

Winifred Pemberton, Bartley's wife, an otherwise conventional character, is interesting for probably coming as close to a description of Isabelle McClung as Willa was ever to provide. "A person of distinction," she is called, "and, moreover, very handsome." Tall like Isabelle, she "carried her beautiful head proudly, and moved with ease and certainty. One immediately took for granted the costly privileges and fine spaces that must lie in the background . . ." There is a "suggestion of stormy possibilities in the proud curve of her lip and nostril."

The captivating Hilda Burgoyne is probably a composite of actresses Willa had seen in London and the description of the London theatrical scene gives an indication of Willa's own social activities during her visits, the receptions and the backstage parties she had attended in the company of William Archer and other English friends. For the book's final tragic episode, the collapse of the bridge over the St. Lawrence River that was to have been Bartley's crowning achievement but that takes his life instead, Willa relied on newspaper accounts of an actual disaster, the crash of the Quebec Bridge in 1907. In that case a commission appointed by the government held the engineer responsible for the bridge's collapse. Bartley, who had been with Hilda when a first warning was delivered, also bears the blame for the crash of his bridge. The bridge's weaknesses are matched by flaws in his own character and in the end he is brought down by them both.

By the autumn of 1911 Willa was worn out. Working on her novel while putting out the magazine had exhausted her energy and left her tense and irritable. You can't know how crushing office work can be, she told a friend, unless you have been crushed by it. She was tired, so awfully tired. In October she had a respite. She and Isabelle went to stay in Cherry Valley, a historic old town in western New York State, the site of a famous massacre in the Revolutionary War, and at one time the western terminus of the coach road from Albany. Mrs. McClung had grown up there and Isabelle had no difficulty finding a suitable house to rent.

For the first time in a long while Willa was free of responsibility. She had not felt so well or enjoyed life so much for years, she wrote to Sam McClure. She called it her winter cure. After six weeks of healthy outdoor activity—they tramped about the woods no matter what the weather—she was sleeping nine hours a night without turning over. And she had begun a new story; it was such a great relief to get back to her writing. McClure had made one of his flying visits to see her and make plans for the future. When she came back he hoped she would not allow herself to be tied up in office machinery, but that she would work out a series of articles "that will give us distinction."

McClure's plans for Willa sound a sad note. The flamboyant publisher was no longer in control of his magazine when he spoke to her of giving *us* distinction. Changes had been taking place that relegated Sam McClure to a figurehead and placed his son-in-law, Cameron Mackenzie, in charge. McClure was putting up a brave front—"I am rather enjoying the new developments, the new body of jealousies that has sprung up . . ." he told Willa—but she knew how much it pained him to see others at the helm of the magazine he loved. He was going abroad with some idea of getting backing for a new magazine devoted exclusively to fiction. She would wait to see what his needs were when he returned. She thought she might go abroad herself in the spring.

Meanwhile, it was Mackenzie with whom she had to work. He

and Willa had not always worked together smoothly. Once Isabelle had had to act as go-between to patch up a misunderstanding. But she was fond of him; she had told Mrs. McClure that he was just the son-in-law she would have liked to have. When she returned to the office in the winter of 1912 she found him well disposed toward her. Apparently he had been receiving favorable comments about her bridge builder, she told Elizabeth Sergeant. She was not certain, however, how he would react to her new story which was completely different. She called it "The Bohemian Girl" and it was all about her neighbors in Nebraska, the Swedes and Bohemians she had grown up with. They were not the usual subjects of fiction, especially not magazine fiction, which tended to deal with Anglo-Saxon men and women from middle- and upper-class backgrounds, not with the farmers and small-town characters she had written about.

Willa brought the story with her when she returned to New York from Cherry Valley but she hesitated before giving it to Cameron Mackenzie. It was too highbrow, too remote, she insisted when he pressed her. But he provoked her finally by asking if she had nothing to show for her stay in the country, and, with some trepidation, she let him have it. He read the story overnight and the next day invited her to tea at the Brevoort where he offered to buy it for $750. She could not help laughing at him. She knew more than he did how much a story was worth to the magazine and hers was not possibly worth more than $500, she told him. He said she was silly but agreed to a compromise. He would pay her the $500 she thought the story was worth, but she would receive $750 for the next one.

The success of *Alexander's Bridge* followed by the long story, "The Bohemian Girl," made Willa quite a celebrity among her colleagues. They were eager to know what she planned to do next and they plagued Edith Lewis for details. When Willa talked vaguely about a story of an opera singer, Cameron Mackenzie wrung the plot out of her and told everybody in the office. She hadn't even written it and he wanted to advertise it. She'd never be able to write under those conditions, she told Elsie Sergeant; it was giving her a severe case of stage fright. Nevertheless, she was enjoying the attention. William Heinemann, the London publisher whose opinion she thought highly of, was bringing out *Alexander's Bridge* in England

and she considered the illustrations in the English edition a great improvement on the American illustrations which, in her opinion, were dis-gus-ting.

An indication that she had begun to achieve a measure of recognition in literary circles came with an invitation to a dinner in honor of the seventy-fifth birthday of William Dean Howells. Howells was leaving Boston for retirement in Maine, and the dinner on the evening of March 1 was in the nature of a farewell tribute to the man considered by many the preeminent literary figure of the day, novelist, editor and critic. "Such a gathering of distinguished men [sic] assembled last night at Sherry's," reported the New York *Times*, "as few occasions in the past have called together in the city." President William Howard Taft came up from Washington for the occasion and "practically every literary celebrity in the country" attended.

Colonel George Harvey, the editor of *Harper's Weekly*, presided and speeches were made by the President himself and by William Allen White, the American Winston Churchill, Basil King and Hamilton Wright Mabie. James Barnes appeared in costume as Silas Lapham to thank Howells in verse for creating the character. "Nearly everyone in the hall knew everybody else," said the *Times* of the four hundred guests whose names were listed in the article. They included Mary Austin, Ray Stannard Baker, Ellen Glasgow, James Cabell, the actor Richard Le Gallienne, Willa's old friend Ida Tarbell, Emily Post, Mary Roberts Rinehart, Woodrow Wilson's friend Colonel Edward Mandell House, Mark Twain's niece Jean Webster (the creator of Daddy-Long-Legs) and Margaret Deland with her husband and her daughter. Edith Wharton was in Europe, as was Henry James. But there in the *Times*, between Hayden Carruth and George W. Chadwick, was the name Miss Willa Cather.

The evening had its share of irreverence as well as sentiment. The speeches were endless and full of hyperbole. Margaret Deland wrote to Willa afterward that she regretted they hadn't had a chance to compare notes. Next to the portly figure of the President the unassuming little man from Boston had been overwhelmed. "Did you ever see anything more cunning than the way in which he stood and clasped his hands tightly while he waited for that storm of applause to subside?" asked Mrs. Deland. Willa sent the letter to Carrie Miner

Sherwood in Red Cloud. After all, Margaret Deland was a famous author and Willa knew that Carrie would like to have her autograph.

Willa stayed in New York longer than she intended in order to be present at the Howells dinner. She had been hospitalized in February for a minor operation and she was still feeling weak. The accommodating Mr. Mackenzie encouraged her to take as much time as she needed away from the office until she was completely fit, and she left for Pittsburgh immediately following the dinner. There she found a household plunged in gloom. Mrs. McClung had suffered a stroke and lay unconscious in her bedroom, although she did not appear to have suffered any paralysis. Willa's own regimen required that she have care and large amounts of rest, which must have put a strain on the harassed family, but as always she was treated as a member of the family and her presence was not only accepted, it was assumed. It was impossible to lead a normal life in a household that was waiting rather than living, she wrote to Elsie Sergeant, but she was eating and sleeping well and taking long walks which seemed to act upon her like a soporific. In addition she was getting lots of reading done. Michelet's history had been a life preserver one week and she also recommended the autobiography of Richard Wagner. The composer's story had lots of action and little reflection. It was just what Willa thought a man's "life" ought to be!

Her own plans had to wait on Mrs. McClung's condition; she was counting on a trip out West with Douglass, but she couldn't leave Isabelle while her mother was so ill. It became evident, however, that any improvement would come slowly, if at all, and in April Willa set out to join Douglass in Arizona. She had wanted Elsie Sergeant to come along and try the desert country with her, but Elsie too had been ill and was in the South recuperating when Willa was ready to start out.

That journey with her brother, even more than her first trip to Europe with Isabelle, affected the way Willa viewed the world. It was an affirmation of her feeling for the past and a renewal of her sympathy for the primitive devotion of men and women to the land. In Edith Lewis' words, a whole new landscape opened up for her, and it was as much a landscape of the mind and spirit as a physical landscape of rugged terrain and stunning natural features. Willa was to carry bits and pieces of the experience with her for the rest of her

life, and many of the things she saw and the people she met on that
first trip to the Far West are fixed forever in her books and stories.

DRUNK UP BY DESERT SANDS

Willa began her trip in Winslow where Douglass shared a house
with a brakeman named Tooker. The third member of the household
was a drunken Englishman who served as cook and housekeeper.
While Douglass was out with a construction gang, as happened
often, Willa and Tooker lived in the house together, an arrangement
that was in accord with proprieties in Winslow, Willa informed Elsie
Sergeant. In the way she sometimes did, Willa took a strong dislike
to Tooker and to the town. On the other hand, her brother's Cock-
ney cook amused her and she overlooked his constant drinking. He
had worked at one time in his life in a stable in Paris and he spoke a
rather odd, but fluent, French. He also had a favorite poem that he
would recite to her, weeping bitterly when he reached the line
"Where ere I look, on sea or skies, / I see them fair, deceivin' eyes."
Willa remembered him when she wrote *The Professor's House* and
created the castaway Englishman, Henry Atkins, who cooks for
Tom Outland and Roddy Blake. Henry had none of the mean ways
of a bum, she wrote. He was defenseless and innocent and held no
grudge against anyone, even those who had abused him. That was
written more than ten years later. In the flesh she found he could
grow tiresome.

Winslow depressed her terribly. She hated the sandstorms and the
wind and the tin cans whirling about the streets. The people lived in
flimsy, run-down shacks and while Douglass' house was more commodious than most, there was no spot in it for her to work. The air
of the place was off, she wrote to Elsie. The Mexicans were her only
compensation, even though, with her Midwestern prejudice, she considered them an inferior lot. Nevertheless, they had good manners, at
least they went their own way, and she liked the sound of their musical speech. She was learning Spanish from a priest who took her with
him on his round of the little Indian and Mexican churches. Their
villages delighted her after the hideous little railroad town.

It was Tooker, however, who was her real nemesis. He was the kind of self-taught man who had digested information whole and he would discourse stolidly on topics he thought would interest her. She had to grit her teeth when he told his endless stories. He never did things in one syllable, she said. He arrived; he removed his hat and he reflected. When he wasn't talking he buried himself ostentatiously in a volume of Emerson, bound in full Morocco. She supposed that his square jaw and the proud way he held his head made him one of nature's noblemen, but she didn't think she could stand either his information or his nobility much longer. She spent her time at target practice while Douglass was away and she was afraid that one of these days she would turn on Tooker with a pistol. She was hoping that Douglass would rescue her soon and take her to Flagstaff where she longed to see the Cliff Dwellers.

When Douglass did finally return they went camping in the hills and on the trip Willa did something that was very rare for her; she changed her opinion of Tooker. Her own mood had undoubtedly improved—she had been lonely back in Winslow—and she was able to appreciate Tooker's qualities. Once they left town, she told Elsie, he was a different man. No doubt he thought the same of her. All the miserable information he had gleaned from countless magazines dropped away, she said, as boys drop their clothes when they go swimming. Without his pretentious baggage he was actually a very decent sort, strong, active, with lots of verve. He was also very important on the trip because they did some steep climbing, once inching their way along a hundred-and-fifty-foot cliff by handhold, and Tooker was the only one who really knew the terrain. Without his help they might have been in serious trouble. Willa never changed her mind about Tooker again, and he served as the model for one of her most endearing characters, Ray Kennedy, the railroad brakeman in *The Song of the Lark* whose legacy makes it possible for Thea to study voice.

* * *

Willa enjoyed Arizona, especially the ancient houses of the Cliff Dwellers, and she thought the Grand Canyon was the most attractive place she had seen in America. It was wonderful for walking and riding—she took a mule trip down into the canyon—and, best of all, it had been let alone, without a single shop or amusement and with only two hotels. She was staying at Old Bright Angel Camp which was comfortable but very simple. It cost three dollars a day with an additional two-fifty for a riding horse and five dollars for a team and open wagon.

But it was New Mexico, big, bright and consuming, that thrilled her and excited her imagination. After Winslow, Albuquerque was a revelation, reminding her of the French countryside between Marseille and Nice. All around it were thriving Indian villages and ghost towns that had been Spanish missions in Queen Elizabeth's time. There was a pull about the place, Willa told Elsie Sergeant, something Spanish in the air that teased and captivated. The Lord set the stage so splendidly, she said, there must be a new hope coming, a new tragedy, a new religion or perhaps a crusade. It was too glorious to have been put there without a purpose.

Her feeling for the color and the splendor of the country was somehow all mixed up with her feeling for a young Mexican she and Douglass met who became her special friend, her Mexican sweetheart. His name was Julio, pronounced Hulio, please, she said to Elsie, and in her letters she rhapsodized about his romantic looks. His skin was the pale bright yellow of very old gold—and old races, she added. He had the long strong upper lip of Aztec sculpture. And his eyes were somber with lots of old troubles buried in them. He wasn't soft and sunny like the Latin boys people were always writing home about from Italy. Julio was indifferent and opaque. He was a cool and graceful young man who carried his great beauty lightly. And he had a personal elegance such as she had never known in anyone before.

He had never read anything but a prayer book, Willa wrote, so he had no stale ideas. As a matter of fact, he had very few ideas at all, but a good many fancies and feelings and a grace of expression that she found exotic, like listening to a new language. One night he told her the legend of the Forty Lovers of the Queen. She planned to write it as soon as she reached the place where it had happened, but it was not until many years later that she told the story herself in "Coming, Aphrodite!" Nevertheless, hearing it from Julio in his gentle, lilting voice must have been peculiarly seductive.

On the night before she left Winslow he took her to a Mexican dance. It was the prettiest dance she had ever seen, she wrote to Elsie, a curious pantomime in which a man danced with two women. Such music, such dancing, she wrote, and she was the only white person there. That night Julio serenaded her with a song that was meant to be sung by a married lady to her husband or her lover and she translated it into English for Elsie. She wished she could give it to her in Spanish, she wrote, with the stars and the desert and the dead Indian cities on the mesa behind it. Willa never used the song in any of her books or stories. Her poem "Spanish Johnny," which appeared in *McClure's* a few months after her return from the Southwest, was written earlier and was set on the long red grasses of the plains, not on the desert where Julio sang to her. A little of Julio is in the character of Johnny Tellamantez in *The Song of the Lark* and she may have been thinking of him when Johnny sings the refrain of an old railroad ditty: "For there's boys that's bold and there's some that's cold, / But the gold boys come from Spain, / Oh, the gold boys come from Spain."

Clearly, Willa was infatuated with her "gold boy" from Mexico, but just as clearly, his appeal was to her imagination rather than to her emotions. He was like all the things in the Naples museum, she told Elsie Sergeant, and having him about was like living in another civilization. She may even have been teasing Elsie a little for not coming with her on the trip. A Mexican sweetheart of her own would have done Elsie far more good than Tryon, North Carolina, Willa had no doubt of that. Yet an undercurrent of passion was certainly suggested, and years later, after Willa's death, when Elsie gave her letters from Willa to the Morgan Library in New York, Edith Lewis was distressed that she had included the letter about Julio. She may have felt that the letter showed Willa in an undignified light and Edith always considered it her responsibility to protect Willa's reputation. But it was also a part of Willa's life that Edith had not shared and she tended to be jealous when she felt left out, especially when the person in whom Willa confided was Elsie Sergeant.

In the end, Willa escaped from Julio's strong Egyptian fetters and from the Southwest. She was not utterly drunk up by desert sands, she said. All her life she feared being consumed by people and by places. When she was home she sometimes was afraid she would never get away, that she might die in a cornfield. She felt some of that same fear in the desert with its swift yellow excitement that threatened to carry her along with it. She was sitting beside the Rio Grande one day, she told Elsie, just outside the Indian village of Santo Domingo, when she looked up and saw a sentence from Balzac written in the sand: *Dans le désert, il y a tout et il n'y a rien; Dieu, sans les hommes.* Those words told her what she needed to know. People are the only interesting things in the world, but you have to come to the desert to find it out. Julio was a wonder but he couldn't for very long take the place of a whole civilization. You can play with the desert, love it, be quite tipsy with it, but there comes a moment when you must kiss it goodbye and go. Go bleeding, but go, go, go. It's a sudden change, like a norther, and when it comes you have to trek.

Perhaps the last lines of Julio's lullaby were in her thoughts on the day she said goodbye and put Julio and the desert behind her: *The eyes of night are shut / So thine should be. / The tired stars fade but / To dream of thee. / Dew-drenched blossoms spill / Their odors deep. / The heart of night is still— / Beloved, sleep.*

VIII

---　❖　---

The Fortunate Country

THE BOHEMIAN GIRL

On her way East, Willa stopped off in Red Cloud to see her family. Roscoe came down from the Wind River Mountains to spend a week with her but her sister Elsie was in Maine visiting classmates. She and Elsie had seen each other often during the last two years, however, while Elsie was in the East finishing her undergraduate degree at Smith College. A young woman now of twenty-two, in the fall Elsie was going to teach Latin in the high school at Lander, Wyoming, where Roscoe lived, and the following year she planned to do graduate work in Lincoln under Louise Pound.

For the first time in several years Willa was home for the wheat harvest. A great sight, she told Elsie Sergeant. After the desert the Bohemian country seemed more benign, somehow more manageable. Perhaps she was making peace with it at last. She felt that she had got the people and the country right in "The Bohemian Girl" which appeared in *McClure's* in August. The story was really like the people, Willa told Elsie Sergeant. She had seen them again and they were just the way she described them—"fat, rosy women who looked hot in their best black dresses; spare, alert old women with brown, dark-veined hands." And the land too was as she had described it. You could feel the undulation of the ground.

Willa put a lot of her own feelings into Clara Vavrika, her Bohemian girl, who must decide whether to go with Nils when he asks her to run away with him or to stay behind. "The great, silent country seemed to lay a spell on her. The ground seemed to hold her as if by roots . . . She felt as if her soul had built itself a nest there on that horizon at which she looked every morning and every evening . . ." Suddenly her restlessness and discontent are very dear to her and she recognizes that they are the things that have kept her alive. Nevertheless, like Willa, Clara breaks away and passes like a shadow on the great, still, indifferent land that never even knows she has departed.

Even before "The Bohemian Girl" was published Willa already had a new story in mind, one that was sure to terrify Ferris Greenslet, she told Elsie. It too was a foreign tale, but colder, chillier than "The Bohemian Girl." She had started it in Cherry Valley and went back to it again when she returned to Pittsburgh. Pittsburgh was still the place where she worked best. It seemed such a simple thing, she said, four walls in which one could write, and yet it was almost unattainable. Douglass had nursed a wistful hope that she might be able to work in his house in Arizona, but she couldn't and she knew he would never understand why. In Pittsburgh, however, in her study upstairs at the McClungs', with Isabelle close by to guard her privacy and provide for her every comfort, the "air" was right and she could work.

Meanwhile, things were not going well at the office and although her own situation was not affected, she was distressed for McClure. His trip to London had been a failure, Hattie McClure was in ill health and needed medical attention, and his own financial woes were mounting. Willa had written him a long and loving letter from Lamy, New Mexico. She could not make herself believe that at his age, with such a career behind him, everything should be going to pieces. She urged him to let her know when he was in New York and she would go to him from wherever she happened to be. She felt sure that if they talked things over, they would find a way out. He had always been so generous with others it made her not just sad but fighting Irish mad that he should be tormented and deviled about money.

In truth, there was little Willa could do to help McClure other than to reassure him of her loyalty and personal affection and promise to assist with his autobiography. By fall she was already occupied with what she called her writer's move. Her plan was to remain in Pittsburgh on leave of absence until January, go back to the office for five or six months and then give up the job for good and devote herself entirely to her writing. In the end, she never did go back to *McClure's*, although she continued to contribute articles and stories until the magazine finally went out of business during the First World War.

The remarkable thing is not that Willa was ready to give up her job, but that she stayed with it for as long as she did. Only her attachment to McClure himself and the skillful way he catered to her needs—the leaves, the trips abroad—explain those six years of essentially uncongenial labor. The magazine had changed her life. Without it she might have stayed behind in Pittsburgh or gone back home to Red Cloud. The experience had been important to her, but *McClure's* had served its purpose. She had been a good editor as she had been a good critic and a good teacher. Now she wanted one thing only, to be a writer, and a good one.

HER WRITER'S MOVE

One important requirement had still to be met before Willa's writer's move could be accomplished. Having decided she could afford to leave the office, she must now find a proper place to work.

The situation was delicate. She had given up her share of the apartment on Washington Place before she went out West in the spring. Besides, although she had managed to write *Alexander's Bridge* there, the place was uncomfortably cramped, "boxlike," Edith Lewis called it, and Willa had never thought of it as permanent. Willa's moods depended greatly on her surroundings and it never gave her pleasure to see even people she cared about under the wrong conditions. She liked to be in control of every situation, and that included choosing the right setting in which to see friends, as well as in which to work.

As always there was a place for her with Isabelle in Pittsburgh but it was a sad home now, shadowed by Mrs. McClung's hopeless illness. Willa also knew that she had been on her own for too long to go back to living under Judge McClung's parental roof. She could do it as a guest from time to time, she could still take refuge in her study there, but she could not give up her independence to become a daughter of the house again.

Meanwhile, she decided to let things take their course and she did not discourage Edith from apartment hunting for them. When Edith, in her competent fashion, came up with an ideal place—seven spacious rooms at Number Five Bank Street—Willa was enthusiastic. It was the perfect apartment, she told Elsie Sergeant, large, old-fashioned, roomy. It had a good fireplace, good windows, good woodwork and wide stairways. The location was a good one, too, off Greenwich Avenue and only two blocks from the Jefferson Market. "My apartment," Willa called it in her letters, but in fact it was "theirs," hers and Edith's. The arrangement was becoming permanent.

The brick, five-story house had originally been a wedding present from a rich brewer to his son. In time, with minor changes, the sumptuous dwelling was converted into an attractive apartment building, having two apartments to a floor. Willa and Edith made the three front rooms into one large living room and they had a separate dining room besides. The high-ceilinged rooms, on the second floor, were light and airy with windows facing east, south and west. There was no central heating and they depended on a coal grate to heat the living quarters, carrying the coal up the stairs themselves. They bought little copper-lined gas stoves for the two bedrooms and used gas for lighting also. It was a solid house, wrote Edith Lewis in her memoir, with thick walls that shut out the cold in winter and the heat in summer and shut out noise as well, which was especially important to Willa. They installed a telephone when they moved in but Willa always considered it an intruder.

When Elsie Sergeant came to visit a few months later, Willa was saying that this was where she hoped to live for the rest of her life. Elsie described the flower-filled rooms suffused with the fragrance of a spicy perfume. "My first impression of Bank Street was a sensuous one," she wrote. "Rightly so, for Willa's work was carried on, at any season, within a fragile screen of hovering flower-scents and gay petals." In winter there were always orange blossoms, camellias, violets and freesias. In spring "jonquils and narcissus stood on the table, and lilac and dogwood branched on the mantel." It was as if the blossoms in the garden at South Berwick had migrated to Bank Street, Elsie said.

Between them, Willa and Edith furnished the apartment modestly, buying what furniture they absolutely had to have at auction rooms on University Place where it was possible to get good bargains. Among the necessities were a few mahogany chests, a round mahogany dining table and some comfortable chairs. Several large oriental rugs gave the whole apartment a feeling of warmth and generosity. For their small library they found a local Italian carpenter to build low open bookshelves. Above the marble mantel in the living room Willa hung an etching of George Sand by Couture that she liked especially. She had also brought back photographs from Italy and she framed and hung them along with some Piranesis she had come across in a print shop in the Village that was going out of business.

Having made the apartment "fairly comfortable," writes Edith Lewis, "we gave no more thought to acquiring new things, or getting better ones than those we had. What money we had we preferred to spend on flowers, music and entertaining our friends." Certainly Willa's work habits were austere. She wrote sitting at a small writing table that held a sheaf of papers and a typewriter. Years afterward, close to the end of her life, Willa was staying in an inn on the tree-lined coast of Maine's Mount Desert Island. She was to be there for several months and the proprietor was trying to do everything he could to make her comfortable. She was a well-known author by then and he assumed she would have to have a desk to write on. He had secured the finest one available and had it waiting for her in her cottage when she arrived. "No, no," she pleaded. "Please take it out. I want a table, just a table, nothing more."

A DELIGHTFUL FRIEND

While the apartment was being made ready Willa spent the fall shuttling between Pittsburgh and New York. Rather to her surprise "The Bohemian Girl" was proving more popular than *Alexander*. She could not believe that people preferred reading about Swedish and Bohemian immigrants to civilized Bostonians or that they should care anything about Nebraska. It upset all her theories about what people wanted. Yet she knew the story's worth herself. Don't bother with *Alexander,* she told her old friend Louise Pound, but if she had the time, she hoped Louise would read "The Bohemian Girl." That was the real thing, at least as far as it went. She was already deeper into the country and the people than she had ever been before in the new story which she had begun in Pittsburgh. It had started out as two separate tales, "Alexandra's Story" and "The White Mulberry Tree," but she had decided to combine them. She hadn't finished it and already it was three times as long as "The Bohemian Girl." As always when she was working on a story, Willa was totally absorbed and to friends like Elsie Sergeant and Zoë Akins with whom she was accustomed to discuss her writing, she spoke of little else.

It was *McClure's* that brought Zoë into Willa's life. Their first exchange, however, was hardly prophetic of enduring friendship. Zoë had submitted some poems to the magazine and Willa had rejected them with a terse comment that they were not quite up to "our standards." She went on to wonder whether "Miss Akins" would ever settle down and do some hard work. Zoë was also writing plays and must have mentioned it because Willa replied that, as for herself, the older she grew the less she cared about the theatre. Indeed, it was a harsh, blunt-sounding letter and Willa admitted as much in a charming and generous apology. It was always hard for her to send things back when she liked them at all, she said, and she realized that she often sounded curt when what she felt was really just regret. Zoë had said kind things about *April Twilights* for which Willa thanked her. She liked young writers to care for her work; who wouldn't? She invited Zoë to send her some more poems and recommended that she read the work of Louise Imogen Guiney, particularly *A Wayside Harp.* Miss Guiney, said Willa, showed a richness and delicacy and a restraint that they could all learn from.

Zoë Akins began her career as an actress and a writer in St. Louis where she grew up and where her father was the postmaster. Clever and high-spirited, Zoë was a sophisticate in a conventional town, and her love affairs, her provocative dress and the rakish society in which she moved inevitably made her a target of local gossip. Sara Teasdale was also from St. Louis and had gone to school with Zoë.

According to Teasdale's biographer, the poet never forgot the sight of Zoë "with a cigarette, legs crossed in a delicately revealing fashion and her most Frenchy manner," entertaining friends with a reading of suppressed poems by Baudelaire that somebody had lent her. The inhibited Teasdale was amazed that Zoë and her set would talk openly of homosexuality and " 'excesses' " all the time, "as calmly as any ordinary happening."

Willa's more sober personality nevertheless responded to Zoë's spontaneity and she was drawn to Zoë Akins as she had once been drawn to the young Dorothy Canfield so many years before. Where Zoë was concerned, Willa was at her least judgmental and demanding. She might scold when she thought Zoë was being frivolous, spending too much money or shopping when she had a temperature, but Willa was more apt to be indulgent of Zoë than of anybody else she knew. For many years Zoë's great friend was the actress Jobyna Howland. Jobyna was a heavy drinker and it was one of Willa's worries that Zoë might drink too much also. Nobody could keep up with Jobyna, she warned Zoë. When Jobyna died quite suddenly, Willa sympathized with Zoë's loss, but she could not help feeling that a bad influence had been removed from Zoë's life.

Zoë's success on Broadway was one of Willa's greatest satisfactions and even when she did not totally approve of Zoë's sophisticated outlook, she recognized a fellow craftsman and found things to praise in Zoë's plays. For all Zoë's superficial smartness and theatricality, Willa took her seriously enough to talk to her about her own work. She also knew her own life would be much drabber without Zoë Akins in it.

"THE GENIUS OF THE DIVIDE"

It pleased Willa that Zoë loved "The Bohemian Girl." Her new story, Willa said, was about the same country, only this time it was the country itself that was the hero. Or the heroine, she added. The country was also the subject of a verse that would appear in *McClure's* in December, she told Zoë. Written in the fullness of her feeling for the land, "Prairie Spring" is one of the most beautiful poems Willa ever wrote and when her new story grew into the novel *O Pioneers!* she used it as an epigraph.

While she was working on the book Willa's mood kept changing. It was either pretty good, she told Elsie Sergeant, or an utter fizzle. It was all about crops and corn but it still seemed interesting, she thought. The best thing was that she had done with it exactly what she wanted, without being afraid of anybody. The story had told itself. She had merely taken the little themes that were hiding in the long grasses and worked them out as well as she could. That's what Anton Dvořák had done in the New World Symphony. She had learned only this past summer, she said, that Dvořák had spent several weeks in Nebraska in the early 1880s when it was truly a wild land. Progressives were always saying he had based his theme on Negro melodies, but Willa felt that she knew otherwise. She knew where the Largo came from, she told Elsie; it came from the long grass!

Nevertheless, she was nervous about the story. Perhaps it was not the sort of stuff that ought to be written down at all. Maybe it was too slow and sounded too much like J. R. Wyss's *Swiss Family Robinson*. Sometimes she thought that not more than six people would be interested in it. Yet it was the story she always wanted to write, and she was desperately afraid of failing with it. She had decided to name it after Walt Whitman's "Pioneers! O Pioneers!" and that too added to her sense of responsibility.

In early February she sent a copy of the manuscript to Elsie Sergeant, who was traveling in France, with a plea to give her an absolutely honest opinion. She was not sentimental about things just because she made them. She was aware the writing might seem glossy or too emotional and she encouraged Elsie to come down hard on the offending passage. Elsie was one of the few people whose judgment she cared a snap of the finger about and she awaited her verdict with terror. When Elsie wrote back from Avignon to say how much she liked the book, Willa's reaction was a great sense of relief and gratitude. "To Elsie Sergeant, the first friend of this book," she wrote in Elsie's copy. While she was gratified by her approval she also conceded that Elsie had put her finger on the book's weak spot when she said that the skeleton did not stand out enough. But that was because the country itself had no skeleton, explained Willa, no rocks or ridges. It was a fluid black soil that ran through your fingers. The country was all soft and that influenced the mood in which one wrote about it and the very structure of the story.

Ferris Greenslet was delightfully enthusiastic and Houghton Mifflin was rushing the book into print for publication in June 1913. Mr. Greenslet, said Willa, was just like all the men in the book; he had a weakness for the amber-eyed Marie Shabata. But it was surly, brooding Frank Shabata who satisfied her more than any of the other characters. In the beginning the critics were uncertain what to make of *O Pioneers!* Accustomed to thickly plotted, lengthy tomes, they were unprepared for Willa's subtlety and compression. What Elsie had called the absence of a skeleton seemed to some a lack of any form at all. To others it was less a novel than a series of vignettes, loosely strung together. In the end, however, few did not succumb to the intensity of feeling and the poetic power of the narrative.

The Boston *Transcript* spoke of the book's "magnificent sufficiency." *The Nation* called it "far above the ordinary product of contemporary novelists," and the New York *Times* said it was American "in the best sense of the word." One of the most glowing reviews came from Floyd Dell in the Chicago *Evening Post* who wrote, "It is touched with genius." The *Transcript* critic remarked on the "simplicity, almost severity of the treatment" and, indeed, the influence of Willa's beloved Vergil is marked throughout. It was not until she wrote *My Ántonia* five years later that Willa made the debt explicit, but it is clear that with *O Pioneers!* she too had brought the Muse into her country. In Alexandra Bergson, she had created a character to match the spirit of the Divide, the dignity, the strength, the sweetness and the simplicity. In the words of Carl Linstrum, the childhood friend who marries her, there had always been something "triumphant" about Alexandra.

Here is Alexandra returning home after a visit, singing a little Swedish hymn. Her brother Emil marvels at his sister's radiance: "For the first time, perhaps, since that land emerged from the waters of geologic ages, a human face was set toward it with love and yearning. It seemed beautiful to her, rich and strong and glorious. Her eyes drank in the breadth of it, until her tears blinded her. Then the Genius of the Divide, the great, free spirit which breathes across it, must have bent lower than it ever bent to a human will before.

The history of every country begins in the heart of a man or a woman."

It was just ten years since *April Twilights*, Willa's first book, had appeared. She had been almost thirty then. Now nearing forty, she was the author of three more books, one, a superb collection of short stories, and two very different novels. Age was not something that Willa ever took lightly. She was very conscious of the two-score mark. No longer young herself, she felt a special sense of sympathy for youth. *O Pioneers!* begins and ends with a kind of paean to the young. "Youth with its insupportable sweetness /," goes the epigraph, "Its fierce necessity, / Its sharp desire." Marie Shabata and Emil Bergson, shot to death by Marie's husband, the tormented Frank, die young, just like those other Cather characters who have to be protected from the erosion of time. "Why does it have to be my boy?" cries the heartbroken Alexandra, and Carl answers, "Because he was the best there was, I suppose." The last lines of the book read like a prayer: "Fortunate country, that is one day to receive hearts like Alexandra's into its bosom, to give them out again in the yellow wheat, in the rustling corn, in the shining eyes of youth!"

IX

❊

The Song of the Lark

At forty Willa's life was taking on the shape it was to have for many years to come. She and Edith were settled comfortably in Bank Street with a remarkable Frenchwoman, Josephine Bourda, to come in daily to cook and keep house for them. "She was an important figure in our lives," writes Edith Lewis. "Her personality was so pervasive and uncompromising that she created a sort of French household atmosphere around us . . ." Josephine's splendid cooking made it possible for Willa and Edith to entertain at formal dinner parties which became quite popular among their little circle. Later Willa was "at home" more informally on Friday afternoons, but even then a few favored guests would linger to sample one of Josephine's *specialités* at dinner. Willa made a point of inviting old friends from home who happened to be in New York, and it was not uncommon to find Nebraskans sipping tea with Boston publishers or with one of Willa's colleagues from *McClure's*. Willa never mingled much with other writers, but creative people interested her. She had met George Arliss, the distinguished British character actor who was to make a great hit in motion pictures, when she lived near him on Washington Place and she continued to see a great deal of him and his wife.

The artist Henry Hoyt, Elinor Wylie's younger brother, and his painter wife, Alice Parker, were also favorites. Talented and bright, from Willa's point of view they were also unique in that they were the only married people she knew who were both nice. She was tired of having to put up with stupid wives for clever husbands and vice versa, she complained to Elsie Sergeant. The Hoyts, however, were different; there was never any strain between them, no feeling of tension.

Sadly, that was not to be the case for very long. The marriage that Willa found so idyllic ended tragically. The vivid personality of Henry Hoyt that she and others found so appealing was blighted by severe mental illness. In despair Alice left him, taking their two small children with her. Henry's condition grew worse, his behavior became increasingly erratic and he spent some weeks in a sanatorium. And then, on August 25, 1920, at the age of thirty-three, Henry Hoyt tidied his brushes and his easel, put his papers in order, and turned on the gas in his studio at 37 West Tenth Street. William Rose Benét, who had shared the apartment with him and would later marry Henry's sister Elinor, wrote of the friend he dearly loved that "the individuality with which he did or said anything marked him out immediately from among all the other men I knew." Willa was fortunate to know Henry Hoyt during the few years of happiness he and Alice had together before disaster overtook them.

FREMSTAD

Sometime during the winter of 1913 a new enthusiasm entered Willa's life. She had been assigned an article for *McClure's* on three American opera singers, Louise Homer, Geraldine Farrar and Olive Fremstad. She enjoyed the interviews with Homer and Farrar but it was Fremstad who excited her imagination. To find a new kind of human creature, to get inside a new skin was like discovering a new country, only even more exhilarating, she told Elsie Sergeant. Fremstad's colleagues may have found the singer overbearing and difficult to get along with—she was famous for insisting on being paid in cash before each performance at the Metropolitan—no cash, no Fremstad —but Willa declined to be put off by Fremstad's temperament. What she discerned in the dramatic soprano from Minnesota who had been born in Stockholm were the very qualities she had first seen in the fearless women she admired on the Divide. To Willa, Fremstad was like those pioneers, suspicious, defiant, far-seeing. Her physical presence alone might have been intimidating. Unpolished and untamed, she had a way of sweeping things before her, of dismissing people and objects that bored her. The fierce concentration when she was working took all the energy she possessed and she had no interest in anything but music except when she was at her home in Maine. Then she cooked and gardened and chopped wood like the farm woman Willa always said she was.

Willa already had the outline of her next book in mind when she and Fremstad met. She had long planned to write about an opera singer and now she studied Fremstad, trying to discover what it was that transformed the stolid "battered" Swede into an artist. In her personal life Fremstad was intelligent but unimaginative. Her rooms were like Alexandra Bergson's, Willa told Elsie Sergeant, a mixture of Mission and gold leaf. There was no evidence of taste or even a feeling for comfort. Her secretary told Willa that when Fremstad took the apartment she had some twenty sets of furniture sent up before she selected the objects Willa found so agonizing. And yet she was a woman of supreme musical gifts, a brilliant Kundry, a magnificent Isolde and an unforgettable Elisabeth. Willa and Edith went to the Metropolitan again and again to hear her sing.

One performance in particular made a lasting impression on Willa. It was the day on which she went to interview Fremstad for the first time. Appearing by appointment at four-thirty, she found the singer arriving late from a motor trip. Fremstad was exhausted, barely able to speak above a whisper, and so pale and wan she looked like an old woman. Feeling sorry for the poor soul, Willa suggested it might be better to postpone the interview. Fremstad did not argue and Willa left the apartment, in time to join Edith and Isabelle, who was visiting, at the opera for a performance of *Tales of Hoffmann*. Before the second act began the manager came out with the announcement that the soprano had been taken ill but that Mme. Olive Fremstad had consented to sing in her place. Edith Lewis described the experience:

"The curtain went up—and there, before our astonished eyes, was Fremstad—whom Willa Cather had left only an hour before—now a vision of dazzling youth and beauty. She sang that night in a voice so opulent, so effortless, that it seemed as if she were dreaming the music, not singing it."

"'But it's impossible,'" Willa Cather kept saying. "'It's impossible.'"

Another time Willa saw Fremstad just after a performance as she was getting into her car. Willa was about to greet her but something stopped her and she merely bowed to Fremstad's secretary. The singer's eyes were empty glass, said Willa; she had simply spent her charge. Her personality renewed itself each night upon the stage, but the experience was draining and when the curtain fell she could not sustain the illusion she had created. Willa was to use that strange duality of the creative artist which she observed in Fremstad in the heroine of *The Song of the Lark*, Thea Kronborg.

THE WORLD WAS TOO MUCH WITH HER

Willa spent the spring and summer of 1913 in Bank Street working on articles for *McClure's*. She was also working with S. S. McClure on his autobiography, which began to appear in the magazine in installments in July. In Pittsburgh the suspense in which the family had lived for more than a year was over; Mrs. McClung was dead. Her gaiety had always been a counterpoint to the judge's somber nature and Willa knew that she would miss her. Isabelle, who had borne much of the brunt of her mother's suffering, needed a change of scene and came to stay with Willa for the month of April. When she went back to Pittsburgh Willa took the train to Boston for one of her hasty trips to see Annie Fields. Willa never liked to "visit" and rarely stayed longer than one or two days with Mrs. Fields or Mary Jewett. It was different in Pittsburgh; the McClungs did not consider her a visitor, nor did she think of herself as such. She did enjoy being a hostess, however, and having others visit her. In June, Elsie Sergeant stopped off in New York on her way home from Europe. It was then that Willa met her at the boat and brought her back to Bank Street for a splendid two-day visit. For something to be "splendid" in Willa's vocabulary meant that it was endowed with the very highest quality. It was her most superlative adjective.

The summer in New York took its toll on Willa's disposition. She was unaccustomed to working without relief and the heat was difficult to bear. It was not until September, however, that she could finally escape and make a long-planned trip to her Virginia birthplace with Isabelle. Even that began badly. She was uninterested in the social idiosyncracies of the people she had known when she was small, she wrote to Elsie. And she didn't think that even the most remote province in Russia could serve such wretched food. Since she refused to visit—most of the people she loved were dead—she was forced to put up with the accommodations. It would be different if she had a house. As it was, she had no patience for the romantic South with its elaborate courtesies and its eternally budding Southern belles. The male of the species was almost extinct from what she observed, or so cowed and housebroken he was useful only to carry wraps, dance and touch his hat.

Vacations were a trap anyway, she decided, and far more tiring than work. She was already bored with loafing and impatient to lead an industrious life again. The trip improved, however, when they went into the mountains. Walking in the woods always acted as a tonic to her and in Gore the woods were particularly fine. She and Isabelle walked at least six miles every day, rain or shine. Nevertheless, she was glad to get back to Pittsburgh and to work, although there were distractions even there. Edith McClung, Isabelle's sister, was getting married—her brother, Samuel Alfred Jr., was engaged to a niece of Andrew Mellon—and in the midst of all the excitement Sam McClure arrived for further work on his autobiography. Yet despite the interruptions Willa managed to write 28,000 words of her new novel by the time she returned to Bank Street in November.

Before she could settle down to work again, however, she received shocking news from Washington, D.C., that her cousin Howard Gore's Swedish wife, of whom she was so fond, had died during an operation in Paris. Her cousin had made a tragic trip across the ocean to bring her body back on the *France*. Even a temporary stop in work was a torture but Willa felt she had no choice but to go to Washington to spend a few days with the bereaved husband. On her return to New York there was an invitation from Mrs. Fields but she felt she simply could not take the time. The world was too much with her, she told Elsie Sergeant, and in desperation she had the telephone disconnected. Unfortunately that only resulted in Fremstad wearing down her $2,000 vocal cords trying to call Willa at 2036 Chelsea and always getting a brewery!

In early 1914 Willa was forced to put her work aside when she suffered one of the frightening and debilitating illnesses that would plague her in the years to come. This one did not seem serious to begin with, merely a scratch on the back of her neck under the hair, but the scratch became infected and, after seeing two specialists, Willa found herself in Roosevelt Hospital with a case of blood poisoning. In her own words she considered the experience a degrading one. The pain was abominable, she wrote to Elsie Sergeant, like forty toothaches in the back of her head. Her one interest while she lay in bed, wracked with fever, was to wheedle all the narcotics she could get from the doctors, but the side effect of the medication was a sense of such profound depression and disgust that she told Elsie she felt almost like a freak.

As daunting as the pain was the necessity of having the back of her head completely shaved. It was an ugly and agonizing business and made her feel unclean. She had always had a horror of deformity. As a youngster in Virginia she had been terrorized by the child of a servant who slipped into her room with a knife and threatened to cut off her hand. She had talked him out of it by distracting his attention, but the memory had haunted her. Mildred Bennett, in her introduction to Willa's collected short stories, cites several instances where a mutilated hand figures in her fiction. A shaved head hardly seems in the same category, but in Willa's morbid imagination she was as disfigured by the loss of her hair as if she had lost a limb. Illness not only took away precious working time, it also robbed her of her self-respect.

Her friends, once they were assured she was out of danger, did what they could to cheer her up. Isabelle had come in great alarm from Pittsburgh to be with her, and almost every day brought a visit from Fremstad, unannounced and unheralded, bearing armloads of spring flowers to the hospital. If it had been a railroad wreck one could enjoy it, had been Fremstad's comment, but a pin scratch was simply silly. The kindest thing that practical-minded woman did, however, was teach Willa how to tie a scarf over her bandages in the style of Elisabeth in the last act of *Tannhäuser*. Best of all, Fremstad showed so little horror at her ugly head, said Willa, that she too lost her horror of it.

In those days before the advent of antibiotic drugs a patient might be hospitalized for a month or more with blood poisoning. Willa could consider herself lucky to be home in three weeks. She still required care, however, and Isabelle remained with her until mid-March, when she no longer had to go to see the doctor every day. While she was in the hospital her room at Number Five Bank Street had been done over with a fresh coat of white paint and new wallpaper which made it a cheerful place to come home to. The world had turned a different color and she apologized to Elsie for the letters she had written when it seemed a cloud of madness must have descended on her brain. She was working a little every morning, she told Elsie, and managed to take a bus ride or sit in the park every afternoon when the weather was fine. She had even been to the opera twice, she wrote on March 19. She was feeling like a bear in winter, not a cross bear as she was during those dreadful weeks in the hospital, but a sleepy bear, stupid and contented.

In April the work that had gone so well earlier came to a halt. She reached an impasse in the story and for two weeks did no writing at all. Elsie Sergeant, who stopped in to see her, found her tense and low-spirited, although a visit to the Museum of Natural History, where an exhibition of Cliff Dweller finds had been assembled, seemed to lift her out of her depression, at least temporarily. For the most part she used the time when she was unable to write to talk to young singers, attend singing lessons and rehearsals and steep herself in the backstage operatic world that was the center of her heroine's existence. By the time she was working well again, she had learned a good deal about an opera singer's regimen and also about opera politics. In mid-April came the dramatic announcement of Fremstad's retirement from the Metropolitan and Edith and Willa were present at her final performance. She sang one of her great roles, Elsa in Lohengrin, and the audience brought her back before the curtain nineteen times for an ovation that lasted forty minutes.

In May, tired of New York, Willa went back to Pittsburgh. As always, Isabelle and Murray Hill Avenue worked their magic. Willa was perfectly happy there, working regularly, sleeping well and enjoying a limited but pleasant round of social engagements. She had plans to go out West but first she accepted Fremstad's invitation to visit her in Maine. At Fremstad's camp they did things every mortal minute except when they were asleep and even then, said Willa, she dreamed hard. Fremstad fished as if she had no other means of getting food; cleaned all the fish; swam like a walrus, rowed, tramped, cooked and watered her garden. It was the grandest show of human vigor and grace, Willa said, that she had ever watched. Fremstad was always claiming to want peace, she told Elsie Sergeant, but peace was where Fremstad was not! Willa was so exhausted that she stopped off in South Berwick to spend a few days recuperating in Mary Jewett's quiet garden.

July found Willa tramping through Wyoming and the Sangre de Cristo Mountains in Colorado, although she had barely gotten back her strength. Her deepest pleasure that fateful summer of 1914, however, came from a visit she made to the French and Bohemian country around her own home in Nebraska. For two weeks, with the thermometer often up to 110° Fahrenheit and never below 90°, she was on the road or in the fields, seeing old friends and places that she hungered for when she was in the East. The people were like characters in a book to her, she told Elsie; she had begun their story when she was little and it went on and on like *War and Peace*, rich and various and so much stranger than any invention of hers. It was probably on that visit that she renewed her friendship with Annie Pavelka, whom she had lost touch with, and met Annie's husband and her children.

WAR AND A CHANGE OF PLANS

When war broke out in August, Willa was in Nebraska. For the first time events in Europe and what she referred to as the Kaiser's high Napoleonic mood were too threatening to be ignored, and they found their way into her letters. It was impossible to get away from the war, she wrote to Elsie; everything one cared about seemed in danger and under test. At the same time there entered into her correspondence with Elsie a new note, at once sharp and somewhat petulant. She had always been interested in her friend's career and had been generous with editorial advice on where to submit her articles and which publishers were apt to be most receptive. But recently Elsie had become more independent. She had talked to Willa about a prospective new weekly magazine of opinion for which she had been approached to contribute articles on the French literary scene. Willa was suspicious of liberals like Herbert Croly and Walter Lippmann, who were among the publication's chief backers, and she suggested with some asperity to Elsie that she could hardly expect to go to Europe now with the situation as it was. She also thought it unlikely that there would be much talk of woman suffrage for a while, another of Elsie's preoccupations. And in her perverse way, she recommended to her Francophile friend that she read the last several issues of *Punch*. Willa said they had given her a fresh appreciation of the English, like reading *Henry Esmond* after Galsworthy.

This time when Willa returned to Pittsburgh from the West she brought Jack, her youngest brother, with her and enrolled him at the Carnegie Institute of Technology. A handsome, twenty-year-old six-footer, he had not been off the farm before, but he was totally lacking in self-consciousness and went on happily about his horses and his Bohemian neighbors. Since he never tried to talk of things he didn't know about, said Willa, there were no difficulties. And he always said, "Yes, ma'am," to older women, meaning anyone older than twenty, according to his indulgent sister. She had her work cut out for her, however, teaching him enough grammar to get by and correcting his pronunciation. The Nebraska farm speech, she explained to Elsie, was a slightly inflected grunt!

In October she made a hasty trip to New York to see some plays for an article she had promised to do for *McClure's*, but she hurried back to Pittsburgh as soon as she could get away. It had been a long while since she had spent so much time with a member of her family and she couldn't seem to tear herself away from Jack. She often dropped in on him in his rooms when she was out walking and she frequently brought him back to the McClung house with her. It did him good to be with older people, she decided, it made him more manly and serious. He told her he had never been so happy before and it gave her the greatest pleasure to watch him among her friends.

The war, however, kept intruding. A Belgian friend of Willa's wrote to say her family was starving in Brussels and she could get no word or money to them. The wife of the Belgian Minister of State, who was in America to raise money for her starving countrymen, gave a talk in Pittsburgh and impressed Willa with her personal gallantry as well as with the desperate situation in her country. She would not give Christmas presents, Willa decided, but would send money to the Relief Committee instead. She wished there were a way to rouse the little towns of Nebraska. If every family in Red Cloud alone were to give a dollar or a half dollar, it would mean so much.

In spite of the shadow of events abroad and her very real concern, it was a happy period in Willa's life. Pittsburgh for her was simply the best place to be. She could write better there, spend more time out of doors and even read more there than in Bank Street. She thought *The Awkward Age* was the best of Henry James, she wrote to Elsie; she and Isabelle had been reading it aloud. Her book was writing itself so well she was afraid to risk an interruption. Besides, she hated the thought of leaving Jack.

She broke away at last, however, and spent most of the winter and spring in New York. She was still there in June when the proofs of *The Song of the Lark* began to dribble in from Houghton Mifflin. Fortunately the weather was uncommonly benign, green and gray like London, or blue and breezy like Denver. She had never seen anything like it in New York before, she wrote to Elsie Sergeant. Elsie's article on the mistral had appeared, not in *The New Republic* after all, but in the sober *Century*, and Willa thought it was the best of her Provence studies, lovely, warm and satisfying. She also shared with Elsie her enthusiasm for a new poet whose work she had encountered for the first time. She did not always react so favorably to new forms of expression—Elsie had tried in vain to interest her in the Cubists—but in *North of Boston* she heard a voice that thrilled her. Robert Frost, she wrote to Elsie, was a "really, truly poet" with something fresh to say and a style that showed great individuality and verve. Out of the unlikeliest material he fashioned real verse, tight and tough and with a rhythm all its own. When *A Boy's Will* came out, she thought it even finer than *North of Boston*. She never ceased to admire Frost's poetry and she liked the man himself when she met him.

In July she had plans to go to Germany on an assignment for *McClure's*. Isabelle was to accompany her but at the last minute

Judge McClung had a change of heart. He became nervous about the war situation and refused permission. Willa did not want to go alone so the trip was canceled. It was another reminder of Isabelle's dependence on her family. Whatever transpired between the friends, when Willa arranged to go out West instead, she went with Edith, not with Isabelle. The abrupt alteration of her plans proved to be a watershed in Willa's life. She and Isabelle never made another trip together. After this she traveled everywhere with Edith and only when Willa went to see her family, were she and Edith separated.

THE ANCIENT PEOPLE

Years later Edith could still recall every detail of that first trip with Willa to the Southwest. They rode the Burlington from Chicago, traveling all day across Nebraska and the Colorado desert to Denver. Alongside the train the Republican River wound "like a snake back and forth from one side of the tracks," and orange milkweed bloomed along the banks. From Denver they went by the narrow-gauge road of the Denver and Rio Grande, over the Continental Divide to Durango and from Durango as far as Mancos. Their destination was the Mesa Verde, some twenty miles or so from Mancos, and they engaged a team and driver to take them there. On the evening before they started on their journey, Willa paid a visit to a brother of the famous explorer of Southwestern ruins, Dick Wetherill. The discoverer of the cliff dwellings of the Mesa Verde, Dick Wetherill had been murdered by Indians in 1910, but five years later his brother, probably Clayton Wetherill, was still living in Mancos. He told Willa the story of how Dick Wetherill had made his great discovery, how he swam the Mancos River on his horse and rode into the Mesa after lost cattle, to find an entire city of cliff houses that had been hidden there for centuries.

The Mesa had always been a place of myth and mystery. When Willa wrote about it in "The Enchanted Bluff" she had not seen it, but it haunted her imagination. A prehistoric people had lived among the clouds on its green-capped summit for centuries before moving into villages of stone, cut with exquisite detail and workmanship right into the caves and cavities of the porous rock. What catastrophe of man or nature caused them to abandon their stone dwellings is unknown. The semi-nomadic Utes and other Indians who came later and roamed the Mesa and its canyons preferred to make their camps in the valleys and along the river streams.

Willa and Edith spent a week in the Mesa Verde, exploring the ruins. They devoted one entire day to the great tower Dick Wetherill had named the Cliff Palace. Ten years later Willa described it in *The Professor's House*, recreating the moment when Wetherill, in the person of Tom Outland, first set eyes upon the ruin. "Far above me, a thousand feet or so," goes Tom Outland's story, "set in a great cavern in a cliff, I saw a little city of stone, asleep." He saw the pale houses first, perched on top of each other, their flat roofs, narrow windows and straight walls. Then he saw the tower, its swelling, beautifully proportioned shape, its color the red of winter oak leaves in the sunlight. "The tower was the fine thing that held all the jumble of houses together and made them mean something . . . Such silence and stillness and repose—immortal with the calmness of eternity . . . It was more like sculpture than anything else. I knew at once," says Tom to the professor, "that I had come upon the city of some extinct civilization, hidden away in this inaccessible mesa for centuries, preserved in the dry air and almost perpetual sunlight like a fly in amber, guarded by the cliffs and the river and the desert."

Willa and Edith had an adventure of their own that was reported widely, even in the New York press. The two women had set out with a strange guide to visit an unexcavated dwelling known as the Tower House. Their trail took them down into Soda Canyon where, in many places, they had to hang from a tree or rock and then drop several feet to the next rock. To return the same way without ropes would have been impossible, and their guide said he would take them back a different route. They walked for several miles before he admitted he could not find the trail. "The sides of the canyon were everywhere precipitous," wrote Edith Lewis, "and for several feet beneath the rim the bare rock generally overhung." They had come to a point where Cliff Canyon opened up at right angles to Soda Canyon and, as evening was coming on, Willa decided that she and Edith would wait at the intersection of the two canyons while their guide went in search of help. They found a large flat rock at the mouth of Cliff Canyon and settled themselves comfortably, probably with the idea, said Edith, that they would be able to spot rattlesnakes if they "came racing up."

They spent four or five hours on the ledge, sitting in the dark, not talking, watching the full moon as it rose above the canyon's rim, before they were rescued by two men their exhausted guide had sent to find them. The trip back was arduous but the men, diggers from an archaeologist's camp, proved splendid guides over the rocks. "Occasionally we would stop for a short rest," wrote Edith, "and then the men would quickly build a little fire, for an icy wind swept down the canyon at night." At two in the morning they reached the archaeologist's camp. "Our two diggers then went out into the pasture, caught a couple of horses, hitched them to a wagon and drove us back to [our] camp."

Edith thought it had been the most rewarding part of their whole trip for Willa, and Willa herself said that although it had been a rough twenty-four hours, she had never learned so much in a single day before, and most of it had been glorious. Four days later, just a little bruised, she was back on her horse and ready to test herself once more against the Mesa's massive power and brutality. It was a country that drove you crazy, she told Elsie, and that was all there was to it. She was not pleased, however, with the newspaper account of the incident. She had an aversion, that in time became almost obsessive, to revelations of her personal life. She was reticent even in her letters to her closest friends. She had not mentioned to Elsie, when she wrote to her about the Western trip, that Edith would be with her. Now to find the story of her "rescue" in newspaper headlines seemed a distasteful invasion of her privacy that caused her intense distress.

Before returning to New York, Willa stopped in Red Cloud to see her family while Edith went directly back to Bank Street. Edith had an office job she could no longer stay away from and, besides, she never visited Red Cloud with Willa. The little town found Willa's relationships with women too ambiguous for comfort. The Cather family came to accept the way Willa lived in New York and members of the family, especially the younger generation of nieces, were frequent visitors at Bank Street, but it was understood that when she went home to Red Cloud, Willa went alone.

THE SONG OF THE LARK

In October, Willa's new book, the story of an opera singer's life, was published by Houghton Mifflin. She had dedicated *O Pioneers!* to the memory of Sarah Orne Jewett. She dedicated *The Song of the Lark* to Isabelle McClung with a charming verse expressing her gratitude to the friend in whose home so much of the book was written. Willa had been happy working on the story and she found herself missing the companionship of her heroine to a degree that surprised her. She may not have realized how much of herself had gone into the character of Thea Kronborg. Thea's career as a singer, her training and the development of her art were inspired by Willa's association with Olive Fremstad, but the young Thea and the circumstances of her early years are drawn from Willa's own life. In the book she placed Moonstone in Colorado, but the town is plainly Red Cloud. Thea had pulled at her, Willa said, until she sometimes felt that she belonged to Thea more than Thea belonged to her.

It is in their ambition, the passionate desire to do great things, that the three personalities fuse, Fremstad's, Willa's and the fictional Thea's. "Living's too much trouble unless one can get something big out of it," Thea says to Dr. Archie. "I only want impossible things. The others don't interest me." Willa saw it as a kind of fierceness in the blood. She recognized it in Fremstad, she knew that she possessed it too, and she had given it to Thea.

The crucial episode in Panther Canyon that marks the transition from the Thea who is Willa to the "Kronborg" who is Fremstad, came directly out of Willa's trips to the Southwest. Fremstad had never been in the country of the ancient people but Willa knew it well, and she made Thea's visit to the cliff dwellings the same liberating experience for her heroine that it had been for her. To live among the fragments of pottery that had survived the centuries stretches one's own past, Thea realizes. And she begins to understand that "one ought to do one's best, and help to fulfill some desire of the dust that slept there." The potsherds were like fetters binding one "to a long chain of human endeavor." The question in Thea's mind is one that had teased Willa since her college days and her essay on Thomas Carlyle. "What was art but the effort to make a sheath, a mound in which to imprison for a moment the shining, elusive element which is life itself?" wrote Willa Cather in *The Song of the Lark*.

The critics were divided about *The Song of the Lark* but, in general, they were kinder than the author was herself in later years. She had come to agree with her English publisher, William Heinemann, who turned it down, though he admired it personally, because he considered she had taken the wrong road in trying to tell everything about everybody. The full-blooded method was not natural to her, he felt. At the time Willa was too close to her story to be grateful for such criticism. "One is always a little defensive about one's last book," she said. But for a new edition in 1937 she made extensive revisions and eliminated some of the details her critics had found burdensome. "Too much detail is apt, like any other form of extravagance, to become slightly vulgar," was her verdict.

It was a harsh judgment to make on a book that had given her so much pleasure in the writing. Edith Lewis thought the faults Willa found in the book came from her having worked "too directly from immediate emotions and impressions." None of her other novels was written in the same fashion. Yet it is the sense of the author's intense personal involvement with her heroine that makes *The Song of the Lark* so appealing and helps to explain why generations of readers have taken Thea to their hearts. Few novelists have written more perceptively about small town society and family relationships than Willa Cather did in *The Song of the Lark*. And few novels have evoked more sympathetic understanding of what it was like for a radiant and gifted girl to grow up in the narrow provincialism of the Middle West in the early years of the century. As always, Willa was ambivalent about her own small town. But Red Cloud liked *The Song of the Lark*. She was home when the book came out and flattered by the enthusiasm of her neighbors. Though she had written a portrait of an artist, she liked to think the heart of the story was not the development of Thea's genius as much as it was what Thea got from Moonstone and what she gave back to it.

The musical aspects of the book had come out well, she thought.

She had shown the galley proofs to a well-known critic who told her the points she made in Thea's singing lessons were correct and very telling to anyone who had worked with voices. Knowing nothing about the story, he could tell from her early lessons exactly the characteristics Willa wanted Thea's voice to have in later life. Another compliment, and perhaps the most rewarding, came from the formidable Madame Fremstad herself. Willa was afraid Fremstad might be furious with the liberties she had taken, but when they met in Lincoln after a recital the singer was glowing with excitement. She had bought a copy of the book in Brentano's in New York, she said, and had read it on the train coming West. It was the only book she had ever read about an artist, she told Willa, in which she felt there was something doing in the artist. Willa might think it was old stuff to her, but she knew just what Thea was up against and she kept wanting her to pull it off. Willa felt as if she had received a decoration.

X

❀

Loss and Change

TWO DOORS CLOSED

The year 1915 began and ended with the death of someone close to Willa. In February, Annie Fields died, bringing that association to a close. Sometime during the next twenty years a garage would go up on the site of 148 Charles Street, but Annie Fields was spared the destruction of her gentle world. She "rounded out her period, from Dickens and Thackeray and Tennyson, through Hardy and Meredith to the Great War, with her standards unshaken," Willa wrote, and she died "in that house of memories, with the material keepsakes of the past about her."

In October, Judge McClung died. Willa was bereft. Not only did his death deprive her of the stern affection and protection of the judge—he had made her a member of his household against all the disapproval of his Presbyterian relatives—but, more ominously, the breaking up of the house on Murray Hill Avenue spelled the end of her cherished haven, the place where Isabelle sheltered and sustained her and where she worked so well. Nevertheless, her sadness at the death of her two old friends, with all that their loss implied, seemed almost inconsequential compared to a blow that was soon to befall her.

NOTHING WOULD EVER BE THE SAME

In the unhappy days following her father's death, Isabelle had turned to a friend who had been a frequent guest in the McClung home during the past year. A suave and cultivated young man, Jan Hambourg came from a family of Russian Jews who had become British subjects and lived in London and Toronto. Michael Hambourg, the father, taught music and had raised his three sons to be musicians. The eldest, Mark, became a well-known pianist. Boris was a violin-cellist, and Jan, a violinist. Together they gave concerts as the Hambourg Trio. Willa had heard Mark Hambourg when he played in Pittsburgh on his first American tour in 1899. She had been dazzled by the virtuosity of the twenty-one-year-old performer as well as by his intellectual attainment. He had made her think of Stevenson's remark about Kipling, that all the fairy godmothers must have been present at his christening. But she had not found his temperament congenial.

Now Mark Hambourg's younger brother, Jan, had appeared on the scene and was about to carry off Willa's Isabelle. It seemed a strange match. Jan was thirty-four and Isabelle was nearing forty when they were married in New York on April 3, 1916. The Reverend John Haynes Holmes officiated at the ceremony in the Church of the Messiah and a reception was held at Sherry's. Samuel A. McClung, Jr., gave his sister away and many Pittsburgh friends came East to attend the wedding. For Willa, on the best terms that one could figure out, as she said of it, it was a devastating loss. Isabelle's marriage was hard and always would be, she told Elsie Sergeant, and Elsie said that when Willa spoke of it her face was bleak, her eyes spiritless and drained of expression. To Dorothy Canfield Fisher Willa said flatly that she and Jan were not congenial. He was the kind of strong personality one either liked very much or not at all, and she did not like him.

How could Willa possibly like Jan Hambourg? He was taking from her the most important person in her life. She had always seen

Jews as intruders and despoilers and while there was no way to make the scholarly Jan Hambourg fit her stereotype of a coarse and predatory race, still, on the most intimate level, Willa must have seen his relationship with Isabelle as a violation. It was almost more than she could bear. For more than fifteen years Isabelle had always been there for her. Willa would travel, go home to Red Cloud or to New York, but always she had returned to Pittsburgh, to the house on Murray Hill, to Isabelle. For all that time, Pittsburgh had been her anchor. Now she, to whom change of any kind was abhorrent, was faced abruptly with the necessity of altering her working patterns and, more acutely, her habit of emotional dependency on Isabelle. It is no wonder that she cried that nothing would ever be the same again.

Jan Hambourg could not possibly have been unaware of the anguish he was causing Willa. He knew her position in the household and how close she was to the woman he was marrying. Besides, Isabelle had her own ideas; she had fought her parents in the past in order to have Willa with her, and she did not intend her marriage to make a difference to their friendship. Why couldn't Willa come to live with her and Jan? Nothing need change and they could go on as they always had. Jan was essentially a kind man. On more than one occasion he invited Willa to make her home with them. While the war was on he and Isabelle would be in the United States and Canada. Afterward they would probably live in Europe. Wherever they were, he hoped that Willa would be with them.

Willa never did accept Jan's offer as a permanent arrangement, but she was a frequent guest in the Hambourg home. When Jan and Isabelle were in New York, Willa went with them to concerts and the opera, and they regularly attended her Friday afternoons in Bank Street. Over the years her attitude toward Isabelle's husband became somewhat more accommodating. After her initial resistance she confessed to Carrie Sherwood that she and Jan got on well together, although she would not allow herself to be totally won over. Like most people, she said, he had many good qualities, once you got to know him. Willa dedicated two books to Jan Hambourg, *A Lost Lady* and *The Professor's House*, though the dedications were removed in later editions. Nevertheless, in the end, try as she might to overcome her resentment of Isabelle's husband, the publisher Alfred

Knopf, reminiscing more than sixty years later, could state emphatically that Willa Cather did not like Jan Hambourg.

In the months immediately after Isabelle's marriage Willa was in too much turmoil to start a new book. She had to write to keep her sanity, but it was short stories and not another novel that occupied her. She had begun writing short stories again during the period after the completion of *The Song of the Lark*. They were uncharacteristic, facile tales of New York office life. Now she turned her attention once again to the leading ladies of the concert and opera stage, but the background does not have the warmth of the vibrant world she created for Thea Kronborg. There is a hard edge to the stories of Cressida Garnett and Kitty Ayrshire, a suggestion of depleted patience and a bitterness impossible to conceal. In two of the stories major roles are played by Jews. The portrait of Miletus Poppas, the Greek Jew who is Cressida's Svengali in "The Diamond Mine," is mean-spirited, but so is the portrait of Cressida's relatives who, in the end, outdo even Poppas in their greed. But if Willa relents in the case of Poppas, she indulges in what can only be described as an outburst of anti-Semitism in her portrayal of Siegmund Stein, the unscrupulous garment manufacturer who compromises Kitty Ayrshire in "Scandal." The clever plot does not conceal the author's savagery. Her raw wounds are painfully evident.

Poppas and Stein are in no sense modeled on Jan Hambourg but they probably owe their very existence to the residue of anger Willa felt toward Jan that she could not express in more direct ways. She did have Jan very much in mind, however, when she created Louie Marsellus, Professor St. Peter's son-in-law in *The Professor's House*. Louie too is a Jew. Thoughtful, attentive, assured, he has all the attributes of Jan Hambourg. With whatever irony Willa dedicated the novel to Jan, the artist was firmly in control when she wrote it and she made Louie a fully rounded character, not a caricature. Louie's values may not be the professor's, but he is a likable fellow nonetheless and his father-in-law is fond of him.

The decline of the old values that she cherished and that the professor represents, preoccupied Willa for many years before she sat down to write *The Professor's House*. The dislocation in her own life had coincided with the war and the disappearance of a world she loved. More and more, in the difficult months of 1916 and 1917, she was obsessed with the suffering and heroism of people whose stories she heard from European friends. The misery let loose in the world seemed to have its counterpart in the misery in her own heart.

A GOOD FIRST MATE

Nevertheless, Willa was resilient. She had made a good life for herself in New York and she had her work. She also had too much pride to give in to her despair. Whatever her feelings, it was not her nature to display them. She was helped as well by having Edith, and she came to depend increasingly on Edith's presence. The spunky, independent Edith was as unlike Isabelle as Willa was herself. But she was a good companion and Willa was comfortable with her. As the years went by the attachment grew stronger, and if the romantic image of Isabelle persisted, it did not mean that Willa felt any less tenderness for Edith. Their life together was undoubtedly a marriage in every sense. But Willa was too conscious of her ties to home and family, and too much a conservative Midwesterner herself, to live openly with Edith. And, in this regard, she never changed.

In Greenwich Village she would have seen many avowed lesbian couples, but it would not have suited Willa to expose her own most intimate relationship. She and Edith had their own rooms, respected each other's privacy and maintained independent professional lives. Elizabeth Sergeant wrote that seeing them together reminded her of a comment William Allen White had once made, that a captain must have a first mate who does a lot the captain never knows about to steer the boat through rocks and reefs. It is an apt description of Edith's role in Willa's life, but it does not tell the whole story.

A CHANGE OF SCENES

In the summer of 1916 Willa and Edith went out West again, spending a month in Santa Fe and Taos. Taos was a quiet Mexican village then, not yet discovered by the Mabel Luhans and the Witter Bynners. It was difficult to reach and the accommodations were limited and tended to be fairly primitive, but the one adobe hotel proved to be clean and comfortable—in the Southwest you need a cool, shadowy adobe house to come back to after you've been out in the blazing sun, Willa told her friends. The food was poor but possible and the water, though questionable, produced no ill effects. "It was not a tourist country then," wrote Edith Lewis. "The distances were too great, the roads too rough, to get about easily by team . . . It was difficult to get any information about places not on the beaten track; one picked it up here and there from drivers, railroad men, an occasional Indian trader. Willa Cather had a great talent for this sort of discovery; a name, a sentence let drop would start her off on some ambitious new exploration." Saddle horses could be rented cheaply and she rode around the hilly countryside, visiting the homes and churches of the Mexicans and Indians as confidently as she used to ride on the prairie to see her European neighbors.

When she finally tore herself away from New Mexico she went up to wildest Wyoming, as she called it, to visit Roscoe and his family in the Wind River Mountains. The camping was good but the country was tame compared to the Southwest. She enjoyed being with her brother and his interesting German wife, however, and the children were adorable, a girl of five and twin babies, also girls. The house was cozy and attractively situated with two rivers flowing through the backyard, one of them filled with trout. To the east there were fine sand hills and on the west was the Wind River that gave its name to the mountains where she and Roscoe rode. She had time for only a brief visit in Red Cloud before getting back to New York in late August.

The following year Willa made the round trip between New York and Red Cloud twice. The journey was becoming routine although it wearied her increasingly as she grew older. She usually managed to be home for Christmas and she spent three or four weeks with the family in the summer. She would take the New York Central to Chicago and stay overnight there with Irene Miner Wiesz. When Irene was not available there were other friends in Chicago, many of them former classmates, whom she enjoyed seeing. The following afternoon she would board the Burlington for the second half of the trip. In New York, Edith Lewis took charge of getting tickets. In Chicago it was Irene who made Willa's travel arrangements and reserved a lower berth for her on the Burlington Number One. Her father usually met her at the station in Hastings and they drove to Red Cloud together.

In June 1917 Willa received an unexpected invitation to come to Lincoln to accept an honorary doctorate on the occasion of the University's semicentennial commencement. She and Edith Abbott, who was Jane Addams' assistant, were the first women ever given honorary degrees by the University. Willa was to receive many such honors in her life but none gratified her quite as much as her first Doctor of Letters from the University of Nebraska, because it came from that school and that state. The commencement was followed by ten exhausting days of parties and visiting with old friends. There was an innocent sameness to the festivities, said Willa, the green lawns, the oldish girls in white dresses, the stranded professors from Maine, New Hampshire, Rhode Island and Vermont. After Lincoln she had another round of calls to make in Red Cloud, which was experiencing one of the worst heat waves in years. The amorous sinners of Dante were no more persistently scourged by fire, she wrote to Elsie Sergeant, than the corn-dwellers of Nebraska.

In the fall she was back again in Red Cloud. Her mother was seriously ill and it fell to Willa to take charge of the household, cooking and keeping house for a family of eight. Margie was helpful but she had never learned to cook. On the whole, Willa told her friends, she rather enjoyed it. She thought she'd got the secret of good pastry at last and, one thing was certain, she'd never be intimidated by a kitchen range again. It was characteristic of Willa that although she enjoyed, and even demanded, comforts in New York, she begrudged no effort where her family was concerned. If Fremstad could roll up her sleeves and cook and clean, so could Willa Cather. She had to confess, however, that once her mother was better she was not unhappy at the prospect of having Thanksgiving dinner in Bank Street.

ANOTHER PLACE TO WRITE

During the summer of 1917, between her two trips West, Willa was persuaded to visit Isabelle and Jan in the little village of Jaffrey, New Hampshire, where they were vacationing for several weeks.

Two Pittsburgh friends had rented a house called High Mowing and Willa and the Hambourgs stayed nearby in the Shattuck Inn. Willa was strongly attracted to the New England countryside. There was not the drama or the novelty of the Southwest, but she found that Jaffrey gave her something that was even more important. It was another place, associated with Isabelle, that offered her the peace and privacy she had depended on so much in Pittsburgh. To her intense pleasure, she found that she could work there.

After that first visit she went back often, in later years spending the autumn months there. The Shattucks who ran the inn, and later their daughter and her husband, the Austermanns, who took it over, saw to it that she was protected from intrusion. "The fact that she was a celebrity meant, I think, little to them," wrote Edith Lewis; "they were too much New Englanders for that. They had a great admiration and liking for her character." The two small attic rooms that Willa and Edith occupied over the years had sloping ceilings and reminded Willa of her room at home. From the windows she could look out on woods and pastures and in the distance the brooding shape of Mount Monadnock. When it seemed there might be too many guests in the inn, her friends at High Mowing put up a tent for Willa in their meadow where she could work in seclusion. It proved an ideal arrangement. She loved the half mile walk every morning from the inn to the tent. She would work there at her table for two or three hours and in the afternoons go for long walks in the woods.

Edith Lewis understood just what Jaffrey meant to her. "The fresh, pine-scented woods and pastures, with their multitudinous wild flowers, the gentle skies, the little enclosed fields, had in them nothing of the disturbing, impelling memories and associations of the past—her own past. Each day there was like an empty canvas, a clean sheet of paper to be filled. She lived with a simple sense of physical well-being, of weather, and of country solitude."

MY ÁNTONIA

It was in Jaffrey, during that first visit, that Willa wrote much of *My Antonia*. The idea for the book had taken shape gradually in the year since Isabelle's wedding. Even before she went to stay with the

Hambourgs in Jaffrey the acute pain of the marriage had diminished somewhat and the world had begun to look bright again. Elsie Sergeant was living in New York at the time and she recalled Willa coming to tea one afternoon, "flushed and alert from one of her swift wintry walks." She took an apothecary jar that Elsie had filled with orange-brown flowers of scented stock and placed it in the center of a small antique table. "'I want my new heroine to be like this,'" Elsie recalled Willa saying, "'like a rare object in the middle of a table which one may examine from all sides.'"

Her visits home in recent years had reawakened her interest in the friends of her childhood and her imagination had fastened in particular on Annie, the daughter of the suicide Anton Sadilek. Seeing Annie with her husband and children the summer before had brought back vividly those days when, as the Miners' hired girl, she had been an important part of Willa's life. Annie became for her, she said, the embodiment of all her feelings about the early years and the immigrants she had known on the prairie. She supposed she was destined to write *My Antonia* if she ever wrote anything at all.

Ferris Greenslet said of *My Antonia* that it gave him "the most thrilling shock of recognition of the real thing" of any manuscript he had ever seen. But Willa was not yet a writer who received immediate attention and the critics did not rush to embrace *Antonia*. The front page of the New York *Times Review of Books* for Sunday, October 6, 1918, ran a banner headline to announce the "latest works of fiction" by Albert Payson Terhune and Willa's old friend Dorothy Canfield, among others. On an inside page appeared an unheralded review of *My Antonia* by Willa Sibert Cather that did little more than summarize the plot of this almost plotless novel, calling attention to its carefully detailed picture of daily life on the farm. Indeed, Dorothy Canfield's collection of short stories, *Home Fires in France*, drew far warmer notices generally than Willa's *My Antonia*. There were exceptions, of course, even at the beginning. The critic of *The Nation*, contrasting the portrait of Ántonia with Elizabeth Robins' *Camilla*, a sophisticated story of divorce and adultery on both sides of the Atlantic, concluded in Willa's favor that her style had "distinction, not manner." It was the style of "an artist whose imagination is at home in her own land among her own people . . ." The Chicago *Daily News* told its readers that "if . . . you want to brush away stiff-jointed literary puppets and live for a while with real people, you will read and give thanks for *My Antonia*." The New York *Sun* put the case for the book and its author in language that proved prophetic: "If a writer is so blessed as to be able, only one or two times, to recapture the past and rekindle the ancient fires he will leave a name remembered and loved from generation to generation. Of living American writers there is particularly one who has this great gift."

In time, the chorus of acclaim for *My Antonia* was to overwhelm the naysayers among Willa's critics. In 1934 when the International Mark Twain Society held a contest to decide on the most memorable and representative American novel of the century, the majority vote went to *My Antonia* and won a silver medal for its author. Typically, Willa had misgivings about how Red Cloud would receive the news. She sent one of the announcements to Carrie but warned her against showing it to the town cats, as she called them, or putting it in the local paper. It would only make people go out to look Annie over and decide that Willa was a liar.

People could not seem to understand, she said to Carrie, that a story was not made out of legs and arms and faces of an author's friends and acquaintances, but out of an emotion or an excitement. She did not describe actual people; it was their effect on her as a child that she tried to communicate. And while Annie is the book's central character, *My Antonia* is woven out of many people's lives. These were the personalities and events that had teased her imagination, just as Sarah Jewett knew they would, and out of them Willa wrote her most human story. "There is a time in a writer's development," she wrote long after, "when his 'lifeline' and the line of his personal endeavor meet." They met most memorably for Willa Cather when she wrote *My Antonia*.

The scenes that stay longest in the reader's mind are those that Willa too recalled most vividly or that had been described to her when she was a child: the long railroad journey from Virginia; Mr. Shimerda's burial at the crossroads; Pavel's horrifying tale of the wedding night in the old country, when his sled was being pursued by hungry wolves and he and Peter tossed the bride and bridegroom out to appease the animals and save their own skins; Blind d'Arnault making his way to the piano in Mrs. Gardener's Boys' Home Hotel;

Ántonia and Mrs. Harling working quietly together in the Harling kitchen. And who can forget the waltzing feet of the hired girls? "To dance 'Home, Sweet Home,' with Lena," says Jim Burden, "was like coming in with the tide."

The drowsy afternoon when Jim and the girls share a picnic on the river ends with one of Willa Cather's most enduring images, the great black figure of a plough standing alone in a field on the rim of the horizon. "The sun was sinking just behind it. Magnified across the distance by the horizontal light, it stood out against the sun, was exactly contained within the circle of the disk; the handles, the tongue, the share—black against the molten red. There it was, heroic in size, a picture writing on the sun."

The writing in *My Ántonia* has a buoyancy and freshness that is perfectly suited to the simplicity at the heart of Ántonia and her story. "When a writer once begins to work with his own material," Willa Cather was to write, "he finds that he need have little to do with literary devices. He comes to depend on something else—the thing by which our feet find the road home on a dark night, accounting of themselves for roots and stones which we had never noticed by day." *My Ántonia* was important to Willa. Writing it helped her to escape from the war and from the changes taking place in her personal life. She had found a way to go home. It was her genius that she made of her personal past a place not only that she could return to, but that would draw readers from all over the world, long after she was dead and towns like Black Hawk had been left behind to dwindle in the hot Nebraska sun.

While she was working on *My Ántonia* Willa received word of Mrs. Miner's death. It touched her to realize that she had been thinking of Mama Miner almost every day for weeks, trying to recall certain tricks of voice and gesture for the character of Mrs. Harling. She hoped that Carrie and Irene would like the portrait of their mother as Willa first remembered her. And she hoped they would not mind seeing their own names in print along with hers, because she intended to dedicate the book to them. One has to live about forty years, she wrote to Carrie, to find out which things are temporary excitements and which are the lasting affections. Their friendship, she believed, was simply one of those that last for life and as the years went by it became more precious.

In a letter to Will Owen Jones, who always interested himself in her career and who was one of those to whom Willa was not afraid to speak frankly, she had some provocative things to say about *My Antonia* and about Jim Burden in particular. Her narrator had to be a man of worldly experience, she said, for only those who knew the world could see the parish as it was. Sarah Jewett had said that, of course, and it became one of Willa's tenets. Her next comment is more personal and curiously suggestive. She had deliberately made Jim Burden a man without children to plan for and one who was not fortunate in his domestic life. If he were, she went on, he would not dwell upon the years of his first youth either so minutely or so sympathetically. It is impossible to escape the implication that Willa also felt unfulfilled in her adult life. Why otherwise, she seems to ask, would she too have continued to recreate those scenes of childhood over and over again? She paid a price for clinging to the skirts of her art. She did not regret it, but she was aware of it.

XI

※

Endings and Beginnings

America's entrance into the war brought changes in the daily life of Bank Street. Because of the fuel shortage Willa was forced to move out of her study and write in the dining room so that she and Edith would only have to keep one coal grate going. Anything that disrupted her work was difficult for Willa and adding to the general inconvenience was the fact that Josephine was sick for a month and Willa's time was taken up with the iceman and the laundryman and other domestic concerns. Then, before Josephine was well enough to come back to work, Willa fell ill herself with bronchitis. Again Fremstad came to the rescue, sending her car down to Bank Street every evening to bring Willa up to her apartment on Eighty-sixth Street, where she gave her a good dinner and a little music before sending her home again.

Willa had tried not to think about what was going on in Europe, but now she and Edith followed the war news avidly. It was always individual experiences that mattered most to Willa; she could never grasp a canvas that was too crowded. The tragic deaths in training camps seemed especially cruel and senseless. When she was home during the summer of 1918 there were seven funerals in one week of boys sent home from Camp Dodge, Iowa. The most astonishing news of all, however, came from Elsie Sergeant. Just a month before the armistice Elsie had been touring a battlefield with a group of correspondents when an innocuous-looking souvenir turned out to be a lethal grenade. The official French guide, a woman who was standing beside Elsie, was killed instantly when it exploded. One of the French officers had an arm blown off and Elsie's legs and ankles were filled with steel fragments. When Elsie's letter describing the event reached her, Willa was speechless with amazement. She was ashamed to recall how she had fussed about her shaved head and how degraded it had made her feel. Compared with Elsie's cruelly shattered bones it seemed a trivial thing. Her heart went out to her poor friend who had cared so much for France and was now suffering for it in her own way. It seemed as though she were fated to have the war get through her skin, said Willa, even as it had already tortured her mind and heart.

Still, life went on and Willa never liked to dwell on infirmities, her own or anyone else's. The *Mauretania* arrived in New York on December 2 with five thousand soldiers on board, the first big homecoming of troops. One met them all about the town, she told Elsie, in hotels and theatres, and they were all that one could want them to be, jolly boys, modest and awed at everything. "Ours," she said, were so much nicer than the French, though she quickly added that the French were fine fellows too. But the Americans seemed to her wonderfully, unexpectedly picturesque and so much more alive than anything she had ever seen before. New York, she said, was never so gaudy and extravagant as during those early postwar days. Meanwhile, there was the soaring cost of living to be coped with. Elsie, lying in pain in a hospital in Neuilly, must have grimaced at her friend's characteristic lament that the monthly meat bill was to weep over!

A NEW PUBLISHER

Undoubtedly *My Antonia* suffered by coming out in October 1918, when the country was occupied with the ending of the war

and the return of its soldiers from abroad. Sales were poor during the
first months, but Willa did not think it was entirely because the public's attention was on other things that the book was doing badly.
For some time she had not been happy with the way her books were
treated at Houghton Mifflin. She had no complaint to make with
Ferris Greenslet, who had always been a staunch supporter, but it
seemed to her that others in the company did not share his enthusiasm for her work and that, as a consequence, her books were not
properly promoted. To do her best work she needed to feel appreciated and she knew she would have to find another publisher.

Since 1916, when she had come upon an attractive edition of
Green Mansions bearing the imprint of Borzoi Books, she had been
following the career of its young publisher, Alfred A. Knopf. "He
seemed to be doing something new and doing it with conviction,"
she said years later. One of her quarrels with Houghton Mifflin had
been the way her books were designed and illustrated. The appearance of a book was of great importance to Willa and she liked the
look of the early Borzoi Books. Fanny Butcher, the Chicago critic
who was a friend of hers, suggested still another reason for Willa's
interest in Knopf. She saw him frequently at concerts, apparently
as much immersed in music as she was herself. "I decided that any
young man who cared enough about music to neglect his business to
go to an afternoon concert was someone whom I would be happy to
have as a publisher," Fanny Butcher recalled her saying.

Having made her choice, at least in her own mind, she had next to
meet the man himself. Accordingly, one morning in the early spring
of 1920 she took the West Side subway up to Forty-second Street
and walked in, unannounced, to Knopf's informal office in the Candler
Building. Up to that time he had made no gesture in her direction, as
she expressed it, but she was not unknown to him. While recuperating from flu in 1918 he had been attracted by what he described as
"an oddly dignified advertisement" for *My Ántonia* and had read the
book with great admiration and enjoyment, although he had never
been west of the Missouri. The author's unexpected appearance in his
office a year later, he said, was "one of those things a publisher
dreams about but doesn't often experience." Their conversation that
first morning was entirely impersonal. They talked about books they
liked and some they didn't. He told her what he had been doing,

how he had gone to the Metropolitan Museum to find exactly the right shade of blue for a book of Chinese poems. "We haven't much money to spend here," he told her, "but we'll take any amount of pains with a book." Those were the words that meant everything to Willa. Before she left his office, "without so much as a hint from him that he would like to have [her]," she asked him to be her publisher. It was the beginning of the closest professional relationship in Willa's life.

In Edith Lewis' opinion Willa's choice of Alfred Knopf as her publisher influenced her career more than any action she ever took, save for writing novels in the first place. Knopf described their relationship in his own way: "From small beginnings it grew into something so close that to the day of her death some twenty-seven years later we never wavered in our respect and affection for each other."

* * *

Willa's first book for her new publisher was a collection of short stories rather than a novel. Knopf told her it was not customary for a publisher to accept stories without getting a commitment for the author's future work, but Willa felt she owed the next novel to Houghton Mifflin. After that, she said, Knopf would be her publisher. As it happened, she never did go back to Houghton Mifflin, although she and Ferris Greenslet remained good friends. *Youth and the Bright Medusa*, the title of her first Knopf book, includes the best of *The Troll Garden*—"A Wagner Matinee," "The Sculptor's Funeral," "A Death in the Desert" and "Paul's Case"—with the addition of her most recent work, "The Diamond Mine," "A Gold Slipper" and "Scandal." "Coming, Aphrodite!" which H. L. Mencken ran in *The Smart Set* in August 1919 as "Coming, Eden Bower!" became the first story in the book, which was published the following year. Willa's own mood may be judged by the common theme that links the tales, the passion of the artist to create and the thwarting of his desire by a hostile and mercenary society. She repeated the dark verse of Christina Rossetti's that had served as one of the epigraphs for *The Troll Garden:* "We must not look at Goblin men, / We must not buy their fruits; / Who knows upon what soil they fed / Their hungry, thirsty roots?" The "bright

Medusa" of success lured its victims every bit as relentlessly as the Goblin men with their evil fruit. Not just society's indifference, but its material rewards, could be the enemy of art.

The book's reviews more than justified Knopf's faith in his new author. Inevitably she had her detractors—even at the height of her career Willa was not to everybody's taste—but the majority of critics were excited by the stories of big dreams and bold ambitions and found much to admire in the style. *The Bookman* praised her faculty of getting under the skin of her characters and her firm sense of detachment. *The Dial* considered that "as studies of success, of the successful, of the victims of big careers . . . above all of the quality of ambition in women," the stories were unsurpassed. And *The Nation* described the book as constituting "one of the truest, most serious and most poetical interpretations of American life."

A FRIENDSHIP RENEWED

One of the most generous reviews came from Dorothy Canfield Fisher, writing in *The Yale Review*. "She is a plant of our own American garden to her last fiber," said Dorothy of her old friend, "an American writer to whom European culture is but a food to be absorbed and transformed into a new product, quite different, unique, inimitable, with a harmonious perfection of its own." Praise from Dorothy meant more to Willa than just another good review. For one thing, no other critic was as important in Red Cloud, which had always loved Dorothy and her mother. But more personal reasons also played a part in Willa's pleasure and the gratitude she felt toward Dorothy. With her warm admiration so wholeheartedly expressed, Dorothy bridged an awkwardness that had grown up between the two friends. Married since 1907 to John Redwood Fisher, Dorothy was already a prolific author herself, having published *Gudrun*, her first novel, the same year that she was married. Her fifth book, another novel, *The Brimming Cup*, came out less than a year after *Youth and the Bright Medusa* and by 1922 there was a sixth.

It was natural that the two women, writing their novels of small-town American lives, should be considered rivals. Willa said her readers insulted Dorothy's and Dorothy's insulted hers and that Dr. Tyndale's life was one long warfare against Dorothy's more numerous fans. But though she was popular with the public and the critics responded to what one of them referred to as "the rich, sweet philosophy" of her books, Dorothy Canfield Fisher never attained Willa Cather's stature as a writer. Fanny Butcher said she lacked greatness but had "fineness," and Rebecca West called her "one of those saved by works, not grace." For her own part, Dorothy stayed cheerfully impervious to either envy or resentment. She only wanted others to recognize her friend's genius as she did.

To have Dorothy in her life again was a great joy to Willa, although their communication was largely through the mails. She wished they could see more of each other and talk as they used to. She knew that there were years when she had been sullen and difficult, like Paul in "Paul's Case." She was mixed up in those days, but doing her own work had straightened her out and she invited Dorothy rather charmingly to try her on for size; she was more reasonable now. With a complete lack of self-consciousness—Freud never penetrated Willa's view of the world—she told Dorothy that she had been dreaming about her. She rarely dreamed, she said, at least not the kind of convincing dreams one remembers on waking. But in her vivid dreams of Dorothy there was no change in their relationship, no misunderstanding. When she awoke there was not the bitter feeling of being fooled, but only a sense that a delightful part of her life had been revived for a while. She was sure it meant they would be in touch.

Repeating the theme she had so often stated in her letters to Carrie and other old friends, Willa questioned whether our endings in life were ever as glowing as our beginnings. She had been thinking a great deal about such things in connection with a new book that had been stirring in her mind since the last days of the war. Though she had never seriously contemplated writing a war story—it was not like Willa to allow public events to enter into her private imaginative life—the death of a cousin in battle at Cantigny in May 1918 had pierced her isolation and started a train of association that grew into an obsession. She felt that she must write about her cousin in a way that would give meaning to his life and his death. For the next four years, his story became her life.

CLAUDE

Grosvenor, known as G.P., Cather was the third and middle child of Aunt Franc and Uncle George. He was ten years younger than his cousin Willa and she had sometimes taken care of him when he was a small boy. She felt a kinship with him at the same time that she was repelled by his behavior. It was to escape him and his kind that she wrote at all, she told Dorothy, in whom she increasingly confided about her work. He couldn't escape the misery of himself except in action, yet it seemed that whatever he did turned ridiculous. He had no use for her way of escape and for many years they avoided each other. But she happened to be staying on his father's farm when the war broke out and for the first time in a long while she and G.P. talked. When she heard that he had been killed, leading his men in the first American offensive, she could not shake the notion that anything so glorious could have happened to one so disinherited of hope. She kept thinking about him, believing that some of her died with him in France and that some of him was in her still. After his death his mother let Willa read the letters he had written home and they brought him close again. At times she felt that G.P. had been in her blood for so long, she might never be herself again.

She wanted to call the new book simply by its hero's name, but Knopf considered *Claude* a poor title. Willa remained stubborn until she had a talk with Fanny Butcher, who agreed with the publisher. Butcher persuaded her to change the title, but although the book became *One of Ours*, for Willa it was always *Claude*. Claude is selling well, she would say. Or Claude might do something handsome for his ma. She had greater personal affection for Claude Wheeler, the ordinary Nebraska boy who went off to war and died bravely far from home on a French battlefield, than for any of her other characters. He took over her life so completely that every morning when she awoke she would think, how is Claude today? And paraphrasing Shakespeare's Romeo, she would tell herself, if he were well, nothing could be ill. She said once that she wished she could spend the rest of her life writing about him. During the winter of 1918 it happened that a number of Western boys were in Polyclinic Hospital in New York. Willa visited them and listened to their stories. To her they all were Claude.

Other soldiers came to call on her at Number Five and she encouraged them to tell her about their experiences while they were still fresh in their minds. When Elsie Sergeant came home, hobbling on crutches, Willa besieged her too to talk about the war. Elsie, however, did not entirely sympathize with Willa's curiosity. She could not escape the feeling that the war, which had injured her so cruelly, was only a story to Willa. It seemed to her that Willa showed a lack of sensitivity to the true cost of those four years. It was obvious to Elsie that Willa and she were never likely to agree about the war, about politics or the League of Nations—Elsie was a confirmed Wilsonite—and that books, as always, remained their safest topic.

But if Elsie Sergeant would not indulge her, Willa found other sources of human interest stories about the war. The newspapers were filled with dramatic acts of heroism. In her personal copy of Victor Chapman's *Letters from France*, which had been sent to her by The Macmillan Company in advance of publication, she pasted pictures of flyers and Legionnaires she had clipped from the New York *Times*. One such photograph of an American "Ace," with eighteen German planes to his credit, was accompanied by an Associated Press dispatch describing in detail the flyer's burial "near a certain French village." Three American and three French aviators had carried his flag-draped coffin, the newspaper reported. While the service was being read at the grave, "one American aviator after another planed down from the sky, his motor off, until he was just overhead. Each threw out great bunches of red roses, which floated down on the coffin and the bared heads of the officers and caps of the soldiers, who were drawn up at attention." Still another clipping, slipped between the pages of Chapman's book, told of the suicide following domestic troubles of an American veteran who had served with the British Flying Corps and had made a daring escape from a German prison. For seventy-two days he had traveled behind enemy lines before reaching neutral Holland. In a suicide note to his wife he wrote that in the end he had discovered he was just "a little piece of clay."

There is no doubt that stories such as these fed Willa's own romantic view of the war as an opportunity for young men to redeem dull, ordinary lives by dying gloriously in the service of their country and her great ally. It was still another variation of the theme that the good die young. Victor Chapman, whose letters were important in providing her with details of army life in training camp and on the battlefield, had been struck down himself at Verdun, the first American aviator to be killed. In a memoir of his son, printed with the letters, John Jay Chapman recalled that Victor had wanted to enlist at once, as soon as war was declared, but that he had discouraged the idea. It was his wife, Victor's stepmother, who saw something in the young man's voice and manner that gave her "a vision of a ruined life" if he did not go. "I had rather see him lying on the battlefield than see that look on his face," she said of the boy she dearly loved. In the end even the grieving father wrote, "It was the cause that made a man of him. Here was a thing that was big enough."

In 1917 Charles Scribner's Sons published a posthumous volume of Alan Seeger's poems with an introduction by Willa's friend, the critic William Archer, who wrote that the young poet, who died the year before in the village of Belloy-en-Santerre on his country's Independence Day, was to be envied: "Youth had given him all that it had to give, and he met the death he had voluntarily challenged, in the cause of the land he loved, and in the moment of victory." Seeger himself had written in his "Ode in Memory of the American Volunteers Fallen for France" that France had given them *that grand occasion to excel, / That chance to live the life most free of stain / And that rare privilege of dying well.* In *One of Ours* Willa wrote that Claude "used enviously to read about Alan Seeger and those fortunate American boys who had a right to fight for a civilization they knew."

Willa worked on *One of Ours* steadily through 1919 in Bank Street most of the year and in Jaffrey in the fall. Her stay at the Shattuck Inn was longer than she had anticipated because while there she came down with a serious attack of influenza and was confined to her room for several weeks. Always somewhat fierce-tempered when she was ill, this time she had a stroke of luck that helped to brighten even the days she felt most miserable. The local doctor who attended her turned out to have served as a medical officer during a flu epidemic on board a troopship crossing the Atlantic. Willa plied him for details of the experience and the doctor was so impressed with his patient's interest that he allowed her to borrow his diary of the voyage. The doctor's journal was the most important source of information for Claude's trip to Europe on the *Anchises*.

Willa was still weak when she returned to New York and her father came East to be with her until she was strong again. For both of them it was a rare opportunity to spend unbroken time together and Willa treasured his visit. She worked at Number Five in the early months of 1920, finishing most of the Nebraska portions of the book, but for Claude's experiences in France she felt that she must personally acquaint herself with the scenes that meant so much to her hero. Edith took a leave of absence from her job and together they sailed for France in June, landing at Cherbourg. For the next six weeks they lived in Paris at the Hôtel du Quai Voltaire on the Left Bank. Edith wrote later that Willa said she wanted to live in the Middle Ages, and so they did, rarely venturing beyond the Tuilleries except to get money or see a performance at the Opéra-Comique.

Isabelle and Jan arrived sometime during the summer and took Willa with them on a tour of battlefields. Edith went to Italy to visit friends. Willa joined her in the South of France and they traveled back to Paris slowly, spending a few more weeks at the hotel. It was already mid-November when they returned to Bank Street. The seventeen-day voyage home was one long storm, according to Willa. Edith suffered terribly from seasickness and had to stay in bed for ten days, and Willa came home with a sprained ankle. Willa set to work at once, finishing *One of Ours* in the spring of 1921.

STILL A NEBRASKAN

By then Isabelle and Jan had come home from Europe and were living in Toronto where Willa went to stay with them for almost two months in early summer. Isabelle fitted out a little study for her and she worked there happily under the eaves. She had revisions to make in a French translation of *My Antonia* that was to be serialized in *La Nouvelle Revue Française* the following spring. It wasn't dreadful, she told Elsie Sergeant, but it wasn't first-rate either, and she was having trouble with the language. Typically, Willa let Elsie have her unvarnished opinion. To Laura Hills she wrote warmly about the splendid translation and described the publication as quite the best of the French literary magazines. It made her feel rather "chesty," she said, using one of her favorite expressions. She had other cause for pride as well. Sinclair Lewis gave a lecture in Toronto in which he said so many admiring things about her books that three reporters were at her door before breakfast the next morning. In fact, she told Carrie once, Lewis never missed a chance to throw her a bouquet and she hoped Carrie would forgive him *Main Street*. Not many writers were able to see anything good in another writer's work, she added.

Willa did not spend August as usual in Red Cloud that summer. Her mother, who knew the heat made her short-tempered, wrote almost begging her not to come home until it was over. Instead Willa went to Grand Manan, the island in the Bay of Fundy, barely seven miles off the coast of Maine, where she and Edith would one day build a house. No one had lived on Grand Manan until the late eighteenth century when loyalists from New England, fleeing the Revolution, took refuge in New Brunswick. From there a few of the hardy ones found their way to Grand Manan. The French, the English and the Americans all claimed it at one time, but in 1817 it was officially recognized as part of New Brunswick, Canada. When Willa knew it first, the fishermen of the island still referred to their countrymen on the mainland as "foreigners" and few tourists cared to brave the primitive accommodations that were all the island provided.

Willa loved it from the first moment she set eyes upon it. Wrapped in fog, the island, with its cliffs rising two to three hundred feet, had the appearance of a ghostly fortress, mysterious, remote, impregnable. Yet behind the cliffs stretched acres of woods and meadowlands with bright green grass, sweet-smelling field flowers and a profusion of wild strawberries. Edith and Willa stayed in a guesthouse at Whale Cove run by a Miss Sarah Jacobus. The next summer they rented a small cottage known as Orchardside, but they continued to have their meals with the other guests at Whale Cove.

14. The George P. Cather house, north of Red Cloud on the Divide, was the setting for *One of Ours*. Here it is today, viewed on a tour of Catherland.

15. The author of *April Twilights* in Pittsburgh, her hair piled becomingly on top of her head like a Gibson Girl, the tie a characteristic addition to her wardrobe. (Willa Cather Pioneer Memorial Collection, Nebraska State Historical Society)

16. & 17. Judge Samuel Alfred McClung and his wife, Fannie Merritt McClung. Isabelle's mother was a gentle, kindly woman. The judge was stern but Willa was fond of him. For five years she lived with the McClungs as a daughter of the house. (Photos courtesy of Samuel A. McClung III)

18. The horse carriage had not yet disappeared when Willa took her first apartment on the south side of the Square, seen here at Sullivan Street, in one of the modest red brick buildings where artists and writers had their studios. (Courtesy of The New-York Historical Society, New York City)

19. On the north side of Washington Square the great marble arch served as a gateway to the spreading city beyond. But New York's first families still resided in their "very solid and honorable dwellings" in an atmosphere of Georgian tranquillity. (Courtesy of The New-York Historical Society, New York City)

20. Willa's friend Elizabeth Shepley Sergeant noted her fondness for brightly patterned fabrics and elaborate dress. In this informal pose Willa's strong face is softened and her gaze is dreamy and a little wistful. (Courtesy of The New-York Historical Society, New York City)

21. The managing editor of *McClure's* in all her dignity, c. 1912. The necklace was a gift from Sarah Orne Jewett. (Willa Cather Pioneer Memorial Collection, Nebraska State Historical Society)

22. Every captain needs a first mate: Edith Lewis was Willa's companion for forty years.

23. Willa thought the painter Léon Bakst was quite the most interesting man around. She enjoyed sitting for him in his beautiful studio. Paris, October 1, 1923. (Willa Cather Pioneer Memorial Collection, Nebraska State Historical Society)

Willa is wearing the mink coat that she ght with money from *The Professor's House*. said it was the first valuable thing she had owned and she quickly had it insured.

25. The Menuhin children were among the chief treasures of her later years, Willa often told her friends. Here Yehudi stands between Hephzibah, left, and Yaltah, possibly in the park where Willa often went walking with them. (The Bettmann Archive, Inc.)

26. S. S. McClure (left) was eighty-seven when he and Willa posed with Theodore Dreiser and Paul Robeson in 1944 at the annual awards ceremony of the National Institute of Arts and Letters, just three years before Willa's death. (Willa Cather Pioneer Memorial Collection, Nebraska State Historical Society)

During their stay at Grand Manan, Willa and Edith read the proofs of *One of Ours* and in September when she was at home in Red Cloud she received a telegram from Knopf congratulating her on a "masterly, perfectly gorgeous novel." She gave Dr. Tyndale a copy of the telegram, knowing that praise of her was always a delight to her old comrade. While at home she was invited to give a talk at the Women's Club of Hastings before an audience that included her mother and two of the Miner sisters, Carrie Sherwood and Mary Creighton. If her listeners expected a literary lecture they were disappointed. She took as her topic the "Conservation of Native Timber" and spoke in eloquent defense of the cottonwood tree, esteemed in France and in New York's Central Park, but in Nebraska on its way to becoming extinct. In Paris they held *fêtes* in honor of the cottonwood and called it "summer snow" when the cotton began to fly, but in Red Cloud and Hastings, said Willa, they chopped it down.

Before returning to New York she stopped off in Omaha for a festive two days during which she addressed the Fine Arts Society at a luncheon in the Hotel Fontenelle and that evening was guest of honor at a dinner given by the League of Women Voters. Carrie went with her from Red Cloud and Irene came from Chicago for the occasion. In her talk to the Fine Arts Society she gave vent to her disenchantment with the Nebraska of the present, denouncing the tendency in the West toward conformity and rigid conventionality and deploring the rage for novelty. "What better reason can you want for staying in a house than that you have lived there for forty years? New things are always ugly." On a lighter note, she denied to a reporter for the Omaha *Daily News* that she lived in Greenwich Village. "The village doesn't exist," she said. "How could it in these times when the last cellar is empty?" To the *Daily Bee* she spoke words of reconciliation: She was not an Eastern, Western, Northern or Southern writer. She was a Nebraska writer, first and foremost a Nebraskan.

The presence of Carrie and Irene made the Omaha visit especially sweet to Willa. Nothing on earth, she wrote afterward to Carrie, strengthens one's arm like having one's old friends be a part of one's lifework. It was particularly so for her, she said, because her old affections were the very springs out of which her best work flowed. She had been with her family and childhood friends for two months and on the train back to New York she wrote to Dorothy Canfield that there was no spot in the world she liked so well as the Divide. You know it's *your* place, she said, when your tummy turns over. She had gone to live among writers and musicians to learn her trade, but her heart never got across the Missouri River.

THE WORLD BROKE IN TWO

Knopf waited to bring out *One of Ours* until September 1922, when he thought the timing was propitious. Willa had urged him all along not to let word get out that the book touched on the war. By underplaying Claude's experiences as a soldier, she hoped readers would see the novel for what she meant it to be, the story of a boy's life. Knopf tried unsuccessfully to sell serial rights to all the major magazines. But the war aspects discouraged interest. On the one hand, the public was surfeited with war. And on the other, the Nebraska portions of the book were not compelling enough to make editors like George Horace Lorimer of the *Saturday Evening Post* willing to take a chance with it. Lorimer "would have none of it," wrote Knopf. A little of the dreariness of Claude's life crept into Willa's prose and even Sinclair Lewis was forced to confess that "from Miss Cather" the book was disappointing.

Actually, Willa was subjected to some of the harshest criticism she would ever receive, for *One of Ours*. Much of it echoed Elsie Sergeant's sentiments that she had romanticized a cruel conflict. By 1922 the image of young men going proudly to their "rendezvous with death" had lost its appeal to a generation that had seen the fighting in the trenches at firsthand. A new spirit of isolationism was settling on the land along with a revulsion against war. "She did not know the war for the big bow-wow stuff it is," wrote Sidney Howard in *The Bookman*. "She should stick to her farms." H. L. Mencken was kinder, but he said essentially the same thing. He thought the first half of the book deserved to rank almost with *My Antonia*, but that the second half, the part about the war, dropped to the level of the

Ladies' Home Journal. Edmund Wilson, who later was to grant that Willa Cather was one of the only writers to bring any real distinction to the life of the Middle West, nevertheless considered *One of Ours* a total failure.

Although her dissenters were vociferously outspoken, they were, happily, in the minority. Most of the reviews around the country were glowing. Burton Rascoe in New York's *Tribune* was typical when he called *One of Ours* "the best sustained and most powerful novel Miss Cather has written . . . the high-water-mark of her achievement as a literary artist." The reviewer for the influential New York *Times* was Dorothy Canfield who, not unexpectedly, found the book "amazingly rich . . . rich as no other living American could write." Readers would not suspect, of course, how close the critic was to the author and especially to *One of Ours*. Months before the book came out Willa had asked Dorothy to read the proofs and check the French sections in particular. Dorothy, said Willa, was the first to know her Claude except for the poor three, as she called them, Edith, Isabelle and Jan, who had had to adjust their lives to his needs.

One of the most savage attacks on the book came from Heywood Broun in a review that appeared in the New York *World* on September 13, 1922. Not only did he not like *One of Ours* as well as *My Antonia*, he didn't like it at all. He too felt that Willa had sentimentalized the war. "The hero loses his life and finds his soul. We happen to believe that there is such a thing as setting too high a price even upon souls and war is too high a price," wrote Broun. Yet the same newspaper, on the very next day, carried a decidedly contrary opinion: "Nothing has been written on this side of the Atlantic since we have been a nation that can approach in value, both as art and history, this version of America's performance in the great war." Once again a friend had risen to Willa's defense; the review was written by Zoë Akins.

It took a reviewer who was not a friend to see through to the essential bleakness of Willa's attitude toward the postwar world and to recognize one of her recurrent themes. The novel was a tragedy, wrote L. M. Field in the *Literary Digest's* International Book Review, not because Claude was killed but because its point of view was "that in this world there is no place for the idealist, that just because Claude was fine and sensitive, clean-souled and aspiring, the best that can be wished for him was death."

Yet for all the controversy it aroused, this disputed novel became Willa's first best-seller and won for her the coveted Pulitzer Prize in 1923. Even the sales of *My Antonia* picked up significantly after *One of Ours* was published. With *One of Ours* Willa achieved at last that measure of financial security she had hoped for when she gave up her job at *McClure's* for a full-time writing career. Though she was always careful about money, from this time on she earned enough not to have to worry about finances. Together she and Edith could afford to live comfortably if not extravagantly. She could buy theatre and concert tickets, entertain her friends and travel as she pleased. She could also help out her old Nebraska friends, people like the Lambrechts and the Pavelkas, when they came upon hard times. She was never one for large charities. She preferred to give gifts to individuals she knew who needed help rather than to institutions. In later years, when she no longer went back to Red Cloud, she would send a check at Christmas and ask Carrie to buy the dried fruits, coffee and other provisions for the families she had known as a child. But in the twenties and early thirties she sent the packages herself to as many as fourteen or fifteen families who had come to depend on her generosity. And she made it possible for more than one farmer to hold on to his farm during the Depression by helping with the mortgage payments.

THE CATHERS CELEBRATE

In late November 1922 Willa went home for her parents' fiftieth wedding anniversary. She had not been well in New York and she was grateful to Irene for traveling with her from Chicago. It would also relieve Isabelle, who always worried about her, to know that she would have Irene in Red Cloud. The visit proved to be one of the happiest times in Willa's life. Her parents were in good health and seemed "absurdly young." A local newspaper commented that the Cathers had never lost a child and now they were surrounded by grandchildren as well as by their seven sons and daughters. With *One of Ours* published so recently Willa could not help but attract attention along with her father and mother. Red Cloud especially enjoyed the portraits of Mrs. Wheeler and Mahailey, clearly recognizable as Aunt Franc and Margie. If Uncle George saw himself in Nat Wheeler and did not feel flattered, his niece could always fall back on her disclaimer that she never wrote about real people!

Willa considered Claude and his mother the best compliment she could pay Nebraska. She hoped that *One of Ours* proved to her own people how much she loved them. Carrie wrote so effusively that Willa immediately sent the letter to Isabelle in France. Isabelle would know how much it meant to her to have touched her old friend's heart so deeply. It was good, too, to be able to give pleasure to her parents. She feared that she had not been a very thoughtful daughter, that she had always been too full of her own ambitions and had taken her parents for granted. She knew that her mother, in particular, had often suffered on her account and she was happy that she could make it up to her a little. For once she had written a book that did not set the neighbors' tongues wagging and her mother did not have to apologize for her.

Nevertheless, 1922 was an exhausting year for Willa. She had been ill a good part of the time and for a while seemed on the verge of mastoiditis. The doctors thought her tonsils might be the cause of the infection and she had gone to the hospital to have them removed. After a difficult operation that weakened her severely she spent some weeks recuperating in a sanatorium in Pennsylvania, but was ill again on her return. Once again her reaction to illness was that same curious sense of shame she had experienced when her head was shaved. She consoled herself with the thought that seasons of good-for-nothingness came to everybody and it was because she was so strong that they seemed more desolating to her. She had hoped to combine her visit home for her parents' golden wedding anniversary with a speaking engagement in Omaha before the Press Club, but she realized that she did not have the strength for it and canceled the speech at the last minute.

It was perhaps because she was feeling wretched physically that Willa had been wounded by the temper of the criticism *One of Ours* received. She had never allowed unfavorable reviews to upset her to such an extent before, but she very much wanted her first novel for her new publisher to be a success. In addition, her emotional identification with her hero was so complete that she felt keenly the rebuff to Claude as well as to herself. But what most disturbed and even puzzled her were the attacks on her interpretation of the war and the role the war played in giving meaning to Claude's life. It seemed to Willa as if she and her critics dwelt in different worlds and spoke entirely different languages. She had no intention of accommodating them, however. She expressed herself to Elsie Sergeant in her usual combative manner. The highbrow critics accused her of not knowing how to write anymore. Their trouble, Willa said, was that they were incapable of recognizing writing unless it had the usual emotional signs. As far as she was concerned, she declared passionately, she was just learning how to write in *One of Ours* and she intended to go right on doing it.

LOOKING BACKWARD

Years later Willa made an observation that was widely quoted and that helps to illuminate her state of mind. "The world broke in two in 1922 or thereabouts," she wrote, and she was one of those who belonged to the earlier time, one of "the backward." Just as she romanticized her own childhood, she glorified the past in general. The present may be difficult, she liked to say, but we had a beautiful past. She had always seen the world in absolutes and that rigidity of her personality made it increasingly difficult for her to come to terms with new ways and new ideas. Though she made exceptions for individual examples of talent and creativity, her deepest instinct was to reject the modern world—modern art, modern literature, modern institutions. She felt the division between the world before 1914 and the postwar world as if the line had been drawn through her own soul. She took her stand deliberately but, given her nature, she had no choice.

The year ended for Willa with an act of faith that was an affirmation of her most cherished ideals. On December 27, 1922, she and her parents were confirmed in the Episcopal Church by the Bishop of Nebraska, Dr. George Beecher. Willa had been raised as a Baptist, but she felt a strong affinity for the Anglican Church, as much for the beauty of its ritual as for its position as the historic church in the New World. Undoubtedly, too, a certain amount of social prestige

accrued to membership in the Church, which had been established
only recently in Nebraska but had already won a sizable following in
Red Cloud. But the great attraction for Willa was the sense of con-
tinuity with an old religious community. It was a Church that placed
a high value on the past. In spiritual matters too, Willa was looking
back.

XII

❧

Fine Undertakings and Bright Occasions

HER OWN QUIET CENTER

The twenties were a time of quiet, intense creativity for Willa. It was as though she did indeed inhabit another planet, working with total detachment from the frenetic mood of the times. She produced an extraordinary body of work between 1920 and 1930—five novels, superb short stories, essays, reviews and poetry. She had become one of the most prominent women in America, considered among the country's foremost novelists. To many she had no peer. When Sinclair Lewis was awarded the Nobel Prize for Literature in 1930, he said publicly that it should have gone to Willa Cather.

Yet to a remarkable degree she maintained her privacy in spite of her celebrity, and held herself aloof not only from the times in which she lived but also from most people. Those who were invited to her Friday afternoons knew they had been singled out and felt themselves privileged. She might send a warm-hearted reply to a stranger whose letter touched a responsive chord, but woe betide the unwary soul who had the temerity to approach her unbidden. Her coldness could be shattering. Mildred Bennett quotes Robert Frost as saying, "With Carl Sandburg it's the people, yes; with Willa Cather, the people, no." The novelist Fannie Hurst who met her in the early twenties at the home of still another writer, May Wilson Preston, later described Willa as a smooth-haired, middle-aged woman of "vast serenity," who looked as if she had never been very young. "Her era," wrote Miss Hurst, "seemed to swirl about her stately intellectual isolation like a noisy storm" and her Bank Street apartment was "no more a part of Fitzgerald's twenties than of Mars."

More and more, as time went by, Willa clung to her old friends. The Miner sisters never failed to keep in touch and provide the fond attention that was so necessary to her. Carrie was her closest link to Red Cloud outside of her family and she rejoiced at having Mary Miner Creighton and her husband near her in New York one winter, but it was Irene who occupied a unique role in her life. Irene was the only person, Willa said once, who knew her as a child who had gone on being a part of her life. Isabelle and Edith and Mr. McClure did not go so far back, and the ones who did, like Carrie and Mary, had not been so much in her later life. But Irene spoke both her languages. Irene knew the names of all the people dear to her in childhood and the names of most of those who had come into her life afterward. It was important to her, Willa said, that someone from Sandy Point should go along with her to the end.

In New York she tried to keep distractions to a minimum but she enjoyed an evening with congenial people from time to time. She liked the Henry Seidel Canbys who lived not far away, and she saw the William Allen Whites when they were in town. But more than writers, Willa was attracted to musicians and at the home of Blanche and Alfred Knopf, who shared her love of music, she met many of the great performers of the day, some like Josef Hofmann whom she had first heard during her reviewing days in Pittsburgh. She was always among the invited guests when the Knopfs held their annual reception for Serge Koussevitsky, the virtuoso conductor who became director of the Boston Symphony in 1924, when he brought the orchestra to New York. It was also through her publisher and his wife that Willa met the English pianist Myra Hess who was to become one of her good friends. With people like the Knopfs whose tastes were similar to hers, Willa was at her best, warm, responsive, at ease. She was always slightly formal—it was not until she had known him for ten years that she addressed the publisher as Alfred, and he and his associates never called her anything but Miss Cather—but that was out of habit and did not preclude a genuine affection. True, she was held in awe by the younger people in the office and she expected them to defer to her, but the Knopf family knew her as a friend.

For Isabelle her attachment never weakened. Even when they were separated by an ocean, as they were to be increasingly, Willa's first thought when something happened in her life, whether it was an honor she received or a marriage in the family, was to share the news with Isabelle. In the summer of 1923 she sailed on the *Berengaria* for France to stay with Isabelle and Jan who had bought a house at 19 rue de Sèvres in Ville d'Avray outside Paris. Another old friend, Dorothy Canfield, appeared suddenly and unexpectedly to say good-bye, bearing flowers that filled Willa's stateroom and lasted the entire trip. The crossing on a soft summer sea was dreamy, she told Dorothy, and the days were enlivened by having Frank Swinnerton as a table-mate. She had landed in France and was with the Hambourgs when a reporter brought her the news that she had won the Pulitzer Prize for *One of Ours*.

It made Willa happy to see how Jan fussed over his wife, and she enjoyed their lovely home, but when they entreated her to make it her home too, she declined the invitation. They did everything to make her comfortable, even arranging a small study for her where she would not be disturbed, but Willa found she could not work at Ville d'Avray. "Indeed," Edith was to state with a note of satisfaction, or maybe only of relief, "she felt she would never be able to do any work there." It appears that Willa was beginning to transfer her dependence, if not her feelings, to Edith.

While she was in Paris, Willa decided on Léon Bakst to do a portrait of her which the Omaha Public Library had commissioned. Bakst was better known for his costumes and sets for the Russian Ballet than for portraits, which he seldom did, but he had heard about Willa from some French friends who admired her books and he said he'd like to paint her. He was modern and rather fanciful, Willa told her friends, and would not do a photographic likeness of her, but she was sure the picture would be like her in the end. In the end, unfortunately, the portrait was generally adjudged a failure. Bakst himself was unhappy with it and would probably have bowed out, said Edith Lewis, except that half a dozen fellow Russians in

Paris at the time were depending on him to support them, and he needed the money. As it was, "he went on painting desperately at the portrait," according to Edith, "sitting after sitting, while all the while it grew worse—stiff, dark, heavy, lifeless, everything that Willa Cather was not, and indeed, everything that Bakst was not." And yet, Bakst had caught something of Willa's stolidity and a stubbornness that Edith might not have been pleased to acknowledge.

Mrs. Cather disliked the portrait so much that Willa said she acted exactly as though her daughter had committed an indiscretion. The Omaha Library people, however, seemed satisfied and behaved graciously. Perhaps it was enough for them that the artist's name was well known. At least that is what Willa thought. It was typical of Willa to have chosen an artist whose conversation entertained her and whose beautiful studio she enjoyed being in. The artist's personality and his surroundings were more important to her than his appropriateness for the commission.

Three years later when Edward Steichen photographed her he saw a very different Willa. In middy and tie, her arms folded placidly, the candid eyes gazing straight at the camera from her broad wholesome face, she might be one of her own prairie heroines. If Bakst sought to show the author in all her dignity, Steichen caught the country girl she also was at heart.

THREE NOVELS

In April 1923 Knopf brought out a revised edition of *April Twilights,* and that same month the first installment of *A Lost Lady* appeared in *The Century.* Willa had pressed Knopf to sell serial rights to her new book because she wanted to be able to afford a secretary, and before she left for France she hired Sarah Bloom. She had worked on *A Lost Lady* all through 1922, beginning as soon as she finished *One of Ours.* Much of it was written in the cottage she and Edith rented on Grand Manan. The writing had not come easily at the start and she tried a first-person version before deciding finally that she could tell the story best from a single point of view that was to be Niel Herbert's, but using the third person. After that the book went smoothly.

Willa's customary method was to write a first draft in longhand, not stopping for revisions, and starting every morning where she had left off the morning before. (She still worked, at most, three or four hours a day.) When she finished the draft she would rewrite it at the typewriter, keeping the handwritten version next to her, but not always following it. It was this typewritten version that Sarah Bloom would copy and it was on the copy that Willa made her changes and corrections. Sarah might retype a book several times before Willa judged it ready for the publisher.

Willa thought *A Lost Lady* was too slight to make a book and should be published along with some of her short stories, but Knopf had firmly discouraged the idea. " 'Mrs. Knopf and I both agree that you ought to be restrained by law, if necessary, from publishing this book with anything else. It belongs, alone, exactly as *Ethan Frome* belongs, alone, and you are very unjust to it and to yourself, I think, for feeling otherwise.' " The most sensuous and delicate of her novels, in it Willa returned to the Nebraska of her childhood and the tantalizing figure of Silas Garber's wife, whose bewitching presence had lent so much color to those days. The setting of *A Lost Lady* and the period are similar to *My Ántonia* but the clear morning light that bathed Black Hawk and that shines over Sweetwater in the early scenes of *A Lost Lady* is shadowed long before the book's conclusion. The subtle nuances of Marian Forrester's personality are in sharp contrast to Ántonia's uncomplicated nature. For Jim Burden Ántonia had the virtue of never disappointing him, but Niel Herbert has to live with his "long-lost lady's" betrayal of his illusions. She lets him down by trafficking with men like Frank Ellerton, in whose arms he spies her, and the crude, contemptible Ivy Peters. Yet Niel can never forget her and in the end he is grateful for having known her. "She had always the power of suggesting things much lovelier than herself, as the perfume of a single flower may call up the whole sweetness of spring."

Willa's own mood was darker when she wrote *A Lost Lady* and the book reflects her disillusion with the times. The spirit of the pioneer generation of railroad men, represented by Captain Forrester, had disappeared. "All those who had shared in fine undertakings and bright occasions were gone," Willa wrote. She caught to perfection that melancholy time between the passing of one age and the coming to birth of another. The book was widely hailed as a small master-piece. "Hardly a novel and yet too full and good for a short story, simply a little work of art," said the New York *Times*. Joseph Wood Krutch, writing in *The Nation*, considered it, if not a great novel, at least "that very rare thing in contemporary literature, a nearly per-fect one." And Heywood Broun extended a hand to welcome Willa back "safe and sound" from the war. "She has never done a better novel than *A Lost Lady*," he wrote, "nor is she likely to nor anyone else. Truly a great book . . . To know Captain Forrester and Marian Forrester is to have an understanding of an age and a class in America."

The book sold well and became the only one of Willa's books to be made into a motion picture. She was so distressed with the 1925 Warner Brothers silent film, however, that she expressly forbade her publishers to sell movie rights to any of her other books or stories and she saw to it that the prohibition was written into her will. In April 1925 she received a startling letter from an author whose work she admired but whom she had never met. *The Great Gatsby* was about to be published by Scribner's and F. Scott Fitzgerald wrote to Willa explaining what he feared might be interpreted as "an instance of apparent plagiarism." He was afraid Willa would think that his de-scription in *The Great Gatsby* of the effect of Daisy's voice on the men who cared for her had been copied from the passage in *A Lost Lady* that begins with Niel's recalling the "promise of wild delight" in Marian Forrester's eyes and ends with his tribute to her power of suggesting lovely things. Fitzgerald said he had already written his paragraph about Daisy when he read *A Lost Lady* and noted the similarity, and he sent Willa two pages from his working manuscript to prove his point. Calling himself one of her greatest admirers, Fitz-gerald assured her that his expression of the effect of a woman's charm was "neither so clear, nor so beautiful, nor so moving" as hers but that he had nevertheless shown the two passages to Ring Lardner and several others before deciding finally to retain them. Willa sent a gracious reply, complimenting Fitzgerald on *Gatsby* and denying that she had detected any plagiarism. The only way to describe beauty was to describe its effect, not the actual person, she told Fitz-gerald. It was what she had been telling people for years when they charged her with drawing her characters too closely from life.

By the time *A Lost Lady* was published Willa was already hard at work on her next novel. *The Professor's House*, she was to say, was written in a middle-aged mood. The professor himself was fifty-two, just the age of his creator. Weary, played-out, his fires banked, he resigns himself to learning how "to live without delight." "Theoretically he knew that life is possible, may be even pleasant, without joy, without passionate griefs. But it had never occurred to him that he might have to live like that." The book was never one of Willa's favorites. A nasty, grim little tale, she called it. And yet she put a great deal of herself into her professor, not just the way she was, but the way she would like to be. Along with a subtle and discriminating mind she gave St. Peter qualities that she admired and had striven to acquire all her life, a cool temperament, reserve, detachment. And though she placed Hamilton, the university town where the professor and his family live, not in Nebraska but along the shores of Lake Michigan, she and the professor shared similar experiences. As a child he too had been taken—"dragged," wrote Willa—by his parents to an unfamiliar country and had nearly died of it. "No later anguish . . . went so deep or seemed so final." He worked, as she had worked in Pittsburgh, in an attic studio that was sometimes a sewing room. No doubt dress forms like the ones that provide a cheerful topic of conversation for St. Peter and the "sewing-woman" had stood in a corner of Willa's study in the McClung house.

Like Willa too, St. Peter had found in the Southwest the springs of his imaginative life. St. Peter had been led to the Blue Mesa by his student, Tom Outland, a young scientist and inventor who comes into his life "just when the morning brightness of the world was wearing off for him." Through Tom, whose own life ends in Flanders fighting with the Foreign Legion, the professor feels he has been granted, if only briefly, a second youth. Had he lived, Tom would have become the professor's son-in-law and St. Peter might have found his creative life extended. But after Tom is killed Rosamond, the professor's daughter, marries Louie Marsellus and Tom's invention, the Outland engine, which he bequeathed to Rosamond, makes them rich. His family prospers but the professor is impoverished, spiritually and emotionally.

Some critics were disconcerted by Willa's insertion in the narrative of a self-contained section which was Tom Outland's own story of his discovery of the Blue Mesa, the tale Willa first heard from Dick Wetherill's brother. She explained that it was an experiment in form, but that the device of inserting the *Nouvelle* into the *Roman* was actually an old one that had been used by early French and Spanish novelists. Beyond that, however, she said she had been inspired by Dutch paintings which she had seen in Paris just before she began the book. Most of the interiors showed a warmly furnished living room or a kitchen filled with copper pots, but there was usually "a square window, open, through which one saw the masts of ships, or a stretch of grey sea." She had deliberately made St. Peter's house overcrowded and stuffy, with not only possessions but also "proprieties . . . petty ambitions and quivering jealousies." She had meant it to be stifling so that she could then open the square window and "let in the fresh air that blew off the Blue Mesa and the fine disregard of trivialities which was in Tom Outland's face and in his behavior."

Edith Lewis calls *The Professor's House* the most personal of Willa's novels. And to Irene, who had seen the book in its early stages, Willa wrote that it was a satisfaction to her that her friend had so quickly grasped the fierce feeling that lay behind the dry and impersonal manner of the telling. Indeed, although she considered it a despairing book, Willa made her professor the spokesman for some of her most affirmative and deeply held beliefs: "A man can do anything if he wishes to enough . . . Desire is creation, is the magical element in that process." To a student St. Peter says, "Art and religion (they are the same thing, in the end, of course) have given man the only happiness he has ever had." Ten years earlier Willa had written almost the same thing in *The Song of the Lark;* Professor St. Peter and Thea Kronborg were not very far apart.

Willa confided to Irene that the serial rights to *The Professor's House* had been sold for ten thousand dollars, but she cautioned her against letting others know. If one's family found out about one's prices, she said, they expected one to do all sorts of absurd things. They didn't understand that it wasn't easy money. In fact, when the book began selling well Willa bought herself a mink coat. Her professor bought it for her, she told Irene; wasn't he extravagant? Irene's husband was in the insurance business and Willa asked her to have him send up a man to appraise the coat. It was the first valuable thing she'd ever owned and she was afraid of losing it.

In 1925, the same year that *The Professor's House* came out, Willa was represented in Knopf's *Borzoi 25* by an essay on Katherine Mansfield. She also wrote a preface to *The Best Stories of Sarah Orne Jewett* and an introduction to *The Wagnerian Romances* by Gertrude Hall which Knopf published. Early in the year "Uncle Valentine" had appeared in six parts in the *Woman's Home Companion*. In 1924 she had written an introduction for Knopf to a new edition of Defoe's *Fortunate Mistress*, which was a favorite of hers. In 1926, when Knopf brought out "Wounds in the Rain and Other Impressions of War," the ninth volume of *The Works of Stephen Crane*, Willa provided an introduction. Then in October, just a year after *The Professor's House*, *My Mortal Enemy* was published.

Although it was an even shorter book than *A Lost Lady*, this time Willa was confidently insistent that it be published by itself and Knopf agreed. *My Mortal Enemy* is the best example of principles Willa had enunciated in a 1922 essay she wrote for her old nemesis, *The New Republic*. "The novel, for a long while, has been overfurnished," the article began. Art, she wrote, was a matter of selection and simplification and in the story of Myra Driscoll Henshawe she stripped the characters and the scenes of all but the most essential details. Although one critic complained of "a creative tautness that robs it of warmth," Willa felt that she had achieved the effect she wanted, and she considered *My Mortal Enemy* an exceptional book. She had written it rapidly while getting *The Professor's House* ready for publication, and in some ways it serves both as a coda to her previous work and as an overture to the books that were to follow.

The marriage of Myra Driscoll and Oswald Henshawe is what the professor's marriage might have been like if his wife had not had money. "A few memorable interregnums between servants had let him know that Lillian couldn't pinch and be shabby . . . ," St. Peter had reflected. "Under such conditions she became another person and a bitter one." In *My Mortal Enemy* headstrong Myra Driscoll renounces her uncle's fortune to marry for love and, in time, poverty does indeed turn her into a bitter figure. The brief story is told in two parts. In the first Myra is seen a quarter of a century after her elopement, a worldly woman in her middle years, vain, imperious but still beautiful and infinitely intriguing to the young narrator, Nelly Birdseye, who comes to New York with her aunt to visit Myra and Oswald in their comfortable apartment on Madison Square.

Willa enjoyed writing about New York as it was when she first knew it—a better time than this, she said—and she drew a memorable picture of Madison Square at Christmastime, with snow clinging to the bushes, the fountain splashing and St. Gaudens' Diana stepping out "freely and fearlessly into the grey air." The second part of the book shows Myra ten years later, at the end of her life, far from the glitter of New York. All splendor gone, crippled and dependent, she and Oswald are living in shabby quarters along the California coast. By chance, Nelly is there too to witness the last chapter of the great romance. "People can be lovers and enemies at the same time. We were," Myra says to Nelly. But at the end she and Oswald have ceased to be lovers, ceased even to be friends. They have long since destroyed each other and, in her sickness, Myra whispers the fateful words: "Why must I die like this, alone with my mortal enemy?" Knowing death is near, she turns to Catholicism, the faith in which she had been raised, and at the last she makes the supreme effort to leave her squalid room so that she may die alone on a bare headland overlooking the sea, a crucifix clasped in her hands.

In her last years Myra came to bitterly regret the romantic adventure of her youth. "I should have stayed with my uncle," she says. "It was money I needed. We've thrown our lives away." But for Willa Myra's tragedy was not that she had been cut out of her uncle's will; it was that she had cut herself off from her past. In the end she finds her way back to where she belongs, to her own people and the world she left behind, by returning to the religion of her fathers. From Willa's point of view, that made Myra a less despairing figure than Professor St. Peter, who was allowed no such consolation. Significantly, Willa never thought of *My Mortal Enemy* as she thought of *The Professor's House*, that it was a grim, middle-aged book.

In spite of a mixed critical reception, the short novel sold well. A debate over whether Myra's "mortal enemy" was Oswald or Myra herself was waged by both the critics and the public and the controversy probably helped sales. In a captious letter Willa's old friend

George Seibel put the matter to her squarely. He had personally decided that Myra's husband was her enemy, but he found that most readers thought it was Myra, and he had had a heated argument on the subject with one opinionated lady "of literary propensities." He pressed Willa to tell him exactly what she had intended. " 'Of course you are quite right,' " she answered, and then went on to state with some impatience: " 'I can't see much in this particular story unless you get the point of it. There is not much to it *but* the point.' " So much for ladies of literary propensities!

AN AUTHOR'S LIFE

The restless pattern of Willa's year continued through the twenties. She would spend the early months writing in New York and she invariably worked in Jaffrey for several weeks in the fall. As a rule she went home to Red Cloud in June and returned for Christmas, but her summers were reserved for travel, which generally meant either going abroad or to the Southwest. As her reputation grew, she was inevitably in demand for public appearances of one sort or another. She rarely submitted to interviews but she accepted carefully chosen lecture dates and honorary degrees when they were offered by institutions she felt she could not turn down. In June 1924 she went out to Ann Arbor to receive an honorary degree from the University of Michigan, sharing the platform on that occasion with one of the Wright brothers. A few years later she was honored at Columbia University in a ceremony she described to Carrie as dignified and impressive although it rained and the exercises had to be held indoors. Each time she received an honorary degree she would send the diploma and academic hood to Carrie, who was accumulating a fine collection of Cather souvenirs and memorabilia in her Red Cloud home.

In the summer of 1923 Willa had consented to give a series of talks to students at the Breadloaf Writers Conference in Middlebury, Vermont, recuperating afterward by spending a few quiet days with Mary Jewett. The following fall she begged Irene to stand by her, help her dress and hold her hand, when she gave a lecture at the University of Chicago. From Chicago she went on alone to Cleveland, where she spoke before a large and distinguished audience, mostly young and very dressy. About a fourth of them were men, she told Irene. The hall, she said, was particularly lovely, done in deep shades of blue with splendid soft lights. She would never speak in an ugly hall again—apparently she had not been pleased with the Leon Mandell Auditorium in Chicago—it made her wretched and all she could do was stutter. The Cleveland lecture, on the other hand, went along like a rippling stream.

In 1926 she accepted one of the much coveted invitations to the MacDowell Colony, the retreat for writers, artists and musicians, established under the will of the composer Edward MacDowell and run on the couple's estate in Peterborough, New Hampshire, by his formidable widow. Admission was by invitation only and conferred undeniable prestige, which probably accounts for Willa's willingness to spend several weeks there although her own work habits were rather different from those of most of the other residents. Guests were housed by gender in separate quarters, the women in a red farmhouse called the Eaves. After a community breakfast they scattered to assigned studios on the wooded grounds where they were expected to work in solitude until dinner. Lunch was delivered in a basket to each studio at midday. It was expressly forbidden to use the studios except in the daytime as a precaution against fire, or so it was said. The poet Elinor Wylie thought otherwise. It was quite a different kind of fire, she observed, that caused the rule to be imposed upon "the company of excellent old maids and worthy bachelors" who gathered in the summertime. Nevertheless, Wylie and others found the spartan accommodations and the long silent days conducive to hard work, and the convivial evenings a welcome release, relaxing and entertaining.

Willa, however, worked her usual two or three hours in the morning, after which she was ready for a walk and a good lunch. Without regard to custom, she simply left her studio a little after noon and walked into town, where she found a local inn that served a hearty meal. Her basket lunch she saved for tea. And although she found one or two guests congenial, the evening social activities were an ordeal she steeled herself to endure. She never went back to the

Colony, but she retained her friendship with Mrs. MacDowell, and they would see each other when Willa was at Jaffrey.

INTO THE MORNING

Of all her experiences during the twenties, the years of her most abundant creativity, none was more important to Willa than her rediscovery of the Southwest. Ever since the trip she made with Edith in 1916 Willa knew that she would return one day to New Mexico. When she did go back in 1925 it was to find that, in the interim since her last visit, others too had fallen under the spell of the desert country she loved so well—Mabel Luhan, Mary Austin, Witter Bynner and a writer Willa very much admired, D. H. Lawrence. She had met Lawrence in New York that spring and he had come to Bank Street several times for tea. On one occasion he and his wife, Frieda, brought along the English painter Dorothy Brett, who had come from Europe with them. In her diary Brett recorded that Willa and Edith had been kind and hospitable and had served very good tea. Willa wanted to talk to Lawrence seriously about his work but he would not allow himself to be engaged and kept evading her in a teasing way. Finally, according to Brett, he said, " 'I hate literature and literary people. People shouldn't fuss so much about art.' " As Willa became more indignant, Lawrence became increasingly outrageous. " 'I hate books and art and the whole business,' " he said. It was all good-humored, however, and before they parted they made plans to see each other in New Mexico in the summer.

Willa and Edith stopped first in Santa Fe and stayed at La Fonda, the historic adobe hotel on the Plaza that marked the end of the old Santa Fe Trail. The Lawrences were in Taos living on the ranch that Mabel Luhan had given Lawrence in exchange for the manuscript of *Sons and Lovers*. Mabel invited Willa and Edith to stay with her at Taos but Willa never liked to visit and it was not until Mabel offered her one of her guesthouses that Willa accepted the invitation, actually staying an unheard-of two weeks. Mabel had the intuitive sense to understand that the best way to entertain Willa was to leave her alone, but she saw to it that her husband was available to take her guests on long drives about the country.

"Tony would sit in the driver's seat, in his silver bracelets and purple blanket, often singing softly to himself," wrote Edith, "while we sat behind. He took us to some of the almost inaccessible Mexican villages hidden in the Cimarron mountains, where the Penitentes still followed their old fierce customs; and from Tony, Willa Cather learned many things about the country and the people that she could not have learned otherwise. He talked very little, but what he said was always illuminating and curiously poetic."

When she arrived in New Mexico, Willa had no definite idea for a story in mind, but the longer she stayed the more it seemed to her that the real story in that part of the country lay in the Roman Catholic Church. The artist Georgia O'Keeffe felt it too and when she stayed at Mabel Luhan's, a few years after Willa, she said she saw so many crosses, they were like "a veil of the Catholic church spread over the New Mexico landscape." Although the Spanish influence was all around, Willa's interest fastened on the French missionaries and in particular on the Archbishop from Auvergne, whose life-sized bronze image stood before the Cathedral of St. Francis in Santa Fe. In a letter to *The Commonweal* in which she discussed how she came to write *Death Comes for the Archbishop*, Willa said that "Archbishop Lamy, the first Bishop of New Mexico, had become a sort of invisible personal friend." There was in his aspect, she wrote, "something fearless and fine and very, very well-bred—something that spoke of race." It made her curious to know how such an obviously cultivated man had gone about his daily life "in a crude, frontier society."

By good fortune, while she was in Santa Fe she came upon *The Life of the Right Reverend Joseph P. Machebeuf* by William Joseph Howlett in which she learned the history of the two men, Machebeuf and his boyhood friend, Jean Baptiste Lamy; how they had left their native village near Auvergne together; and how they had worked side by side for many years in Santa Fe, Lamy as Bishop and Machebeuf as his Vicar General. Machebeuf's sister had given Howlett her brother's letters and these provided details of the two priests' life in New Mexico. Everything she read about them and everything she saw in the country all around her made Willa know she had to write about the men and about the place. It was as if her story and her characters had been waiting for her to find them.

Calling Lamy "Bishop Latour" and Machebeuf "Father Vaillant,"

Willa followed the life stories of the two men fairly accurately, weaving in Indian legends, old superstitions and certain of her own and her father's experiences. She too had traveled to Acoma and had gazed with wonder at the Mesa Encantada. She made a change in the biography of the two friends for her literary purposes. In her version Father Vaillant dies first while, in fact, Lamy died before Machebeuf. Lamy's funeral had been particularly poignant and Willa wrote that she had often heard from some of the older people that Machebeuf had broken down when he rose to speak and had been unable to go on.

With *Death Comes for the Archbishop* (a title Willa said she took from Holbein's *The Dance of Death*) Willa quite literally turned away from the modern world. Writing the book, she said in *The Commonweal,* was like "a happy vacation from life, a return to childhood, to early memories." But it would be a mistake to think that it was only because he represented the past that Lamy made such a strong appeal to her imagination. His personal qualities were equally significant and she made of them a transcendent story of simplicity, courage and faith. Lamy was that rare combination of connoisseur and pioneer that, as one critic noted, had always been Willa's ideal. But there was yet another aspect of the Archbishop's story, his lifelong friendship with Machebeuf, that evidently stirred Willa deeply. Certainly the devotion between the Bishop and his Vicar is one of the book's most moving themes.

Like their historical counterparts, Latour and Vaillant are a study in contrasts: the gentle, courteous Bishop, reserved, reflective, deliberate, his features "handsome and somewhat severe"; merry little Father Vaillant, a man of quick-silver temperament, friendly, outgoing, with a countenance "that had little to recommend it but kindliness and vivacity." Yet despite their very different dispositions the two men had been drawn to each other from boyhood. When Latour becomes first Bishop of New Mexico he chooses Vaillant to be with him, for the most human of reasons. In the loneliness of his high post in that vast desert diocese, he wants the man's companionship. They are perfectly attuned to each other in the way of old and trusted friends. Latour hopes they will stay together always, growing old in each other's company. But Vaillant is a harvester of souls and his restless missionary feet will not let him retire. Willa describes the poignancy of their last days together in the Bishop's garden at Santa Fe.

Years before, a rich Mexican had made the priests a gift of two cream-colored mules "of singular dignity and intelligence," and ever since, Vaillant had ridden Contento and Latour had ridden Angelica. Before Vaillant leaves with Contento for Denver, Latour asks him to take Angelica also. "They have a great affection for each other; why separate them indefinitely? One could not explain to them. They have worked long together."

Friendship held a place of paramount importance in Willa's life. When she wrote *Death Comes for the Archbishop* she and Edith had been together for twenty years and had reached a rare degree of accommodation. Like her Archbishop who found it difficult to make new ties, Willa tended to put up walls between herself and others, and it was often left to Edith to make overtures of sociability as well as to protect Willa from too assiduous assaults on her privacy. On the other hand, Willa made concessions also in their life together. Nothing speaks more eloquently of her attachment to Edith than the fact that although she would grumble about New York and declare that one day she would leave it behind for good, Edith's job as a copywriter at J. Walter Thompson kept Willa in New York. The love between Latour and Vaillant may well have expressed some of Willa's feeling for her friend.

Edith said Willa worked on the *Archbishop* in a mood of unusual happiness and serenity. In no other of her novels since *O Pioneers!* is there so great a feeling of well-being and delight. The physical environment is a palpable presence and the spirits of light and earth and air seem to suffuse the atmosphere. Willa herself had the gift she ascribes to the Navajo, Eusabio; to travel with her is to travel with the landscape made human. In luminous language she describes Latour's rapture on waking in the desert with a light dry wind blowing and the fragrance of sun and sagebrush and sweet clover. In that air he always awoke a child. It was "only on the bright edges of the world, on the great grass plains or the sagebrush desert" that one could find such air. "Something soft and wild and free, something that whispered to the ear on the pillow, lightened the heart, softly, softly picked the lock, slid the bolts, and released the prisoned spirit of man into the wind, into the blue and gold, into the morning, into the morning!" It was the way Willa felt when she awoke in her bedroom in Red Cloud.

When she brought the manuscript to Knopf she knew its worth, he said, and "remarking that our son would some day be paying royalties on it to her niece," she asked the publisher for special terms. She never asked for the higher rate again, nor did she accept it when Knopf offered it to her. It was also the only time she used an agent, not in dealing with her publisher but in selling serial rights. Paul Reynolds sold it for her to *The Forum* where it began appearing in January 1927, a full nine months before Knopf brought out the book. By mid-September the book had sold thirty thousand copies. The reviews were the best Willa had received since *A Lost Lady*— *The New Republic* called it "an American classic" and the New York *Times*, "a very rare piece of literature." The less enthusiastic notices tended to be harsh and several asserted that the book was not really a novel. Willa was unhappy with the book's reception and complained to Knopf about the advertising. She had not liked the ads for *My Mortal Enemy* and had written her own copy with quotes she selected herself. Now she did the same for the *Archbishop*. Though he says Willa never told him so, Knopf always suspected "the fine hand of Edith Lewis in much of the copy about her books that she supplied from time to time." Edith herself was discreetly silent, but it seems likely that she would have exercised her copywriter's skill on her friend's behalf.

Death Comes for the Archbishop was the last book Willa wrote in Bank Street. The progress she deplored and feared had at last reached her front door. A new subway was being built and Number Five was to be torn down to make way for a high-rise apartment building. In the fall of 1927 she and Edith were forced to move out, and for the first time in many years Willa found herself without an address.

XIII

❋

We Are the Older Generation

A PROP FALLS

In the summer of 1927 before attending to the sad business of giving up the Bank Street apartment, Willa made a trip on horseback with Roscoe through the Big Horn Mountains of Wyoming. While she was in the West news came that her father had suffered a severe angina attack, the first serious illness of his life, and Willa left immediately for Red Cloud to be with him. As soon as he was comfortable and out of danger she could no longer put off the inevitable and she hurried to New York to begin the doleful process of packing. Putting your things in storage, she wrote to Zoë, was a good deal like having a funeral. She and Edith were going to the Grosvenor, an apartment hotel at 35 Fifth Avenue, for what they hoped would be a temporary stay. Had she known in the beginning that they would be there five years, Willa would have been even more distressed than she was. Could anything be a better index of the dreary way she lived, she asked Dorothy, than the awful Grosvenor letter paper? The *Archbishop* was to be released in September, she informed Carrie on Knopf letterhead; she hoped he had more go in him than she had.

In December she went back to Red Cloud to spend a long holiday with her family. A little prairie town in winter was very thrilling, she said, with blinding sunlight all day and crystal moonlight all night. Her father had a car with a heater and he was well enough to drive her about the Bohemian and Scandinavian settlements. She found it oddly satisfying to watch the same human stories go on and on and to see how the lives she knew so well came out in the end. As for the family, although Christmas was a bit like living through *War and Peace*, her parents had celebrated their fifty-fifth anniversary on December 5 and it seemed to Willa that the time they had together was like a gift.

Willa stayed at home until the end of February and then went back reluctantly to New York and the Grosvenor. Perhaps she stretched her visit because she had a presentiment that the family would never again be so happy. A week after she left Red Cloud, Charles Cather suffered a heart attack and lingered only a few hours before he died. Willa turned around and made the sad trip back but she was too late to see her father alive. It was a little after five when she reached the Cather house, just as dawn was breaking. Charles Cather lay on a stretcher in the big bay window of his own room in one of the silk shirts he always wore. The rest of the family was asleep and Willa sat with him alone. When she had left him he had looked so happy and boyish. He still looked happy in death, she thought, so contented and so at home. Her father had never in his life hurt anybody's feelings and he died with as little fuss as he had lived.

Willa had lost people she loved before, but this was the first loss in the family and she found it difficult to bear. Her friends tried to assuage her desolation but Mildred Bennett wrote that "she paced frantically back and forth between the house and the little Episcopal church where his body [was taken], wringing her hands, apparently unable to conquer the grief and panic which overwhelmed her." Especially now, when she felt she had no other home, this first break in the family circle was a bitter blow. She felt that a prop had fallen and she did not see how she could go on without it. Her winter at home seemed like a miracle. She had stayed, not because her parents were ailing, but because they were both so well, and she was grateful for the precious time they had together. Douglass took his mother back with him to California, leaving the house in Red Cloud that had seen so much life empty for the first time.

One refuge remained to Willa. In 1925 she and Edith had decided to build a house on Grand Manan. They had found a local carpenter to build it to their specifications and he had worked throughout the fall and spring to have it ready for them in the summer. "It was a rough little place, with many inconveniences," wrote Edith Lewis, "but it came to have not only comfort but great charm." In the desolate season following her father's death Willa thought only of the summer and Grand Manan. It seemed the last foothold left on earth, said Edith.

THE TRANSIENT YEARS

Willa was sick in the spring and she and Edith decided that when they went to Grand Manan in June they would go leisurely by way of Canada instead of through Maine as usual. Traveling through unfamiliar country always refreshed Willa and her mood was considerably lightened by the time they reached Quebec. "From the first moment that she looked down from the windows of the [Hotel] Frontenac on the pointed roofs and Norman outlines of the town," wrote Edith, "Willa was overwhelmed by the flood of memory, recognition, surmise it called up; by the sense of its extraordinarily French character, isolated and kept intact through hundreds of years, as if by a miracle, on this great, un-French continent." They had barely settled when Edith came down with an attack of flu, and for ten days Willa wandered alone through the winding streets of the picturesque town, soaking up the atmosphere of a place that was new to her, but that had a long history. In the library of the hotel she found Parkman's books on Canada and other accounts of the early days of French settlement. Her reading took her back two hundred years before the missionary priests Lamy and Machebeuf first set foot in New Mexico, to the time when two other Frenchmen, a man of faith and a man of action, led a colony of settlers to the great rock in the St. Lawrence River and there established a little piece of France in the New World that had survived to Willa's own day.

Willa's susceptibility to the spirit of the old city is not surprising. Edith Lewis thought her pleasure in Quebec came from finding a continuation of the Catholic theme that had absorbed her during the writing of the *Archbishop*. There was also her lifelong infatuation with anything French. Even in the Southwest, with the Spanish influence all about, it was a French priest who captured her imagination. When Lamy built his Cathedral in Santa Fe he chose to recreate the Romanesque and Gothic styles that had "always enclosed the religious activities of his early life." Later generations would accuse him of a failure of imagination for using stone and alien architecture in that yellow adobe country. But he built in a manner that was familiar to him and which he believed to be more appropriate and more beautiful than anything he found in New Mexico. Mary Austin, that gossipy defender of the local mores, liked to boast that Willa wrote the *Archbishop* in her house in Santa Fe. "She sat in *that* chair," she would tell visitors. Nevertheless, she was one of those who believed that not only had Lamy dealt a mortal blow to the local culture by building a French cathedral in a Spanish town, but that Willa had perpetuated the affront when she gave her allegiance to the French Archbishop.

In Quebec no such conflict existed. The French had brought their church and their traditions to a barren place and the Cathedral, the Ursuline Convent, the Laval Seminary had an integrity of purpose and design that was deeply soothing to the spirit. By the time Edith had recovered sufficiently for them to continue on their way to Grand Manan, Willa had found the setting, if not yet the story, of her next novel. She worked very little that summer, however. There was a lot to do to furnish the house before she could get down to writing. The cottage stood in a field of daisies on a sloping hillside that dropped two hundred feet into the sea. Every part of the island that was not pine woods, Willa told Carrie, was one soft fluffy hayfield full of daisies and bluebells. Her study was a large attic that held only her chair and table and from which on a bright day she could look across the cliffs to the sea. Here she hoped to find the silence and contentment that were so necessary to her.

She began *Shadows on the Rock* in earnest in the fall at the Grosvenor and went back to Quebec alone at Thanksgiving to do further research. Her peaceful life was discommoded once again in December when her mother suffered a stroke in California. Willa immediately went out to be with her and help Douglass make arrangements for her care. It was the start of the bleakest period in Willa's life, from which she never fully recovered. At first Mrs. Cather was in an apartment hotel in Long Beach with nurses around the clock and Willa stayed at the Breakers. Zoë had moved to California and was in Los Angeles, but Willa felt too heavy-hearted to be social, and she begged Zoë not to betray the fact that she was in that part of the world. She was in no mood to be a literary personage. In March they decided to put Mrs. Cather in a sanatorium in Pasadena. Douglass was nearby and could visit his mother every day, and a cottage on the premises was made available to Willa whenever she came. Having her mother in California meant that Willa once again became a transient. Since she would have to spend a lot of time in California she never even tried to find a permanent apartment in New York but just stayed on with Edith at the Grosvenor.

The travel back and forth across the continent was exhausting, and her mother's piteous condition added to the strain of the next two and a half years. Mrs. Cather's mind was as keen as ever but her body was paralyzed. Relations between Willa and her mother had often been difficult. Mrs. Cather was a demanding woman and Willa could be stubborn. But the Cathers were a close family who drew together in time of trouble. There was never any question but that Willa would be with her mother as often as possible, and she did not complain about the long train trips. Yet it broke her heart to see her proud mother as helpless as a baby, and she told her friends that every time she came away after a visit, she was so knocked out it took months to get over it.

In June she came back to New York and went up to New Haven to receive an honorary degree from Yale. She was painfully tired and told Carrie it was absolutely the last degree she would take. Nevertheless, she boasted a bit that Yale had given a degree to only one woman writer before her, Edith Wharton, and that she was the only woman among six very old boys this year. Edith told her to tell Carrie that she got more than twice as much applause as anyone else when her degree was given. Following the Yale commencement she went to Grand Manan and after a summer on her flowery, bowery isle, as she called it, she stopped in Jaffrey before returning finally to

New York. She was desperate to go to Red Cloud for Christmas but it wasn't possible, she told Dorothy. Her mother had become terribly jealous in her illness and would be hurt if she so much as stopped off there on her way to California. If they were to become the older generation, why could it not be done without so much pain? It was like dying twice. She and Edith spent New Year's in Quebec and she went out West to see her mother early in 1930, this time staying four months.

The other Cather children all came for brief visits and Elsie, who was teaching in Lincoln, came for longer periods during school holidays. In the summer of 1930 Willa felt comfortable enough about the care Mrs. Cather was receiving—she did not think there was another spot where anyone so pitifully helpless could be looked after so beautifully—to make a long-planned trip to France with Edith. She had put *Shadows on the Rock* aside while she was in California, working instead on short stories, but the book was always in her mind. It was to be a historical novel and she considered it important to visit the parts of Paris associated with Count Frontenac's life before he went to Canada. Frontenac and Laval, the Bishop who accompanied him, were to be protagonists in the story.

After several weeks in Paris, Willa went on an excursion to St. Malo with Isabelle and Jan and when they left Paris for the Mozart Festival in Germany she and Edith traveled to the South. They stayed with friends in Marseille first and then went on to Aix Les Bains. It was a lovely quiet place, Willa wrote to Zoë, as worldly as a capital and as simple as a village. It was while she was in the Grand Hotel at Aix Les Bains that Willa encountered Madame Grout, the remarkable old lady who turned out to be Flaubert's niece, his "dear Caro." At first it seemed so personal—Willa had bent over and kissed the old lady's hand when Madame Grout revealed her identity—that Willa thought of telling only a few of her closest friends about the amazing adventure, as she called it. Later she changed her mind, perhaps at Edith's urging, and told the story in an article in the *Atlantic Monthly*, calling it "A Chance Meeting." The piece shows Willa at her most sympathetic and unguarded, as she always was with the very old. Hearing Madame Grout talk about Flaubert and about Turgenev, whom she had known well as a child, must have taken Willa back to the happy hours she had once spent listening to Annie Fields telling stories about Dickens. Willa was herself a recognized and admired literary figure now, but before this fascinating French woman she showed the same tender homage Elsie Sergeant had perceived so long ago in her friend's behavior toward their hostess in Charles Street.

Flaubert's niece and Willa both wept when it was time to part. Willa might have stayed longer but alarming news had come from Paris. Her beloved Isabelle was very ill and Willa once more hurried to the side of someone dear to her. Though Isabelle rallied, Willa felt the shadows falling on her own small circle. Mrs. Canfield died that summer and Willa wrote to Dorothy that the vanishings, one after the other, made the world seem sadly diminished. The landmarks were disappearing and the splendid distances behind were closing. It was as if one were going on in a play after most of the characters were dead.

She and Edith sailed for home on the Canadian Pacific liner, the S.S. *Empress of France*, which stopped at Quebec, where Willa spent several weeks before returning to New York by way of Jaffrey. She hated to leave the country but she had to be back in town by mid-November when the National Institute of Arts and Letters honored her with the prestigious Howells Medal for *Death Comes for the Archbishop*. She was accompanied on that occasion by Wilbur Cross, the governor of Connecticut, who was a great admirer of her work. All fall she worked steadily on *Shadows on the Rock* so that she could finish it by the end of the year before she had to go back to California.

Though she disliked the Grosvenor, Willa found some compensation in its proximity to the New York Society Library which was then on Thirteenth Street just around the corner. She stopped in often while she was working on *Shadows* to consult old herbals, maps and histories of Paris. The librarian, Marian King, remembered her in those days as "a rather short, stocky lady in an apple-green coat and matching green pork-pie felt hat, which she alternated with a similar habit in red . . ." Her voice was husky and rather boyish and seemed to come in little gusts. When she first came into the library she was somewhat shy: "'I'd like to subscribe here if I may,'" she said in her abrupt way. "'My name is Cather. I'm by way of being a writer.'" She evidently found the librarian compatible and when they met, as Willa took her morning exercise, she would turn back and walk to the library for what Mrs. King described as "a succession of five minute chats" about everything from books to green vegetables—Willa wanted them only in season, not covered with cold water and slowly introduced to heat. During one of those chats Willa told Mrs. King that she would always be grateful to *Shadows on the Rock* for carrying her over a hard stretch of her life.

Mary Virginia Auld, her red-haired niece, spent the Christmas holidays with her in New York. Zoë had sent a gorgeous green evening jacket which Mary Virginia kept trying on most of New Year's Eve. But she won't get it, said Willa, and she knows it. Willa finished *Shadows on the Rock* on the twenty-seventh of December and left for California soon after. Her mother's condition showed no improvement. Douglass' devotion was beyond words, she wrote to Dorothy; he would so much rather have her like this than not at all. The proofs of *Shadows* came from Knopf while she was in the West and she repeated to Dorothy what she had said to Mrs. King, that the book had been her rock of refuge, the only thing in her life that held together and stayed the same.

Despite her intention never to accept another honorary degree, she received two in 1931, one from the University of California and one from Princeton. She was in distinguished company in Princeton—Charles A. Lindbergh, Frank B. Kellogg and Newton D. Baker—but according to the New York *Times*, "the conferring of the Doctorate of Letters on Willa Cather seemed to attract the greatest attention." She was, in fact, the first woman ever to receive an honorary degree from that male stronghold. Princeton went off with a bang, she told Zoë. She sat next to Lindbergh at the President's Dinner and the next day she lunched with him and his wife in the students' dining hall. She was taken with both. All her photographs to the contrary, she reported to Zoë, Mrs. Lindbergh was fascinating and quite worthy to be the flyer's wife. When their baby boy was kidnapped and later found dead, Willa was heartsick for them and felt the pain of notoriety for two such private people.

For herself, the occasion of the Princeton degree brought a flurry of publicity. A "Profile" appeared in *The New Yorker*, written by the poet Louise Bogan and subtitled "American-Classic." Bogan found her a "perfectly natural person" and commented on her deep voice, her preference for bright colors and exotic strings of beads and the fact, not mentioned in other interviews, that Willa smoked cigarettes "as though she really liked the taste of ignited tobacco and rice paper." *Time* magazine put her on the cover of its issue of August 3, causing her mother even more displeasure than the Bakst portrait. Willa wrote apologizing for the horrible picture but said she was not responsible. One just had to grin and bear such things. She signed the letter "Willie." It was the last letter she would ever write to her mother.

When her mother died on August 30, Willa was at Grand Manan. Elsie and Douglass made the journey from Pasadena with the body and Roscoe joined them on the way. There was no boat out in time for Willa to get home for the funeral, but in December she opened her parents' house and spent a last Christmas in Red Cloud with Elsie. Lizzie Huffman, a former housekeeper of whom Willa was especially fond, came and kept house. Friends and neighbors called and Willa made a trip in the snow to see Annie Pavelka and her family. Mariel sent a plum pudding which Elsie and Willa saved to have with Douglass who came in time for New Year's. It was a lovely Christmas, Elsie told Mariel, with the old house open and alive. It was hard to think her mother and father were not there.

With her sisters and brothers Willa donated two stained-glass windows to Grace Episcopal Church in Red Cloud in memory of her mother and father. But she also paid another kind of tribute to them in the way that only she could. While she was staying at the sanatorium she had found it difficult to work on *Shadows on the Rock*, which required meticulous attention to historical detail. Her mother's illness and her father's recent death preoccupied her and her mind kept going back to the early days in Red Cloud when the family was whole and life was full of promise. She wrote three stories about those happier times. "Neighbor Rosicky" is about a city-bred Bohemian immigrant who enjoys the bright lights and dissipations of New York but feels a longing for the country and ends his life farming in Nebraska. "He was like a tree that has not many roots, but one taproot that goes down deep." "Two Friends" tells of two businessmen in town—one of them is based on Mr. Miner—who have a falling-out over William Jennings Bryan.

In "Old Mrs. Harris," the most autobiographical story Willa ever wrote, she recreated the Cather house at Third and Cedar and the three generations who had lived there. She had fussed a good deal with the writing but she was satisfied. The simplest was always the most difficult, she said; you had to wait for it and catch it asleep. In the story her parents are young, her grandmother is alive and next door, the Wieners, here called the Rosens, keep a tender watch over the comings and goings of the household and especially the prickly adolescent daughter who stops by in the afternoons to rummage through their library. When the story ran as a serial in the *Ladies' Home Journal* it was called "Three Women." In 1932 Knopf brought out the three Nebraska tales in a single volume with the hauntingly appropriate title, *Obscure Destinies*.

Willa never went back to Red Cloud, although she sometimes thought she might. Her parents had always shielded her from the gossip and animosity of the town and without them she felt undefended. She realized sadly how much their love and pride had meant to her. The strain of the last years had aged her. She was only fifty-four but her friends saw her becoming old. Though she would have liked to slip into town quietly without anyone knowing it, except for Carrie and a very few others, it was impossible. And in the end she knew she was not strong enough for either the pleasure or the pain of it. Now they were the older generation, she wrote to Dorothy.

THE TRANSFIGURING TOUCH

When Willa finished *Shadows on the Rock* she received a letter from Dorothy Canfield, then a judge of the Book-of-the-Month Club, concerning the possibility of the book's becoming a selection of the club. Knowing Willa's disapproval of book clubs in general—she thought they were too much like required reading assignments—Dorothy sought to reassure her, especially in regard to the effect on booksellers. Willa was convinced that the fact that her books were not available through mail-order clubs helped their sales in bookstores, and Knopf agreed. But she was reluctant to offend Dorothy and Henry Seidel Canby, who was chairman of the board of judges. When she came to Knopf with Dorothy's proposal, he cleverly decided to put the matter to the booksellers themselves. Knopf salesmen across the country were asked to inquire of their most important accounts whether Willa Cather's new book, *Shadows on the Rock*, should be sold to the Book-of-the-Month Club. The vote was overwhelmingly in favor of the idea, with booksellers arguing that a club selection would mean increased sales in their stores. Ultimately, according to Knopf, the book had the largest sale of any of Willa's books he published. This, despite almost uniformly negative reviews.

Even the critics who had nice things to say about the author's style and use of language found *Shadows on the Rock* dramatically thin. The relationship between the apothecary and his daughter, which took so much of its tone from the tenderness Willa felt for her own father, was touching but not strong enough to sustain a story that lacked the impetus of conflict and that moved at almost a lethargic pace. The historical figures, the Count de Frontenac and the old Bishop, who had played such grand roles in the affairs of men in their lifetime, were somehow domesticated by being observed through the eyes of a child. "A very delicate and very dull book," said *The New Republic.* Comparing it unfavorably to the *Archbishop*, the critic for *The Outlook* wrote that "*Death Comes for the Archbishop* was a bell ringing between heaven and earth, its deep reverberations going on and on and on into space." *Shadows on the Rock* was a bell too, the critic said, "a pure thin tinkle in a sanctuary; beautiful, but not great." Even the devoted Edith felt that *Shadows* and the novels that came after it betrayed Willa's weariness. Willa had always suffered from raising great expectations. Time and again reviewers would remark about a book of hers that it would be considered a triumph for any other novelist, but that it was a disappointment coming from Willa Cather.

Willa was inclined to be philosophical about her treatment by the critics, especially as her books kept selling well. Every day brought letters from appreciative readers all over the world telling how much her stories meant to them. She seemed to touch the heart of a large and generous public and she numbered many of the famous among those who called themselves her fans. Thomas Hardy, the greatest living novelist, in Willa's opinion, particularly admired *A Lost Lady.* Tomáš Masaryk, the President of Czechoslovakia, not only read all of Willa's books but also corresponded with the real-life Ántonia, promising Annie that she would be an honored guest if she should visit his country. To Willa he wrote that although as a rule he did not prefer short stories—"I like the whole drama of life"— nevertheless, he liked "Neighbor Rosicky" and could quote the last page of "Old Mrs. Harris." The book, *Obscure Destinies*, had a great success in London. When Myra Hess came to New York for a concert she told Willa that all her musical friends were talking about it and she brought interesting messages about each one of the stories from John Galsworthy.

Death Comes for the Archbishop brought more mail than any of Willa's books except *My Antonia.* In many ways those two books were the cornerstones of her art. James M. Barrie, the creator of Peter Pan, had a special fondness for the *Archbishop* and the actress and writer Cornelia Otis Skinner, whose mother was a friend of Willa's, spoke for generations of readers when she wrote that to read *Death Comes for the Archbishop* was "a benediction." Oliver Wendell Holmes wrote to Willa on stationery of the United States Supreme Court to say that he had just finished the *Archbishop*—his secretary had been reading it to him—and that it had given him great pleasure. "You have the gift of the transfiguring touch," he wrote. "What to another would be prose, under your hand becomes poetry without ceasing to be truth." He had already thanked Ferris Greenslet for introducing him to *My Antonia,* which lifted him "to all [his] superlatives." Greenslet himself said he personally read *Shadows on the Rock* most often, that no other book so completely captured the spirit of a place.

As for Willa, she thought that if her books had to be read year after year in school, though she deplored the idea, probably the *Archbishop* would stand the wear and tear better than the others, which did not mean it was necessarily her own favorite. It was usually the book she had just finished or the one she was beginning to which she gave her heart. It pleased her that people grew attached not only to the books themselves but also to her characters, as though they had taken on a reality quite independent of their author. She loved it when she went to see a new doctor, the head of the Stomach Clinic at St. Luke's, who asked her first name and, when she gave it to him, put down his pen and leaned back in his chair, saying, "Is it really?" He said he had hoped she might be a relative of Willa Cather's, that he would rather have written *My Antonia* than any other book written in America. That kind of serendipitous admiration pleased her more than all the honors she received.

XIV

————— ❦ —————

A Life of Disciplined Endeavor

SPLENDID YOUNG PEOPLE

In the fall of 1932 Willa's transient years came to an end. It had been
a miserable period in her life and she always associated the Gros-
venor with death and illness. In December she and Edith moved to a
commodious apartment on Park Avenue at Sixty-second Street.
Willa was never as attached to 570 Park as she was to Number Five
Bank Street, but when the furniture came out of storage and her
George Sand engraving and the head of Keats were over the mantel,
she began to feel at home. Nevertheless, she was a very different
Willa from the young woman who had settled so exuberantly in
Greenwich Village in the early 1900s. Then she had looked out at
the world with pleasure and anticipation. The windows of the Bank
Street apartment had opened to the street and the rooms seemed always to be flooded with sunlight. The Park Avenue apartment was
in the rear of the building and the heavily curtained windows all
faced the blank wall of the exclusive Colony Club next door. The
apartment turned its back on the fashionable avenue below just as

Willa shut herself off from the life around her. Even in the last years at Bank Street she had rented an empty apartment above hers so that she would not be disturbed by noise overhead. To the public she had become what George Seibel once called her, "an ingrown genius."

Privately, she denied that she ever shut herself away from people she cared about. It was the crowd she shut out in order to be all there for her friends, especially the ones back home who depended on her. Five years of drought in the Middle West had brought great suffering in Nebraska. Willa sent fruits and vegetables and holiday chickens but she knew she could not bring the dead trees and ruined pastures back to life. She wrote to Zoë from Grand Manan that she felt guilty on her cool green flowery island while in Nebraska her friends were enduring another summer of scorching heat. She wished she could increase her gifts but the Depression was taking its toll in New York too, and many of her friends there were down and out. It was desperate to be without money in a big city, she told Carrie, worse than being poor in the country.

Even her rich little niece, as she called Jessica's daughter, was having a hard time in New York and Willa sent her a T-bone steak and fresh vegetables. Mary Virginia had finished college and was working at low-paying jobs but she never complained, never whimpered and her aunt was proud of her. As always, Willa was at her happiest when she had the young around her and her nieces often spent vacations with her in New York or Grand Manan. Splendid young people, she said once, seemed to give her something to live for. In the 1930s Willa's circle of intimates widened to include three young people who were to become as dear to her as if they were her own family. In fact, in later years, she often said they were among the chief treasures of her life.

She had been introduced to the Menuhins—Moshe and Marutha and their children, Yehudi, Hephzibah and Yaltah—by Jan Hambourg during her visit to Isabelle and Jan in 1930. The next winter the girls came to see her in New York with their mother and when Willa was in California she saw Yehudi when he gave a concert in Los Angeles. Yehudi Menuhin had begun to play the violin at the age of four and was seven when he made his debut with the San Francisco Symphony Orchestra. Hephzibah was a prodigy as well and frequently gave concerts with her brother. Both she and Yaltah were pianists. Prodigies had always interested Willa. In the old days she had often written about child performers, although none too kindly. And one of her early stories in the *Home Monthly* had actually been called "The Prodigies," and concerned two musicians, a brother and sister, exploited by an ambitious mother.

The Menuhin parents, however, bore no resemblance to the Mackenzies of the story. Willa admired Moshe and Marutha and approved the way they brought up their three prodigies. When Willa met them, Yehudi was fourteen, Hephzibah was ten and the youngest, Yaltah, was only nine. Edith Lewis wrote that the Menuhins "were not only the most gifted children Willa Cather had ever known, with that wonderful aura of imaginative charm, prescience, inspiration, that even the most gifted lose after they grow up; they were also extremely lovable, affectionate, and unspoiled; in some ways funnily naïve, in others sensitive and discerning far beyond their years." Edith adored them too, and she and Willa kept a Menuhin scrapbook in which they pasted photographs, newspaper items and critical reviews.

To Willa, Yehudi and his sisters seemed almost enchanted, like children in a fairy tale. And they in turn were drawn to her buoyant personality and quickly made her a part of their lives as "Aunt Willa." It was a unique and precious relationship and it lasted until Willa's death. Her letters to friends were filled with tales of the Menuhin family. She wished she could show the dear children to Carrie; Carrie would understand why they were so important to her. Yehudi was growing more beautiful as an artist and a human being all the time, she wrote. On his sixteenth birthday she and Edith were guests at dinner and a few nights later the Menuhin family came to dine with them.

On Willa's birthday they showered her with attention. Flowers poured into the apartment from every member of the family, each one sending his or her own favorite. The box from the father was so huge that Josephine had to dash out and buy more vases. Another year, there was a blizzard on Yehudi's birthday and Willa spent the morning coasting with the children in the park—Yehudi stored his sled with her every year—after which they returned to a luncheon Marutha had prepared with Yehudi's favorite dishes and two bottles of champagne. Only one other guest was invited besides Edith and

Willa. It was a lovely party, Willa said, with the whole world out-side lost in snow and perfect harmony inside.

One of the advantages of the Park Avenue apartment was that it was close to Central Park. The Menuhins were usually at the Ansonia on Broadway, but they sometimes stayed at the Savoy-Plaza on Fifth Avenue at Fifty-eighth Street and then Willa would stop by at the hotel to see if the children wanted to join her on her daily walk around the reservoir. Yaltah, for whom Willa seemed to have a special tenderness, would find a hand-delivered envelope addressed formally to Miss Yaltah Menuhin with a note inside to "My darlingest Yaltah" inviting her to elope for an hour and go walking in the park. Or the little girl might receive a pressed autumn leaf, delivered by "carrier pigeon," who took much love on his wings from Aunt Willa. Sometimes the three children accompanied Willa, taking turns walking alongside and holding her hand. When they were away on tour, as they so often were, they wrote long letters about their experiences and Willa said the quick brightening in the air when a letter came made her realize how dear they had all become to her.

Because the children spent so much time abroad their speech had a somewhat foreign flavor and Willa worried about their lack of familiarity with the English language and especially with the great works of English literature. She wanted to introduce them to Shakespeare and asked Marutha if she might organize an English Club for the children and herself. At first only the girls were to participate, but when Yehudi asked to join they agreed to include him. Years afterward he recalled how they used to gather round the table in a small room at the Ansonia for the Shakespeare readings, "each taking several parts, and Aunt Willa commenting on the language and situations in such a way as to draw us into her own pleasure and excitement." She secured copies of the plays in the original Temple Edition for each of the children, and Edith Lewis, who joined the group from time to time, said that Willa was greatly touched when Yehudi told her once that he had not been able to resist buying a complete secondhand set of the Temple Shakespeare when he came across it in a New Orleans bookshop.

To the Menuhins, Willa's "mannish figure and country tweed-iness, her let's lay-it-on-the-table manners and unconcealed blue eyes, her rosy skin and energetic demeanor" were the embodiment of

America, while what she adored in them, as Yehudi Menuhin observed, was "what she felt had not been her birthright—the old, the European, the multilayered, and above all, music." He might have added that their association with Isabelle was another thing that drew Willa to the Menuhin family.

In 1935 Isabelle's illness, that had begun five years earlier, became acute and Jan brought her to America for medical attention. The case was hopeless; she was suffering from a fatal liver ailment and the most that could be done was to make her as comfortable as possible. Willa visited her daily for the three weeks she was in a New York hospital and then traveled with her to Chicago when Jan went out to give a summer course and Isabelle insisted on accompanying him. The Menuhins were in Australia where Yehudi was enjoying a spectacularly successful tour and Willa sent a heartbreaking letter to Marutha describing Isabelle's plight and her own despair. Life had been pretty dark and difficult for her since Isabelle's arrival, so very, very ill. Marutha replied with words that were like a hand stretched out to pull her from the water, Willa said. Yet in spite of her own pain Willa knew how fearful children often were of sick people and she tried to prepare fourteen-year-old Yaltah. Her Aunt Isabelle, she wrote reassuringly to Yaltah, was not at all forlorn or dismal as some invalids were. She had never been so beautiful in face or manner as she was now in her illness. A kind of nobleness had come to her, said Willa, and Yaltah need never dread seeing her.

Willa's niece, Mary Virginia Auld, was married in the "Little Church Around the Corner" in early June and Isabelle roused herself to be present at the wedding, even attending the little tea afterward. But she was very frail. When Jan's classes ended he brought her to Cherry Valley where her brother and his family were vacationing. Isabelle kept to her bed for most of the visit and Jan spent his time hovering over her possessively, possibly to avoid being with the McClungs, who had never found him endearing, although they acknowledged that Isabelle loved him and that he seemed to make her happy. In July he took her back to Europe for the last time.

A few weeks later Willa and Edith sailed for Italy, spending six weeks in the Dolomites and Venice before joining the Hambourgs in Paris. For almost two months Willa was with Isabelle constantly, keeping her diverted and helping Jan to care for her. As always,

Isabelle responded to her devotion and seemed to rally. In November, Willa left for home. She was never to see Isabelle again.

LUCY GAYHEART

Having an apartment of her own again seemed to release Willa's energies. It pleased her to be able to receive her friends in dignified surroundings and she and Edith began to entertain at small dinners. One of the few bright spots while they were at the Grosvenor had been the reappearance of Josephine in their lives. She was married and had a family but she came in half a day to do the laundry and keep the place in order and, most important, prepare a delicious French meal every night. It was the kind of food, said Willa, that was simple and honest, not over-rich and showy, the kind that was made chiefly out of human brains and a long and glorious national past. Josephine came with them to Park Avenue, but a few years later she and her husband decided to go back to France. By then she had become a friend and Willa felt her loss keenly, though she rejoiced with Josephine that she was back in her own glorious mountains, living out her vigorous life in the country she loved so passionately.

The space, the silence, the sense of peace and privacy were just what Willa needed for her work. In the spring following the move to Park Avenue she began a new book, working on it over the next months in New York, Grand Manan and Jaffrey. The story of *Lucy Gayheart* with its melancholy note of loss and loneliness seemed to spring directly from Willa's mood in the aftermath of her parents' death. But along with the nostalgia for home the book also reflects the direction of her present interests and her increasing preoccupation with music. She went less to the opera but regularly attended concerts, sometimes several a week. The Knopfs made her a gift of a phonograph and Yehudi kept her supplied with his recordings and Hephzibah's. Ethel Litchfield came for dinner at least once a week and they would spend the evening listening to Willa's records. E. K. Brown said that Irene Weisz told him that whenever Willa was unhappy, under strain or fatigued, she would plead, " 'I must have music.' "

Music is important in Lucy Gayheart's bittersweet career, but her experiences in Chicago where she goes to study and her passion for the singer Clement Sebastian are not the reasons for the book's unique appeal. What moves the reader, almost unbearably, are the small details of Lucy's life in Haverford and the memory the town keeps, long after her death, of a figure "always in motion; dancing or skating, or walking swiftly with intense direction, like a bird flying home." Lucy is too frail to be one of Willa's pioneer heroines; she lacks the staying power of women like Ántonia and Alexandra. And while the musical portions of the book inevitably recall *The Song of the Lark,* neither Lucy's talent nor her drive measures up to Thea's. Her old friends in Haverford loved her for her gaiety and grace. "Life seemed to lie near the surface in her. She had that singular brightness of young beauty: flower gardens have it for the first few hours after sunrise."

There is also the other image, of a little prairie town in winter. Haverford on the Platte is an echo of Red Cloud and once again Willa pins down the essential qualities of all such little towns where "lives roll along so close to one another; loves and hates beat about, their wings almost touching. On the sidewalks along which everybody comes and goes," she wrote, "you must, if you walk abroad at all, at some time pass within a few inches of the man who cheated and betrayed you, or the woman you desire more than anything else in the world. Her skirt brushes against you. You say good-morning, and go on. It is a close shave. Out in the world the escapes are not so narrow."

For Lucy herself Willa had two memories to draw upon. One was the girl in Blue Hill so long ago, the young schoolteacher she had met just once, whose last name was similar to Gayheart. And the other was a girl in Red Cloud who often skated on the frozen pond with Willa and her friends. Willa knew that Carrie would remember Sadie Becker and the way she used to skate in the old rink dressed in a red jersey. She wasn't certain whether Sadie Becker had golden-brown eyes like the ones she was giving Lucy, but she could still hear the girl's contralto laugh, as clearly as she did when she was twelve.

Lucy Gayheart came out in February 1935 and the next month began serial publication in *Woman's Home Companion*. Willa never liked to see her stories broken up, but magazines paid well and especially in hard times she didn't see how she could refuse the money. She particularly asked Carrie, however, to read the story over again in book form. The first part didn't mean much, she told her, until you get to the last part; it was built that way. She didn't think *Lucy* was one of her best books, although Myra Hess, the Hambourgs and other musicians thought so. Nevertheless, it held its end up, she reported to Carrie, and was a big success abroad, heading the best-seller list for eight weeks with Anne Lindbergh's *North to the Orient*, which Willa loved, in second place.

While she was working on *Lucy Gayheart*, Willa suffered a relatively minor mishap which was to have serious consequences. She had finished her handwritten copy of the book and was about to start on the typing when she sprained the tendons of her right wrist. She ignored it for as long as she could until the wrist became inflamed and began to cause her considerable discomfort. It was impossible to hold a pencil, and typing was excruciating. The prescribed treatment was to immobilize the hand completely, making it a torture to write or to perform almost any other simple human act. After the first acute attack the inflammation subsided, only to return again, sometimes affecting the right hand, sometimes the left. A noted orthopedist, whom Willa consulted in despair, devised a brace for her that left the fingers somewhat free while immobilizing the thumb. With difficulty she could just manage to sign her name or scrawl a few personal words on a card. It meant, however, that for the last eight or nine years of her life she was forced to dictate all her letters. But she could not dictate her stories. She told Carrie that to compose, she had to see the words forming on the sheet of paper like a picture.

The disability seemed to mock all Willa's worst fears. It crippled her; it made her helpless; and it prevented her from doing her life's work. It was a not uncommon affliction of washerwomen, she said bitterly. People who did small fine mechanical work with repetition of small careful movements of the hand were the ones who suffered from it, not writers, most of whom used typewriters. But Willa, who wrote by hand, was afflicted like any manual laborer and her last years were lived in almost constant pain. She wrote her final book slowly and painfully and after it was published in 1940 she worked fitfully on the last stories, which were published after her death.

As Willa's output slackened and she herself became more reclusive, honors came less frequently, but they did not stop entirely. Smith College gave her a degree, and in 1933 she was awarded the Prix Femina Americain for *Shadows on the Rock*. She was not eager to accept it but Alfred Knopf told her it was one prize she simply could not refuse. Nevertheless, when Edna St. Vincent Millay made the presentation Willa froze in the glare of flashbulbs as photographers crowded round to take her picture. In 1937, after a series of negotiations, Houghton Mifflin brought out a Library Edition of her works, beautifully designed by Bruce Rogers. Willa rearranged the order of her books, making *O Pioneers!* Volume One, but aside from revisions in *The Song of the Lark,* cuts in the Introduction to *My Antonia,* and the elimination of some dedications, she made few other changes, content to let her books speak for her as they always had. The twelve volumes included *Not Under Forty*, a collection of her essays that Knopf brought out in 1936, retitled *Literary Encounters*. A thirteenth volume was added in 1940 with the publication of *Sapphira and the Slave Girl*.

Though her books continued to be translated abroad, which pleased her, the translations invariably involved her in details she found tiresome. They were often beautiful editions, she said, but she was more interested in writing new books. She complained that she had a constant struggle to keep her books from being read on radio and she remained adamantly opposed to dramatizations of any kind. She would also not allow Knopf to accept offers to anthologize her works and she scolded Elsie Sergeant for even suggesting that she permit Viking to bring out a Portable edition. Knopf himself remained her staunch ally, fending off the more aggressive demands and protecting her from assaults on her privacy. Nevertheless, he thought it was sad that Willa "never realized how widely known, admired and respected she was and how many people were eager at least to shake her hand."

A 1936 photograph by Carl Van Vechten shows Willa as she appeared in those years, assured, worldly, a little haughty, no longer the open-faced young woman in a middy that Steichen saw ten years earlier. For Van Vechten, Willa stood fashionably posed, her bearing regal, her head framed luxuriously in fur.

OLD AFFECTIONS

The pleasures that came to Willa in the thirties came principally from friends. Dorothy Canfield Fisher was asked to do a profile of her for the New York *Herald Tribune*'s literary section and, although Willa said that reading the dates made her seem to belong to a bygone era, she nevertheless admitted that Dorothy had done the operation as gently as it could be done. Dorothy sent her a typescript of the article before publication and Willa corrected two dates. By this time she may even have believed the fiction that she was born in 1876 and not in 1873. Loyal friend that she was, Dorothy meekly made the changes. She called the profile "Daughter of the Frontier" and in it she gave her theory of the genesis of Willa's art. "The one real subject of all her books," wrote Dorothy, "is the effect a new country—our new country—has on people transplanted to it from the old traditions of a stable, complex civilization."

Willa had her own ideas, and she wrote to Dorothy that the common denominator of her books was escape. She had always fled the less agreeable for the more agreeable, she said, and she had never made a sacrifice to art. She taught because it was less distasteful than newspaper work. She wanted to see the world so she spent five years at *McClure's* doing it, and when she'd had enough she stopped. She had also spent as much time listening to music as some people spent at their professions. It was important to her that Dorothy had not made her sound noble or pathetic. She wanted neither false praise nor sentiment, but she thanked Dorothy for her kind judgments and loyalties to old memories, and told her that Isabelle, who was certainly the hardest person to please in such matters, had said "a good job" without reservations.

Zoë Akins was another friend who could be counted on to bring color and amusement into Willa's life, and her successful playwriting career was one of Willa's greatest joys. When a telegram arrived one day from California announcing Zoë's unexpected marriage to the

artist Hugo Rumbold, Willa wired back that the news was a delight
and gave her the wildest surprise. Later she wrote at length, as
though Zoë might misunderstand the exclamation of surprise, to say
that she was confident that Zoë, of all her friends, would be able to
make matrimony work. And she suggested in a charming and discerning fashion the qualities Zoë possessed so abundantly that ideally
fitted her to be a wife. She was not fussy about trifles, she was elastic
and she had a natural power of enjoying life that Willa envied. Zoë,
said Willa, had always had a golden glow about her and she always
would.

Less than a year later Zoë's happiness that Willa had so joyously
predicted was cruelly and tragically cut short. Before she and her
husband had celebrated their first wedding anniversary, Hugo Rumbold was killed in an automobile accident. Willa was shocked and
her grief for Zoë came from deep in her own heart. After one is
forty-five, she said, it simply rains death all about one and after fifty
the storm grows fiercer. When she and Zoë first knew each other the
obituary page hadn't the slightest connection with their lives. She
added words meant to comfort, but they sound a bleak note. Personal life was rather a failure always, biologically so. But something
nice happened in the mind as one grew older. It would come to Zoë,
Willa promised, if she kept her courage up; it was a kind of inner
light that compensated for the many losses and the afflictions of the
body.

IT RAINS DEATH

In 1938 Willa suffered two devastating losses that forever changed
the landscape of her private world. In December of the year before,
Douglass had come East to spend her birthday with her; six months
later he was dead of a heart attack. During the ten days they had together they had almost a lifetime of happiness, she told Carrie. On
her birthday she had stuffed the turkey for him herself because her
cook could never make the kind of stuffing that Grandma Boak had
made and that was the way Douglass liked it. One evening she sent
him to the theatre alone because she had a previous engagement. It
was a lost evening she would always bitterly regret.

Still mourning the brother she adored, she received another blow. The news she had been dreading for so long came at last; Isabelle had died in Italy on October 10. Jan Hambourg, the strange, erratic man who had nursed her so devotedly, buried her in the cemetery at Sorrento. Willa's grief was such that she could do no work for months. Writers wrote their books for just one person, she cried, and for her that person had been Isabelle. In time Jan returned the letters she had written to Isabelle over the years. As with all her personal correspondence Willa wanted the letters destroyed. Elsie Sergeant says that she made packs of them which Edith then took to the incinerator in their apartment house and burned.

The words that passed between them were obliterated by the flames but, like all the people Willa loved, Isabelle was preserved for her in memory. She had not seen Isabelle for three years, in part because she did not feel strong enough herself to make the trip. The other, perhaps unspoken reason was that she could not bear to see the alteration in her beloved friend. Death might take her away but it would not change Willa's image of her. For Willa, Isabelle was as beautiful as she had ever been, untouched by time or illness.

The next year her Christmas card to Carrie showed a village scene in winter, the houses and the trees blanketed in snow. Perhaps this little town was Red Cloud, Willa wrote, and perhaps she was among the gay little figures. But despite the effort to be cheerful, she could not escape her loss and she added a note, that if only Isabelle could have lived just a little longer, everything would be easier for her. It was a cry of anguish, of inconsolable bereavement.

THERE SEEMS NO FUTURE FOR MY GENERATION

Willa began her last book and her only Southern story in 1937. She made a nostalgic trip to Winchester with Edith in the spring of 1938, visiting the childhood home she had left so long ago. "It was as memorable an experience, as intense and thrilling in its way," wrote Edith, as her journeys to New Mexico. "Every bud and leaf and flower seemed to speak to her with a peculiar poignancy, every slope of the land, every fence and wall, rock and stream." *Sapphira and the*

Slave Girl did not come out until the end of 1940, almost six years after *Lucy Gayheart*. By then the personal misery that had engulfed her was matched by cataclysmic world events. When the French Army surrendered in June 1940, Edith Lewis said that Willa wrote in a "Line-a-day" diary she had begun to keep, " 'There seems to be no future at all for people of my generation.' "

Sapphira surprised Willa's public. It was not only that she had followed her most artless heroine with her most calculating, but she had never dealt with social or political problems before in any of her books. Now she touched a tender nerve when she set her tale against the background of the pre-Civil War, slave-owning South. Those critics who had always considered her irrelevant because she ignored the great causes of the day now attacked her for seeming to romanticize a pernicious society and for failing to come to grips properly with the institution of slavery. What they did not perceive was the author's crushing weariness and her urgent need to get her story told. Edith Lewis described her working on *Sapphira* "with a resoluteness, a sort of fixed determination . . . different from her ordinary working mood; as if she were bringing all her powers into play to save this, whatever else was lost."

Most of the reviews were favorable, however, as if the reviewers were grateful to meet the writer on her own terms. "[She] bucks the trend, swims upstream, walks by herself and does very nicely, thank you," wrote Clifton Fadiman in *The New Yorker*. And Henry Seidel Canby compared her work with the French art of the *nouvelle* "in which Voltaire triumphed and Turgenev excelled." "Miss Cather," he wrote, "has triumphed in it also." Alfred Knopf received a note from C. C. Burlingham, the courtly member of the bar and generous citizen of New York, then close to ninety, who wrote that he had just finished *Sapphira* " 'non sine lacrimis . . . what a marvelous book it is.' "

After autographing a special deluxe edition of two hundred copies of *Sapphira*, Willa was forbidden by her doctor to use her right hand at all. She sent advance copies of the book to Laura Hills and Elsie Sergeant, apologizing for not signing them personally. Her thumb was a serious factor in her life, she told Elsie, she couldn't even write her signature on checks. She was ill during much of 1940 and spent several weeks in French Hospital which she seemed almost to enjoy.

The nurses were becoming old friends and made her escape from the active world a pleasure rather than a misfortune. Nevertheless, a reporter who was sent to interview her found her querulous and distant.

During the winter, when she was suffering from a cold at home, Yehudi came almost every day bringing his young wife Nola. He would keep the wood fire going while Nola made the tea. Willa approved Yehudi's choice of a wife. He had often talked to her about his romances and after one unhappy episode she had told him, "'A little heartache is a good companion for a young man on his holiday.'" She had also offered him advice about the sort of woman he should marry. She thought that fundamental honesty was the most important quality, by which she seemed to mean a realistic attitude toward life that would accept the fact that two and two made four and that no amount of sighing or dreaming could turn it into five. Real love, she told him, was less admiration than a desire to help and make life easy for the other person. As *Time* had said of her, Willa Cather may have been a spinster, but she was not an old maid.

The following year Roscoe suffered a heart attack and Willa had no peace of mind until she went out to San Francisco to see him. She had a happy visit with Roscoe and his wife but she had no strength to visit her brothers Jim and Jack who lived in Southern California. She had made the trip out on the Santa Fe from Chicago, but she returned home on the northern route by way of British Columbia. At Lake Louise, Edith was ill for a week and they were both exhausted when they reached New York. Edith had accompanied her, Willa told her friends, because she needed help with her brace. After all their years together Willa still felt obliged to explain Edith's presence, as if it could never simply be taken for granted.

Thirty years after her death a book about lesbian writers would include a chapter on Willa Cather along with Radclyffe Hall, Gertrude Stein and others. A university lecturer would call her talk on Cather, "Problems of Interpretation in an Undeclared Lesbian Writer." And at a public hearing on gay rights a speaker would cite Willa Cather as one of the homosexuals whose presence in New York had enriched the city's cultural and intellectual life. But such openness was unthinkable in Willa's lifetime. Willa was silent about her sexual nature, keeping her most private feelings hidden. She never felt free even to dedicate a book to the friend with whom she lived for forty years. The writer Truman Capote, telling how he used to see her in 1942 at the Society Library, could recall his first impression. "'A lesbian?'" he remembered asking himself. "'Well, yes,'" he had decided. Capote was a boy of eighteen when he and Willa became friends, but he did not tell the story in print until 1981. By then such casual surmises had become acceptable in a way that was not possible in Willa's day.

"NON SINE LACRIMIS"

With failing health, life became increasingly difficult for Willa and she retreated more than ever into her private world. Content to be with Edith and one or two close friends, she saw fewer and fewer people and rarely accepted invitations or extended them. The Knopfs and the Menuhins were exceptions. And she kept up her correspondence through her secretary, Sarah Bloom. In July 1941 her gall bladder and appendix were taken out at New York's Presbyterian Hospital. Yehudi came on the subway to visit her, greatly impressing her surgeon. She was unaccustomed to the city in the summer and the intense heat and dampness slowed her recovery. She lost eighteen pounds and was down to one hundred and ten, her little niece's weight. All her dresses were miles too big for her, she told Elsie Sergeant, but she had neither the moral nor the physical strength to stand to have them fitted. She and Edith went to Williamstown for a month, but it was hot there too, and rained most of the time.

When the war came she suffered for her nieces and their husbands whose lives were dislocated. Once more it seemed the misery in the world was touching her own family. In World War II, just as in World War I, Willa responded to individual acts of gallantry rather than to causes. She made a new friend through the Knopfs who seemed to personify the situation of the exile, of whom there were so many in the world. The writer Sigrid Undset had escaped from occupied Norway in 1940, reaching New York after a harrowing journey through Siberia and Japan to San Francisco. Undset's personality was on a scale Willa had not encountered since the days of Olive

Fremstad. In some ways they were alike, the Norwegian author and the Swedish-American singer. A cook, a gardener and a proficient scholar who spoke four languages, Undset, like Fremstad, seemed to combine in herself an artist's sensibility with the practical nature of a peasant. She reminded Willa of the women on the prairie who had been cut on the same large pattern. It rested her, Willa told Carrie, simply to sit and look at the strength that had survived so much tragedy.

Although she continued to refuse requests for radio and motion picture adaptations of her work and only allowed the smallest possible selections to be included in anthologies, during the war she felt she could not deny permission for special armed forces editions. The result was that she was kept busy answering letters from GIs all over the world who wrote to say how glad they were to have discovered her. She was touched by the messages and by the warmth her books had evoked, and she faithfully dictated replies, but she would far rather have been writing new books. She had long had in mind a story about Avignon and she had begun work on it when she returned from her visit to Roscoe, only to put it aside as her strength declined. A novel proved too ambitious, and although she picked it up from time to time, the only writing she felt strong enough to finish were short stories.

The war brought a major change in Willa's life, one that saddened her but to which she was fortunately able to accommodate without too much disruption of her routine. Grand Manan, where she had spent so many happy days, became impossible after 1942, as the workmen left the island for service in the armed forces and the trip itself became more difficult. She and Edith gave much thought to an alternative and decided finally on the island of Mount Desert on the coast of Maine. The Asticou House, she wrote to Laura Hills in 1943, was heavenly cool and they had a cottage and a garden of their own. Charles Savage and his wife, who ran the inn, were impressed by the modesty of their famous guest. She took the smaller of the two bedrooms in the cottage for herself and declined a table on the popular water side of the dining room. Although she was very frail, she went walking every day with Edith. Charles Savage had built a little map house on a trail above the inn where she liked to stop and enjoy the view. When Savage expressed concern that he had not been able to attract many people to his map house, Willa told him that he should not worry, it was sufficient that she and Miss Lewis enjoyed it!

Willa and Edith spent four summers in Northeast Harbor and became familiar figures in the fashionable little seaside village. In 1945 Willa was there when a telegram reached her that her brother Roscoe had died in his sleep. She was crushed. It may have been an easy way out for him, she said, but it was hard for the people who loved him to realize that he was gone. She kept waking in the night thinking it was all a bad dream. The very day the news came she had been working on "The Best Years," the lovely story of their childhood. Her hand bothered her too much to write personally but she dictated letters informing her closest friends about her brother's death. Their sympathy gave her comfort. One always feels it when a friend cares and wishes one well, she said to Elsie Sergeant. Something passes between friends in silence and she and Elsie were old, old friends, and dear to each other.

In New York she lived a quiet life with Edith. A maid came in four hours a day to clean the apartment and give Willa a good lunch. She also negotiated with all the service and delivery people who came to the back door. Dinner was a problem, however. Edith did not get home from the office until six and then she generally rested for an hour before they set out to find a restaurant. Still, a very good maid for four hours was preferable to an indifferent one for eight, said Willa, who never lost her concern for domestic matters. She missed Mary Virginia who had been in the city most of the war but had now gone off to join her husband. No one could quite take her place but another niece was living in New Jersey and her nephew Charles was at West Point. It was wonderful to see the younger generation looking ahead so hopefully and getting the thrill out of life that they used to get, she wrote in one of her last letters to Carrie. For herself Willa didn't think she wanted to live in the new world they kept promising; it wasn't to her taste. If the young were optimistic about the future, it was because they had no beautiful past to remember.

One morning at the end of March 1947 Yehudi and Hephzibah came with their children to say goodbye before leaving for England, where they were to give a series of popularly priced recitals. The mood that morning may well have been elegiac—Willa was really very frail—but she always roused herself for the Menuhins and the brief visit was a sweet one.

On the seventeenth of April Willa sent a letter to Dorothy Canfield regarding their famous call on Housman forty-five years before. She hoped that Dorothy would help to refresh her memory of the visit to the poet. Perhaps in her Park Avenue apartment, in the poignant softness of a New York spring, Willa had been remembering the time she made her first trip to Europe with Isabelle and Dorothy, how young and dear her friends had been, and how much she had loved them. She had at last agreed to give an editor an account of that distant afternoon, long before she was a famous author, when she too had been ardent and impressionable and thirsting for experience. She was ready to tell the story now; unfortunately, it was too late.

On April 24 Willa was a little tired in the morning, choosing to remain in bed and have her lunch brought in to her. Edith Lewis said: "Her spirit was as high, her grasp of reality as firm as always." That afternoon at four-thirty she was in her room alone when she suffered a massive cerebral hemorrhage. By the time Edith arrived home, Willa was already dead.

In his biography of Archbishop Lamy, Paul Horgan writes that when Lamy died, the seminary at Clermont, where he had studied as a boy, recorded these words: "'Sa mort a été le fin d'un beau jour—his death was the end of a fine day.'" So might it be said of Willa Cather.

Afterword

────────── ❀ ──────────

Not even in death did Willa go home to Red Cloud. Her publisher and a few close friends joined Edith at a simple service in the apartment and four days later Willa Cather was laid to rest on a hillside in the cemetery at Jaffrey where she had requested to be buried. Her surviving brothers, James and Jack, accompanied her body when it was brought by train and automobile from New York.

Edith stayed on alone for twenty-five years—"Life seems nothing but pain since she has gone," she wrote to Hephzibah—keeping the apartment exactly as it was when Willa was alive. She died there on August 11, 1972, and lies beside her friend in the place they both had chosen and which they loved so well.

The words from *My Antonia* are carved on Willa's gravestone: ". . . that is happiness; to be dissolved into something complete and great."

Acknowledgments

───────── ❀ ─────────

Many people have helped to make the last few years a uniquely satisfying time for me. When I undertook the work of research and writing I had no idea the mention of Willa Cather's name would evoke such interest. Yet in almost any gathering I had only to say that I was writing a book about her to release a flow of happy recollections of the pleasure her stories and characters had given. Nothing encouraged me more than to discover that each one of her books was somebody's favorite and that she appealed equally to young and old and to both men and women. To all those who cheered me on with their enthusiasm I am grateful beyond measure.

Special thanks are owed to the individuals who responded so generously to a stranger's bold requests for information and who so willingly shared their knowledge and their memories. Through the kind offices of Joel Ryce I was able to read Willa Cather's letters to Yaltah Menuhin and I am grateful to Yaltah's son, Lionel Menuhin Rolfe, for putting me in touch with his mother and his stepfather. I treasure my correspondence with Professor Alfred McClung Lee and his cousin Samuel A. McClung III, and hope that one day I may have a chance to thank them both in person. Alfred Knopf, who was Willa Cather's publisher, was a gracious host at lunch. The author Jane Rule, who wrote perceptively about Willa Cather in *Lesbian Images,* replied unhesitatingly to my many questions. Her perspective was important in helping me to understand my subject. On a visit to Mount Desert I had the good fortune to make the acquaintance of Mrs. Charles Savage, who charmingly recalled the years when Willa Cather was a guest at the Asticou House.

In Red Cloud, Vi Borton kindly took me on a tour of Cather country and I enjoyed the hospitality of the Willa Cather Pioneer Memorial and its able curator, Ann Billesbach. At the Nebraska Historical Society in Lincoln, as in all the places where the surviving Cather letters are housed—the Huntington in California, the Lilly Library at Indiana University, the University of Vermont, the Morgan Library in New York—I met with the greatest courtesy and interest. The Barrett Library in Virginia and the Newberry in Chicago were expeditious in filling requests for Xerox copies and microfilm. I owe a special debt of gratitude to Dr. Charles Ryskamp, Director of the Morgan Library, and Herbert Cahoon, Curator for Autograph Manuscripts, for making it possible for me to see the Elizabeth Shepley Sergeant letters. As always, the New York Society Library was a pleasant place to do research.

I am the recipient of much hard work done by others and gratefully acknowledge the achievements of E. K. Brown, Leon Edel, Mildred Bennett, Bernice Slote, William Curtin, James Woodress, the late Virginia Faulkner and the University of Nebraska Press. Thanks to their scholarship and dedication, more is known all the time about Willa Cather's life and writings. They have lightened the biographer's task; indeed, they have made it possible. Grateful acknowledgment is also made to Willa Cather's publishers, Houghton Mifflin Company, Alfred A. Knopf and the University of Nebraska Press, for permission to quote from her works.

My dear friend, the late Dr. Leonard Small, discussed with me at length the complex nature of female homosexuality. I recall our conversation, at a time when he was very ill, with gratitude and sadness.

I have been uncommonly fortunate in my agents, Sterling Lord and Patricia Berens, and my editor, Kate Medina, and acknowledge with affection their patience and support.

I am indebted to August Heckscher for sharing work space and for his wise comments on the manuscript. Christine Shipman Doscher typed the manuscript in its early stages so that it began to resemble a book. Robert Witten, with great generosity, allowed unlimited use of his copying machine.

As someone who, like Willa Cather, never learned to drive a car, I would have found it difficult to make the trip to Red Cloud were it not for my friend Mary Perot Nichols, who flew down with me from New York and cheerfully drove me around Nebraska.

My husband's humor, his unflagging confidence and his companionship have seen me through. I am forever grateful.

P.C.R.

Notes

———— ❁ ————

Most of the citations below are drawn from reprints and soft-cover editions of Willa Cather's works. For the original, hard-cover editions, see the bibliography.

The following abbreviations have been used:

Willa Cather   WC
Dorothy Canfield Fisher   DCF
Edith Lewis   EL
S. S. McClure   SSMcC
Elizabeth Shepley Sergeant   ESS
Carrie Miner Sherwood   CMS
Irene Miner Weisz   IMW
Collected Short Fiction   CSF
The Kingdom of Art   KOA
Nebraska State Journal   NSJ
Not Under Forty   NUF
The Song of the Lark   SOL
The World and the Parish   W&P

Introduction

page 3 *Next morning she wrote*   WC to SSMcC, May 26, 1944. Willa Cather's correspondence with S. S. McClure and his wife is in the Lilly Library at Indiana University, Bloomington.

Chapter I   Mea Patria

page 6   *a date long obscured*   For a full discussion of Willa Cather's birth
   date, see Leon Edel, "Homage to Willa Cather" in *The Art of
   Willa Cather*, ed. by Bernice Slote and Virginia Faulkner, University of Nebraska Press, Lincoln, 1974, pp. 192–94.

page 8   *the indulgent father*   Ibid., p. 193.

page 15   *"that was all of it tragic"*   Edith Lewis, *Willa Cather Living*,
   Alfred A. Knopf, New York, 1953, Bison Books, University of
   Nebraska Press, Lincoln, p. 8.
   "every tree and every rock"   Ibid., p. 8.

page 16   *"a highway for dreamers"*   Willa Cather, "Nebraska: the End of
   the First Cycle," *The Nation* 117: 236–38, September 1923.

page 18   *There seemed nothing to see*   WC, *My Ántonia*, Houghton
   Mifflin Company, Boston, 1918, p. 7.

page 19   *young and fresh and kindly*   WC, *The Song of the Lark* (1915
   edition), University of Nebraska Press, Lincoln, p. 219.

page 20   *On Sunday we could drive*   WC, "Nebraska: the End of the
   First Cycle," op. cit.
   Perched on a shelf in Miner Brothers   Mildred Bennett, *The
   World of Willa Cather*, University of Nebraska Press, Lincoln,
   1961, p. 1.

page 22   *flower-laden spring*   WC, "Nebraska: the End of the First
   Cycle," op. cit.

page 24   *Even children in the street*   Mildred Bennett, *The World of
   Willa Cather*, p. 94.

page 25   *as in a hospital ward*   WC, "The Best Years," *The Old Beauty
   and Others*, Vintage Books, Random House, 1976, New York,
   p. 108.
   to be close enough to share   Ibid., p. 108.
   a story in itself   Ibid., p. 106.

page 26   *one of the most important things*   WC, *SOL*, p. 7.
   pleasant plans and ideas   Ibid.
   The mere struggle to have anything   WC, "Katherine Mansfield,"
   Not under Forty, Alfred A. Knopf, New York, 1936, p. 136.

page 27   *Brothers are better*   WC, *SOL*, p. 7.
   Human relationships are the tragic necessity   WC, "Katherine
   Mansfield," *NUF*, p. 136.

page 30   *"It's good for us he does drink"*   WC, *SOL*, p. 16.
   as if the hot wind that so much of the time blew   EL, *Willa
   Cather Living*, p. 17.

page 31   *It was this little town*   Ibid., p. 18.
   peculiarly fitted her   WC, "The Way of the World," *Collected
   Short Fiction, 1892–1912* (revised edition), University of Nebraska Press, Lincoln, 1970, p. 400.

page 33　*"had a remarkable perception"*　　　Edward K. Brown, *Willa Cather*,
　　　　Avon Books, New York, 1980, p. 25.
　　　　"Those unguarded early letters"　　EL, *Willa Cather Living*,
　　　　p. 20.
　　　　Yet it was Edith Lewis　　Edith Lewis was following Willa Cather's
　　　　explicit instructions when she destroyed her letters. In her will
　　　　Willa Cather included a clause that her letters were never to be
　　　　published.

page 34　*the world was full of summer time*　　WC, "O! The World Was
　　　　Full of the Summer Time," with "The Way of the World," *CSF*,
　　　　p. 395.

page 37　*"that simply doubled our pleasure"*　　WC, Letter to the Editor,
　　　　The Commercial Advertiser, Red Cloud, October 28, 1929, Ne-
　　　　braska State Historical Society, Lincoln.
　　　　"The excitement began"　　This quote and the others on the page,
　　　　ibid.

page 38　*"It is generally safe to admire"*　　WC, quoted in the Red Cloud
　　　　Chief, June 13, 1980, Willa Cather Pioneer Memorial, Red Cloud,
　　　　Nebraska.

Chapter II　Endeavor and Bright Hopefulness

page 40　*"that had lifted its head from the prairie"*　　WC, *My Ántonia*,
　　　　p. 258.

page 41　*almost as oppressively domestic*　　Ibid., p. 260.
　　　　The door opened　　The story was first told in Edward K. Brown,
　　　　Willa Cather, Alfred A. Knopf, New York, 1933, p. 38.
　　　　Most girls would have been afraid　　Interview with Louise Pound,
　　　　Lincoln *Sunday Star*, June 29, 1924.
　　　　His story was　　Dr. J. H. Tyndale, ibid.

page 42　*"a little Renaissance world"*　　Bernice Slote, *The Kingdom of Art*,
　　　　University of Nebraska Press, Lincoln, 1966, p. 9.

page 43　*"Well," Norton had replied*　　Ferris Greenslet, *Under the Bridge*,
　　　　Houghton Mifflin Company, Boston, 1943, p. 52.
　　　　"A brilliant freshman . . ."　　Dorothy Canfield Fisher, "Novelist
　　　　Recalls Christmas in Blue and Gold Pittsburgh," Chicago *Sunday
　　　　Tribune*, December 21, 1947. Dorothy Canfield Fisher's papers,
　　　　including her correspondence with Willa Cather, are in the Bailey
　　　　Library at the University of Vermont, Burlington.

page 44　*The idea for the story*　　DCF to Professor James R. Shively, May
　　　　9, 1948.

page 45　*"a careful reading will convince . . ."*　　Quoted in E. K. Brown,
　　　　op. cit., p. 40.

page 46　*he felt the plains were like himself*　　"The Clemency of the Court,"
　　　　WC, *CSF*, p. 518.

pages 46   *"It's mighty hard to lose you, Nell . . ."*   "The Elopement of
& 47   Allen Poole," WC, *CSF*, p. 578.

page 48   *"Not an orange or a bonbon . . ."*   WC, *Nebraska State Journal*,
     November 26, 1893, *The World and the Parish*, University of
     Nebraska Press, Lincoln, 1970, p. 21.

     Ten years later at the height of her career   This story was related
     to the author by Herbert Mayes, March 11, 1980. I am indebted
     to Mr. Mayes for his recollections of Willa Cather and for his
     attentiveness in keeping me informed of current Cather refer-
     ences.

page 50   *not a bad play . . . only driveling*   WC, *NSJ*, June 5, 1894, *The*
     World and the Parish, University of Nebraska Press, Lincoln,
     1970, p. 91.

     unwomanly tirades   WC, *NSJ*, November 18, 1894, *W&P*, p. 63.

     Is there no kind friend   WC, *NSJ*, June 2, 1895, *W&P*, p. 203.

     to see a woman of seventy   WC, *NSJ*, March 11, 1894, *W&P*,
     p. 62.

     when one knows Lillian   WC, *NSJ*, February 25, 1894, *W&P*,
     p. 62.

     "Atrocious"   WC, *Hesperian*, March 15, 1893, *KOA*, p. 174.

     She undoubtedly has a great future   WC, *NSJ*, February 20, 1894,
     KOA, p. 266.

page 51   *It is like red lava*   WC, *NSJ*, October 14, 1894, *KOA*, p. 118.

     one with which a fire worshipper   WC, *NSJ*, February 16, 1896,
     KOA, p. 126.

     under all those thousand little things   WC, *NSJ*, January 26, 1896,
     KOA, p. 121.

     Bernhardt's dissipation   WC, *NSJ*, June 16, 1895, *KOA*, p. 119.

     in this age of microscopic scrutiny   WC, *NSJ*, March 22, 1896,
     KOA, p. 154.

     [gave] herself body and soul   WC, ibid., p. 154.

     She has kept her personality   WC, *NSJ*, November 4, 1894, *KOA*,
     p. 153.

     utterly alone upon the icy heights   Ibid.

page 52   *She offered another explanation*   WC, *NSJ*, October 21, 1894,
     KOA, p. 177.

     "It's queer you should have that one weakness"   Mrs. Harvey
     Newbranch (Evaline Rolofson) in the Omaha *World Herald*,
     February 1, 1920, Nebraska State Historical Society, Lincoln.

     pitiably weak and childish   WC, *NSJ*, February 10, 1894, *W&P*,
     p. 178.

     thoroughly reputable and manly games   This quote and the two
     following, WC, *NSJ*, December 2, 1894, *KOA*, p. 213.

page 53   *to use that inoffensive article*   WC, *NSJ*, May 19, 1895, *KOA*,
     p. 208.

the very things out of which an artist is made   WC, *Courier*, October 26, 1895, *W&P*, p. 186.

"*Art does not come at sixteen*"   Ibid. WC ascribes the statement to Helena von Doenhoff, but she frequently put her own ideas into other people's mouths and her quotes are sometimes suspect.

a little more endurance   WC, *NSJ*, January 27, 1895, *W&P*, p. 176.

married nightingales seldom sing   Ibid.

page 54   *heredity or divorce or the vexed problems*   WC, *NSJ*, December 23, 1894, *W&P*, p. 136.

in the wealth and fragrance of unceasing summer   Ibid.

he wrote of the glory and the hope of effort   Ibid.

genius means relentless labor   WC, *NSJ*, February 11, 1984, *W&P*, p. 50.

page 54   *It would be more encouraging*   WC, *NSJ*, December 23, 1894, *W&P*, p. 138.

Don't hang about our cities   Ibid.

page 55   *The talent for writing*   WC, *NSJ*, October 28, 1894, *W&P*, p. 131.

the healthy commonplace   WC, *NSJ*, November 23, 1895, *W&P*, p. 277.

page 56   *for him alone it was worth while*   WC, *NSJ*, April 29, 1894, *W&P*, p. 84.

Sometimes I wonder   WC, *Courier*, November 23, 1895, *W&P*, p. 275.

emotional in the extreme   WC, *NSJ*, January 13, 1895, *W&P*, p. 147.

a story of adventure   WC, *Courier*, November 23, 1895, *W&P*, p. 275.

to feel greatly is genius   WC, *NSJ*, January 13, 1895, *W&P*, p. 146.

An author's only safe course   WC, *NSJ*, September 23, 1894, *KOA*, p. 407.

page 57   *She liked nothing so much as to sit alone with him*   WC to Will Owen Jones, March 2, 1927.

page 58   *she also had a chance to observe him*   WC to Mariel Gere, October 7, 1904. Willa Cather's letters to members of the Gere family are in the Nebraska State Historical Society, Lincoln.

page 59   *There was something enigmatical*   Hartley Burr Alexander, *Nebraska Alumnus*, October 1933; *Roundup: A Nebraska Reader*, edited by Virginia Faulkner, University of Nebraska Press, Lincoln, 1957, p. 237.

Before she went home   The Pound letters are in the Perkins Library at Duke University, Durham, N.C.

page 60   *In his early youth, he was a notorious bully*   WC, *The Hesperian*, March 10, 1894, *W&P*, p. 122.

page 61   *We do not know*   My suppositions about Willa Cather's motives in attacking Roscoe Pound are purely speculative, but they seem to me a not unreasonable explanation in the absence of any other evidence. Louise Pound referred to the incident in a 1937 interview in the Omaha *World Herald* but gave no explanation, other than to say that Willa had used material gained as a guest in the Pound house, and blaming her banishment from the Pound house on her mother and sister.

came unbidden [and] grew unforced   WC, "Shakespeare and Hamlet," *NSJ*, November 1 and 8, 1891, *KOA*, p. 432.

The great virtue of friendship   WC, *NSJ*, December 14, 1893, *W&P*, p. 28.

In a story written after she left Lincoln   WC, "The Count of Crow's Nest," *Home Monthly*, September, October 1896, *CSF*. The quote is on p. 454.

page 63   *It is just as though the lights were going out*   EL, *Willa Cather Living*, p. 22.

page 64   *Several events during that hot dry summer*   WC to Mariel Gere, August 1, 1893.

pages 65   *In August on a blistering day*   Willa Cather described her trip to
& 66   Brownsville in the *NSJ*, August 12, 1894, *W&P*, p. 103, and again six years later in *The Library*, July 7, 1900. For *The Library* she called the story "The Hottest Day I Ever Spent" and used the pseudonym "George Overing." *W&P*, p. 778.

page 66   *"No real estate ever sells in Brownsville*   WC, "A Resurrection," *Home Monthly*, April 1897, *CSF*, p. 431.

page 67   *Alvin Johnson, who was a prep then, recalled*   Elizabeth Shepley Sergeant, *Willa Cather*, Bison Books, University of Nebraska Press, Lincoln, 1962, quotes Johnson in her 1952 foreword, p. 10.

"Oh, you're moping, are you?"   This quote and the following, *"The detail of a thing,"* are from the article "When I First Knew Stephen Crane," *The Library*, June 23, 1900, *W&P*, op. cit., pp. 772 ff. Willa Cather used the pseudonym Henry Nicklemann.

page 68   *there is every evidence*   WC, "Stephen Crane's *Wounds in the Rain and Other Impressions of War*," *On Writing*, p. 74.

stuff that would sell, a double literary life and *the wonder of that remarkable performance*   WC, "When I First Knew Stephen Crane," *W&P*, pp. 772 ff.

the meeting of youthful minds   Wright Morris, *Earthly Delights, Unearthly Adornments*, Harper & Row, New York, 1978, p. 59.

Chapter III   Nebraska Coda

page 71   *something appears to have gone wrong*   WC to Mariel Gere, January 2, 1896.

Douglass had prevailed on her to go   WC to Mariel Gere, January 2, 1896.

page 72   *well educated and extremely pretty*   WC to Mariel Gere, May 2, 1896.

   the wreck of ten winters on the Divide   WC, "On the Divide," *Overland Monthly*, January 1896, *CSF*, p. 495.

page 73   *Willa gave them a stylish wedding breakfast*   WC to Mariel Gere, March 2, 1896.

   She wanted the job desperately   WC to Charles H. Gere, March 14, 1896.

page 74   *Herbert Bates was sending happy letters*   WC to Mariel Gere, May 2, 1896.

page 75   *The whole category of child literature*   WC, *NSJ*, April 12, 1896, *KOA*, p. 337.

   by any stretch of courtesy or imagination   WC, *NSJ*, January 19, 1896.

   a joyous elephant and from fly-specks to fixed stars   WC, *NSJ*, January 19, 1896, *KOA*, p. 352.

   such a rare anomaly   WC, *NSJ*, February 23, 1896, *KOA*, p. 333.

   Comparisons may be odious   WC, *NSJ*, June 14, 1896, *KOA*, p. 373.

page 76   *The business of an artist's life*   WC, *NSJ*, April 5, 1896, *KOA*, p. 413.

   to know is little and to feel is all   WC, *NSJ*, May 17, 1896, *KOA*, p. 401.

   art itself is the highest moral purpose   WC, *NSJ*, May 17, 1896, *KOA*, p. 378.

   to induce men to live more simply   WC, ibid., p. 402.

page 77   *"she took rather her own way with the curriculum"*   This quote and all the quotes following to the end of the chapter, WC, "Tommy the Unsentimental," *Home Monthly*, August 1896, *CSF*, pp. 473–80.

Chapter IV   Apprenticeship in Pittsburgh

page 80   *the very incandescence of human energy*   WC, "The Namesake," *McClure's*, March 1907, *CSF*, p. 140.
   a feverish, passionate endeavor   WC, ibid.

page 81   *Willa had never seen so much marble*   WC to Ellen Gere, undated, but probably July 1896.

page 82   *They were kind and well-meaning*   Willa Cather's description of life at the Axtells' is from her letter to Ellen Gere.

   she astonished her audience   WC to Mariel Gere, August 10, 1896.

page 83 *On a magical moonlit evening*   Ibid.
    prim old maid   WC to Mrs. Charles H. Gere, July 13, 1896.
    It was all great rot   WC to Ellen Gere, July 1896.
    Besides, it allowed her   WC to Mrs. Charles H. Gere, July 13, 1896.

page 84 *For that she turned confidently*   Ibid.

page 85 *"when you are buying other writers' stuff . . ."*   WC, Interview with Ethel M. Hockett, Lincoln *Daily Star*, October 24, 1915, *KOA*, p. 451.

page 86 *pictures of prize pigs and silos*   George Seibel, "Miss Willa Cather from Nebraska," *The New Colophon*, Volume II, Part Seven, September 1949, New York, p. 195. The account of the French readings and George Seibel's quotes on pp. 117, 118 and 119 are all from the same article.

page 87 *"the most concentrated essence of Christmas"*   Dorothy Canfield Fisher, "Novelist Recalls Christmas . . .", ibid.

page 89 *"some of the most musical lyrics"*   WC, *Home Monthly*, October 1897, *W&P*, p. 358.
    "the strongest and most satisfactory relation"   WC. The discussion of *The Mill on the Floss* is in the *Home Monthly*, November 1897, *W&P*, pp. 362–64.
    All of Pittsburgh is divided   WC, *Journal*, January 10, 1897, *W&P*, p. 505.
    Anyone who has not lived here   WC, *Courier*, October 23, 1897, *W&P*, p. 510. The reference is to the artist Charles Stanley Reinhart.

page 90 *She wrote immediately to her old friend*   WC to Will Owen Jones, September 9, 1897. Willa Cather's letters to Jones are in the Willa Cather Pioneer Memorial, Red Cloud, Nebraska, and the University of Virginia Library, Charlottesville.

page 91 *When an international committee of artists*   Willa Cather's account of the dinner is in the *Courier*, October 30, 1897, *W&P*, p. 513.
    Never before was I present   WC, *Courier*, November 27, 1897, *W&P*, p. 520.
    she was working harder   WC to Louise Pound, October 13, 1897.

page 92 *As for her social life*   WC to Mariel Gere, January 10, 1898.

page 93 *" 'Gad, how we like to be liked' "*   WC to Mariel Gere, April 25, 1897.
    "no man can give himself heart and soul"   WC, quoted by George Seibel, op. cit., p. 203.

page 94 *Willa used the setting of the two houses*   WC, "Uncle Valentine," *Uncle Valentine and Other Stories*, University of Nebraska Press, Lincoln, 1973, pp. 3–38.

"boy-man with the girlish laugh"   WC to Mariel Gere, January 10, 1898.

on one memorable afternoon   Ibid.

page 95 *to sit in the Metropolitan*   WC, *Courier*, March 19, 1898, *W&P*, p. 417.

page 96 *she looked a woman of another race*   WC, *My Mortal Enemy*, Vintage Books, Random House, New York, 1926, p. 45.

with a part of player folks   WC, *Courier*, July 1, 1899, *W&P*, p. 475.

her cousin Howard Gore and his fascinating Norwegian wife   Willa Cather's cousin was a professor at Columbian (now George Washington) University and his wife was a cousin of the King of Sweden. James Woodress, *Willa Cather*, University of Nebraska Press, Lincoln, 1975, p. 93.

page 97 *Isabelle was so good to her*   WC to DCF, October 10, 1899.

page 98 *she is merely a clever ingenue*   WC, *Courier*, March 18, 1899, *W&P*, p. 674.

How has she preserved?   WC, *Courier*, January 28, 1899, *W&P*, p. 671.

Each night you seem to wear   WC, *Courier*, April 22, 1899, *W&P*, p. 677.

an hour to be singled from among the rest   WC, *Courier*, January 14, 1899, *W&P*, p. 660.

this dirty, gloomy city   WC, *Courier*, June 10, 1899, *W&P*, p. 619.

page 99 *less attractive physically*   WC, ibid., p. 620.

Madame Nordica told me   WC, ibid.

I was talking with Mme. Nordica   WC, ibid., p. 622.

Conceive if you will   WC, *Courier*, January 6, 1900, *W&P*, p. 647.

It is a grave matter for a man   WC, *Leader*, November 11, 1899, *W&P*, p. 705.

page 101 *Willa herself expected to spend the winter*   WC to Will Owen Jones, September 29, 1900.

page 102 *She made the decision to go*   Just why she went to Washington remains a mystery. She may have gone for financial reasons; she took on a number of assignments while she was there. Or she may have wanted to see more of her cousin and his wife, who fascinated her. It is also possible that Will Jones suggested a change of scene, knowing that she was growing restless in Pittsburgh.

"all the hundreds of clerks come pouring out"   WC, *The Professor's House*, Alfred A. Knopf, New York, 1925, p. 232.

His widow brought the body back to Pittsburgh   Willa Cather's tribute to Nevin appeared in the *NSJ*, March 24, 1901, *W&P*, pp. 637–42.

page 103   *From Washington just four days after his death*   WC to William V. Alexander, February 21, 1901. University of Virginia Library, Charlottesville.

      "I remember Washington"   WC, *The Professor's House*, p. 234.

Chapter V   At the McClungs'

page 105   *At the appointed hour*   The quotations in this paragraph and the one following are from Elizabeth Moorhead, "These Too Were Here," *Willa Cather and Her Critics*, edited by James Schroeter, Cornell University Press, Ithaca, N.Y., 1967, p. 102.

page 106   *I discovered at once*   Elizabeth Moorhead, ibid., p. 104.

      Dorothy Canfield described   DCF, "Novelist Recalls Christmas . . .", ibid.

      George Seibel called her presence "stately"   George Seibel, op. cit., p. 200.

      "Her voice was deeper"   The student was Norman Foerster, quoted in E. K. Brown, *Willa Cather, a Critical Biography*, Alfred A. Knopf, 1953. A Discus Book, published by Avon Books, 1980, p. 71.

page 107   *"The calculated round of social engagements"*   Ethel Jones Litchfield, quoted in E. K. Brown, ibid., p. 112.

      These informal affairs   Elizabeth Moorhead, op. cit., p. 105.

page 108   *"under canopies, arches and flags"*   WC, *NSJ*, July 13, 1902, *W&P*, p. 890.

      the remoteness, the unchangedness   WC, *NSJ*, July 27, 1902, *W&P*, p. 897.

      Willa took a decidedly jaundiced   The quotes about the English are in *NSJ*, August 10, 1902, *W&P*, pp. 907–11.

page 109   *Burne-Jones never had a valet*   Mildred Bennett, *The World of Willa Cather*, p. 249.

page 110   *Willa sent off an angry letter*   WC to Cyril Clemens, December 11, 1936, University of Virginia Library, Charlottesville.

      A year later she wrote again   WC to Cyril Clemens, January 30, 1937, University of Virginia Library, Charlottesville.

      "Dear dear Willa"   DCF to WC, Bailey Library, University of Vermont, Burlington. The letter was returned to Mrs. Fisher on May 14. "I know that she received it," wrote Sarah Bloom, "and it seems to me that it should be returned to you."

page 112   *"with French people"*   WC, *NSJ*, August 31, 1902, *W&P*, p. 921.

      "so small a body of water"   WC, ibid., p. 921.

      "quite the most magnificent kite"   WC, ibid., p. 922.

"*through miles of brook-fed valleys*"   WC, ibid., p. 923.

"*it seems that a town will forgive*"   WC, ibid., p. 923.

page 113 "*very like the one on which I have acted as super-cargo*"   WC, *NSJ*, September 21, 1902, *W&P*, p. 931.

page 114 "*a sort of Chicago-like vehemence*"   WC, *NSJ*, October 19, 1902, *W&P*, p. 950.

"*with small convulsions*"   WC, *NSJ*, August 31, 1902, *W&P*, p. 921.

"*stout and puffing*"   WC, *NSJ*, September 21, 1902, *W&P*, p. 932.

"*for joy of life and companionship*"   WC, ibid.

"*for a certain small brother*"   WC, *NSJ*, October 5, 1902, *W&P*, p. 939.

in a letter to Mariel Gere   WC to Mariel Gere, August 28, 1902.

page 115 "*sense of immeasurable possession*"   WC, *NSJ*, October 12, 1902, *W&P*, p. 944.

"*not a little like certain lonely*"   WC, ibid., p. 946.

"*One cannot divine nor forecast*"   WC, ibid., p. 944.

"*a great country of shepherd kings*"   WC, *NSJ*, October 19, 1902, *W&P*, p. 948.

"*nearly the whole will and need*"   WC, ibid., p. 948.

"*the strange homesick chill*"   WC, ibid., p. 947.

"*these fine, subtle, sensitive . . . races*"   WC, ibid., p. 951.

page 116 *In January 1903 she told Will Jones*   WC to Will Owen Jones, January 2, 1903.

page 117 *Oh this is the joy of the rose*   WC, "In Rose Time," *April Twilights*, 1903, revised edition, Bison Books, University of Nebraska Press, Lincoln, 1962, p. 7.

or the sighing chant   WC, "Sleep, minstrel, sleep," *April Twilights*, 1903, p. 14.

Across the shimmering meadows   WC, "The Hawthorn Tree," *April Twilights*, 1903, p. 13.

page 118 "*Grandmither, gie me your still, white hands*"   WC, "Grandmither, Think Not I Forget," *April Twilights*, 1903, p. 5.

"*Of the three who lay and planned at moonrise*"   WC, "Dedicatory," *April Twilights*, 1903, p. 3.

page 119 "*Saxon boys by their fields that bide*"   WC, *April Twilights and Other Poems*, Alfred A. Knopf, 1923, p. 48.

"*Joy is come to the little / Everywhere*"   WC, "Fides, Spes," *April Twilights*, 1903, p. 15.

"*a city full of exiles*"   WC, "A Silver Cup," *April Twilights and Other Poems*, p. 64.

"*Long forgot is budding-time and blowing*"   WC, "Autumn Melody," *April Twilights and Other Poems*, p. 55.

page 120 *for the most part they were "passive"*   Bernice Slote, "Willa Cather and Her First Book," *April Twilights*, 1903, p. xxii.

Willa's memorable first visit to the McClure offices   WC to
Will Owen Jones, May 7, 1903.

page 122   *She was in Lincoln . . . when she made the acquaintance*   Edith
Lewis describes the first time she and Willa Cather met in *Willa
Cather Living*, pp. ix–xiii.

page 124   *even Will Jones scolded Willa*   WC to Will Owen Jones, March
6, 1904.

page 125   *"cast ashore upon a desert of newness"*   WC, "The Sculptor's
Funeral," *The Troll Garden*, New American Library, 1961,
p. 43.
Willa told George Seibel   George Seibel, p. 205.
If a young woman sits down in the cornfield   WC to Will Owen
Jones, May 29, 1914.

page 126   *"tepid waters of Cordelia Street*   WC, "Paul's Case," *The Troll
Garden*, p. 135.
The Troll Garden won for its author   Unless noted otherwise,
I have depended for reviews of Willa Cather's works on the
yearly editions of the *Book Review Digest*, edited by Marion A.
Knight and Metice M. James.

page 127   *In a contented letter to Mariel*   WC to Mariel Gere, September
1905.

page 128   *"our necessities are so much stronger than our desires"*   WC,
NSJ, June 14, 1896, *KOA*, p. 374.

page 129   *"a mere name, a sort of far-off benignant deity"*   Elizabeth
Moorhead described the evening in "These Too Were Here,"
Willa Cather and Her Critics, p. 106.
Isabelle and her dazzled parents . . . had been "'McClured'"   "I
will not be lured or McClured," Holmes is quoted as saying in
Peter Lyon, *Success Story*, Charles Scribner's Sons, New York,
1963, p. 124.

Chapter VI   *A Red-hot Magazine of Protest*

page 130   *"a kind of established repose"*   Henry James, *Washington Square*,
Albert & Charles Boni, New York, 1926, p. 23.

page 131   *"very solid and honorable dwellings"*   Henry James, ibid., p. 23.

page 133   *"red-hot magazine of protest"*   WC, "Ardessa," *Uncle Valentine
and Other Stories*, p. 101.
"he was somewhat afraid"   WC, ibid., p. 102.
"Constraint was the last thing O'Malley liked"   WC, ibid., p. 102.

page 134   *"Mrs. McClure is stone blind"*   Peter Lyon, p. 261.
Calling him "conceited, impertinent and meddlesome"   Ibid.,
p. 42.

page 135   *"He's a Mormon"*   Ibid., p. 261.

"ex-schoolteacher from Pittsburgh"   Witter Bynner, "Autobiography in the Shape of a Book Review," *Prose Pieces, The Works of Witter Bynner*, edited by James Kraft, Farrar, Straus & Giroux, New York, 1979, p. 159.

Bynner had been asked by the publisher to cut   Ibid., p. 160.

page 136   *"plenty more words where those came from"*   WC.

In New York she lived the life   I am indebted for biographical information concerning Viola Roseboro to Jane Kirkland Graham, *Viola, the Duchess of New Dorp*, 1955, Columbia, S.C.

page 137   "to listen to Miss Roseboro talk"   Ibid., p. 309.

page 138   *John Chapman's professional association with Mary Ann Evans*   George Eliot's experience as an editor of *The Westminster Review* is told in "A Self That Self Restrains," Ruby V. Redinger, *George Eliot: The Emergent Self*, Alfred A. Knopf, New York, 1975, pp. 163–224.

page 139   *"certain immediate problems of American civilization"*   The advertisement appeared in *McClure's Magazine*, November 1906.

"has made a mark in proportion to its strength"   Ibid.

page 140   *"like the shameful conception of some despairing"*   WC, "The Profile," *CSF*, p. 128.

"'My art is more important than my friend'"   Quoted in Witter Bynner, op. cit., p. 253.

page 142   *The story would take Mrs. Eddy from her birth*   *McClure's Magazine*, December 1906.

Willa was writing to Mrs. McClure   WC to Hattie McClure, January 19, 1907, Lilly Library, Indiana University, Bloomington.

page 143   *All the members of her household*   Mary Baker Eddy, *The Story of Her Life and the History of the Christian Science Church*, XII, *McClure's Magazine*, April 1908.

Many another girl certainly has   Ibid.

page 144   *Mrs. Brandeis explained*   Willa Cather described her first visit to Annie Fields in "148 Charles Street," *NUF*, Alfred A. Knopf, 1935.

page 145   *"aristocracy of letters and art"*   All the quotations in this paragraph and the next, ibid.

"the ideal friend to fill the gap"   Mark A. de Wolfe Howe, *Memories of a Hostess*, Atlantic Monthly Press, Boston, 1922.

page 146   *"Such an alliance I was brought up to hear called"*   Helen Howe, *The Gentle Americans*, Harper & Row, New York, 1965, p. 83.

"Sometimes entering a new door"   WC, "148 Charles Street," op cit., p. 52.

page 147   *An amusing story is told of a visit*   Elizabeth Shepley Sergeant, *Willa Cather—a Memoir*, Bison Books, University of Nebraska Press, Lincoln, 1963, pp. 168–69.

Ferris Greenslet was not a native Bostonian either   For details
of Greenslet's life and career, see his autobiography, *Under the
Bridge*, Houghton Mifflin, Boston, 1943.

page 147   *"a fresh-faced, broad-browed, plain-speaking"*   Ferris Greenslet,
& 148   ibid., p. 116.

page 148   *a little of the outsider's perspective*   For Greenslet's observations, ibid., p. 78.
"quick flashes of humor . . . large, generous, mobile mouth"
WC, "148 Charles Street," op. cit., p. 59.

page 149   *"The quiet village life, the dull routine"*   Sarah Orne Jewett,
quoted in John Eldridge Frost, *Sarah Orne Jewett*, The Gundalow Club, Kittery Point, Maine, 1960. For details of Jewett's
life, see also, Francis Otto Matthiessen, *Sarah Orne Jewett*,
Houghton Mifflin, Boston, 1929.
"a lady, in the old high sense"   WC, "Miss Jewett," *NUF*, p. 85.

page 150   *"living things caught in the open"*   Ibid., p. 78.
"work with nature, not against it"   Sarah Orne Jewett, *A
Country Doctor*, Houghton Mifflin, Boston, 1884, p. 283.
"Nan's feeling toward her boy-playmates"   Ibid., p. 137.
"a rule is sometimes very cruel"   Ibid., p. 138.
" 'Mr. Right' comes along"   Ibid., p. 285.
"Most girls have an instinct"   Ibid., p. 326.

page 151   *"The preservation of the race"*   Ibid., p. 336.
she had also liked the "austere and unsentimental"   George
Seibel, op. cit., p. 202.
"She was content to be slight"   WC, "Miss Jewett," op. cit.,
p. 89.
"No story yet . . . but do not despair"   Sarah Orne Jewett to
WC, August 17, 1908, *The Letters of Sarah Orne Jewett*, edited
by Annie Fields, Houghton Mifflin, 1911.
"I envy you your work"   Ibid.

page 152   *"It is impossible for you to work"*   Jewett to WC, December
13, 1908.

page 155   *Her business letters were patient*   The Barrett Library at the
University of Virginia, Charlottesville, has a number of letters
written on *McClure's* letterhead. Some are signed, "Willa Sibert
Cather for Mr. S. S. McClure."
"His electric energy keyed the whole office"   EL, *Willa Cather
Living*, p. 60.

page 156   *Willa told her former "chief"*   WC to SSMcC, May 26, 1933.
After Willa's death   EL, *Willa Cather Living*, pp. 72 and 73.

page 157   *something of a masquerade*   Jewett to WC, November 27, 1908.

page 158   *"better and truer McClure"*   ESS, *Willa Cather—a Memoir*,
p. 125.

page 159   *"to antagonize and frighten her"*   WC, "Coming, Aphrodite!"

Youth and the Bright Medusa, Vintage Books, Random House, 1975, p. 46.

page 160 *"an intangible residuum of pleasure"*   WC, "Miss Jewett," op. cit., p. 78.

Chapter VII   People and Places

page 161 *"I wasn't out to spy on life"*   WC quoted in Louise Bogan, "American-Classic," *The New Yorker,* August 8, 1931.

page 162 *"splendid and successful stay in London"*   SSMcC to WC, June 18, 1909.

"Willa Cather's Fifth Avenue"   ESS, *Willa Cather—a Memoir,* p. 46.

page 163 *"copper kings from Denver"*   ESS, ibid., p. 47.

Elizabeth Sergeant recalled one such afternoon   ESS, ibid., p. 51.

"blithe made-in-Nebraska look"   ESS, ibid., p. 46.

page 164 *"No trace of the reforming feminist"*   ESS, ibid., p. 33.

"'Aren't short stories more in your line?'"   ESS, ibid., p. 35.

page 165 *Willa's reply was to suggest*   WC to ESS, June 27, 1911. The Elizabeth Shepley Sergeant letters are in the Morgan Library in New York.

page 166 *"'a lucky Bostonian . . . living in a house'"*   ESS, *Willa Cather —a Memoir,* op. cit., p. 43.

page 167 *please like Bartley*   WC to Zoë Akins, March 14, 1912. The Akins letters are in the Huntington Library, San Marino, California.

The trouble was that the story had not come   WC, "My First Novels," *NUF,* pp. 92 and 93.

page 168 *the force that "takes us forward" and "builds bridges"*   WC, *Alexander's Bridge,* Bison Books, University of Nebraska Press, Lincoln, 1977, p. 17.

"powerfully equipped nature"   WC, ibid.

"A person of distinction"   The description of Winifred Pemberton is in WC, ibid., p. 3.

page 169 *She had not felt so well or enjoyed life so much*   WC to SSMcC, November 19, 1911.

"that will give us distinction"   SSMcC to WC, October 14, 1911.

"I am rather enjoying the new developments"   Ibid.

page 170 *Willa brought the story with her when she returned*   WC to ESS, March 1, 1912.

page 171 *"Such a gathering of distinguished men [sic]"*   New York *Times,* March 3, 1912.

"Nearly everyone in the hall knew everybody else"   Ibid.

"Did you ever see anything more cunning?"   Margaret Deland to WC, April 9, 1912, Nebraska State Historical Society, Lincoln.

page 172   *Mrs. McClung had suffered a stroke*   WC to ESS, March 13,
            1912.
            a whole new landscape . . . of the mind   EL, *Willa Cather
            Living*, p. 81.
page 173   *Willa began her trip in Winslow*   Willa Cather described her
            trip to Arizona, the Grand Canyon and New Mexico in letters
            to Elizabeth Sergeant, April 20, April 26, May 21 and June 15,
            1912.

                    Chapter VIII   The Fortunate Country

page 178   *Willa was home for the wheat harvest*   WC to ESS, July 5, 1912.
            "fat, rosy old women who looked hot"   WC, "The Bohemian
            Girl," CSF, p. 29.
page 179   *"The great, silent country seemed to lay a spell"*   Ibid., p. 37.
            Willa had written him a long and loving letter   WC to SSMcC,
            June 19, 1912.
page 181   *It was the perfect apartment*   WC to ESS, October 6, 1912.
            "My first impression of Bank Street"   ESS, *Willa Cather—a
            Memoir*, p. 112.
page 182   *Having made the apartment "fairly comfortable"*   EL, *Willa
            Cather Living*, p. 89.
            "No, no," she pleaded   The story was told to the author by Mrs.
            Charles Savage in Seal Harbor, Maine, July 1980.
page 183   *Don't bother with* Alexander   WC to Louise Pound, June 27,
            1912, Barrett Library, University of Virginia, Charlottesville.
            Their first exchange, however, was hardly prophetic   WC to Zoë
            Akins, January 27, 1909.
            a harsh, blunt-sounding letter   WC to Zoë Akins (early 1910).
page 184   *According to Teasdale's biographer*   William Drake, *Sara Teas-
            dale, Woman and Poet*, Harper & Row, New York, 1979, p. 54.
            The description of Akins "with a cigarette . . ." is in a letter
            from Teasdale to Marion Cummings Stanley, September 25, 1909,
            in the Marion Cummings Collection, Newberry Library, Chicago.
            Quoted by permission of Margaret C. Conklin, Literary Executor
            for the Estate of Sara Teasdale. I am grateful to William Drake
            for his kindness in putting me in touch with Ms. Conklin.
            Nobody could keep up with Jobyna   WC to Zoë Akins, Novem-
            ber 21, 1932, and August 30, 1933.
            Her new story . . . was about the same country   WC to Zoë
            Akins, October 31, 1912.
page 185   *It was either pretty good, she told Elsie Sergeant*   WC to ESS,
            (early January) 1913.
            She was not sentimental about things   WC to ESS (early 1913).

"*To Elsie Sergeant, the first friend*" ESS, *Willa Cather—a Memoir*, p. 113.

page 186 *Mr. Greenslet was just like all the men in the book* WC to ESS, April 22, 1913.

"*For the first time, perhaps, since that land emerged*" WC, *O Pioneers!*, Houghton Mifflin, Boston, 1913, p. 65.

page 187 "*Youth with its insupportable sweetness*" "Prairie Spring," ibid.

"*Why does it have to be my boy?*" WC, ibid., p. 305.

"*Fortunate country, that is one day to receive hearts*" Ibid., p. 309.

Chapter IX The Song of the Lark

page 188 "*She was an important figure in our lives*" EL, *Willa Cather Living*, p. 88.

page 189 *they were the only married people she knew* WC to ESS, April 30, 1914.

"*the individuality with which he did or said anything*" Stanley Olson, *Elinor Wylie, a Life Apart*, The Dial Press/James Wade, New York, 1979, p. 158.

to find a new kind of human creature WC to ESS, April 28, 1913.

page 190 *suspicious, defiant, far-seeing* WC to ESS, April 22, 1913.

Her rooms were like Alexandra Bergson's WC to ESS, ibid.

Appearing by appointment EL, *Willa Cather Living*, p. 91.

page 191 *Another time Willa saw Fremstad* WC to ESS, April 22, 1913.

page 192 *Even that began badly* WC to ESS, September 12, 1913.

she had no patience for the romantic South Ibid.

Her cousin had made a tragic trip WC to ESS, November 19, 1913.

pages 192 *The world was too much with her* WC to ESS, ibid.
& 193

page 193 *she suffered one of the frightening . . . illnesses* The account of Willa's illness is contained in letters to ESS, February 13, February 24, March 2 and March 19, 1914.

As a youngster in Virginia she had been terrorized EL, *Willa Cather Living*, p. 10.

page 194 *Willa was perfectly happy there* WC to ESS, May 26, 1914.

page 195 *At Fremstad's camp* WC to ESS, June 23, 1914.

For two weeks, with the thermometer often up to 110° WC to ESS, August 10, 1914.

Kaiser's high Napoleonic mood Ibid.

page 196 *a handsome, twenty-year-old six-footer* WC to ESS, September 28, 1914.

page 197   *Fortunately the weather was uncommonly benign*   WC to ESS,
               June 27, 1915.
               "a really, truly poet"   WC to ESS, July 28, 1915.
page 197   *at the last minute Judge McClung had a change of heart*   Ibid.
& 198
page 198   *Years later Edith could still recall every detail*   EL, *Willa Cather*
               Living, pp. 93–100.
page 199   *"Far above me, a thousand feet or so"*   WC, *The Professor's*
               House, p. 201.
               "The tower was the fine thing"   Ibid.
               "The sides of the canyon were everywhere precipitous"   EL,
               Willa Cather Living, p. 96.
page 200   *"Occasionally we would stop for a short rest"*   Ibid., p. 98.
               it had been a rough twenty-four hours   WC to ESS, September
               21, 1915.
page 201   *Thea had pulled at her, Willa said*   WC to ESS, December 7,
               1915.
               "Living's too much trouble"   WC, *SOL*, p. 242.
               "one ought to do one's best"   Ibid., p. 306.
page 202   *"What was art but the effort to make a sheath . . . ?"*   Ibid.,
               p. 304.
               "One is always a little defensive"   WC, "My First Novels,"
               Willa Cather on Writing, Alfred A. Knopf, New York, 1949, p.
               96.
               "Too much detail is apt"   Ibid., p. 97.
               "too directly from immediate emotions"   EL, *Willa Cather*
               Living, p. 93.
               She liked to think the heart of the story   WC to DCF, Novem-
               ber 15, 1916.
               The musical aspects of the book had come out well   WC to ESS,
               June 27, 1915.

Chapter X   Loss and Change

page 204   *She "rounded out her period"*   WC, "148 Charles Street," op. cit.,
               p. 75.
page 205   *He had made her think of Stevenson's remark*   WC, *Courier*,
               January 27, 1900, *W&P*, p. 655.
               For Willa, on the best terms   WC to DCF, November 15, 1916.
               Isabelle's marriage was hard   WC to ESS, August 3, 1916.
               her face was bleak   ESS, *Willa Cather—a Memoir*, p. 140.
page 206   *Like most people, she said*   WC to CMS, March 13, 1918.
page 208   *seeing them together*   ESS, *Willa Cather—a Memoir*, p. 202.
page 209   *in the Southwest you need a cool, shadowy adobe*   WC to ESS,
               August 3, 1916.
               "It was not a tourist country then"   EL, *Willa Cather Living*,
               p. 100.

page 210 *Willa received an unexpected invitation*   WC to ESS, June 23, 1917.

Her mother was seriously ill and it fell to Willa   WC to ESS, November 13, 1917.

page 211 *"The fact that she was a celebrity"*   EL, *Willa Cather Living*, p. 104.

"The fresh, pine-scented woods"   Ibid., p. 105.

page 212 *"flushed and alert from one of her swift wintry walks"*   ESS, *Willa Cather—a Memoir*, p. 138.

"I want my new heroine to be like this"   Ibid., p. 139.

she was destined to write My Ántonia   WC to CMS, January 27, 1934.

Ferris Greenslet said of My Ántonia   Ferris Greenslet, *Under the Bridge*, p. 119.

page 213 *It would only make people go out to look Annie over*   WC to CMS, January 27, 1934.

"There is a time in a writer's development"   WC, Preface to *Alexander's Bridge*, Houghton Mifflin Company, Boston, 1922 edition.

page 214 *"To dance 'Home, Sweet Home' with Lena"*   WC, *My Ántonia*, p. 222.

"The sun was sinking just behind it"   Ibid., p. 245.

"When a writer once begins to work"   WC, Preface to *Alexander's Bridge*.

One has to live about forty years   WC to CMS, March 13, 1918.

In a letter to Will Owen Jones   WC to Will Owen Jones, May 20, 1919.

Chapter XI *Endings and Beginnings*

page 216 *America's entrance into the war brought changes*   WC to CMS, March 12, 1918.

page 217 *She was ashamed to recall how she had fussed*   WC to ESS, December 3, 1918.

"Ours" were so much nicer   Ibid.

page 218 *"He seemed to be doing something new"*   WC, "Portrait of the Publisher as a Young Man," *Alfred A. Knopf, a Quarter Century*, 1940.

She saw him frequently at concerts   Fanny Butcher, "The Litterary Spotlight," Chicago *Sunday Tribune*, September 25, 1949.

"an oddly dignified advertisement"   Alfred Knopf's account is in "Miss Cather," *The Art of Willa Cather*, edited by Bernice Slote and Virginia Faulkner, University of Nebraska Press, Lincoln, 1974.

page 219 *Willa's choice of Alfred Knopf*   EL, *Willa Cather Living*, p. 115.

page 220   *"She is a plant of our own American garden"*   DCF, *Yale Review*, April 1921.

page 221   *Dr. Tyndale's life was one long warfare*   WC to DCF, December 2, 1916.

   "the rich sweet philosophy"   Re *The Bent Twig*, *Publishers' Weekly*, October 16, 1915.

   she lacked greatness   Fanny Butcher, Chicago *Daily Tribune*, December 20, 1930.

   "one of those saved by works"   Rebecca West, re *The Brimming Cup*, *New Statesman*, July 23, 1921.

   try her on for size   WC to DCF, April 8, 1921.

   She rarely dreamed, she said   WC to DCF, June 21, 1922.

   questioned whether our endings in life were ever as glowing   WC to DCF, January 26, 1922.

page 222   *She felt a kinship with him*   WC to DCF, March 8, 1922.

   He took over her life so completely   WC to DCF, March 21, 1922.

page 223   *she wished she could spend the rest of her life*   WC to DCF, May 8, 1922.

page 224   *"a vision of a ruined life"*   This quote and the others in the same paragraph are from *Victor Chapman's Letters from France*, The Macmillan Company, New York, 1917.

   "Youth had given him all"   William Archer, "Introduction," *Poems by Alan Seeger*, Charles Scribner's Sons, New York, 1917, p. xi.

   "that grand occasion to excel"   Alan Seeger, "Ode in Memory of the American Volunteers Fallen for France," ibid., p. 170.

   "used enviously to read about Alan Seeger"   WC, *One of Ours*, Vintage Books, Random House, New York, 1971.

page 225   *the seventeen-day voyage*   WC to ESS, November 19, 1920.

page 226   *It wasn't dreadful*   WC to ESS, July 6, 1921.

   It made her feel rather "chesty"   WC to Laura Hills (undated), Morgan Library, New York.

   three reporters were at her door   WC to Mrs. Stanfield, June 12, 1921, Barrett Library, University of Virginia, Charlottesville.

   Lewis never missed a chance   WC to CMS, January 8, 1917.

   Her mother, who knew the heat made her short-tempered   WC to ESS, July 6, 1921.

   No one had lived   Katherine Scherman, *Two Islands—Grand Manan and Sanibel*, Little Brown & Co., Boston, Toronto, 1971.

page 227   *"masterly, perfectly gorgeous novel"*   The telegram from Knopf, dated September 21, 1921, is in the Willa Cather Pioneer Memorial, Red Cloud, Nebraska.

   "What better reason can you want"   WC quoted by Eleanor Hinman, Lincoln *Daily Star*, November 6, 1921, Nebraska State Historical Society, Lincoln.

"*The village doesn't exist*"   WC, Omaha *Daily News*, October
29, 1921, Nebraska State Historical Society, Lincoln.

She was a Nebraska writer, first and foremost   WC, *Daily Bee*,
October 29, 1921, Nebraska State Historical Society, Lincoln.

Nothing on earth strengthens one's arm   WC to CMS, November 10, 1921.

Her old affections were the very spring   Ibid.

You know it's your place   WC to DCF, November 5, 1921.

page 228 *Knopf tried unsuccessfully*   Alfred Knopf, "Miss Cather," op.
cit., p. 207.

"*from Miss Cather*"   Sinclair Lewis, *Literary Review*, September 16, 1922.

H. L. Mencken was kinder   H. L. Mencken, *Smart Set*, October
1922, *Willa Cather and Her Critics*, pp. 10–12.

page 229 *Edmund Wilson, who later was to grant*   The two observations
of Wilson are reprinted from *The Shores of Light* and may be
found in *Willa Cather and Her Critics*, pp. 25–29.

Months before the book came out   WC to DCF, February 6,
1922.

page 231 *Isabelle would know how much it meant*   WC to CMS, September 2, 1922.

Once again her reaction to illness   WC to Mrs. Stanfield, June
10, 1922, Barrett Library, University of Virginia, Charlottesville.

page 232 *She expressed herself to Elsie Sergeant*   WC to ESS, October 4,
1922.

"*The world broke in two in 1922*"   WC, Prefatory Note, *NUF*.

Chapter XI   *Fine Undertakings and Bright Occasions*

page 234 *When Sinclair Lewis was awarded*   Mildred Bennett, *The World
of Willa Cather*, p. 202.

page 235 "*With Carl Sandburg it's the people, yes*"   Ibid., p. 149.

"*Her era seemed to swirl*"   Fannie Hurst, *Anatomy of Me*,
Doubleday & Company, Garden City, N.Y., 1958, p. 256.

Irene was the only person who knew her as a child   WC to
Irene Miner Weisz, March 12, 1931.

page 236 *Dorothy Canfield appeared suddenly*   WC to DCF, November
29, 1923.

"*she felt she would never be able to do any work*"   EL, *Willa
Cather Living*, p. 131.

He was modern and rather fanciful   WC to IMW, August 11,
1923.

page 237 *he went on painting desperately*   EL, *Willa Cather Living*, p. 132.

page 238   *Willa's customary method was to write*   EL, *Willa Cather Living*, p. 126.

"'*Mrs. Knopf and I both agree*'"   Alfred Knopf, "Miss Cather," op. cit., p. 207.

"*She had always the power of suggesting*"   WC, *A Lost Lady*, Vintage Books, Random House, 1972, p. 172.

"*All those who had shared in fine undertakings*"   Ibid., p. 167.

page 239   *In April 1925 she received a startling letter*   Dr. Matthew J. Bruccoli, "An Instance of Apparent Plagiarism," *The Princeton University Library Chronicle*, extracted from Volume XXXIX, Number 3, Spring 1978. I am indebted to Charles Scribner III for telling me this story and giving me a copy of the Princeton extract. It was he who discovered the letter and manuscript pages in the Seven Gables Bookshop in New York City and gave them to the Princeton University Library.

page 240   *The Professor's House was written in a middle-aged mood*   WC to DCF, October 14, 1926.

"*Theoretically he knew that life is possible*"   WC, *The Professor's House*, p. 282.

"*No later anguish . . . went so deep*"   Ibid., p. 31.

"*just when the morning brightness*"   Ibid., p. 258.

page 241   *She explained that it was an experiment*   WC, "On the Professor's House," *Willa Cather on Writing*, pp. 31 and 32.

the most personal of Willa's novels   EL, *Willa Cather Living*, p. 137.

And to Irene, who had seen the book   WC to IMW, February 17, 1925.

"*A man can do anything*"   WC, *The Professor's House*, p. 29.

"*Art and religion (they are the same thing . . .)*"   Ibid., p. 69.

page 242   "*The novel . . . has been over-furnished*"   WC, "The Novel Démeublé," *NUF*, p. 43.

"*A few memorable interregnums*"   WC, *The Professor's House*, p. 257.

page 243   "*freely and fearlessly into the grey air*"   WC, *My Mortal Enemy*, p. 25.

"*People can be lovers and enemies*"   Ibid., p. 88.

"*Why must I die like this, alone?*"   Ibid., p. 105.

"*I should have stayed with my uncle*"   Ibid., p. 75.

page 244   "*Of course you are quite right*"   WC, quoted in George Seibel, op. cit., p. 207.

The following fall she begged Irene   WC to IMW, November 4, 1925.

page 245   *The hall was particularly lovely*   WC to IMW, November 21, 1925.

It was a quite different kind of fire   Stanley Olson, *Elinor Wylie, a Life Apart*, p. 199.

Without regard to custom   ESS, *Willa Cather—a Memoir*, pp. 224 and 225.

page 246   In her diary Brett recorded   Dorothy Brett, *Lawrence and Brett, a Friendship*, The Sunstone Press, Santa Fe, New Mexico, new edition, 1974, pp. 39 and 40.

page 247   Tony would sit in the driver's seat   EL, *Willa Cather Living*, p. 142.

"a veil of the Catholic church"   Georgia O'Keeffe, *Georgia O'Keeffe, A Studio Book*, The Viking Press, New York, 1976.

"Archbishop Lamy . . . had become a sort of invisible personal friend"   WC, "On Death Comes for the Archbishop," *Willa Cather on Writing*, p. 7.

page 248   "a happy vacation from life"   Ibid., p. 11.

combination of connoisseur and pioneer   The critic is David Daiches, *Willa Cather*, Cornell University Press, Ithaca, N.Y., 1951.

page 249   "They have a great affection for each other"   WC, *Death Comes for the Archbishop*, Alfred A. Knopf, New York, 1974, p. 254.

to travel with her is to travel with the landscape made human   Ibid., p. 232.

"only on the bright edges of the world"   Ibid., p. 275.

"Something soft and wild and free"   Ibid., p. 276.

page 250   "remarking that our son would some day be paying"   Alfred Knopf, "Miss Willa," *The Art of Willa Cather*, p. 210.

"the fine hand of Edith Lewis"   Ibid., 211.

Chapter XIII   We Are the Older Generation

page 251   Putting your things in storage   WC to Zoë Akins, fall, 1927.

Could anything be a better index?   WC to DCF, December 20, 1929.

page 252   she hoped he had more go in him   WC to CMS, undated.

A little prairie town in winter   WC to Zoë Akins, December 6, 1927.

Christmas was a bit like living through War and Peace   WC to DCF, January 18, 1928.

It was a little after five   WC to DCF, April 3, 1928.

she paced frantically back and forth   Mildred Bennett, *The World of Willa Cather*, p. 28.

page 253   "It was a rough little place"   EL, *Willa Cather Living*, p. 30.

"*From the first moment that she looked down*"   Ibid., p. 153.

page 254 "*always enclosed the religious activities*"   Paul Horgan, *Lamy of Santa Fe*, Farrar, Straus & Giroux, New York, 1975, p. 387.

Mary Austin, that gossipy defender of the local mores   Mary Hunter Austin, *Earth Horizon, an Autobiography*, Houghton Mifflin, Boston, 1932.

"*She sat in that chair*"   Mary Austin, quoted in ESS, *Willa Cather—a Memoir*, p. 227. Willa told ESS that she used Austin's house merely to write an occasional letter, *not* the *Archbishop*.

page 255 *she begged Zoë not to betray the fact*   WC to Zoë Akins, spring, 1929.

She was so knocked out   WC to CMS, April 21, 1930.

Edith told her to tell Carrie   WC to CMS, June 1929.

page 256 *It was like dying twice*   WC to DCF, December 20, 1929.

she did not think there was another spot   WC to CMS, April 21, 1930.

Willa had bent over and kissed the old lady's hand   "A Chance Meeting" is reprinted in *NUF*, pp. 3–42.

page 257 *Mrs. Canfield died that summer and Willa wrote*   WC to DCF, September 30, 1930.

"*a rather short, stocky lady in an apple-green coat*"   Marian King, *Books and People*, The Macmillan Company, New York, 1954.

page 258 "*the conferring of the Doctorate of Letters on Willa Cather*"   New York *Times*, June 17, 1931.

Princeton went off with a bang   WC to Zoë Akins, June 1931.

a "perfectly natural person"   Louise Bogan, "American-Classic," *The New Yorker*, August 8, 1931.

page 259 *One just had to grin and bear such things*   WC to her mother, August 10, 1931. The letter is in the Willa Cather Pioneer Memorial, Red Cloud, Nebraska.

"*a lovely Christmas*"   Elsie Cather to CMS, December 28, 1931.

"*He was like a tree*"   WC, "Neighbor Rosicky," *Obscure Destinies*, Vintage Books, Random House, 1974, p. 32.

page 260 *Now they were the older generation*   WC to DCF, September 1931.

she received a letter from Dorothy Canfield   Alfred Knopf, "Miss Willa," *The Art of Willa Cather*, p. 212.

page 261 "*I like the whole drama of life*"   Tomáš Masaryk to WC, 1932, Willa Cather Pioneer Memorial, Red Cloud, Nebraska.

page 262 "*You have the gift of the transfiguring touch*"   Oliver Wendell Holmes, March 24, 1931, Willa Cather Pioneer Memorial, Red Cloud, Nebraska.

put down his pen and leaned back   WC to IMW, December 10, 1929.

Chapter XIV   A Life of Disciplined Endeavor

page 264   *She wrote to Zoë from Grand Manan*   WC to Zoë Akins, August 30, 1931.

It was desperate to be without money   WC to CMS, December 14, 1933.

Splendid young people   WC to DCF, June 28, 1939.

page 265   *the Menuhins "were not only the most gifted"*   EL, *Willa Cather Living*, p. 170.

On Willa's birthday they showered her   WC to CMS, February 12, 1934.

page 266   *Yaltah would find a hand-delivered envelope*   WC to Yaltah Menuhin, the winter of 1933–34. Courtesy of Yaltah Menuhin and Joel Ryce.

the quick brightening in the air   WC to Yaltah Menuhin, July 21, 1935.

"each taking several parts"   Yehudi Menuhin, *Unfinished Journey*, p. 130.

Willa's "mannish figure and country tweediness"   Ibid., p. 128.

page 267   *She had never been so beautiful*   WC to Yaltah Menuhin, July 21, 1935.

Isabelle roused herself to be present   WC to Roscoe Cather, June 12, 1935. Willa Cather Pioneer Memorial, Red Cloud, Nebraska.

Isabelle kept to her bed   I am indebted to Samuel A. McClung III for information concerning this visit.

page 268   *It was the kind of food*   WC to IMW, December 10, 1929.

she rejoiced with Josephine   WC to CMS, November 25, 1935.

page 269   *"I must have music"*   E. K. Brown, *Willa Cather*, p. 230.

"always in motion; dancing or skating"   WC, *Lucy Gayheart*, Alfred A. Knopf, New York, 1972, p. 3.

"Life seemed to lie near the surface"   Ibid., p. 5.

"lives roll along so close"   Ibid., p. 167.

Willa knew that Carrie would remember   WC to CMS, June 28, 1939.

page 270   *she had to see the words forming*   WC to CMS, April 29, 1945.

It was a not uncommon affliction   WC to Carrie, Elsie and Roscoe, December 6, 1940.

page 271   *she scolded Elsie Sergeant*   WC to ESS, August 16, 1946.

Willa "never realized . . . shake her hand"   Alfred Knopf, "Miss Cather," *The Art of Willa Cather*, p. 215.

page 272   *Dorothy had done the operation*   WC to DCF, June 22, 1933.

The one real subject of all her books   DCF, "Daughter of the Frontier," New York *Herald Tribune*, May 28, 1933.

page 273   *Willa wired back that the news*   WC to Zoë Akins. The telegram is dated March 11, 1932; the letter, March 20, 1932.

        After one is forty-five, it simply rains death   WC to Zoë Akins, November 21, 1932.

        they had almost a lifetime of happiness   WC to CMS, June 28, 1939.

page 274   *Writers wrote their books for just one person*   WC to Zoë Akins, May 20, 1939.

        "It was as memorable an experience"   EL, *Willa Cather Living*, p. 182.

page 275   *" 'There seems to be no future at all' "*   WC quoted, ibid., p. 184.

        "with a resoluteness, a sort of fixed determination"   Ibid., p. 184.

        " 'non sine lacrimis' "   C. C. Burlingham quoted in Alfred Knopf, "Miss Cather," *The Art of Willa Cather*, p. 219.

page 276   *" 'A little heartache is a good companion' "*   WC quoted in Yehudi Menuhin, *Unfinished Journey*, p. 144.

        She thought that   Ibid., p. 145.

        Edith had accompanied her   WC to CMS and IMW, May 16, 1941.

page 277   *The writer Truman Capote, telling how*   Truman Capote, *Music for Chameleons*, Random House, New York, 1980, p. 257.

page 278   *It rested her, Willa told Carrie*   WC to CMS, May 16, 1941.

        impressed by the modesty   Told to the author by Mrs. Charles Savage.

page 279   *it may have been an easy way out for him*   WC to Mariel Gere, October 19, 1945.

        One always feels it when a friend cares   WC to ESS, undated, 1945.

        A maid came in four hours a day   WC to CMS, January 20, 1945.

        It was wonderful to see the younger generation   Ibid.

        it wasn't to her taste   WC to DCF, March 31, 1945.

page 280   *"her spirit was as high"*   EL, *Willa Cather Living*, p. 197.

        " 'Sa mort a été le fin' "   Paul Horgan, *Lamy of Santa Fe*, p. 440.

Afterword

page 281   *"Life seems nothing but pain"*   Edith Lewis to Hephzibah Menuhin, July 9, 1947. Courtesy of Joel Ryce and the late Hephzibah Menuhin.

        ". . . that is happiness"   WC, *My Ántonia*, p. 18.

Bibliography

———— ❀ ————

BOOKS BY WILLA CATHER

April Twilights, R. G. Badger, Boston, 1903
The Troll Garden, McClure Phillips & Co., New York, 1905
Alexander's Bridge, Houghton Mifflin Company, Boston, 1912
O Pioneers!, Houghton Mifflin Company, Boston, 1913
The Song of the Lark, Houghton Mifflin Company, Boston, 1915
My Ántonia, Houghton Mifflin Company, Boston, 1918
Youth and the Bright Medusa, Alfred A. Knopf, New York, 1920
One of Ours, Alfred A. Knopf, New York, 1922
April Twilights and Other Poems, Alfred A. Knopf, New York, 1923
A Lost Lady, Alfred A. Knopf, New York, 1923
The Professor's House, Alfred A. Knopf, New York, 1925
My Mortal Enemy, Alfred A. Knopf, New York, 1926
Death Comes for the Archbishop, Alfred A. Knopf, New York, 1927
Shadows on the Rock, Alfred A. Knopf, New York, 1931
Obscure Destinies, Alfred A. Knopf, New York, 1932
Lucy Gayheart, Alfred A. Knopf, New York, 1935
Not Under Forty, Alfred A. Knopf, New York, 1936
Sapphira and the Slave Girl, Alfred A. Knopf, New York, 1940
The Old Beauty and Others, Alfred A. Knopf, New York, 1948

* * *

Willa Cather on Writing, Alfred A. Knopf, New York, 1949
Writings from Willa Cather's Campus Years, edited by James R. Shively, University of Nebraska Press, Lincoln, 1950
Five Stories (with an article by George N. Kates on WC's unfinished and unpublished Avignon story), Vintage Books, Random House, New York, 1956
Willa Cather in Europe, Her Own Story of the First Journey, Alfred A. Knopf, New York, 1956
The Kingdom of Art: Willa Cather's First Principles and Critical Statements 1893–1896, edited by Bernice Slote, University of Nebraska Press, Lincoln, 1966
Willa Cather's Collected Short Fiction 1892–1912, edited by Virginia Faulkner, University of Nebraska Press, Lincoln, revised edition, 1970
The World and the Parish: Willa Cather's Articles and Reviews, 1893–1902, edited by William M. Curtin, University of Nebraska Press, Lincoln, 1970
Uncle Valentine and Other Stories: Willa Cather's Uncollected Short Fiction, 1915–1929, edited by Bernice Slote, University of Nebraska Press, Lincoln, 1973

BOOKS ABOUT WILLA CATHER

The World of Willa Cather, Mildred Bennett, University of Nebraska Press, Lincoln, new edition, 1961
Willa Cather—a Critical Biography, Edward K. Brown, completed by Leon Edel, Alfred A. Knopf, New York, 1953
Willa Cather, a Critical Introduction, David Daiches, Cornell University Press, Ithaca, N.Y., 1951
Willa Cather, a Checklist of Her Published Writing, compiled by JoAnna Lathrop, University of Nebraska Press, Lincoln, 1975
Willa Cather Living, Edith Lewis, Alfred A. Knopf, New York, 1953
Willa Cather, Dorothy Tuck McFarland, Frederick Ungar Publishing Co., New York, 1972
Five Essays on Willa Cather, The Merrimack Symposium, edited by John J. Murphy, Merrimack College, North Andover, Mass., 1974
The Landscape and the Looking Glass—Willa Cather's Search for Value, John H. Randall III, The Riverside Press, Cambridge, Mass., 1960
Willa Cather and Her Critics, edited by James Schroeter, Cornell University Press, Ithaca, N.Y., 1967
Willa Cather—a Memoir, Elizabeth Shepley Sergeant, J. B. Lippincott Co., Philadelphia, 1953

The Art of Willa Cather, edited by Bernice Slote and Virginia Faulkner, The Department of English, University of Nebraska, Lincoln, and the University of Nebraska Press, Lincoln, 1974

Willa Cather, Dorothy Van Ghent, Pamphlet on American Writers, No. 36, University of Minnesota Press, Minneapolis, 1964

Willa Cather, Her Life and Art, by James Woodress, Pegasus, New York, 1970

Willa Cather: a Pictorial Memoir, photographs by Lucia Woods, text by Bernice Slote, University of Nebraska Press, Lincoln, 1973

ARTICLES ABOUT WILLA CATHER

"Miss Willa Cather from Nebraska," George Seibel, *The New Colophon*, Volume II, Part Seven, September 1949

"Willa Cather in Pittsburgh," John P. Hinz, *The New Colophon*, Volume III, New York, 1950

"Willa Cather's Early Career: Origins of a Legend," Helen C. Southwick, *The Western Pennsylvania Historical Magazine*, Voume 65, Number 2, April 1982

OTHER REFERENCES

Lawrence and Brett—a Friendship, Dorothy E. Brett with Introduction, Prologue and Epilogue by John Manchester, Sunstone Press, Santa Fe, N.M., 1974

Rhythm in the Novel, Edward K. Brown, University of Toronto Press, Canada, 1950

Witter Bynner—Prose Pieces, "The Works of Witter Bynner," edited by James Kraft, Farrar, Straus & Giroux, New York, 1979

Music for Chameleons, Truman Capote, Random House, New York, 1980

Greenwich Village, Anna Alice Chapin, Dodd, Mead & Co., New York, 1917

Victor Chapman's Letters from France, with memoir by John Jay Chapman, New York, The Macmillan Company, 1917

The Improper Bohemians, Allen Churchill, E. P. Dutton & Co., New York, 1959

A Heritage of Her Own, edited by Nancy F. Cott and Elizabeth H. Pleck, Simon and Schuster, New York, 1979

The Literary Situation, Malcolm Cowley, The Viking Press, New York, 1958

The Sod-House Frontier, Everett Dick, Bison Books, University of Nebraska Press, Lincoln, 1979

Sara Teasdale—Woman and Poet, William D. Drake, Harper & Row, New York, 1979

Surpassing the Love of Men, Lillian Faderman, William Morrow & Co., New York, 1981

Roundup: a Nebraska Reader, edited by Virginia Faulkner, University of Nebraska Press, Lincoln, 1957

Return to Yesterday, Ford Madox Ford, Horace Liveright Inc., New York, 1932

Sarah Orne Jewett, John Eldridge Frost, The Gundalow Club, Inc., Kittery Point, Maine, 1960

The Last of the Provincials, Maxwell Geismar, Houghton Mifflin Company, Boston, 1947

Mabel—a Biography of Mabel Dodge Luhan, Emily Hahn, Houghton Mifflin Company, Boston, 1977

The Gentle Americans—The Biography of a Breed, Helen Howe, Harper & Row, New York, 1965

Memories of a Hostess, Mark A. de Wolfe Howe, Atlantic Monthly Press, Boston, 1922

A Country Doctor, Sarah Orne Jewett, Houghton Mifflin Company, Boston, 1884

The Letters of Sarah Orne Jewett, edited by Annie Fields, Houghton Mifflin Company, Boston, 1911

On Native Grounds, Alfred Kazin, Harcourt Brace & Co., New York, 1942

Success Story, the Life and Times of S. S. McClure, Peter Lyon, Charles Scribner's Sons, New York, 1963

Sarah Orne Jewett, Francis Otto Matthiessen, Houghton Mifflin Company, Boston and New York, 1929

My Autobiography, S. S. McClure, Frederick A. Stokes Co., New York, 1914

Richard Wetherill: Anasazi, Frank McNitt, University of New Mexico Press, Albuquerque, 1966

Unfinished Business, Yehudi Menuhin, Alfred A. Knopf, New York, 1977

Literary Women, Ellen Moers, Doubleday & Company, Garden City, N.Y., 1977

Earthly Delights, Unearthly Adornments, Wright Morris, Harper & Row, New York, 1978

Silences, Tillie Olsen, A Seymour Lawrence Book, Delacorte Press, New York, 1978

Elinor Wylie, a Life Apart, Stanley Olson, The Dial Press/James Wade, New York, 1979

Telling Lives—the Biographer's Art, edited by Marc Pachter, New Republic Books, Washington, D.C., 1979

Garrets and Pretenders, Albert Parry, Covici-Friede, New York, 1933

The Collected Essays and Occasional Writings, Katherine Anne Porter, A Seymour Lawrence Book, Delacorte Press, 1958

George Eliot—the Emergent Self, Ruby V. Redinger, Alfred A. Knopf, New York, 1975

The Menuhins—a Family Odyssey, Lionel Menuhin Rolfe, Panjandrum/Aria Books, San Francisco, 1978

Lesbian Images, Jane Rule, Doubleday & Company, Garden City, N.Y., 1975

Fire Under the Andes—a Group of North American Portraits, Elizabeth Shepley Sergeant, Alfred A. Knopf, New York, 1927

The Eye of the Story, Eudora Welty, Random House, New York, 1978

Nebraska—a Guide to the Cornhusker State, Federal Writers' Project of the Works Progress Administration, Bison Books, University of Nebraska Press, 1979

Index

───── ❈ ─────